MAD ABOUT
TRADE

Daniel Griswold

DANIEL GRISWOLD

MAD ABOUT TRADE

Why Main Street America Should Embrace Globalization

CATO INSTITUTE
WASHINGTON, D.C.

Copyright © 2009 by Cato Institute.
All rights reserved.

Library of Congress Cataloging-in-Publication Data

Griswold, Daniel T., 1958–
    Mad about trade : why Main Street America should embrace globalization /
Daniel Griswold.
        p. cm.
    Includes bibliographical references and index.
    ISBN 978-1-935308-19-5 (alk. paper)
    1. Free trade—United States.   2. Balance of trade—United States.
3. Consumers—United States.   4. Globalization.   I. Title.

HF1756.G66 2009
382'.710973--dc22   2009026023

Cover design by Jon Meyers.

Printed in the United States of America.

CATO INSTITUTE
1000 Massachusetts Ave., N.W.
Washington, D.C. 20001
www.cato.org

Contents

Foreword

This is a book that ought to be read by all Americans. As its author, Dan Griswold, points out, international trade seems often to provoke more anxiety than gratitude. That is unfortunate, for without the encouragement of foreign investment and a concomitant expansion of trade, we'd likely still be a Third World country today. "Globalization," a concept that has provoked more fear than comfort throughout the world, also has far more positive attributes than negative ones. It is ironic that those who loudly protest against free trade and a global economy are often among its beneficiaries. (In fact, one can almost guarantee that protesters will be wearing clothes that are produced in a country other than their own.)

In this tome, Dan Griswold confronts protectionism and methodically demolishes its supportive arguments. Protectionists have always relied on emotion and xenophobia, rather than facts, to carry their agenda. Remember the "sucking sound" of disappearing jobs that was to accompany NAFTA? In the 15 years since NAFTA was passed, our trade deficit with Mexico and Canada has grown (as its critics relentlessly point out), but compared to the 15 years before NAFTA, just about every imaginable economic indicator shows that all three countries—Mexico, Canada, and the United States—have benefited from the agreement. Not all of those benefits are attributable to NAFTA, of course, but there is no denying that NAFTA helped push those indicators in the right direction.

Griswold wears on his sleeve genuine compassion for the poor and empathy for the often forgotten consumer. Throughout his book, he emphasizes that protectionists have little or no concern for the downtrodden of the world, or even for the middle class. Their concerns are for the select producer groups who have the political clout to fend off international competition. When governments kowtow to such groups, they inevitably impose inefficiencies on our society, and that hurts the poor more than anyone else. Competition motivates entrepreneurship and productivity. Protection from competition, in contrast, produces only lethargy and complacency. The result: more costly products and services.

As Griswold so effectively emphasizes, protectionism is really just another tax on working families, often paid unknowingly. The benefits of more-open trade are diffuse, but they're often difficult to quantify, and they may not even be visible. In contrast, the benefits of protectionism are concentrated on a definitive class of producers; they are quantifiable and visible to that group, and the beneficiaries are highly motivated to defend them. So guess who typically gets the most attention from policymakers?

Griswold provides an especially useful discussion of the impact of trade on job creation and job turnover. He points out that the entire discussion of job losses or job gains from trade has been vastly overblown in recent years. Free-trade advocates have oversold anticipated job gains from trade agreements; their critics, in turn, have oversold anticipated job losses. In reality, trade agreements have had little impact on the number of Americans who are employed.

Job churn, or turnover, is another matter. Few of us realize just how much job turnover there is in our dynamic, capitalistic economy. Millions of American jobs disappear every year. But if that is a "sucking sound," it is drowned out by the clatter of even more millions of new jobs being created. Fortunately, the average income level of those new jobs has typically exceeded the level of those that are lost, and they're often more desirable from a quality of life standpoint. That is why our vibrant economy is the envy of the world.

Griswold estimates that no more than 3 percent of our job churn is in any way related to international trade. Most of the other 97 percent represents technological change. Whatever the cause, job churn is not a painless process, and the United States has had a mixed record of success in helping people adjust to it. Where trade is involved, trade adjustment assistance has helped a bit, and we've been trying to improve those programs. But where technology is the agent of change, our public policy response has been unimpressive. Griswold properly notes that if we, as a nation, wish to ease the pain of job transitions, the rationale for doing so is as persuasive when technology is the culprit as it is when job change is trade related.

U.S. manufacturers have taken a big hit in the present recession, so devoting a chapter to that subject may seem incongruous. But it is not. The present recession was in no way caused by global trade, so it is entirely appropriate to analyze what has happened to U.S. manufacturing in the preceding years. Protectionists fret over the loss of manufacturing jobs, but they conveniently forget that the vast majority of those losses are attributable to technology, not trade. And they also conveniently forget that manufacturing continues to be an American success story. Our manufacturing output has been remarkably steady in recent years, so we are not de-industrializing America. We are producing the same level of output with far fewer employees than we did in the past. Our productivity in manufacturing has skyrocketed. As Griswold points out, that is a mark of strength, not weakness. Furthermore, we've "moved up the food chain" in manufacturing. We're now producing more capital-intensive, technologically advanced, higher-quality products, where the operating margins are higher. That, of course, enhances our international competitiveness.

I am especially appreciative of Griswold's comprehensive discussion of the trade deficit and its counterpart, our capital account. Many Americans are worried about both. They wonder whether the trade deficit is ever going to peak and begin to decline, and whether we can forever depend on the rest of the world to finance that deficit. These are provocative, but relevant, questions. Griswold answers by noting that for much of our history, capital flows may have been the drivers of trade flows, rather than vice versa. The United States has been "the global frontier" for more than 200 years. Investors from throughout the world have sought to march across that economic frontier, and they've needed dollars to do that. The only way to get those dollars is by selling merchandise or services to us. In addition, the U.S. dollar has long been the world's leading currency, reflecting the strength and stability of our economy. So it is not surprising that the dollar is strong, which makes the rest of the world's goods and services attractive to U.S. consumers. The bottom line: So long as we welcome and encourage foreign investment—and use it wisely— our trade deficit will be manageable.

Griswold also makes the salient point that we have only ourselves to blame for our low savings rate: that is, the situation where our domestic investment consistently exceeds our domestic saving. To make the two balance, we must attract savings from abroad. If we really wish to do something about that, we could start by reducing government "dissaving," which is reflected in our federal budget deficit. That'll be a little difficult in the near term, of course, in light of recent stimulus packages! We could also generate greater private-sector savings through changes in tax policy, but that will not likely be on the Congressional agenda anytime soon.

This book has a superb chapter on the importance of investment flows. U.S. politicians have had a field day recently with their demagogic comments on outsourcing. But we insource as well as outsource. To encourage one and condemn the other would be utterly foolish! Foreign investors have created huge numbers of jobs in the United States throughout the years and have brought new technology, new business management techniques, and a myriad of auxiliary benefits to our shores. Without that input, our economy would not be nearly so vibrant and productive, and our personal incomes would all be a lot lower. At the same time, we need to recognize that U.S. investment abroad is also in our self-interest. Without it, we would not sell nearly as much in the way of either products or services. Griswold notes that for every $1 billion worth of goods that we export from the United States, we sell $6 billion from the overseas base that foreign investment has provided. That, in turn, creates jobs in the support structure here in the United States. So, outsourcing typically turns out to be a benefit, rather than a drag, on the U.S. economy.

Finally, this book does more to articulate the intangible benefits of trade and globalization than any I have ever read. Griswold draws attention to the interactions of people, business firms, and governments—all of which help to develop understanding, tolerance, fidelity, prudence, respect for cultural differences, and a whole host of other positive attributes. Over time, this contributes to peace, freedom, and civility, thereby also reinforcing democratic trends. Beyond that, more-open trade helps to pull people out of poverty and boosts them to middle-class incomes, where they can see a better life ahead for their children. That, too, is a "peace dividend" of major importance to the entire world.

Dan Griswold discovers a lot of good in globalization and international trade, and he lays it out for the reader in understandable language. We should all be grateful for his contribution.

—Clayton Yeutter
Former U.S. Trade Representative and Secretary of Agriculture

Preface

Until I left home for college at age 18, I had spent my entire young life in two small midwestern towns of no more than 4,000 souls each. My family life was quintessentially small-town, middle-class America. In the 1870s, my great-grandfather, Henry Daniel Griswold, migrated from Connecticut to become a successful dairy farmer in La Crosse County, Wisconsin, establishing his farm on the edge of the town of West Salem. My grandfather, Harry W. Griswold, bought and sold dairy cows throughout western Wisconsin. The connections he made servicing the dairy farms enabled him to win a seat in the state legislature in 1932 and then in Congress in 1938. He died of a heart attack the following year at age 53 after only six months in office.

My dad, Donald W. Griswold, left the farm for good after serving in the Aleutian Islands in Alaska as a captain in the Army during World War II. He saved enough during the war to buy the local weekly newspaper, the *West Salem Journal*. When I was 13, he sold the newspaper, and he, my mother, and I moved to Sauk Centre, Minnesota, a small town with a more vibrant business district, where he bought another weekly newspaper. The *Sauk Centre Herald* office was downtown, two blocks east of the boyhood home of Sinclair Lewis, the Nobel Prize–winning author of the 1920 novel *Main Street*, and a block west of the town's only stoplight, at the intersection of Sinclair Lewis Avenue and the Original Main Street.

Hanging around the newspaper office as a kid, I caught the bug and spent more than a decade in the business—one year as assistant editor of the *Sauk Centre Herald* and a dozen years as editorial page editor of the daily *Gazette Telegraph* in Colorado Springs, Colorado. I wrote editorials that landed on 100,000 doorsteps every morning and spoke around town to schools, Rotary Clubs, the Breakfast Optimists, and other civic groups. In 1995, I left newspapering to earn a diploma in economics and a master's degree in the Politics of the World Economy at the London School of Economics. Since

1997, I've supported my family by researching and writing about trade, globalization, and immigration at a think tank in Washington, D.C.

My family story is worth recalling not because it is unusual, but because it is so typical. In four generations, my line of Griswolds moved from the farm to manufacturing (newspapers and publishing, Standard Industrial Classification no. 3371) to a research job in a nonprofit educational institution in a metropolitan area of 5 million. I don't know where my three children will find their vocations, but it will probably not be on a farm or in a factory.

During the past century, our country has made a similar journey. A hundred years ago, my great-grandpa Henry Daniel was among the 40 percent of Americans still earning their living in agriculture. As more Americans left the farm, along with my father, those working in factories and the service sector grew. Then, as the 20th century matured—during a time of rapidly expanding trade and foreign investment—the number of factory jobs peaked and began to decline, while my brothers and I and millions of other baby boomers found our calling in the service sector. This book will try to explain the largely positive role that trade and globalization are playing in this economic transition that continues to shape our country and our daily lives.

Allow me one more personal story. A few years back, a counterpart at another Washington nonprofit, Stephen Canner of the United States Council for International Business, invited me to lunch to talk about U.S. trade policy. Stephen told me he wanted "the clean view from ten thousand feet," which stuck with me as a neat description of what I may have to offer in the current debate about America's place in the global economy. Journalists write their stories from ground level about particular workers and businesses, whereas academic economists write their research papers from a "cruising altitude" of 35,000 feet (or sometimes deep space). But if you press your nose against the window as the plane is descending, you know that some of the most revealing views of your destination occur at 10,000 feet. From there, you can drink in the whole landscape and yet also see the individual parts—the backyard pools, the lay of the subdivisions, the fields and farmhouses, the traffic snaking along the highways, and what lies over the ridge—and how they all fit together.

This book offers a clean view from a vantage point that strives to make sense of America's changing place in the world economy and the effect this change is having on families and workers across America. This book is also unapologetically American centered. It examines every aspect of the globalization debate from the perspective of what it means for millions of typical American families. This book is written for my fellow Americans living in small towns, farmhouses, cities, and suburbs who wonder where we are all heading in this more open world of ours.

—May 18, 2009
Washington, D.C.

Acknowledgements

During the course of writing this book, I incurred a string of professional and personal debts large and small. First in line among my creditors are Cato President Ed Crane and the thousands of people who support the Cato Institute for making it possible for me to do the work I do. Offering helpful comments on the manuscript, from missing commas to misplaced chapters, were my Cato colleagues Brink Lindsey, Sallie James, Dan Ikenson, and David Boaz. (Thanks, David, for suggesting the main title.)

Also providing valuable comments and encouragement were Clayton Yeutter, Douglas Irwin, Jim Bacchus, and Bill Lane. Helping me gather the material I needed were Cato research assistant Tanja Stumberger and Cato research interns Corey Sheahan, Tatiana Kryzhanovskaya, Joseph Sullivan, Jordan Phipps, Nimish Adia, Carl Oberg, Silvana Gross, Ben Sonley, William Clinton, Austin Duus, and Scott Grandt. Cato's manager of information services, Tito Colon, bailed me out of more than one technological jam. I owe intellectual debts to Professors Timothy Tregarthen, Donald Boudreaux, Douglas Irwin, Jagdish Bhagwati, and Razeen Sally. Any errors of fact or logic between these covers are entirely my own. Finally, I want to thank my wife Elizabeth and my children, Emily, Michael, and Paul, for reminding me daily what is most valuable in this world. I dedicate this book to them.

1. Introduction: Main Street Meets the Global Economy

Welcome to my closet—my multinational, middle-class closet. If you had cared to look inside on a Saturday afternoon in early 2009, you would have found:

- Ten business suits and blazers: two of them made in China, two in Canada, two in the United Kingdom (my tweed jackets from the 1990s), and one each in Mexico, Guatemala, India, and parts unknown (the label fell off).
- Fourteen dress shirts: four made in Bangladesh, two in Honduras, and one each in China, Mexico, Nicaragua, Vietnam, Peru, Costa Rica, Korea, and Egypt.
- Seventeen neckties: nine made in the U.S.A. (several of those from imported fabric, including "finest Italian silk"), three in China, and one each in Costa Rica, South Korea, the United Kingdom, Italy, and parts unknown.
- Sixteen casual button shirts: five from India, three from Canada, two from Malaysia, and one each from the U.S.A., South Korea, the Philippines, Thailand, China, Bulgaria, and parts unknown.
- Thirteen knit shirts with collars: three each from India and Egypt, and one each from Thailand, the Philippines, Honduras, Bulgaria, Vietnam, Brunei/Darussalam (time to get out the atlas), and China—the last with Lou Dobbs' worst nightmare on the label: "Hecho en China."
- Twenty-seven colored and printed T-shirts: nine from Honduras, six from Mexico, three from El Salvador, two from Thailand, one each from China, Singapore, Australia, and four from parts unknown.
- Six sweaters: two from China, one from Mexico, one from Italy, one knit by my dear wife, and one from parts unknown.
- Twelve pairs of jeans and other pants: seven from the Dominican Republic, four from Mexico, and one from Guatemala.

1

- Six pairs of shorts: two each from Sri Lanka and Nicaragua and one each from El Salvador and Egypt.
- As for shoes, if you include my spouse's to increase the sample size, almost all come from China and the rest from India, the Dominican Republic, and that export powerhouse, parts unknown.

If you were to snoop in my dresser drawers, you would find various undergarments and furnishings from Costa Rica, the Dominican Republic, Honduras, and Thailand. On the coat rack inside our front door hangs outerwear from Israel, Jordan, Macedonia (with fabric woven in Italy), the Philippines, Portugal, Sri Lanka, Ukraine, and Vietnam.

In the kitchen, you would find a drip coffee machine from Mexico, a quarter-century-old coffee grinder from Germany, and from China, an electric tea kettle, a toaster, an electric griddle, an electric sandwich grill, a food processor, a bread machine, and a hand vacuum. As you move through the rest of the house, items made—or at least assembled—in China are everywhere: two laptop computers and accessories, a label maker, a table lamp, a DVD player, a steam iron, folding chairs, an indoor/outdoor thermometer, a plastic electronic barking guard dog, three basketballs, and a football. A year-old desktop computer and a decade-old TV are from Mexico, and the 4-in-1 printer is from Malaysia.

Peek over my shoulder as I check the balance of our 401(k) online— alas, not what it was in the fall of 2007—and you will see 10 percent of our retirement assets parked in an international index fund. According to the fund portfolio, our modest savings are providing capital to Japan, the United Kingdom, France, Switzerland, Germany, Spain, Australia, the Netherlands, Italy, and Hong Kong. In the upper left corner of the web page is the logo for the Dutch insurance conglomerate that administers the plan. Inside my health insurance file nearby is paperwork from a South African company that used to administer our health savings account. My wife's home page on her laptop is set to the BBC website.

And sitting outside our townhouse in our two parking spots on a late winter day are a Dodge minivan and an Oldsmobile sedan. Both were made by Detroit-based automakers, but if they are typical of even "American-made" cars, they contain plenty of parts from

Mexico, Canada, and even a few from outside North America. And before it went out of business, a Venezuelan-owned CITGO down the road is where we would occasionally gas them up.

An inventory of your own closet, home, and life would probably tell a similar tale. Whether you live in Manhattan, a small town in the Midwest, or anywhere other than a primitive mountain cabin, you are plugged into the global economy and it is plugged into you.

America's Growing Globalization . . .

Growing trade and globalization have come to Main Street, and not just in how we spend or earn our money. Through our TVs, newspapers, and Web browsers, the global economy has become a major subject of coverage and controversy. TV personalities such as Lou Dobbs and Pat Buchanan and a growing chorus of politicians and interest groups blame trade and globalization for a long list of real and imagined ills afflicting our nation. They blame the trade deficit and our growing inventory of foreign products for the loss of millions of well-paying jobs, declining real wages and household incomes, a shrinking middle class, deindustrialization, and the exploitation of poor workers in distant countries. They tell us that multinational companies are "shipping our jobs overseas," and now millions of white-collar service jobs are at risk of being "outsourced." Polls show that their message resonates with a majority of the public.

Much of this book will be spent examining the merit of those claims as we shine a light on just what trade and globalization mean for the typical middle-class American family.

We can all agree that America is a more globalized place today than it was in the past. The trend is true whether we look at the narrower measure of international trade—the movement of goods and services across our borders—or the broader measure of globalization, which includes not only trade but also the movement of capital and the growing integration of production across borders. In 2007, 18.7 million standard shipping containers arrived at U.S. ports carrying many of the shirts, shoes, toys, and consumer electronics that fill our closets and family rooms. That figure is an average of 2,133 containers arriving every hour of the year, 24/7. Almost half arrived from one country.[1]

Figure 1.1 shows total annual U.S. imports and exports as a percentage of our gross domestic product going back to 1900. The share

3

Figure 1.1
AMERICA'S GROWING GLOBALIZATION
(imports and exports as a percentage of GDP)

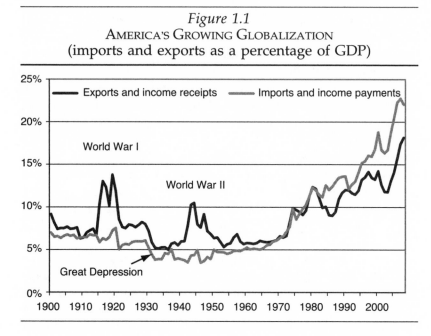

includes not only trade in goods but also services and income earned on investments, such as profits, dividends, and interest. U.S. exports spiked during both World Wars as Americans exported arms and other war supplies to our allies, whereas both imports and exports plunged during the Great Depression of the 1930s as output fell and trade barriers rose. As recently as the 1960s, both imports and exports were only about 6 percent of our GDP. In 2007, after four decades of historic growth, exports reached 17.4 percent of GDP and imports 22.8 percent.[2] Not since colonial days have Americans earned or spent a higher share of our income in the global economy than we do now.

On foreign investment, the story is the same. Cross-border ownership of assets has soared since the United States and most other developed nations lifted controls on foreign investment in the 1970s. In 1976, the sum of U.S.–owned assets abroad and foreign-owned assets in the United States was less than $1 trillion, equivalent to about 40 percent of our GDP. The current sum total of cross-border assets is $38 trillion, nearly three times our GDP.[3] To grease the

4

global exchange of goods, services, and assets, about $3 trillion change hands *daily* on foreign exchange markets.[4]

America's growing globalization has been driven by three fundamental changes—growth of the global economy, reduced government barriers to international trade and investment, and the spread of new technologies. The first cause may be the least obvious, but one reason why we do more business with the rest of the world today is because there are so many more people in other countries who are able to do business with us. The recovery of Japan and Europe after World War II, the explosive growth of the "Little Tiger" economies in East Asia and the formerly sleeping giants of China and India, and the emergence of former Communist countries from their self-imposed isolation have multiplied the opportunities for Americans to buy, sell, and invest abroad.

Meanwhile, trade and investment barriers have been coming down in the United States and most other countries in the world. Trade agreements have played a part. Eight rounds of negotiations through the General Agreement on Tariffs and Trade since it was established in 1947 have helped to bring global tariffs on manufactured goods down sharply. Those agreements now limit tariffs and other barriers to trade for more than 150 members of the successor World Trade Organization. The United States has signed and implemented free trade agreements with 16 other countries, cutting tariffs to zero on most goods we trade with those countries and opening markets even more widely to foreign investment. Many developing countries cut their barriers to trade and investment unilaterally in the 1980s and 1990s, most spectacularly China and India, but also Chile, Vietnam, and Mexico before the North American Free Trade Agreement.

Powering America's globalization have been advances in transportation, telecommunications, and computing technology. International shipping costs have declined sharply since the 1950s for both air and ocean freight. On the high seas, the introduction of container shipping in the 1960s has allowed manufactured goods to be transported more quickly and cheaply. Containerization enables goods to be packed once in a standard container and then shipped by a variety of modes—usually by truck, rail, ocean liner, rail, and finally truck again to the final destination. This process speeds loading and unloading at the docks, so ships spend less time in port and more

5

time plying the oceans from one port to another. Gains in efficiency continue to accumulate as more ports in developing countries modernize to accommodate container shipping. The open registry of ships to countries such as Panama and Liberia has allowed shippers to circumvent high regulatory and manning costs imposed by rich nations. And higher trade volumes have allowed ships to grow bigger, moving goods with greater economies of scale and enabling the creation of a global hub-and-spoke system for moving goods.

In the air, the development of jet aircraft engines after World War II dramatically raised the speed at which goods can be delivered, at a cost that continues to fall. Because jet engines are faster, more fuel efficient, and more reliable and require less maintenance than piston props, the actual cost per ton-kilometer to transport goods has fallen by more than 90 percent in the past half century, from $3.87 in 1955 to $0.30 in 2004, according to a comprehensive study by David Hummels of Purdue University.[5] Air transport still represents less than 1 percent of the weight and ton-kilometers shipped, but it is grabbing a larger and larger share of the market to ship smaller but more valuable manufactured goods and other high-value items. As a result, the value of U.S. exports going outside of North America via air has jumped from 12 percent of total exports in 1965, to 28 percent in 1980, to a majority of 53 percent by 2004. Almost a third of the value of U.S. imports from outside North America now arrives by air.[6]

The spread of the Internet and the plunge in the cost of international communication has allowed companies to coordinate operations around the globe. This coordination has led to a dividing up of the "supply chain" so that the various parts of a final product, from an iPod to a jumbo jetliner, can be made in dozens of countries to take advantage of differences in costs and capabilities. Services such as writing software, entering medical data, and providing technical support can now be "shipped" electronically across the globe at almost zero cost.

Falling transportation costs have stimulated trade at least as much as falling tariffs. Technological progress in the air and seas has cut the aggregate expenditures on freight for U.S. imports from 8 percent of their total value in 1974 to 4 percent in 2004. Even after those gains, importers in 2004 were still paying three times as much for shipping costs as for tariffs, leaving even more potential gains for the future.[7] As Professor Hummels concluded in his study, "[T]echnological change in air shipping and the declining cost of rapid transportation has been a critical input into a second era of globalization during the latter half of the twentieth century."[8]

... and Growing Opposition

The growth of trade and other measures of globalization has stirred more anxiety than gratitude among Americans. Polling data on trade paints a mixed and sometimes contradictory picture. Most polls show a majority of Americans expressing some degree of skepticism that free trade and globalization benefit most Americans, and yet other polls show a majority holding a favorable if qualified opinion. Some polls show the skepticism growing, yet polls from the early 1990s revealed widespread fear about imports and foreign investment from Japan. From the Civil War to the 1920s, Republicans won election after election running on protectionist platforms, which were popular not only with the public but also with much of the business community. Skepticism toward trade and the global economy is an American tradition dating back to our founding as a nation.

One reason why skepticism remains is the difference between "what is seen and what is unseen." The transition costs of moving to free trade are visible and lend themselves to images and anecdotes: a factory closing in North Carolina, the anxiety on the face of a laid-off steel worker, and the sweatshop conditions in factories making shirts in Honduras and soccer balls in Bangladesh. Yet the benefits that flow from free trade and globalization, while real and substantial, are diffused and often hidden from view: a dozen jobs created at a small business serving an American exporter or foreign-owned plant, lower interest rates on a loan, and $20 saved on a Saturday-afternoon shopping trip because of import competition.

Another related reason for the skepticism is the emotional appeal of arguments against trade. In a November 2007 essay, "Why Lou Dobbs Is Winning," the generally pro-trade Third Way Foundation tried to explain why the skeptics have been winning the rhetorical debate. Advocates for open trade "have lost the debate on values," the authors concluded. "While neopopulists and 'fair' traders speak compellingly of 'justice' and 'fairness,' we speak of dollars per household in economic gains, job growth, and economic efficiency. . . .'Fair' traders fight with values; free traders fight with data."[9]

That depiction is not quite right. "Fair" traders also fight with data, much of it wrong or misleading, as we shall see. But it is certainly true that those of us who advocate the embrace of free trade and globalization as the best policy for America too often confine ourselves to data. We fail to close the deal by drawing a connection from the facts to our deepest American values of fairness, compassion, competition, freedom, progress, peace, and the rule of law. The mission of this book is to make that connection.

As we build that connection, this book will challenge much of what we hear and read about trade in the American media. Here are some facts and themes from *Mad about Trade* that you will not hear on cable TV, talk radio, or the most popular blog sites.

Free trade is the working family's best friend. Import competition delivers lower prices and more variety, empowering consumers to get the most from their paychecks. Greater product variety from imports boosts our incomes by $400 billion a year. Those Americans who benefit the most from being able to buy imports from China through big-box retailers are the poor (chapter 2).

Trade has delivered better jobs for American workers. Most of the net new jobs created in the past decade pay more than the average manufacturing job. The American middle class today is built on millions of well-paying service-sector jobs. Despite the most recent recession, Americans today enjoy significantly higher real hourly compensation, household incomes, and family net worth than 15 years ago (chapter 3).

Most American manufacturers have managed to thrive in a global economy. Trade has helped American factories move up the value chain. We're producing more planes, pills, appliances, chemicals, semiconductors, and sophisticated equipment than in decades past. The volume of U.S. manufacturing output was 50 percent higher in 2008 than when Congress passed NAFTA in 1993 (chapter 4).

America's big trade deficit is not a scorecard for U.S. trade policy. It reflects a steady inflow of foreign investment and continued domestic demand for goods and services, whether made at home or abroad. Since 1982, America's unemployment rate invariably rises when the trade deficit shrinks and falls when the trade deficit grows. Despite what Warren Buffett says, raising trade barriers cannot "fix" the trade deficit (chapter 5).

American companies that invest abroad are not "shipping jobs overseas"; they are reaching new customers for U.S.–branded goods and services. For every $1 billion in goods that U.S. companies export, they sell $6.2 billion through their foreign affiliates—and 90 percent of those sales go to foreign buyers. Foreign capital flowing into the United States cuts almost a full point off long-term interest rates, saving a typical homeowner $1,000 a year and federal taxpayers $40 billion (chapter 6).

High U.S. trade barriers in the 19th century were a drag on growth and bred anticompetitive domestic monopolies. The Great Depression occurred on the protectionists' watch. America's economic performance has been superior during the era of lower tariffs since World War II, including the past 15 years since NAFTA was enacted. Nearly a quarter of a million small and medium-sized U.S. companies are now exporting to global markets, including China (chapter 7).

Membership in the WTO has not compromised U.S. sovereignty. It has served our national interest by opening markets abroad to U.S. exports and restraining the U.S. government's abuses of our economic liberty. A global "rule of law" in place today has prevented a repeat of the disastrous trade wars of the 1930s (chapter 7).

The spread of trade and globalization has helped to cut world poverty in half since 1981. Fewer children are dying, fewer are heading for work on the farm and in factories, and more are in school, especially girls, than in decades past. Once the world shakes off the current recession, a growing middle class in developing countries will be hungry to buy U.S.–provided goods and services (chapter 8).

Thanks in part to expanding trade, our world is more democratized and peaceful. More people enjoy full political and civil rights under democratic governments around the world than in any previous era. Trade has promoted peace among nations, making it less likely that America's sons and daughters will fight in future wars (chapter 8).

America is not yet a "free trade" nation. American citizens remain fettered by anticompetitive regulations and thousands of restrictive tariffs on everyday products that protect politically connected domestic producers. Existing tariffs fall especially hard on low-income families struggling to buy the necessities of life (chapter 9).

Many Americans these days are "mad about trade"—mad as in angry. They perceive that trade is reducing our welfare by eliminating good jobs in a global race to the bottom. By the end of this book,

I hope that readers open to persuasion will see that we really should be "mad about trade" in quite a different way—mad as in crazy in love with the opportunities that our new and more open world is creating before our eyes, not only for ourselves but, more importantly, for our children. We should have the same positive feelings toward free trade and globalization as we do toward digital cameras, iPods, email, online shopping, a well-fed child going off to school, and peace on earth.

2. America's Consuming Interest in Trade

Free trade is the American consumer's best friend. Whereas trade barriers limit competition, free trade keeps producers honest by forcing them to work hard to offer consumers more and better products at lower prices.

Millions of American families benefit from free trade every day. We benefit whenever we buy a cart of groceries, a new shirt, a TV, or a car. The receipt doesn't say, "You have saved $30 (or $300 or $3,000) because of import competition," but the savings add up to hundreds of billions of dollars every year for American households.

Most Americans believe in competition. We are better off when a dozen restaurants and half a dozen auto repair shops compete for our business instead of only one or two. By expanding the number of producers selling goods and services in the domestic market, trade safeguards and intensifies competition. The result is lower prices, more variety, and better quality for tradable products. We should think of trade as the market's trust buster. In a recent annual report for the Dallas Federal Reserve Bank, Michael Cox and Richard Alm wrote, "Globalization erodes market power. Natural monopolies that might rise in national economies—airlines, electricity, or telephone service, for example—don't exist on a global scale."[1]

Consumer benefits are the most important and yet least appreciated payoff of trade. One reason is that the benefits are largely invisible. They are diffused throughout the economy in millions of daily transactions that are small and often hidden but collectively deliver a huge boost to our standard of living. Producers pinched by trade often join together, hire lobbyists, and buy advertisements to get the attention of Congress. Consumers are simply too numerous to organize and generally unaware of the stake they have in defending an open and competitive market.

The other reason why the consumer benefits of trade are too often dismissed is that "consumption" has a bad reputation. There

11

is something ignoble, even grubby, about wanting more and wanting it "cheap." We liken consumption to acquisitiveness and greed. Consumption in the minds of many means four cars in the driveway, a triple-decker cheeseburger, and a 52-inch flat screen TV bought with a credit card at 18 percent annual interest.

Consumption can be abused, but it is also life itself. Without consumption, we would all be starving, naked, homeless, and quickly dead. Consumption is the proper end of all economic activity. We do not start a business or show up at work every day just to be there but because we seek to be rewarded in a tangible way. And the paychecks or profits we earn do us no good unless we can translate them into goods and services with real value—a place to live, a car, clothes, food, that big-screen TV, tuition for the kids, a donation to church or charity. Production divorced from consumption is akin to slavery.

The founder of modern economics, Adam Smith, understood clearly that the argument for free trade begins with the consumer. As he wrote in his 1776 book, *An Inquiry into the Nature and Causes of the Wealth of Nations*:

> Consumption is the sole end and purpose of all production; and the interest of the producer ought to be attended to, only so far as it may be necessary for promotion of the consumer. The maxim is so perfectly self-evident, that it would be absurd to attempt to prove it. But in the mercantile system, the interest of the consumer is almost constantly sacrificed to that of the producer; and it seems to consider production, and not consumption, as the ultimate end and object of all industry and commerce.[2]

By the "mercantile system," Smith meant one based on protecting domestic producers against their foreign competitors regardless of the impact on consumers. The multiple trade barriers that still exist are holdovers from the mercantilist thinking of the 17th and 18th centuries that Smith intellectually demolished in his great work. We can't begin to understand the benefits of free trade without shedding the old, producer-focused way of thinking and instead consider the well-being of American families as consumers. Here is where trade delivers the greatest benefits to the widest possible number of Americans.

Benefits of Import Competition

Politicians and critics of trade tend to belittle the consumer benefits. Their sympathies lie with producers, or more accurately, certain noisy producers, and so they are quick to dismiss any argument that trade broadly benefits consumers. For example, in his 2004 book, *Exporting America*, CNN host Lou Dobbs dismissed any concerns for consumers. "I don't think helping consumers save a few cents on trinkets and T-shirts is worth the loss of American jobs," he wrote.[3]

When he was running for president in 2007, then-Sen. Barack Obama was equally dismissive of consumer worries about higher prices. At a Democratic primary debate in Chicago, moderator Keith Olbermann of MSNBC asked the reasonable question, "If buying American costs more, and in many cases it does, how do you convince a working family that's struggling to get by on a tight budget and in part makes ends meet using $10 T-shirts for their kids, that buying American is still best for them no matter what the price is?"[4]

Before a stadium full of cheering union members, Senator Obama basically said, "let them pay more": "Well, look, people don't want a cheaper T-shirt if they're losing a job in the process. [Applause.] They would rather have the job and pay a little bit more for a T-shirt. And I think that's something that all Americans could agree to."[5] Like most politicians, he chose to favor the noisy producer interests over the silent, suffering consumer.

When it comes to T-shirts, most Americans have a consuming and not a producing interest. Virtually all of America's 114 million households (most of them "working families") buy shirts every year. In fact, Americans buy 4.5 billion T-shirts and other apparel tops each year, 94 percent of them imported.[6] That's an average of almost 40 shirts per household. But very few American workers, less than half a million, make their living producing T-shirts, other apparel, and textiles.[7]

Yet Senator Obama and the union audience clearly sided with the one-third of one percent of American workers (many of them still unionized) who make shirts and other clothing rather than the 99.7 percent who unambiguously gain from being able to buy their clothing at more affordable prices. Democrats and their union allies were not representing "working families" against big corporations but a small and declining share of U.S. producers and their employees at the expense of the vast majority of American households.

13

Lou Dobbs and Barack Obama are both guilty of exaggerating the impact of imports on American workers and of minimizing the benefits of imports for American consumers. A well-paid television personality in New York City or a politician in Washington need not care about the price of a T-shirt or other everyday consumer items, but millions of American families, especially those living on low and middle incomes, do care. Our freedom to buy in the global marketplace benefits American families in three major ways.

Lower prices

Open markets keep a lid on prices. A domestic producer who tries to raise prices runs the risk of being undercut by a foreign competitor. An open market makes it more difficult for domestic producers to "conspire" with one another to raise prices at the public's expense. As a result, the prices we pay for goods and services exposed to global competition tend to rise more slowly or even fall compared to prices paid for goods and services where competition is limited to the domestic or local market.

Table 2.1 shows the change in prices between 2000 and 2007 for an assortment of products and services. Price changes cover a wide spectrum, from an 81 percent fall in the (quality-adjusted) prices paid for personal computers and accessories to the 71 percent jump in what we pay for college tuition and fees. By comparison, the overall price index for all urban consumers during that same period rose 24 percent.[8]

With a few exceptions, the unmistakable pattern is this: The prices we pay for goods most exposed to international competition rise more slowly than overall prices, and for many categories, the prices actually fall. Meanwhile, the prices we pay for goods and services that are insulated from global competition tend to rise faster than inflation.

Among the goods globally traded are consumer electronics, toys, clothing, shoes, household goods, and new cars. Those are the same sorts of goods that have gone up the least or even fallen in price. This trend is no coincidence. Among the goods and services least likely to be traded across borders are college tuition, medical care, electric utilities, cable TV, admission to sporting events, and auto repair. Again, it is no coincidence that those services also lead the

Table 2.1
COMPETITION AND PRICE CHANGES
PERCENTAGE CHANGE, JANUARY 2000 TO DECEMBER 2007

Price Changes below Inflation	% Change	Price Changes above Inflation	% Change
Personal computers and peripheral equip,	−80.7	Laundry and dry cleaning services	24.6
Televisions	−70.8	Haircuts and other personal care services	25.6
Toys	−36.0	Full-service meals and snacks	25.6
Dishes and flatware	−25.3	Fruits and vegetables	30.8
Wireless telephone services	−20.6	Motor vehicle repair	31.5
Infants' and toddlers' apparel	−14.6	Rent of primary residence	32.0
Men's and boys' apparel	−13.3	Garbage and trash collection	32.2
Sports equipment	−12.2	Admission to movies, theaters, and concerts	32.5
Men's footwear	−5.7	Prescription drugs	33.3
Women's and girls' apparel	−5.7	Cable and satellite television and radio service	35.8
New cars and trucks	−4.7	Household electricity	40.9
Music instruments and accessories	−3.5	Bread	41.0
Women's footwear	3.8	Admission to sporting events	44.7
Breakfast cereal	7.4	Dental services	44.7
Roasted coffee	9.9	Veterinarian services	58.8
Peanut butter	12.0	Inpatient hospital services	65.9
Sugar and artificial sweeteners	16.8	College tuition and fees	71.5
Eyeglasses and eye care	16.9		
Consumer Price Index	**24.4**		

SOURCE: Bureau of Labor Statistics, U.S. Department of Labor.

list of steepest price increases. Many of those services are not "protected" by government-imposed trade barriers but rather by the nature of the service, yet the result is the same: less domestic competition and a greater ability on the part of producers to saddle consumers with higher prices.

Higher prices mean that we can buy less with our paychecks and other earnings. A higher consumer price index translates into lower real wages, compensation, and household incomes. Erecting barriers to trade may "protect" certain industries and their workers, but they rob workers in every other sector by diminishing the value of what they earn.

Some of the tradable items in the table do face trade barriers, but the tariffs our government imposes on shoes, clothing, tableware, and musical instruments have not stifled trade completely but only slowed its growth. Without tariffs, prices would have fallen even further, to the benefit of American consumers. And prices have also gone up, sometimes sharply, for such freely tradable commodities as fruits and vegetables and crude oil. But commodities are more prone to natural price swings than manufactured goods, and we can be certain that prices would have been even higher if import competition had been curbed by artificial trade barriers.

Another seeming anomaly on the list is prescription drugs. In 2007, Americans imported $71 billion worth of medicinal, dental, and pharmaceutical preparations, making it one of the more heavily traded product categories. Yet the average price level for prescription drugs since 2000 has risen faster than inflation. One plausible explanation is a trade restriction of sorts—the U.S. government's granting of patents for brand-name drugs. Patents are in essence temporary monopolies granted by the government to the creators of an innovative product such as a new medical drug.

The purpose behind patents is to encourage investment in breakthrough products by allowing the people and companies that develop the new products to benefit the most. Otherwise, one company would invest heavily in researching and developing a new drug, only to have other producers immediately co-opt the formula, driving down prices. Companies would then lose the incentive to innovate, depriving the public of potential medical advances. To make drug patents effective, the U.S. government has also imposed restrictions on the "re-importation" of U.S.–made drugs that have been sold abroad at prices lower than what they are sold for here in the United States.

Without taking sides on the re-importation issue, it's worth noting that some of the same members of Congress who complain the loudest about free trade and "unfair" import competition are also leading the charge to lift restrictions on drug re-importation so that American consumers can enjoy the benefits of lower prices. If only they cared as much about lowering prices for food, clothing, and shoes as they do for lowering prices for Viagra.

Import competition might be one reason that inflation rates are lower than in past decades. As the late Nobel Prize–winning economist Milton Friedman explained, inflation is ultimately caused by the creation of too much money by the central bank, but lower trade barriers can help to moderate price increases by breaking the power of domestic monopolies and oligopolies to charge higher prices. As the United States and other major economies have become more globalized in the past two decades, global inflation fell from 30 percent in the early 1990s to 4 percent by 2003. Inflation ticked up recently during the spike in oil and food prices, but it is nowhere near where it was 15 or 30 years ago. By making workers more productive and prices more flexible, open markets have reduced pressure on central banks to inflate the money supply. Our expanding freedom to trade assets and currencies has given Americans more options to shield themselves from the impacts of inflation.[9]

More Choice and Variety

Free trade delivers real benefits for American families not only through lower prices but also by enriching the variety of products and brand names we can buy. More choices among similar products increase our satisfaction as consumers. Instead of one-size- or one-taste-fits-all, we can choose the brand or flavor that gives us the greatest satisfaction. Consider imported beer. Even if imports did not cause the price of a six-pack to drop, consumers are still better off if they can choose among not only Miller High Life, Old Milwaukee, and Coors but also Heineken, St. Pauli Girl, and Newcastle Brown Ale. Increased variety can have the same effect on our well-being as a drop in prices.

Free trade means we can buy fresh-cut flowers from Colombia in the middle of winter along with fresh fruit from Chile and fresh vegetables from Mexico. Free trade means we are more likely to find the style and size of shirt we want on the shelves at the department store. A more sophisticated global supply chain has allowed such retailers as J.C. Penney to cut the time it takes for a junior fashion design to go from concept to the store from 70 weeks a decade ago to 17 weeks today.[10]

The consumer benefits of variety can be harder to quantify than a simple drop in price, but they are just as real. Two economists for the National Bureau of Economic Research calculated the consumer benefits of increased variety in a 2004 study, and the benefits add up to hundreds of billions of dollars. Authors Christian Broda and David E. Weinstein built their study on the pioneering insight of the liberal Nobel Prize–winning economist and *New York Times* columnist Paul Krugman that consumers do not care just about the price of imports but also even subtle differences in similar products. As the NBER authors succinctly put it, "Consumers value variety," which free trade delivers in abundance.[11]

If trade delivers more brands while keeping prices in check, we are better off. In fact Broda and Weinstein calculate that the global varieties available to Americans multiplied four-fold between 1972 and 2001. "Roughly half of this increase appears to have been driven by a doubling in the number of goods and half by a doubling in the number of countries supplying each good," the authors found.[12] Adjusting for the benefits of increased variety, they calculate that import prices actually fell 1.2 percent faster than official statistics showed. As a result, the real incomes of American families are about 3 percent higher because of the greater variety that imports bring.[13] That's not "a few cents"; it's nearly $400 billion in our current economy. That figure translates into a real gain of $1,300 per person or more than $5,000 for a family of four just from the expanding varieties that trade has brought to the marketplace. Trade with China has done more to expand the variety of imports we enjoy than trade with any other country, but more on that in a moment.

Better Quality

A third benefit of free trade for American consumers is higher quality. Nowhere have Americans witnessed the improved quality from trade more noticeably than in the automobile market. When I first began to drive in the mid-1970s, the American market was dominated by the Big Three. American automakers and their unions had grown fat and happy with their exclusive franchise of making big and powerful cars for the world's largest domestic car market. Imported Volkswagens and Toyotas were seen back then as rather exotic. Now it is the boxy, unreliable, and gas-guzzling American cars of that day that seem exotic, like four-wheeled dinosaurs destined for extinction.

Three decades of oil spikes and vigorous foreign competition have transformed the U.S. auto market. Today foreign-brand vehicles account for more than half the cars and light trucks sold in the United States. Along with the increased competition have come more moderate price increases, greater variety, and, yes, better quality. Today's cars are safer, better designed, more loaded with extra features, and more fuel efficient for their class. It was Japanese automakers who introduced crossover utility vehicles, hybrid vehicles, and small light trucks to the American market. According to an October 2008 poll commissioned by the Japanese Automobile Manufacturers Association, 79 percent of Americans agreed that competition from

Japanese automakers has spurred the Big Three to offer hybrid technologies and more fuel-efficient vehicles.[14]

Trade skeptics have been quick to jump on safety concerns about toys and pet food imported from China. Those concerns are real, but they spring from breakdowns in quality control, not from trade itself. U.S. regulators have every right under international law to impose exactly the same safety and health standards on imported products as they do on products made domestically. Poisoned pet food or toys with lead paint are just as much a safety concern whether they come from abroad or another state. In the past three years, Americans have been sickened and even killed by baby spinach from California and ground beef from Nebraska tainted by E. coli bacteria, chicken from Pennsylvania tainted with listeria, and peanut butter and peanut products from Georgia tainted with salmonella. The regulatory challenges are no different. Importing goods from less-developed countries need not lead to any lowering of health and quality standards.

How Imports from China Improve Our Daily Lives

It seems an American cannot go shopping today without buying something "made in China." Our store shelves brim with products made, or at least assembled, by workers in the world's most populous nation. Factories in China specialize in goods that are especially attractive to consumers in the United States, so it only makes sense that the world's richest consumer nation would buy lots of stuff every year from one of the world's leading makers and exporters of consumer goods. Of those 2,133 containers that arrived every hour in 2007, slightly more than 1,000 came from China.[15]

Most of what we import from China are everyday consumer goods that make our lives better at home and work. As Table 2.2 shows, more than 80 percent of the goods imported from China in 2007 were consumer products: laptop computers, iPods and MP3 players, furniture, shirts, shoes, sporting goods, TVs and DVD players, and office products.[16] China was the source of 80 percent of America's imported toys, sporting goods, and bicycles; 73 percent of imported footwear; 68 percent of imported radios, CD players, and other audio equipment; and more than half of imported computers, furniture, and household items.[17]

19

Table 2.2
WHAT WE BUY FROM CHINA
(2007 imports in billions of U.S. dollars)

Consumer Products	
Computers and telecommunication equipment	72.4
Furniture, appliances, household goods	56.4
Apparel and footwear	51.6
Toys and sporting goods	27.6
TVs, radios, dvds, cameras	23.5
Vehicles and parts	9.5
Printed matter, writing supplies	7.1
Food, paper and energy	5.7
Jewelry, artwork, and miscellaneous	4.8
Miscellaneous	3.9
Total	262.3
Industrial Goods	
Industrial machinery	30.9
Steel and other metal products	11.0
Building materials	5.2
Packing materials	4.7
Chemicals	4.4
Textiles	2.9
Total	59.2
Total Goods Imported	321.5

Although China is now the number one source of imported goods for the U.S. economy, 85 percent of what we import still comes from countries other than China. And Chinese imports must be seen in the context of the U.S. economy that in 2008 produced $14 trillion worth of goods and services. There is nothing wrong with the fact that Americans spend the equivalent of 2 percent of our national income on things put together by the one-fifth of mankind that lives in China.

Imports from China have delivered lower prices on goods that matter most to the poor, helping to offset other forces in our economy that tend to widen income inequality. In a 2008 study, two economists from the University of Chicago confirmed the pro-poor bias of imports from China. Christian Broda and John Romalis calculated that between 1994 and 2005, the inflation rate for goods bought by U.S. households in the lowest tenth percentile of income was 6 percentage points lower than inflation for goods bought by families in the top tenth percentile. Lower-priced imports from China were a big reason why. "Since Chinese exports are concentrated in low-quality non-durable products that are heavily purchased by poorer Americans, we find that about one-third of the relative price drops faced by the poor are associated with rising Chinese imports," they concluded.[18] Broda and Romalis found that trade with China has helped to offset nearly a third of the official rise in income inequality during this period. Lower prices on goods imported from China have more than compensated for any downward pressure on low-skilled wages because of U.S.–China trade.

Imposing punitive tariffs on imports from China would be a direct tax on tens of millions of working families in America. Some members of Congress have proposed that the U.S. government drastically raise tariffs on Chinese goods. Sens. Charles Schumer, a New York Democrat, and Lindsey Graham, a South Carolina Republican, offered a bill in 2005 that would have imposed a 27.5 percent tariff on Chinese goods unless Chinese authorities allowed their currency to rise in value compared to the dollar. Sen. Byron Dorgan, a North Dakota Democrat, has proposed revoking "normal trade relations" with China, which would expose Chinese imports to prohibitively high tariff rates.

Imposing steep tariffs on imports from China would, of course, hurt producers and workers in China, but it would also punish millions of American consumers through higher prices for shoes, clothing, toys, sporting goods, bicycles, TVs, radios, stereos, and personal and laptop computers. It would disrupt supply chains throughout East Asia, invite retaliation, and jeopardize sales and profits for thousands of U.S. companies now doing business with the people of China. Sanctions of the kind contemplated in Congress would also violate the same set of international trade rules that members of Congress accuse China of violating.

Exchange-rate policies can also bite into family budgets. Certain U.S. producers tend to favor a weak dollar vs. China's yuan because it makes U.S. exports more competitive abroad and Chinese imports less competitive in our domestic market. But the exchange rate is a double-edged sword. A weak dollar also drives up import prices for American families and import-using producers. It is no coincidence that the upward spike in global food and energy prices in 2007 and 2008 followed a major decline in the value of the U.S. dollar. When the dollar is worth less compared to other currencies, foreign producers will demand more dollars before they sell us a barrel of oil or a ton of rice. American families lose when the dollars in their pockets and checking accounts buy less in global markets.

Imports from China are just the kind of consumer goods that millions of low- and middle-income families buy at discount stores throughout the year, but especially during the Christmas shopping season. Imports from China tend to spike upward in August through November compared to the rest of the year as importers rush to fill store shelves in anticipation of the holiday shopping rush. Whereas imports from our other major trading partners also typically rise 10 to 15 percent on a seasonal basis, peaking in October, imports from China surge an average of 20 to 30 percent from August through October each year compared to average monthly imports throughout the year.[19] If the Grinch who tried to steal Christmas were in the U.S. Senate, he would gladly co-sponsor higher tariffs on imports from China!

How Big-Box Retailers Deliver the World

The principal channel through which American families enjoy the benefits of imports is American retailers, especially the "big box" stores such as Wal-Mart, Home Depot, and Best Buy. Access to global markets has allowed retailers to expand the range and variety of products we can buy and keep prices significantly lower than they would be if they were not able to source abroad.

Wal-Mart, for example, buys its products wholesale from a network of 60,000 suppliers worldwide. It now imports more than $20 billion a year from China alone. But sourcing from abroad is not just a Wal-Mart phenomenon; Target, Home Depot, Sears, Lowes, Kmart, Best Buy, Office Depot, Staples, and Costco are also major importers. IKEA furniture stores import a large share of their furniture from China.[20] In fact, imports bound for Wal-Mart stores accounted for less than 4 percent of those 18 million containers entering U.S. ports in 2006.[21]

Imports have allowed big box retailers to multiply the variety of goods on their shelves, especially compared to the corner hardware and grocery stores that were the only option when I was growing up in a small town in the Midwest. A typical Wal-Mart store today will stock 60,000 different items, a supercenter 120,000.[22] As we saw earlier, more choice means more customer satisfaction per dollar spent. In his sometimes critical but fair-minded book, *The Wal-Mart Effect*, author Charles Fishman accurately captured the phenomenon: "Step inside a Wal-Mart, pause briefly at the threshold—with two, or three, or four acres of brand-new goods before you piled to the ceiling—and at that moment you command a cornucopia from every corner of the globe that wasn't available, not even to the richest and most powerful, one hundred years ago."[23]

The price savings from the big-box retailers are just as striking, especially when it comes to groceries. Food prices at a Wal-Mart supercenter are typically 15 to 25 percent lower than at traditional grocery stores and supermarket chains. Even families that do not shop at a Wal-Mart benefit because the competition keeps prices lower than they would be otherwise at the traditional stores. Savings are greatest for lettuce, ham, butter/margarine, apples, yogurt, coffee, ice cream, potatoes, tomatoes, and bottled water.[24] Fishman estimates a family of four with an income of $52,000—middle class by any definition—saves about $900 a year by shopping at a Wal-Mart.

Those cost savings enabled in part by global sourcing are even more important for low-income families. In a 2005 study for the U.S. Department of Agriculture, authors Jerry Hausman and Ephraim Leibtag found that buying groceries at a supercenter allowed upper-income families to save the equivalent of 20 percent of their food expenditures, but for low-income families, the savings approached 30 percent. As the authors concluded, "The spread of supercenters has the greatest impact on poorer households and minority households. Thus, the spread of supercenters has favorable distribution effects across the population."[25] The pro-poor impact of the big-box retailers is one reason why spending at Wal-Marts continued to increase in the depths of the 2008-09 recession as sales plunged at other, more expensive retailers. As one major newspaper noted in a headline, "Wal-Mart Flourishes as Economy Turns Sour."[26] Affordable, imported staples have extended a more immediate and effective lifeline to families struggling to stay afloat during tough economic times than any lumbering government stimulus package.

Others in the political arena understand the consumer and distributional benefits of big-box retailers plugged into a global market.

Jason Furman, who now serves as a top economic adviser to President Obama, remarked at a public debate in 2005: "The lower prices at Wal-Mart are staggering. They are eight to 40 percent lower than what people would pay elsewhere. The total annual savings in one recent study ... for consumers are $263 billion. That's $2,300 for every household in America. There are very few public policies that I've advocated in my life that would make as big a difference as that."[27]

Political opposition to big-box retailers has been spearheaded by organized labor. Workers at Wal-Mart and other mass retailers tend to be nonunion, while workers at many grocery-store chains belong to the United Food and Commercial Workers International Union. The union sees double competition in the supercenters, both from their nonunion workers as well as the goods they sell that are produced by foreign workers and farmers. Domestic unions have caught the ear of politicians who tend to ignore the consumer benefits of competition while responding to the noisy producer interests who want to stifle competition at the expense of most working families.

Trade Policy As If Consumers Mattered

After he dismissed concerns about the cost of clothing during the 2007 primary debate, then-candidate Obama asked rhetorically, "[O]n whose behalf is the president negotiating [trade agreements]? Is he or she negotiating on behalf of the people in this stadium, or are you only negotiating on behalf of corporate profits? And that is an important issue and it's an important distinction that we've got to make."

Good question. Should we design our policies toward imported T-shirts and other "sensitive" products in order to pad the profits of the few domestic companies that still make those products and thus benefit the small slice of the U.S. workforce they still employ? Or should our policies be designed for the benefit of the tens of millions of Americans, including poor families living on the edge, who buy those T-shirts, shoes, and socks to clothe themselves and their children? Barack Obama won the cheers that day of union members, but who in that stadium was representing the single mother who must struggle to pay the duties our government imposes on imported goods that loom large in her budget?

Unfortunately, for all his talk about change, Sen. Obama that day sounded like most politicians who typically ignore the interest of Americans as consumers. They pander to the squeaky wheels, and in the trade debate, that almost always means a few producers rather than consumers. As we've seen, the benefits of free trade are diffused widely among more than 100 million households. Although the cumulative savings are huge, they are realized in small doses—just the right product available when you want it, increased satisfaction with that new car or laptop, or a $20 dollar savings from a Saturday trip to the shopping center. But many consumers are not even aware of those benefits or the threat posed to them by protectionist legislation. And even if awareness did grow among consumers, it is daunting to organize millions of diverse people into an effective political coalition.

Adopting a pro-consumer, pro-middle-class position on trade would transform the debate in Washington. Lowering our own trade barriers to imports would not be seen as a "concession" we make to other countries in order to coax them to lower their barriers to our exports. Free trade is a policy we can adopt right now to make our lives better. When other countries keep their trade barriers higher than we keep ours, that is not evidence of "unfair trade" but of misguided trade policies on the part of the other governments, policies that hurt our exporters, to be sure, but that are just as damaging to the other countries' consumers and overall economies.

Just because other countries pursue trade policies that hurt the large majority of their own citizens is not an argument for our own government to do the same to us. To insist on a "level playing field" is to demand that our government adopt or maintain trade policies that are as misguided and self-damaging as those of other countries. We should insist that our government adopt trade policies that are best for most Americans, regardless of what other countries do. And that means pursuing trade policies that spread benefits to the widest possible number of Americans, especially the poor and middle class who have the most to gain from removing the final remaining barriers that separate us from the global marketplace.

3. How American Workers and Families Have Traded Up

Even when Americans can see the consumer benefits of a more open market, fears remain that more vigorous competition may cost us our jobs. What good do lower prices do me if I don't have a paycheck? Those anxieties multiply during times of economic distress such as those that Americans are facing now.

Critics of trade and globalization hammer away that the real wages earned by most American workers have been stagnant or in decline for decades. They claim that higher-paying manufacturing and white-collar jobs are being destroyed by imports and outsourcing, whereas the jobs left behind are lower-paying service jobs such as flipping hamburgers or cashiering at a big-box retailer. In the verdict of public opinion, trade and globalization are held partly, if not primarily, responsible for the perceived loss of jobs, downward pressure on wages, and a middle class under siege.

Before we reach for trade barriers as an elixir for what ails our economy, we need to ask ourselves: What is the real story of jobs, living standards, and the middle class in the United States today, and what role has expanding international trade played in the changing number, composition, and compensation of American workers? By any reasonable and objective measure, American workers and families are better off than during comparable periods in the past, and expanding engagement in the global economy has played an important role in the upward trend in American employment and living standards.

Trade and Jobs: Why Both Sides Are Wrong

Trade is not about more jobs or fewer jobs, but about better jobs. Advocates of trade liberalization who claim that lower barriers boost the total number of jobs in our economy are as wrong as skeptics who argue that lower barriers mean fewer jobs. During the debate

over NAFTA in 1993, people on both sides were guilty of this fundamental mistake. Independent presidential candidate H. Ross Perot
famously predicted that passage of the agreement would create "a
giant sucking sound" of jobs and investment heading south across
the border. Advocates of the agreement, including the Clinton White
House, countered that NAFTA would create hundreds of thousands
of net new jobs. Both sides were wrong to the extent they predicted
the agreement would cause a net change in jobs either way.

Trade a Net Wash on Total Employment

Trade does cause certain jobs to disappear, certain companies to
go out of business, and certain sectors of the economy to shrink.
That's to be expected from increased competition, domestic as well
as international. But trade as a rule does not affect the total number
of jobs or the overall rate of employment or unemployment. Studies
that claim that trade expansion, trade deficits, or trade agreements
have caused the loss of a specific number of jobs during a certain
period are misleading if they leave the impression that the economy
today has that many fewer jobs than it would have otherwise. Trade
does not affect the total number of jobs in an economy for three
reasons.

First, if workers, capital, and resources can shift within the domestic economy, jobs eliminated by import competition will quickly be
replaced by jobs created elsewhere. Focusing merely on jobs lost
because of imports ignores the offsetting jobs that trade and globalization create through other channels. One channel is expanding
exports as U.S. producers ramp up production to meet demand
abroad as well as at home. Trade competition also reduces costs for
U.S. producers by allowing them to buy raw materials, intermediate
inputs, and capital machinery at lower, more competitive global
prices. Lower producer costs translate into higher profits, attracting
more investment and creating more employment in those sectors
that benefit from open markets. Trade also delivers lower prices on
imported and import-competing consumer goods, giving households more money to spend on domestic goods and services, stimulating further employment gains. Globalization also means more
international investment flowing into the United States. Inward foreign direct investment creates jobs by establishing foreign-owned
production facilities in the United States, whereas inflows of financial

capital create jobs by reducing long-term interest rates, thus promoting greater investment and job creation by domestic companies.

Second, the much misunderstood reality of "comparative advantage" means that our economy will always be globally competitive in a range of sectors. If we lose our competitive edge in one sector or industry because of shifting technology and factor prices or the emergence of new global competitors, the competitive edge of other sectors will be enhanced. The insight of comparative advantage, first expounded by David Ricardo in 1817, is that a country will tend to export what it can make more efficiently relative to what else it could produce domestically given its own endowment of land, labor, capital, and institutions. If the United States loses its shoe industry to lower-cost global competition, we will likely gain competitiveness and export share in pharmaceuticals, civil aircraft, financial services, and other sectors where we are relatively more efficient than making shoes.

Third, trade does not tend to affect the overall number of jobs because of other more powerful and counterbalancing factors in the broader economy such as monetary policy and foreign exchange rates. If a surge in imports did cause widespread layoffs in certain sectors, the resulting increase in unemployment would push the Federal Reserve to tilt toward a looser monetary policy and lower interest rates to stimulate the overall economy. Increased imports would also have the effect of pumping more dollars into international markets, causing the dollar to depreciate in foreign currency markets. A weaker dollar, in turn, would make U.S. exports more attractive, stimulating employment in export sectors while dampening demand for imports, offsetting initial job losses. For all those reasons, changes in trade flows have not determined the overall level of employment in the U.S. economy.

Even the most cursory glance at the employment numbers during recent decades should dispel any fear that trade and globalization threaten overall employment. Across the decades, against a backdrop of rising levels of trade and repeated business cycles, a central truth has stood out: In the long run, job growth in the United States tends to keep pace with growth in the labor force. As new workers have entered the labor market, U.S. producers have found profitable ways of employing them. Job growth invariably reverses during

Figure 3.1
U.S. EMPLOYMENT GROWS WITH LABOR FORCE

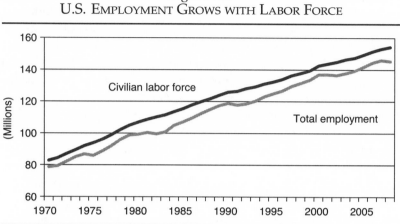

SOURCE: Bureau of Labor Statistics.

recessions, as we have painfully witnessed during the current downturn, but then catches back up with labor-force growth during expansions, driving the unemployment rate back down to a level consistent with "full employment."

In the past four decades, during a time of expanding trade and globalization, the U.S. workforce and total employment have each roughly doubled. As Figure 3.1 shows, total employment has closely followed labor-force growth. Since 1970, the number of people employed in the U.S. economy has increased at an average annual rate of 2.22 percent, virtually the same as the 2.25 percent average annual growth in the labor force.[1] Despite fears of lost jobs from trade, total employment in the U.S. economy during the recession year of 2008 was still 8.4 million workers higher than during the 2001 recession, 27.6 million more than during the 1991 recession, and 45.8 million more than the 1981–82 downturn.[2]

Nor is there any long-term, upward trend in the unemployment rate. In fact, even counting the recession year of 2008, the average unemployment rate during the decade of the 2000s has been 5.1 percent. That rate compares to an average jobless rate of 5.8 percent in the go-go 1990s and 7.3 percent in the 1980s (see Figure 3.2). After decades of demographic upheaval, technological transformations, rising levels of trade, and recessions and recoveries, the U.S. economy has continued to add jobs, and the unemployment rate shows

Figure 3.2
AVERAGE UNEMPLOYMENT RATES BY DECADE

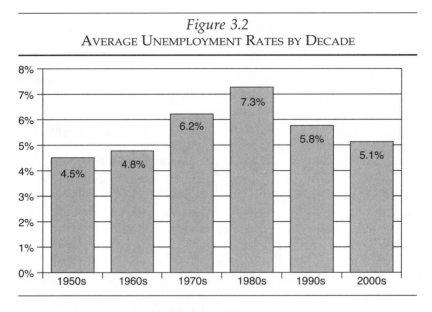

no long-term trend upward.[3] Obviously, an increasingly globalized U.S. economy is perfectly compatible with a growing number of jobs and full employment.

Trade's Small Role in "Job Churn"

Expanding international trade does eliminate a certain number of jobs each year. We can see that reality often in the news media and sometimes in our own communities: An auto parts supplier downsizes its workforce, an apparel factory closes its doors, a marketing firm outsources a call center to India. Affected workers are real people with bills to pay and dependents to support. But the number of people dislocated from their jobs each year because of shifting trade patterns is relatively small in America's dynamic market economy where "job churn" is a fact of life even in the best economic times.

The number of workers who lose their jobs each year because of expanding trade, offshoring, and outsourcing probably falls in the range of 300,000 to 500,000 a year. The Economic Policy Institute, a left-of-center research organization in Washington, claimed in a 2001 paper that rising imports had eliminated 3 million "actual and potential jobs" from 1994 to 2000—an average of 500,000 per year.[4] In a more recent study, EPI claims that our economy lost 200,000 jobs a year just from trade with China in the past decade.[5] Lori Kletzer, in a 2001 study for the Institute for International Economics, estimated that trade accounted for 320,000 job losses annually from 1979 to 1999.[6] Even if we accept the highest of those figures, jobs lost because of expanding trade are a relatively small component of the underlying churn in the U.S. labor market.

Every year, the U.S. economy creates and destroys millions of jobs. According to the U.S. Department of Labor, an average of 32.1 million jobs were created and 30.4 million were eliminated annually between 1992 and 2006, creating an average annual net job gain of 1.7 million.[7] About half the churn is seasonal, but the other half is permanent, meaning that each year about 15 million jobs disappear, never to be seen again.[8] If changing flows of trade account for the loss of 500,000 jobs a year, trade would be responsible for about 3 percent of the overall churn in the labor market.

Job displacement because of expanding trade also appears small when compared to weekly filings for unemployment compensation. If the estimates of job losses from trade expansion are correct, about 10,000 workers lose their jobs in a typical week from trade-related causes. Those job losses provide plenty of sound bites and TV images for the critics of trade. And yet in a typical week, even when the economy is humming, more than 300,000 people file claims for unemployment insurance. By that yardstick as well, workers displaced by expanding trade account for only 3 percent of total displaced workers in good times and an even smaller share during recessions. For every American standing in the unemployment line because of trade, 30 are standing directly ahead who have lost their jobs for reasons that have nothing to do with imports or the global economy.

Technology, not trade, accounts for most of the job turnover each year in the United States. The introduction of the personal computer 30 years ago eliminated hundreds of thousands of jobs for typists, secretaries, and telephone operators. Kodak, the camera company headquartered in Rochester, N.Y., has laid off 30,000 workers since 2004—not because of unfair trade by foreign competitors but because of the proliferation of digital cameras and plunging sales of film. Brick and mortar record and book stores have closed their doors, not because of imports but because online retailers such as Amazon.com and iTunes have captured an expanding share of the market. The daily newspaper business that once supported my family has seen venerable papers declare bankruptcy or shut down entirely as readers and advertising migrate to the Internet. The Pew Project on Excellence in Journalism predicted in a recent report that "by the end of 2009, a quarter of all newsroom jobs that existed in 2001 will be gone."[9]

Workers also lose their jobs because of changing consumer tastes and domestic market competition as one American company cuts into the market share of another. Trade plays only a bit part in the ongoing upheaval in the American workplace.

Trade, like technology, affects the types of jobs in our economy but not the total number. If workers and capital can move freely between states and between sectors, jobs lost in one area will tend to be replaced by jobs created in another. The overall number of jobs depends on the growth rate of the economy and the labor force, business investment, flexibility of employers to hire or lay off workers, and other broader factors. A nation open to the global economy can enjoy low unemployment, just as a nation with a relatively closed economy can suffer high unemployment (like America during the Great Depression). It is simply wrong to blame trade for causing a net loss of jobs or anything other than a small fraction of job displacement.

Higher Pay, Better Jobs

Critics of trade respond that our economy may have been creating jobs in our more globalized era, but the new jobs pay less than the jobs being destroyed. The result is stagnant or falling real wages and living standards and a shrinking middle class. The belief that most American workers are earning less than in years past rests on a faulty understanding of how trade affects the economy and living standards and a misinterpretation of recent wage and income data. Greater freedom to trade, in practice as well as in theory, has helped to lift the wages and incomes of most Americans to levels above what they would be had markets remained less open. Contrary to the common tale, expanding levels of trade in recent decades have been accompanied by rising real hourly compensation for American workers and a higher median income for households.

How Trade Raises Incomes

Trade raises the general wage level by expanding the opportunity for Americans to work in sectors where productivity and pay exceed the average. Because of comparative advantage, American workers tend to be most productive in those sectors that are the most capital intensive—those that require large investments in physical and human capital and intellectual property. Examples of such industries are pharmaceuticals, chemicals, civilian aircraft, sophisticated machinery, microprocessors, and professional services in finance, insurance, accounting, and other sectors. Those industries also tend to pay higher than average wages. As the more competitive industries expand output and employment, the overall wage level tends to rise as they compete in the labor market to hire new workers.

Where Americans find it hardest to compete internationally is in sectors that are relatively labor intensive, such as toys, sporting goods, shoes, and apparel. Those industries tend to pay wages that are lower than average. As the American economy opens itself to global competition, we tend to import more of the labor-intensive goods, reducing relative employment in lower-paying sectors, while we export more of the capital-intensive goods, promoting greater employment in higher-paying sectors. Thus expanding trade tends to raise overall wage and income levels. Even for the majority who work in nontrade sectors, global competition delivers lower prices for everyday consumer goods, allowing workers to stretch their paychecks further.

Yet official statistics show that the average real hourly wage paid to American workers—wage earnings adjusted for inflation—is lower today than in the 1970s. From a peak of $8.99 an hour in 1972, the average real wage (in 1982 dollars) declined steadily to a low of $7.52 in 1993 before rising again to $8.32 in 2007.[10] The statistic that the average real wage remains below its peak of more than 30 years ago has become a rhetorical battering ram against trade liberalization. It is a prime example of where the critics of trade readily seize upon a piece of data to make their case no matter how flawed it may be.

The Unreality of the Real Wage Data

The average real wage is a fundamentally flawed measure of the well-being and progress of American workers, for three reasons: First, the real wage does not include benefits. Second, it relies on cost-of-living estimates that have tended to systematically overstate inflation in recent decades and thus understate gains in real earnings.

Figure 3.3
RISING COMPENSATION FOR AMERICAN WORKERS

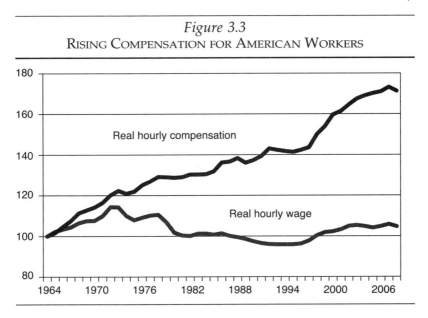

Third, today's real wage is often compared to past peaks that were deceptively high.

By excluding benefits, the real wage data underplay the real gains made by American workers. Although money wages remain a majority of total compensation, benefits have grown as a share of the average worker's compensation package. Those benefits help Americans pay for medical care and retirement. More companies than in decades past are also offering dental and eye care benefits and more generous paid leave and matching 401(k) contributions. The average real wage numbers fail to capture those real benefits.

A more accurate measure of earnings is "real hourly compensation," which includes not only wages but benefits. The BLS data on wages and benefits combined tell a more accurate and encouraging story about the well-being of the average American worker. Since 1973, average real hourly compensation for American workers has increased by 41 percent, and by 23 percent since 1991.[11] Figure 3.3 shows that real hourly compensation has not only climbed since 1973, but its rise began to accelerate in the 1990s along with America's growing economic openness. The average American worker has not suffered from "stagnant" earnings in the past three decades but in fact has enjoyed real gains.

Even the more comprehensive compensation numbers tend to understate the real gains American workers have enjoyed in recent decades. Economists have long realized that the consumer price index (CPI) tends to overstate the cost of living compared to past years because it often fails to accurately capture the increased quality of new and improved products. As Michael Cox and Richard Alm explain in their 1999 book, *Myths of Rich & Poor*, new products do not show up in the CPI shopping cart until several years after they have become popular with consumers. For example, pocket calculators were not added until 1978, VCRs until 1987, and cell phones until 1998 (by which time nearly 40 percent of households already owned one).[12] That means the CPI fails to capture the steep price declines that often mark new electronic consumer goods as they become ubiquitous.

Thanks in no small part to international trade, American workers today benefit from an ever-expanding and improving array of products on which they can spend their paychecks. In the mythical golden era of 1973, the average American worker earning a supposedly higher real wage could not buy a microwave oven, personal computer, cell phone, laser printer, CD, DVD, or MP3 player, iPod, digital camera, camcorder, a car with air bags and antilock brakes, or a cheap cross-country ticket on a discount airline.[13] When we fully account for benefits as well as wages and the wider and more useful array of products we can buy today, the average American worker is much better compensated than his counterpart in decades past.

A third way the real wage data are misused is by the constant comparison to the peak of 1972–73. If more recent real wage data have been distorted by an overstating of inflation, the data of the early 1970s were distorted in the opposite direction. The year 1973 marked the final sprint of a Nixon-era, election-cycle expansion fueled by easy monetary policies and wage and price controls that kept inflation temporarily bottled up (only to see it explode into double digits in 1974). The price controls caused real wages to appear deceptively high that year, making it a misleading benchmark to judge subsequent years.

The Growth of Middle-Class Service Jobs

Behind the rise in average real compensation is a changing mix and growing number of middle-class service jobs. The common story

Table 3.1
MORE JOBS, BETTER-PAYING JOBS

| Employment Sector | Number of Jobs (thousands) | | | Average Hourly Wage |
	1991	2008	Change	(2008)
Information	2,677	2,987	310	$24.74
Natural resources and mining	739	774	35	$22.42
Construction	4,780	7,175	2,395	$21.86
Professional and business services	10,714	17,863	7,149	$21.15
Financial activities	6,558	8,192	1,634	$20.28
Education and health services	11,506	18,878	7,372	$18.78
Subtotal	36,974	55,869	18,895	$20.52
Manufacturing	17,068	13,455	−3,613	$17.72
Trade, transportation, utilities	22,281	26,332	4,051	$16.19
Other services	4,249	5,520	1,271	$15.86
Leisure and hospitality	9,256	13,615	4,359	$10.83
Subtotal	35,786	45,467	9,681	$14.54
Government	18,545	22,457	3,912	

SOURCE: U.S. Bureau of Labor Statistics.

is that trade has caused the loss of well-paying, mostly unionized, middle-class manufacturing jobs, whereas the service economy creates mostly lower-paying, nonunion jobs in food service or retail. That is one of the big lies of the current trade debate. Although some better-paying manufacturing jobs have indeed disappeared, the trend in recent decades has been for lower-paying factory jobs to be replaced by better-paying service jobs.

Since the beginning of the 1990s, the U.S. labor market has in fact shed a net 3.6 million manufacturing jobs. But that loss has been overwhelmed by the creation of 18.9 million net new jobs in mostly service sectors where the average wage is higher than in manufacturing (see Table 3.1). Education and health services alone added 7.4 million jobs between 1991 and 2008. Another net 7.1 million new jobs were created in the professional and business services sector, 2.4 million in construction, and 1.6 million in financial activities—

all sectors where average wages are significantly higher than in manufacturing.[14]

Two-thirds of the net new jobs created in the past two decades of rapid globalization are in sectors where the average wage is higher than in manufacturing. For every one job lost in manufacturing since 1991, our economy has created five in better-paying service sectors, three in less well-paying sectors, and one in government. That pattern was not just a phenomenon of the 1990s. During the Bush years of 2001–2008, two-thirds of the net new jobs were also created in sectors that paid more than manufacturing.

In recent years, economists and politicians have raised the specter that millions of those better-paying white-collar service jobs are now "at risk" because of outsourcing. It is true that the Internet and the falling cost of international telecommunications have made it possible to trade services that were not tradable before. This development has allowed U.S. companies to outsource call center work to the Philippines and computer programming to India. But only a small share of American service jobs could be easily outsourced, and Americans are more likely to sell outsourcing services to the rest of the world than to buy them. Because of our continuing comparative advantage in knowledge-based sectors, we continue to run a large trade surplus with the rest of the world in higher-end services. In 2008, Americans exported $85 billion more in "other private services" than we imported, including big margins in financial, business, professional, and technical services.[15]

In contrast to the nostalgia about manufacturing, the American middle class today earns its keep from better-paying service sector jobs. Knock on doors in a typical middle-class American neighborhood, and you will meet people who work not in factories but in the service sector: teachers, managers, carpenters, architects, engineers, computer specialists, truck drivers, loan officers, vocational counselors, public relations specialists, automotive service technicians, accountants and auditors, police officers and fire fighters, insurance and real estate agents, registered nurses, physical therapists, dental hygienists and other health care professionals, and self-employed business owners.[16] Those are the occupations that now form the backbone of the American middle class. Those are the jobs our children aspire to fill.

Middle Class and Moving Up

A related theme repeated by critics of trade is that global competition has "squeezed" the American middle class. Large sections of Lou Dobbs' book, *The War on the Middle Class*, and many of his nightly homilies are devoted to criticizing trade expansion as a major battle front. As trade and globalization destroy higher-paying manufacturing jobs, the story goes, the great American middle class finds itself shrinking and in threat of disappearing altogether.

As with the employment and wage data, truth about the size and state of the American middle class has become another casualty of anti-trade propaganda. America remains a solidly middle-class country, with a large and growing number of middle-class households earning their living in the service sector. To the extent that trade has affected the middle-class job market, it has tended to create better-paying jobs while eliminating lower-paying jobs. Real household income in America, like real hourly compensation, has continued to trend upward through the ups and downs of recurring business cycles.

The Upward Trend in Household Incomes

Opponents of trade expansion frequently compare the latest median household income figures with those of the year 2000, a peak year at the end of a decade-long expansion. But when compared with previous years at similar stages in the business cycle, the latest household income numbers fail to provide any support for dire warnings about a shrinking middle class or declining household income.

According to the most recent numbers from the U.S. Census Bureau, the median income of America's 117 million households was $50,233 in 2007. That figure was indeed slightly below the median of $50,557 in 2000 (expressed in real, 2007 dollars).[17] That fact has allowed ideological opponents of trade to say, "The median household income has been dropping for eight years!" But that isn't quite right. Median household income did decline in the wake of the 2001 recession, as it does during every downturn, but it had been rising again since 2004 as the economy gained steam. In fact, median household income in 2005, 2006, and 2007 rose almost exactly in line with the long-term trend stretching back 40 years, as we can see in Figure 3.4.

Figure 3.4
MEDIAN HOUSEHOLD INCOME, 1967–2007

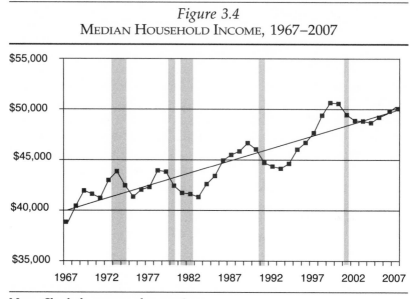

NOTE: Shaded areas mark recessions.
SOURCE: U.S. Census Bureau.

As the graph reveals, median household income fluctuates with the business cycle as it trends upward. Like the waves of an incoming tide, household incomes retreat during recessions, then climb back during the recovery and expansion to eventually exceed the previous peak, only to repeat the cycle. During the previous five cycles of recession and expansion, median household income fell an average of 4.5 percent from peak to trough and then expanded 8.7 percent until the next peak and downturn.[18] Two steps forward, one step back, two steps forward—and through it all, American households have reaped an average gain of $246 in real spending power each year.

The positive trend in household income probably understates the standard-of-living gains of individuals within households. The average number of people per U.S. household has been declining for decades because of more single-parent households, more young single people living outside their parents' home before they marry, more elderly widows, and fewer children per family. Between 1970 and 2005, the average number of people per household fell from 3.2 to 2.6. That number means that the higher incomes earned by today's households are supporting fewer members, allowing even more

Figure 3.5
THE REAL STORY OF THE "SHRINKING MIDDLE CLASS"

NOTE: Household incomes in real 2007 dollars.
SOURCE: U.S. Census Bureau.

purchasing power per person. After decades of expanding trade and globalization, American households, like individual workers, are earning more. There is no reason to doubt that trend will resume once we recover from the current recession.

Behind the "shrinking" middle class

The American middle class is not disappearing but moving up. The same government numbers that show an upward trend in median household income also show a rising share of households moving up to the middle class and beyond. According to the Census Bureau, just under one-third of American households earned a middle-class income of between $35,000 and $75,000 in 2007. That share was indeed down slightly from the 35.8 percent of households that fit that definition of middle class in 1990 (all incomes again in real, 2007 dollars) (see Figure 3.5). But if the middle class has been shrinking, it is not because more families have been squeezed by globalization and other pressures into lower income brackets. The share of households earning less than $35,000 also shrank during the period,

41

from 38.5 percent to 35.5 percent. Meanwhile, the share of households earning \$75,000 or more jumped from 25.6 percent to 32.1 percent.[19]

If we define the middle class more broadly, say \$35,000 to \$100,000; or \$25,000 to \$75,000; or \$25,000 to \$100,000; the same pattern emerges: The middle class continues to slowly shrink over time, while the share of households earning less also shrinks and the share earning more continues to grow. As we see in Figure 3.5, the "decline" of the middle class has been remarkably gradual and steady. During times of recession, the lower-income brackets grow, whereas during good times, the upper-income brackets swell. Over time, the great American middle class has been shrinking not because more households have slipped down the income ladder but because more have moved up.

Contributing to that upward mobility has been the growth of two-earner households. Some critics decry the trend of women joining the workforce as another negative result of globalization, claiming that the alleged downward pressure on wages has forced wives and mothers to leave home for the workplace to help the family pay its bills. But this argument ignores the ample evidence that real hourly compensation and the number of higher-paying service sector jobs have been rising over time, not falling. Critics also ignore the many positive reasons why so many women have decided since the 1970s to work outside the home for pay. Those reasons include growing levels of education among women, growing career opportunities in the expanding service sector, and the wider availability of labor-saving appliances and prepared foods that have reduced labor demands at home—reasons that have nothing to do with globalization and a "middle-class squeeze."

Most women have always labored, whether in the home, farm, or workplace. The difference today compared to four or five decades ago is that a significantly larger share now get paid in dollars in the labor market, which has expanded the financial opportunities of American families. As Cox and Alm observe in their book *Myths of Rich and Poor*,

> When men went to work outside the home, the family's living standards rose because of the tremendous gains from specialization and exchange. Why do we insist that the same transition for women can only mean a pinch on household's

42

possibilities? It makes no sense to suggest that the economic rules flip-flop when a second adult takes a job. Working women are a sign that families are making themselves better off, not slipping toward poverty.[20]

America remains a solidly middle-class country. A majority of Americans see themselves as middle class. They earn middle-class incomes and lead middle-class lives. Through recurring business cycles and the changing composition of employment, median household income has trended upward as a rising number of families move into the middle class and an even larger number move to the upper-income brackets. Expanding trade and globalization have played a positive role in helping Americans make the transition to a middle-class service economy.

Improving Our Household Balance Sheets

Even when the critics acknowledge the longer-term income gains of American households, they claim those gains have come at the expense of the household balance sheet. They charge that Americans have boosted their consumption primarily by borrowing, and as a result, middle-class families "are drowning in debt."[21]

That claim has more than a ring of truth. Too many American households borrowed too much money in recent years based on the mistaken assumption that home values would keep rising at double-digit rates. When housing prices began to fall in 2006, Americans were forced to curtail consumption and even give up their homes to foreclosure.

The resulting economic recession has been brutal on the balance sheets of American households. Over the course of 2008, the double whammy of falling home and stock prices reduced the net worth of American households and nonprofits by more than $11 trillion, or 18 percent.[22] But the recession and loss of wealth cannot plausibly be blamed on trade and globalization, and in fact the global market for assets has helped American families build and keep their wealth.

Globalization has helped to boost the net worth of American households in two main ways: first, by raising household income above what it would be without expanded trade, and second, by enlarging opportunities to tap into global capital markets directly and indirectly. As we will see in more detail in chapter 6, outward foreign investment has boosted returns for U.S. companies that invest abroad as well as individual and institutional U.S. investors who have added foreign holdings to their portfolios. Inward foreign investment has created well-paying jobs for American workers while increasing demand for real estate, business, and financial assets held by American households. The lower interest rates delivered by the inflow of foreign capital have boosted asset prices for Americans while lowering their borrowing costs and debt service payments.

Even when we account for the recent loss in household wealth, the balance sheet of the typical American family is still healthier than it was 10 or 20 years ago. Every three years, the Federal Reserve Board conducts a "Survey of Consumer Finances," a detailed look at the changing incomes and wealth of American households. According to the most recent survey, released in March 2009, the net household wealth of the median U.S. family rose from about $75,000 in the early 1990s, to $100,000 by 2004, to $120,000 in 2007 (all figures in real 2007 dollars). The recent dive in stock and housing values dropped the median net wealth of U.S. households back to just below $100,000 in late 2008, according to the survey's authors. Despite the drop, the median family net worth is still 10 percent above a decade ago and a solid 30 percent above what it was 20 years ago[23] (see Figure 3.6).

A closer look at the typical household balance sheet shows that families have not been "drowning in debt," nor have they been borrowing just to pay for daily necessities. More than 70 percent of debt accumulated by American families has been used to purchase and improve our primary residences, and 11 percent has been used to finance other residential property. Another 6 percent of our debt went to buying vehicles and 4 percent to financing education. Only about 6 percent of family debt in 2007 had been used to buy goods and services.[24]

Credit card debt has been rising in recent years but only at about the same rate as our overall incomes, as one might expect. According to the latest Survey of Consumer Finances, less than 4 percent of family debt is owed to credit card issuers. Less than half of American families owed any balance on their credit cards as of 2007,[25] and the median outstanding credit card balance for families in the middle quintile of income was a manageable $2,400.[26]

The share of family income needed for debt payments, including principal and interest, has held steady during the past decade. The

Figure 3.6
MEDIAN NET WORTH OF AMERICAN HOUSEHOLDS

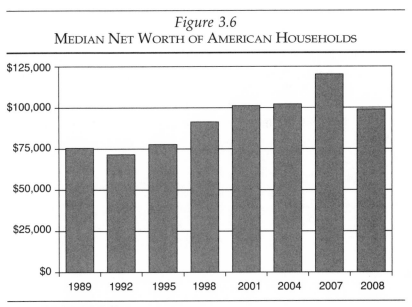

NOTE: Real 2007 dollars.

SOURCE: 2007 Survey of Consumer Finance, Federal Reserve Board.

ratio of debt payments to family income for all U.S. households was 14.9 percent in 1998 and 14.5 percent 2007. The ratio for families in the middle quintile of income rose slightly during the same period, from 18.7 percent to 19.8 percent. By keeping interest rates lower, our openness to the global economy actually makes it easier for American families to manage their debt.[27]

The opportunities offered by our engagement in the global economy have raised incomes and asset values and lowered the cost of borrowing for middle-class American families. The latest recession has brought hardship to millions of American households, but we would be in even worse condition if our government deprived us of access to global markets.

Those who blame trade for "declining real wages" and a "shrinking middle class" are guilty at the very least of a lack of perspective. They have confused the passing pain of a cyclical downturn with the long-term, ongoing, upward trend in U.S. living standards. Trade cannot be blamed for causing recessions. Even the best economists have not figured out how to repeal the business cycle. Trade does, however, boost the overall productivity of the economy and individual workers, allowing more goods and services to be produced in an average hour of work, leading to higher real compensation per hour and a higher median household income than if our economy were not as open to trade. In part because of expanding trade, American workers and households emerge from each recession and recovery in a better place economically than they would be without trade.

4. U.S. Manufacturing in a Global Economy: More Stuff, Better Stuff, Fewer Workers

"We just don't make things anymore!" That common refrain captures the widespread perception that America is "deindustrializing." We hear repeatedly that our manufacturing base has been shrinking, and as a result our economy, our security, and our identity are all in jeopardy. Exhibit A is the fact that more than 3 million net manufacturing jobs have disappeared in the past decade as we continue to run a huge trade deficit in manufactured goods with the rest of the world.

Super Bowl rocker Bruce Springsteen captured the angst in his 1984 song, "Hometown":

> Now Main Street's whitewashed windows and vacant stores
> seems like there ain't nobody wants to come down here no more
> They're closing down the textile mill across the railroad tracks
> Foreman says these jobs are going boys and they ain't coming back
> to your hometown.[1]

Two decades later, the critics of trade are still singing the same mournful tune. In a 2003 column titled "The Death of Manufacturing," conservative Pat Buchanan wrote, "Across America, the story is the same: steel and lumber mills going into bankruptcy; textile plants moving to the Caribbean, Mexico, Central America, and the Far East; auto plants closing [here] and opening overseas; American mines being sealed and farms vanishing."[2] On the left, Sen. Byron Dorgan (D-ND) asserts in his 2006 book, *Take This Job and Ship It*, that "America's manufacturing base is being dismantled. . . . Our manufacturing base is shrinking. . . . Our nation is in danger of having the world's strongest manufacturing and industrial base destroyed."[3]

At the center of anxiety about U.S. manufacturing is the trade deficit. In 2008, Americans imported $1,628 billion worth of manufactured goods from abroad and exported $1,000 billion worth, resulting in a trade deficit of $628 billion.[4] Opponents of trade expansion cite the deficit as all the proof they need for the failure of U.S. trade policies. In fact, our trade deficit tells a misleading story about American manufacturing. The aggregate trade numbers disguise the huge domestic market that U.S. manufacturing firms continue to serve and the comparative advantage of U.S. producers in higher-end products. By virtually every measure but employment, the long-term trend for America's manufacturing and industrial base has been one of growth, not decline.

Cars, Planes, Steel, Computers, Refrigerators, Chlorine Gas, and Pills

Contrary to the popular picture, U.S. manufacturing in the past decade has been more than surviving in a global economy. Although the recession that took hold in 2008 has been brutal for many U.S. manufacturers, as recently as 2006, American factories were producing more output, more sales, more profit, and a higher return on investment than ever before. It's true that certain sectors have contracted and factories have closed in the face of global competition, dislocating workers and impacting real lives. But other sectors of U.S. manufacturing, in fact most sectors, have found a profitable place serving global and domestic markets. Stories of the demise of U.S. manufacturing can be found in the popular press, on TV, and in the halls of Congress, but not when we actually count and measure what we make.

As part of its monitoring of the national economy, the Federal Reserve Board each month estimates the volume of manufacturing produced by U.S. factories. Volume means the actual quantity of output after adjusting for quality changes. According to the Fed, the volume of manufacturing output in the United States in the recession year of 2008 was still 10 percent higher than during the previous recession of 2001. Since the earlier downturn of 1991, the total volume of U.S. manufacturing output has expanded by two-thirds, and since 1980, output has more than doubled. Although output rises and falls with the overall economy, as we can see in Figure 4.1, the long-term trend for U.S. manufacturing output in our more globalized world—like the trends for real hourly compensation for workers and median income for households—continues to point upward.

Behind the aggregate index are millions of tangible "made in the U.S.A." goods that we buy and use every day. In 2007, U.S. factories and workers manufactured:[5]

Figure 4.1
U.S. MANUFACTURING OUTPUT, 1970–2008

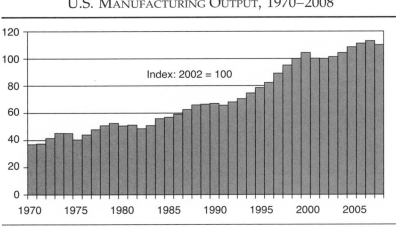

SOURCE: Federal Reserve Board.

- 5,250 complete civil aircraft valued at $7.83 million each and 15,341 complete civil aircraft engines valued at $589,998 each[6]
- 81 million metric tons of raw steel and 113 million tons of shipped steel products[7]
- 10.7 million motor vehicles[8]
- 25,657,243 computers (digital, analog, hybrid, and other) valued at $1,437 each[9]
- 11,594,319 household refrigerators and refrigerator-freezers; 11,618,088 washing machines; 7,097,709 water heaters (electric and nonelectric); 8,415,134 dishwashing machines; 7,133,988 household gas and electric ranges; and 1,366,231 clothes dryers[10]
- 10,403,942 motor-vehicle air conditioning systems; 3,959,624 split system air-conditioning condensing units; 3,664,663 natural gas, forced-air furnaces; 2,132,547 room air-conditioners; 1,861,941 air source heat pumps (excluding room air-conditioners); 727,598 commercial refrigeration units and mechanical drinking water coolers; and 592,174 year-round, central air-conditioners[11]
- 31,361,195 electric (nonindustrial) fans[12]
- 1.61 billion square yards of carpet and rugs, enough to cover 6.1 million average-sized U.S. homes wall to wall[13]

49

- 11.9 million short tons of chlorine gas, 8.9 million tons of sodium hydroxide, 4.7 million tons of hydrochloric acid, and another 2.6 million tons of commercial aluminum sulfate, sodium sulfate, finished sodium bicarbonate, and sodium chlorate[14]
- 1.5 billion gallons of paint and allied products at $13.60 a gallon[15]
- $123 billion worth of pharmaceutical preparations (except biologicals)[16]
- And a large share of the 3.13 billion books sold in the United States that year[17]

That's a lot of stuff. Some of those numbers have been falling and others rising in recent years, but nobody can say that Americans don't make anything anymore. American workers produce millions and millions of big and complicated manufactured goods every year in a relatively open U.S. market. We don't appreciate all the manufactured goods our fellow Americans produce because most of it is not the kind of stuff we put in our closets or living rooms. We are much more likely to buy a shirt made in Bangladesh or a DVD player made in China than an American-made jet engine or a ton of steel or chlorine gas. Many of our heavy appliances are made in America, but the labels of origin are not as obvious.

The American companies and sectors producing all those products have (in recent years, up to the current downturn) enjoyed a growing and profitable business. According to a recent study by my Cato colleague Daniel Ikenson, U.S. manufacturing companies in 2006 enjoyed record real output, record real revenues, and record real operating profits.[18] Against a backdrop of record imports of manufactured products that year, America's domestic manufacturers earned a collective $350 billion in after-tax profits.[19] That is not the profile of a dead or even a dying industry.

U.S. factories have even managed to hold their market share of global manufacturing value added as China and other emerging economies rapidly expand their output. According to the United Nations Industrial Development Organization, America's share of the world's manufacturing value added has remained steady at about 21 percent since the early 1990s. Despite all the attention paid to China's rise as a manufacturing power, U.S. factories in 2006 cranked out two and a half times the value added of all the factories in China.[20]

Productivity Up, Employment Down

Critics of trade typically ignore output and instead complain about declining employment. As we saw in the previous chapter, 3.6 million fewer Americans were employed in manufacturing in 2008 than in the early 1990s. But a declining number of workers in a particular sector need not be a problem for the economy or for the nation as a whole, or even for the sector that is losing the jobs.

More output from fewer workers points to one inescapable fact—manufacturing output per worker has been rising, and rising smartly. U.S. factories employ fewer workers than a decade ago, not because the factories are producing less (they are in fact producing more) but because the workers they still employ are producing so much more per hour of work.

In recent decades, productivity in the manufacturing sector has been galloping ahead of productivity in the rest of the economy. Manufacturing productivity grew at about the same pace as productivity overall up until 1973, but from 1973 to 1995, it grew about 1 percentage point faster, and since 1995, it has grown nearly 2 percentage points faster than overall nonfarm business productivity.[21] Behind the surge in productivity has been the interplay of automation, more skilled workers, computer-guided production systems, and just-in-time inventory management, among other production improvements. The result has been a relative as well as absolute decline in manufacturing employment.

Rising productivity is not a mark of weakness in U.S. manufacturing but of strength. In fact, rising productivity is the essence of economic progress and competitiveness. Higher productivity allows U.S. manufacturers to compete effectively in global markets even though workers in other countries are paid less. It allows U.S. companies to pay more to their workers for an hour of work than what factory owners pay in countries where workers are less productive.

The real test of a nation's manufacturing might is not how many workers it employs in the sector but the real value of what it produces. Consider which of these two countries would be more of a manufacturing power: The first employs 20 million workers churning out 1 billion widgets a year, the second 10 million workers producing 2 billion widgets. Unless your job is to collect union dues from as many workers as possible, the answer is obviously the second country—the one that produces twice as many widgets through the effort of workers who are four times more productive (200 widgets per worker per year vs. 50).

If employment is the measure of success, then America would be more of a manufacturing power than it is today if half the American workforce earned its living cobbling shoes, sewing shirts, and finishing tables in our garages. Such a cottage-industry economy would reverse America's progress by a couple of centuries. In contrast, expanding global trade has helped to make America the manufacturing powerhouse that it remains to this day.

The Not-So-Telling Anecdote of the Swingline Stapler Factory

Instead of acknowledging the general progress of U.S. manufacturing, the critics spin anecdotes. A factory closing down and hundreds of workers losing their jobs can create powerful and sympathetic images. But anecdotes can obscure a more accurate picture of the underlying transformation of American manufacturing.

In his 2000 book, *The Selling of "Free Trade": NAFTA, Washington, and the Subversion of American Democracy,* author John R. MacArthur spends the first 50-plus pages recounting in great detail the story of a stapler factory in Queens, New York, forced to shut down a decade ago because of competition with Mexico. With a reporter's eye for detail, MacArthur, the publisher of *Harper's* magazine, recounts how Swingline, Inc., was founded earlier in the 20th century, how the staplers were made for decades at the company's Leemar Building on 33rd Street in the Long Island City section of Queens, and how the famed "Classic 747" Swingline staplers themselves were fabricated and assembled at the main plant and headquarters nearby at 3200 Skillman Avenue. He even describes the huge, 60-foot-high Swingline sign that dominated the neighborhood's skyline for decades. (A photo of the sign, rusted and in disrepair, serves as cover art for the book and a metaphor of the decrepit state of U.S. manufacturing under the ravages of free trade.)[22]

In the summer of 1998, the happy story of the Swingline stapler factory came to an end. In the midst of the chapter titled, "Death of a Factory: Long Island City," MacArthur writes:

> As I walked into the fluorescent-lit habitat of Swingline's Leemar Building on July 30 [1998], the Dow Jones Industrial Average was still giddy from a record high of 9,338 on July

17, U.S. unemployment had fallen to 4.5 percent, and the U.S. dollar was the dominant currency of the world. At the same time, Swingline Inc., a division of ACCO USA, in turn a subsidiary of Fortune Brands, was shutting down its two Long Island City plants, laying off 450 people and moving the operation and all its jobs to Nogales, just across the U.S. border, in the Mexican state of Sonora.[23]

Here, supposedly, was the giant sucking sound for all to hear. Just as critics of trade had warned, or so MacArthur explains, the lower tariffs brought about by NAFTA had encouraged U.S. companies to move operations to Mexico in search of the cheapest labor possible, putting downward pressure on wages in the United States. In fact, the demise of the Swingline factory in Queens a decade ago provides a perfect example of comparative advantage at work for the greater good.

Although the factory's closing caused temporary hardship for several hundred workers, it was not indicative of a general decline in U.S. manufacturing. Over the course of 1998, the year in which the Swingline plant closed its doors, the real volume of output at U.S. factories was 7 percent higher than the year before and 36 percent higher than output in the final pre-NAFTA year of 1993. Stapler factories may have been moving to Mexico, but many more U.S. factories were staying put and actually ramping up production and employment.

Manufacturing growth was so strong that the number of total jobs was actually growing along with booming productivity gains. In the first five years after NAFTA took effect on January 1, 1994, the U.S. economy *added* a net 500,000 manufacturing jobs. The "death of a factory" in Long Island City that MacArthur chronicled may have typified a certain subsector of manufacturing, but for manufacturing overall, it was more a sideshow than the main story.

Swingline's departure was certainly not the death of Long Island City. The New York City neighborhood has managed to survive and thrive in the years after the last fluorescent light was turned off at the stapler factory. On an October 2007 visit to New York, I rode the Number 7 subway line from Manhattan just a few short stops to the 33rd Street/Rawson Street Station in Queens, just down the street from both former Swingline plants. At 10:00 a.m. on a normal weekday, I emerged along with a throng of other passengers onto a bustling Queens Boulevard. The neighborhood is an eclectic mix of upscale delis; computer, appliance, and furniture stores; a YMCA; a McDonald's; and LaGuardia Community College.

The former Swingline headquarters building on Skillman Avenue has seen better days, but the three-story industrial plant is no empty hulk, either. Inhabiting the space where staplers were once made are now Ames Tools and Supplies Service, the City View Tennis Club, and shipping and receiving facilities for Mercury Beach-Maid Inc., S&S Industries, and Krysman Inc. In front of the frame at the top of the building that once displayed the Swingline sign is now one for North Fork Bank. The Leemar Building down the street became semifamous in the post-Swingline era as the temporary home of the Museum of Modern Art from 2002 to 2005 while the main museum site in Manhattan was being remodeled. The spruced-up facility continues to serve as a storage site for the museum.

The real lesson of the Swingline stapler factory in Long Island City is not that free trade inevitably closes factories. Moving to free trade will cause some factories to close, but it will allow others to expand production. The factories and sectors that expand will generally be those that enjoy a comparative advantage in the U.S. economy—those that are more technology and capital intensive, that require innovative product development and not just rote assembly, and that locate in regions of the country where land, labor, and transportation costs allow profitable operations.

The Swingline factory was not just crowded out by competition from Mexico. It also faced competition from other producers in New York City competing for the same land, workers, and capital. Manufacturing low-tech staplers a 15-minute subway ride from Manhattan was probably not viable in the long run given the city's prospering service sector. If the Swingline operation had not moved to Nogales, Mexico, or another low-wage country, it probably would have moved to a lower-cost region of the United States the way the textile mills moved from New England to the South a hundred years ago. Swingline's 450 workers would still have lost their jobs, but they would have had the cold comfort of knowing it was not because of international trade.

Moving Up the Value Chain

As the tale of the Swingline factory in Long Island City really illustrates, expanding trade has not reduced manufacturing output, but it has upgraded the mix of what we make. While output has continued to rise decade after decade, growth has been especially robust for high-tech goods such as semiconductors, computers and peripheral equipment, information and audio/visual equipment, medical equipment and supplies, oil drilling equipment, pharmaceuticals, chemicals, and nonautomotive durable goods such as major household appliances.[24] In contrast, a more globalized economy has not been so kind to American makers of clothing, textiles, leather goods, footwear, and pottery ceramics—all products where Americans enjoy no comparative advantage in global markets.

Despite the evidence, the myth still lingers that American manufacturing has lost its high-technology edge. At a congressional hearing in March 2007, the chairman of the House Foreign Affairs Subcommittee on Terrorism, Nonproliferation, and Trade, Rep. Brad Sherman (D-CA), unleashed a broadside against the impact of trade on U.S. manufacturing. Quoting a newspaper column, the chairman said "[T]he United States 'has the export profile of a 19th-century Third World economy.' . . . Our chief exports are not value-added high-tech goods. They are scrap metal, waste paper, cigarettes, rice, cotton, coal, meat, wheat, gold, soybeans, and corn."[25]

Talk about misleading. The only sense in which those commodities could be considered "our chief exports" would be by weight or volume. But that is not how the world measures trade. No country would trade away a ton of semiconductors for a ton of soybeans, or a container of name-brand pharmaceuticals for a container of scrap metal. What matters is value—what others are willing to pay—and by that measure, our chief exports are almost all high-technology manufactured goods. By Chairman Sherman's measure, air freight accounts for only a trivial 2 percent of global trade (by weight), but according to Frederick W. Smith, chairman and CEO of FedEx, air freight now carries 40 percent of the value of international trade, much of it the high-tech, high-value-added components fueling the information economy.[26]

In 2007, America's top ten exports by total value were, in descending order: semiconductors, civilian aircraft, passenger car parts and accessories, passenger cars (new and used), industrial machines, pharmaceutical preparations, telecommunications equipment, organic chemicals, electric apparatus, and computer accessories (see Table 4.1). Every one of those categories, except perhaps organic

Table 4.1
AMERICA'S CHIEF EXPORTS 2007
(in billions of U.S. dollars)

Exports by End-Use	Value
Semiconductors	$50.2
Civilian aircraft	$48.8
Vehicle parts and accessories	$44.2
Passenger cars, new and used	$43.7
Industrial machines, other	$38.3
Pharmaceutical preparations	$35.0
Telecommunications equipment	$31.4
Chemicals-organic	$31.4
Electric apparatus	$31.1
Computer accessories	$29.4

chemicals, would comfortably qualify as high-tech. None of them would typify a commodity-exporting Third World country from the 19th century. Together, they accounted for more than a third of total U.S. exports.[27]

In terms of their actual value, the commodities Representative Sherman cited as "our chief exports" rank far down the list. Nonmonetary gold ranks 26th out of 139 categories of exports, corn 34th, soybeans 35th, meat 38th, wheat 42nd, and raw cotton, coal, tobacco, rice, scrap metal, and waste paper even further back in the pack.[28]

Come to think of it, why should our country be embarrassed about exporting millions of tons of corn, meat, soybeans, cotton, wheat, and coal? America today is blessed not only with cutting-edge, high-tech industries employing millions of well-educated workers but also with rich and ample farmland and abundant natural resources. The fact that those commodities have found a place in our export mix is nothing to apologize for but rather more evidence that comparative advantage works. Perhaps it is the subcommittee chairman who owes an apology to America's farmers, coal miners, and scrap metal and waste paper dealers who have found successful niches in world markets. We should celebrate and not denigrate their global success.

Other members of Congress pine for a past when we manufactured a less sophisticated array of goods. In his 2006 book, Senator Dorgan lamented that America now imports certain name-brand manufactured products that it once made at home. The senator described the demise of domestic production of such icons as Huffy bicycles, Etch-a-Sketch, Fig Newton cookies, Pennsylvania House Furniture, Levi's blue jeans, Fruit of the Loom underwear, and Radio Flyer Classic Red Wagons.[29] All were once made in the United States but are now imported from China and other lower-wage countries.

Of course, moving production of those products offshore has cost certain workers their jobs, bringing hardship to families and to communities where those industries were concentrated. But those job losses were relatively small compared to the overall size and churn of the U.S. labor market. As we saw in chapter 2, a growing reliance on imports for those lower-tech items has kept prices low for millions of consumers on modest incomes. More American kids in small towns in North Dakota can enjoy a bicycle or a wagon or name-brand blue jeans because of imports.

Like the closing of the Swingline stapler factory, the demise of factories producing Huffy bicycles, Etch-a-Sketches, and Fruit of the Loom underwear has freed workers, land, and investment capital to go to work for other, more competitive producers—creating more fulfilling jobs for today and tomorrow rather than preserving the jobs of yesterday. U.S. manufacturing has been moving up the value chain, not down, producing and selling more and better stuff as our nation becomes ever more integrated in the global economy.

Assembled in China, Created and Enjoyed in America

Nothing illustrates America's move up the manufacturing value chain more than our growing trade with China. Despite the fears about the $266 billion bilateral trade deficit with China, U.S. manufacturing has not been under threat from alleged "unfair" Chinese imports. Our growing trade with China has probably accelerated the decline of the more low-tech, labor-intensive sectors of U.S. manufacturing, whereas the growth of the Chinese economy has provided a major export market for higher-end U.S. manufacturers.

Everyone can agree that imports stamped "made in China" have soared in the past decade. In 2007, the total value of goods imported from China surpassed $300 billion, a huge increase from the $60 billion we imported in 1996. During that same period, imports from China as a share of total U.S. imports rose from 6 to 15 percent.

During the past decade, imports from China have grown more than twice as fast as imports from the rest of the world.

Despite their rapid increase, imports from China have not been a major source of competition for most major sectors of U.S. manufacturing. Chinese factories specialize in lower-tech, labor-intensive goods, in contrast to the higher-tech, capital-intensive goods that are the comparative advantage of U.S. manufactures. Many of the hard-hit industries, such as apparel, footwear, toys, games, and sporting goods, have been in decline for decades, long before China became a major source of imports. Rising imports from China have not so much replaced domestic production in the United States as they have replaced imports that used to come from South Korea, Taiwan, and Hong Kong. The biggest job losses in manufacturing during the 2000–2003 downturn, when many of those 3 million jobs were lost, occurred in export-intensive industries for the United States where imports from China are only a small presence. (Apparel was the one exception.)[30]

Higher up the quality scale, China has become the final assembly and export platform for a vast and deepening East Asian manufacturing supply chain. Even in mid-range products such as personal computers and DVD players, rising imports from China have typically displaced imports from other countries rather than domestic U.S. production. Final products that Americans used to buy from Japan, South Korea, Taiwan, Hong Kong, Singapore, and Malaysia are now being put together in China with components from throughout the region.

China's more economically advanced neighbors typically make the most valuable components at home, ship them to China to be combined with lower-value-added components at a foreign-owned factory, and then export the final product from China to the United States and other destinations. Thus in the trade statistics, the entire value of the product is counted as an import from China, when in fact most of the value of that product originated outside China. As China imports more and more intermediate components from the region for final assembly, its growing bilateral trade surplus with the United States has been accompanied by growing bilateral deficits with its East Asian trading partners.

The sharp rise in imports from China is not driven primarily by China's currency regime but by its emergence as the final link in

Figure 4.2
CHINA AND THE EAST-ASIAN SUPPLY CHAIN
IMPORTS TO THE UNITED STATES AS A SHARE OF TOTAL U.S. IMPORTS

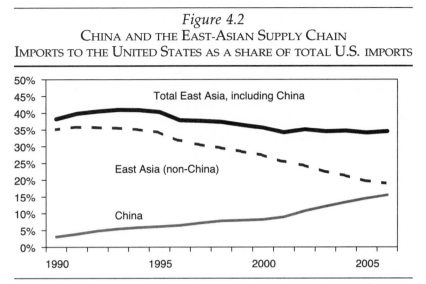

SOURCE: U.S. Department of Commerce. Major East Asian sources of imports include Japan, South Korea, Taiwan, Hong Kong, Malaysia, Indonesia, Thailand, and Singapore.

the supply chain. Although imports from China have been growing rapidly compared to overall imports, the relative size of imports from the rest of East Asia has been in decline. In 1994, the year China fixed its currency to the dollar, imports from East Asia accounted for 41 percent of total U.S. imports. By 2006, imports from that part of the world— including those from China—accounted for 34 percent of total U.S. imports. China's rising share of U.S. imports has been more than offset by an even steeper fall in the share of imports from the rest of Asia, as shown in Figure 4.2.[31]

The "made in China" label we see on so many products today fails to tell the full story. Most of the products we import from China are assembled in non–Chinese-owned factories from components that are typically made outside China. Of China's top 200 exporting companies in 2005, 70 percent were foreign owned or joint ventures.[32] China's own Ministry of Information Industry reports that foreign-owned factories now account for two-thirds of China's exports of electronic products, whereas joint ventures accounted for another 16.5 percent. That means that only one in six factories in China

59

that produce electronic products for export is purely "Chinese" in ownership terms.[33]

Goods made in those foreign-owned factories are typically stuffed with non-Chinese components. Consider a typical laptop computer sold in the United States and stamped "made in China." A look under the hood would reveal processing chips made by Intel, software from Microsoft, an LCD display screen and memory chips from South Korea or Taiwan, and a hard drive from Japan, all assembled in a factory owned by a Taiwanese company.[34] According to the Peterson Institute for International Economics, "On average, about two-thirds of the value of these so-called 'processed exports' originates outside China, mostly in other Asian countries."[35]

Something To Smile About

American companies have managed to claim their share of value-added in the bourgeoning East Asian supply chain. In the lingo of people who do business in the region, Americans have managed to grab the high ends of the "smiley curve," while the Chinese perform the lower value-added tasks in the middle. In a July 2007 cover story for the *Atlantic*, author James Fallows explains the differing roles of American and Chinese producers in the global manufacturing process:

> The [smiley] curve is named for the U-shaped arc of the 1970s-era smiley-faced icon, and it runs from the beginning to the end of a product's creation and sale. At the beginning is the company's brand: HP, Siemens, Dell, Nokia, Apple. Next comes the idea for the product: an iPod, a new computer, a camera phone. After that is high-level industrial design—conceiving of how the product will look and work. Then the detailed engineering design for how it will be made. Then the necessary components. Then the actual manufacture and assembly. Then the shipping and distribution. Then retail sales. And finally, service contracts and sales of parts and accessories.
>
> The significance is that China's activity is in the middle stages—manufacturing, plus some components supply and engineering design—but America's is at the two ends, and those are where the money is. The smiley curve, which shows the profitability or value added at each stage, starts high for branding and product concept, swoops down for manufacturing, and rises again in the retail and servicing stages. The

simple way to put this—that the real money is in brand name, plus retail—may sound obvious, but its implications are illuminating.[36]

What are the implications of the smiley curve for Chinese and American workers? "In case the point isn't clear," Fallows concludes, "Chinese workers making $1,000 a year have been helping American designers, marketers, engineers, and retailers making $1,000 a week (and up) earn even more. Plus they have helped shareholders of U.S.-based companies."[37] Exactly so.

The lesson of the smiley curve was brought home to me after a recent Christmas when I was admiring my two teenage sons' new iPod Nanos. Inscribed on the back of each was the telling label, "Designed by Apple in California. Assembled in China." To the skeptics of trade, an imported Nano only adds to our disturbingly large bilateral trade deficit with China in "advanced technology products," but here in the palm of a teenager's hand was a perfect symbol of the win-win nature of our trade with China.

Assembling iPods obviously creates jobs for Chinese workers, jobs that probably pay higher-than-average wages in that country even though they labor in the lowest regions of the smiley curve. But Americans benefit even more from the deal. A team of economists from the Paul Merage School of Business at the University of California-Irvine applied the smiley curve to a typical $299 iPod and found just what you might suspect: Americans reap most of the value from its production. Although assembled in China, an American company supplies the processing chips, a Korean company the memory chip, and Japanese companies the hard drive and display screen. According to the authors, "The value added to the product through assembly in China is probably a few dollars at most."[38]

The biggest winner? Apple and its distributors. Standing atop the value chain, Apple reaps $80 in profit for each unit sold—an amount higher than the cost of any single component. Its distributors, on the opposite high end of the smiley curve, make another $75.[39] And of course, American owners of the more than 100 million iPods sold since 2001—my teenage sons included—pocket far more enjoyment from the devices than the Chinese workers who assembled them.[40]

Handling an "assembled in China" iPod also exposes the myth that China has somehow become an "advanced technology superstate." As the chronically alarmist U.S.–China Economic and Security

Review Commission warned in a 2005 report, "U.S. producers of advanced technology products are also subject to the growing pressures posed by China. In 2004, the U.S. trade deficit in advanced technology products with China grew to $36.3 billion."[41] The message sounds ominous, but it misses the fact that most of the "advanced technology products" we import from China are what have become everyday consumer items stocking the shelves of a Best Buy or Wal-Mart. In fact, 91 percent of such products imported from China are in a single sector—information and communication products, with notebook computers the single largest item by value. A distant second in the category are so-called "opto-electronics" items such as CD and DVD players. And even if we include those off-the-shelf items, the high-tech guts are made outside China. More than 90 percent of China's exports of electronics and information technology products are produced in foreign-owned factories that have little interaction with domestic Chinese firms.[42]

Would members of the U.S.–China commission be happier if iPods had been designed by a Chinese company in Shanghai, assembled at a Japanese-owned plant in California with major components from Canada, Mexico, and Europe, and exported by the millions back to China for the enjoyment of their teenagers instead of ours? Under that scenario, our deficit with China in "advanced technology products" would be a bit smaller, but it would be the Chinese who would reap the biggest gains while we would content ourselves with the lower-paid tasks at the bottom of the smiley curve.

China As a Customer

For American manufacturers, China has become more than an assembly and export platform; it has also become a major export market for American-made goods. In the past decade, China has lowered its tariffs on goods of the greatest importance to U.S. industry from a base average of 25 percent in 1997 to 7 percent in 2006.[43] Fueled by more open and liberalized markets and double-digit economic growth, China has become the fastest growing major export market for American goods. Since Congress approved permanent normal trade relations with China in 2000, American exports of goods to China have grown at an annual rate of 23 percent, a rate almost twice as fast as in the 1990s and more than four times faster than the growth of U.S. exports to the rest of the world since 2000.[44]

By the end of 2007, China had surpassed Japan as the fourth largest market for U.S. goods exports, behind only Canada, the European Union, and Mexico.[45]

Of the $55.2 billion worth of goods that American companies exported to China in 2006, a third were industrial machinery and components, with semiconductors the single largest item, composing more than 10 percent of total U.S. exports to China. Another third of U.S. exports to China were industrial supplies, such as plastic materials, chemicals, and steelmaking supplies. Another 10 percent were civilian aircraft and parts (think Boeing). Of the remaining quarter of U.S. goods exported to China, more than half were agricultural products—with soybeans and cotton leading the way—with other transportation equipment and miscellaneous goods composing the rest.[46]

America's trade relationship with China has been good for Americans as consumers and producers. Trade with China has accelerated American industry's climb up the value ladder, opening up new export markets for leading-edge U.S. producers while filling the void left by the decline of lower-value-added industries that have been in retreat for decades.

U.S. Manufacturers Need Imports, Too

U.S. manufacturers not only sell and compete successfully in global markets, they also scour those same markets for huge amounts of raw materials, capital machinery, and parts and components. More than half of what Americans import each year are not final consumer products sold by retailers, but goods used by American companies to produce their final products here in the United States. Of the $2,117 billion in goods we imported in 2008, 21 percent were capital goods (not including automobiles), 21 percent were petroleum and other energy products, and 15 percent were industrial supplies and materials.[47] Less than half were consumer goods, automobiles, and food.

The critics of trade usually glide over the fact that U.S. manufacturers and other producers are also major importers. Instead, we are told that imports are universally bad because every good we import displaces domestic production and leads to the layoff of American workers. A dreaded "flood of imports" should mean slower growth or outright contraction of manufacturing output, whereas a slowdown

Figure 4.3
MANUFACTURING IMPORTS AND OUTPUT RISE AND FALL
TOGETHER

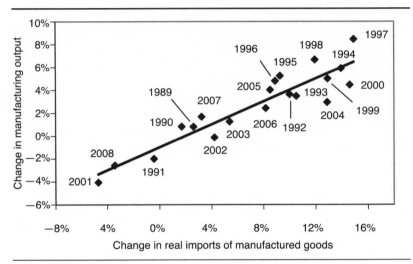

SOURCE: Bureau of Economic Analysis; Federal Reserve Board.

of import growth should bring relief to domestic producers and thus faster domestic output. The story sounds plausible, but it is almost 180 degrees wrong.

If the critics of trade were correct, a rise in the growth of manufacturing imports should lead quite directly to a decline in the growth of manufacturing output. By the same reasoning, a decline in imports should stimulate domestic output, as consumers substitute domestic-made goods for foreign-made goods. But an analysis of manufacturing imports and output during the past two decades plainly refutes this pillar of protectionist thinking.

Figure 4.3 compares the annual change in the volume of manufacturing imports to the change in manufacturing output for each year since 1989. Manufacturing imports are defined as industrial supplies and materials, capital goods, automotive vehicles and parts, and consumer goods.[48] Manufacturing output is measured by the annual average of the Federal Reserve Board's monthly index of manufacturing output.[49] The percentage change in real manufacturing imports from the previous year is plotted on the horizontal axis, and the

64

percentage change in manufacturing output from the previous year is plotted on the vertical axis. Each dot represents a specific year, showing its change in imports and output.

If the trade skeptics were right, the trend line would be sloping down—that is, the more rapidly imports grow in a particular year, the more depressed we would expect manufacturing growth to be in that same year. But something funny happened on the way to the anti-trade rally. In the past two decades, years of rapid growth in manufacturing imports are also years of rapid growth in manufacturing output, and years of slower growth in imports are years of sluggish growth, or even declines, in domestic output. The positive slope of the line means that every 2 percent uptick in the growth of manufacturing imports is, on average, associated with a 1 percent increase in manufacturing output.

One reason why manufacturing output and imports grow together is that American producers themselves are major importers. As American-based companies ramp up production to meet rising domestic demand, they must import more capital goods, intermediate inputs, and raw materials to keep the assembly lines humming. And when factories cut their production, they also cut their demand for imports. Another reason that output and imports grow together is that both track the health of the overall economy. As demand rises among American businesses and consumers, they buy more domestically made goods and more imported goods. During a downturn like the one we are suffering now, demand falls for imports as well as domestic output. American and foreign suppliers to the U.S. economy prosper and suffer together.

When it comes to manufacturing, we either enjoy years of high import and output growth, or we suffer years of low import and output growth. For most of the 1990s and again in 2004–06, we enjoyed healthy growth; in 1989–91, 2001–03, and now again during the current recession, we are suffering through low growth or declines in both imports and output. If forced to choose between the two scenarios, and it seems they are the only alternatives, I would choose more imports and output.

The critics of trade are selling an illusion. They suppose that if imports are reduced, through higher tariffs, a depreciated currency, or other policy tools, Americans will instead buy more domestically produced goods and create more and better-paying jobs at home.

But the reality of the American economy is closer to the opposite. The protectionist dream is really a nightmare for U.S. manufacturers. Slower growth of imports typically means slower growth in domestic output and vice versa. Any efforts to restrict the access of Americans to global markets—either through higher tariffs or an artificially depreciated currency—would cripple rather than protect U.S. industry. Indeed, for American manufacturers, imports and output are a package deal: The more we prosper, the more we trade; the more we trade, the more we prosper.

Manufacturing and National Security

Beyond the economic arguments, skeptics of trade warn that America's "deindustrialization" threatens our national security. The U.S. –China Security and Economic Review Commission predictably advocates that:

> Congress should consider imposing an immediate, across-the-board tariff on China's imports at the level determined necessary to gain prompt action by China to strengthen significantly the value of the RMB [its currency]. The United States can justify such an action under WTO Article XXI, which allows members to take necessary actions to protect their national security. China's undervalued currency has contributed to a loss of U.S. manufacturing, which is a national security concern for the United States."[50]

Duncan Hunter, a former Republican congressman from California and presidential candidate in 2008, cited trade as one way he differed from President Bush. "You know, we won World War I, World War II, and the Cold War with a major industrial base. We're losing our industrial base through bad policy right now."[51] When in Congress, Hunter sponsored "Buy American" amendments to defense spending bills that would require that a significantly higher share of Pentagon purchases be of American-made manufactured products rather than imports. Advocates of such a policy argue that America must retain the capacity to produce sufficient amounts of war-related materials should we be cut off from global supplies during a conflict.

One obvious weak spot in the national defense argument against trade is that America's manufacturing and industrial base is not shrinking but in fact has been expanding decade in and decade out.

Our manufacturing output and capacity are greater today than 10, 20, or 30 years ago. As we saw earlier in the chapter, America remains a formidable manufacturing force in the world. American workers produce impressive amounts of steel, chemicals, and plastics and huge numbers of aircraft, motor vehicles, appliances, semiconductors, and computers. With America's flexible internal labor and capital markets, production of items needed in wartime could ramp up quickly.

Advocates of the Buy American approach and other restrictions on trade in the name of national security are fighting an imaginary war detached from today's global realities. America is unlikely to face an embargo of shipping routes between us and our major trading partners. No Iranian, North Korean, or al-Qaeda U-boats are prowling off our shores ready to block access to global markets. Most of our imports come from a stable and diversified list of friendly countries such as Canada, Mexico, Japan, South Korea, Australia, and members of the European Union. The chances are negligible that any of those countries would cut us off commercially in wartime.

Steel provides a perfect case for what is wrong with the Buy American approach. In January 2002, the U.S. government ruled on a so-called Section 232 case that had alleged that foreign imports of steel were jeopardizing U.S. national security. As part of the Trade Expansion Act of 1962, Section 232 allows the president of the United States to "adjust the imports" of an article or good "so that such imports will not threaten to impair the national security."[52] After receiving a petition, the Secretary of Commerce investigates and then makes a recommendation to the president.

In its 2002 report, the Commerce Department weighed the needs of the U.S. military and other agencies for iron ore and semifinished steel products and found no cause for action. The investigation found no evidence that America is dependent on imports or that imports in any way impair the ability of domestic producers to satisfy our national security requirements. The United States draws its steel imports from a diverse and dependable stable of foreign suppliers, the largest being our neighbors in the Western Hemisphere—Canada, Mexico, and Brazil. Even with imports, U.S. production dwarfs our nation's defense needs. According to the Commerce Department report, the U.S. Department of Defense consumes only about 300,000 tons of steel per year, and demand has been flat for several years.

67

That amounts to an almost trivial 0.3 percent of domestic production of 100 million tons in a typical year. As the report concluded, "There is no probative evidence that imports of iron ore or semifinished steel threaten to impair U.S. national security." [53] And that story is repeated across a wide swath of U.S. industry.

In the name of national security, Congress would cut the U.S. military off from global suppliers of needed goods preemptively in the name of promoting more plentiful supplies during a hypothetical war.

America's Post-Industrial Economy

In his 2006 book, Senator Dorgan laments that "America cannot be great if most of its workers are in the service sector or cashiering at Wal-Mart."[54] That statement is both misleading and, on a deeper level, simply false. It's misleading in the way it equates the typical service job with cashiering at a big-box retailer, when in fact—as we saw in the previous chapter—most of the new jobs being created in the service sector pay higher wages than the manufacturing jobs being lost. The statement is simply false because nearly four out of five American workers earn their living in the service sector today at a time when America remains a great country.

Do the senator and those Americans who agree with him really pine for the days when more than half of Americans worked outside the service sector? That would take us back to about 1930 when our incomes and our standard of living were far lower than they are today. Around the world, the nations with the lowest share of their workforce in services are invariably among the poorest, and those with the highest share of workers in services are among the richest. Most Americans would rather be in the latter group than in the former.

Expanding trade and globalization are helping to speed America toward a brighter post-industrial economy, and that future is nothing to fear. It appears to be a law of human development that, as incomes rise, we spend a smaller share on goods, such as food and manufactured products, and a higher share on services. At the same time, we are turning to foreign producers for a larger share (although still a minority) of the manufactured and agricultural goods we continue to purchase. This one-two effect guarantees that manufacturing will constitute a declining share of our economic output for as long as our

Figure 4.4
THE CHANGING AMERICAN WORKFORCE
(share of workforce by sector)

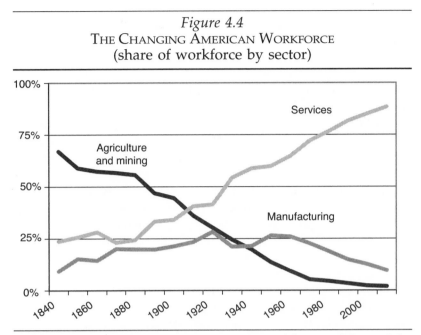

SOURCES: U.S. Census Bureau; Historical Statistics of the United States, Colonial Times to 1970 Bicentennial Edition; and Council of Economic Advisors, 2008 Economic Report of the President, Tables B-35 and B-46.

economy keeps growing. And the faster-than-average productivity growth in manufacturing means that manufacturing employment as a share of total employment will continue to fall.

None of those trends should worry us. We should embrace the relative rise of the service sector compared to manufacturing as natural and positive in an advancing economy. Virtually every developed economy today has long passed the stage where manufacturing constituted a majority or a growing share of economic output. In the United States, manufacturing peaked at 28.3 percent of the economy in 1953—more than half a century ago. Since then, it has been steadily declining to a level of 12 percent today.[55] Manufacturing employment as a share of the workforce peaked in the late 1940s at more than one-quarter of overall U.S. employment and has also been in steady decline ever since.[56] Meanwhile, employment in the service sector has been rising inexorably as employment in farming has been falling (see Figure 4.4).

69

The world's most advanced economies are all following the same path. Manufacturing's share of employment peaked for the United Kingdom and France within a decade or two after its peak in the United States, followed by Japan and Germany in the early 1970s and Taiwan and South Korea in the 1980s. Its share is already declining in Brazil and China.[57] On average, the share of workers in manufacturing in the 23 most advanced economies in the world peaked in 1970 at 28 percent.[58] For most countries, the share of the economy accounted for by industry peaks at the equivalent of $10,000 to $15,000 GDP per capita.[59] Just about every country with a standard of living above that range is "deindustrializing." The share peaked earlier in the United States than other countries not because we were somehow a less successful economy or were declining more rapidly but precisely because we were more advanced. A declining share of workers in manufacturing is not a sign of economic failure but of success.

A major reason why manufacturing is relatively less important in what Americans produce is that it is less important in what we consume. The share of personal income spent on durable and nondurable goods has been in steady decline for decades. In 1950, Americans spent two-thirds of their personal consumption income on durable and nondurable goods and one-third on services. Today we spend 60 percent of our personal income on services and 40 percent on goods. The share of personal income Americans spend on food, clothing, and shoes has dropped in half since 1950, from 38 percent to 18 percent, and the share spent on durable goods such as motor vehicles and furniture has dropped from 16 percent to 11 percent. Americans in the past half century have shifted more than a quarter of their spending from stuff grown or manufactured to services delivered.[60]

About half the increase in spending on services has been for increased medical care in the form of doctors, dentists, other medical professionals, hospitals, nursing homes, and health insurance. We have also increased the share of our spending on housing, recreation, education and research, religious and other charitable activities, domestic and foreign air travel, and "personal business"—brokerage charges, investment counseling, and banking, financial, insurance, and legal services.

We've shifted a big chunk of our household budgets from food, clothing, and other basic necessities to nurturing our health, educating our minds, and improving our finances. That sounds like progress. The increased share of spending on services has helped to spur output and employment in the domestic service sector, creating millions of those well-paying service-sector jobs discussed in the previous chapter. Those who mourn the relative decline of U.S. manufacturing shouldn't blame foreign competition but the evolving preferences and resulting spending habits of their fellow Americans.

U.S. manufacturing is going through a transition similar to American agriculture in middle of the past century. From 1940 to 1970, soaring productivity on American farms allowed agricultural output to grow by 60 percent, while actual employment on the farm declined by 6 million. During those three decades, two-thirds of farm-related jobs disappeared, probably never to return barring some sort of economic cataclysm. Agriculture's share of total employment plummeted from 19 percent of workers to 4 percent as America "de-agriculturalized." At the same time, like prices in manufacturing, real prices paid for farm goods also fell as labor productivity quadrupled, allowing consumers to reduce the share of their personal consumption expenditures on food.[61]

Although that transition destroyed millions of agricultural-related jobs, can anybody seriously argue that Americans are not better off because of it? We should view the transition of manufacturing in our more globalized era with the same hopeful expectation.

5. America's Trade Deficit: Accounting Abstraction or Public Enemy No. 1?

No aspect of international trade is so widely discussed by Americans yet so little understood as the trade deficit. Year after year, Americans spend more on imports than we earn from our exports. That's plain enough. But what that means for our economy, our jobs, and our future is open to a wide range of interpretations. Behind only "13" and "666," the U.S. trade deficit has struck more fear into the hearts of Americans than any other number.

The trade deficit has become the trump card of the critics. They present it as proof in itself that U.S. trade policy has failed and that Americans are losing in the global game of trade. When the final trade numbers were released for 2006, showing yet another record deficit, House Democratic leaders wrote to President Bush as though a plague of locusts had descended on the American landscape: "The United States has run record-setting trade deficits for each of the last five years. The consequences of these persistent and massive trade deficits include not only failed businesses, displaced workers, lower real wages, and rising inequality, but also permanent devastation of our communities."[1]

That is quite an indictment to lay at the feet of what is basically an accounting abstraction. Even in the best of economic times, a camera crew does not need to look far in our nation of 300 million to find any one of those signs of economic distress, but it is misleading to blame trade in general and the trade deficit in particular for our nation's economic troubles. The trade deficit is not a primary or even a secondary cause of economic hardship in the United States. It is the result of deeper economic currents that have little connection to trade.

What the Trade Deficit Is—and Isn't

First, let's define what we mean by the trade deficit. Those who keep track of our trade with the world measure three balances:

- The *merchandise trade balance* counts the flow of goods across our borders, including manufactured products but also agricultural goods and commodities such as lumber, minerals, and crude oil.
- The *trade balance* includes goods and services, such as travel, transportation, royalties, banking, finance, education, and technical services.
- The most comprehensive measure of trade, the *current account balance*, includes goods and services along with income earned from investments, such as interest, dividends, and profits, and unilateral transfers, such as worker remittances, foreign aid, and military transfers.

In a typical year, Americans will run a big merchandise deficit with the rest of the world, approaching $800 billion in recent years. The goods deficit typically includes large deficits in manufactured goods and crude oil partially offset by a small surplus in agricultural goods. The trade deficit is always smaller than the merchandise deficit because we typically roll up a surplus in services trade of $100 billion or more. The broader current account deficit usually clocks in close to the trade deficit, with a net outflow of unilateral transfers offset by a small net surplus earned on America's foreign investments abroad compared to what we pay out on foreign investments in the United States. (For this reason, I'll use the terms "current account deficit" and "trade deficit" interchangeably.)

Table 5.1 shows what America's trade accounts looked like in 2008:[2]

An obsession with the trade deficit obscures the important fact that Americans buy and sell in two distinct but interconnected global markets, one for current transactions for goods and services, and a much bigger market for assets, which is reflected in what is called the financial account. The key to understanding America's trade deficit is the counterintuitive fact that it is much more about investment flows than trade.

For every nation, the two markets are bound together in mirror-like fashion. A nation that runs a current account deficit, like the United States, will inevitably run a nearly equal surplus in the financial account, and a nation that runs a current account surplus, like China, will inevitably run a nearly equal deficit in the financial account.

Table 5.1
AMERICA'S TRADE ACCOUNTS FOR 2008

Merchandise balance	− $820.8 billion
+ Services	+ $139.7 billion
= Trade balance	− $681.1 billion
+ Investment income	+ $127.6 billion
+ Unilateral transfers	− $119.7 billion
= Current account balance	− $673.3 billion

The reason springs from the inherent nature of trade. We acquire things of value by surrendering things of similar value. Trade could not occur otherwise. The Japanese will not send us cars, the Chinese will not send us shoes, and the Canadians will not send us natural gas unless we give them something tangible that is of at least equal value in their eyes. Foreigners who give us things of value ultimately want to be left holding something more than little pieces of green paper.

Let's follow the money. When an American buys a $3,000 big-screen TV from Japan, the producer ultimately wants something of equal or greater value; otherwise, the trade won't happen. If the Japanese buy $3,000 worth of soybeans or engineering services, our current account is balanced and congressional leaders are happy. But if the Japanese invest the $3,000 in GE stock, a U.S. Treasury bill, or a New York City condo, the result is a $3,000 deficit in our current account and a $3,000 surplus in our financial account. Global trade accounts have become "unbalanced."

Of course, the foreign producer who provides us with the big-screen TV may not want or need anything from the United States. Because they probably can't pay their workers or suppliers in the U.S. dollars they earned by selling in our market, they exchange them for local currency on the international foreign currency market with somebody who does want to acquire something in the United States. The party who bought the dollars will then buy an American-made good or service or a U.S. asset. The result is the same: Americans acquire a good, service, or asset in exchange for a good, service, or asset.

The current and financial accounts are inextricably tied together. When we import goods and services from the rest of the world, we ultimately pay for them by either surrendering goods and services or title to assets. Our nation's international accounts are merely the sum total of millions of just those kinds of mutually beneficial transactions. Before he became a newspaper columnist, Nobel Prize–winning economist Paul Krugman wrote sensible books about international economics. As he wrote in his 1994 book *The Age of Diminished Expectations*: "As a matter of straightforward accounting, the United States always buys exactly as much as it sells from the rest of the world. If it sells foreigners more assets than it buys, it must correspondingly buy more goods [and services] than it sells."[3]

Americans practice unbalanced trade every day. Consider two businesses next door on Main Street. Jack, the owner of the USA Appliance Store, spends $1,000 to buy services from his neighbor Joe, the plumber. If Joe spends that $1,000 for a new refrigerator at his neighbor's store, their trade is "balanced" and everybody is happy. But perhaps Joe is in a saving mood and instead buys $1,000 worth of shares in the appliance store. Or he puts his earnings in the local bank, which then lowers its lending rates and extends a line of credit to USA Appliance. Jack then uses the money to install a new sign or upgrade his accounting software. But Jack's wife begins to nag him at the dinner table: "You buy from Joe, but he doesn't buy from you. That's unfair!" She urges him to boycott Joe and take his business to a competitor whose rates are higher and service inferior but who promises to spend money at the appliance store. Our nation's trade deficit debate is the same story but on a global scale.

Investment Flows Drive the Trade Account

As with the two neighbors on Main Street, savings and investment decisions are the hidden hand behind our nation's trade accounts. In 2007, the two-way trade of Americans in goods, services, and investment income totaled $5.6 trillion, but two-way cross-border investment flows—that is, the trading of assets—totaled $58 trillion.[4] In other words, our trade in assets is more than 10 times our trade in current transactions.

The exchange rate acts as a transmission belt between the two markets. When foreign demand for U.S. assets increases, so does demand for the U.S. dollars needed to buy those assets, which bids up the value of the dollar. A stronger dollar tends to make U.S. exports less competitive in global markets and imports more attractive, which together cause the current account deficit to widen. A wider trade deficit accommodates the greater net inflow of foreign investment. In effect, foreigners seeking to invest in the United States outbid foreigners seeking to purchase U.S. goods and services for the limited dollars in global exchange markets.

The reason why more investment flows into the United States each year than flows out is because the pool of domestic U.S. savings falls short of available investment opportunities. Foreign savers fill the gap. In other words, the current account is equal to the difference between domestic savings and domestic investment. If we save more than the level of domestic investment in a year, we will send our extra savings abroad and we will run a current account surplus. If we save less than the level of investment, a net surplus of capital will flow into our economy and we will run a current account deficit.

What that all means is that the trade deficit is not determined by unfair trade barriers, bad trade agreements, currency manipulation, or the alleged declining competitiveness of American industry. We run a trade deficit because our domestic level of savings falls short of domestic investment. Period. If politicians want to shrink or eliminate the trade deficit, they must find a way to either decrease domestic investment or (a better idea) increase domestic savings. But urging Americans to save more does not have the same rhetorical ring on the campaign trail as denouncing a trade agreement with Mexico or imports from China.

Why Is America's Trade Deficit So Large?

U.S. trade deficits have grown so large in recent decades for three reasons: 1) America has retained its appeal as a haven for investment, 2) domestic savings in the United States have persistently lagged behind domestic investment, and 3) the pool of global savings available to fill the gap has been overflowing. Let's briefly look at each phenomenon.

Despite its problems, the U.S. economy remains an attractive place for Americans and foreigners to put their money to work in the form of investment. Gross investment in the U.S. economy averaged $2.5 trillion a year during 2004–08, an amount equal to about 19 percent of GDP.[5] Our economy is not only by far the largest in the world but also (at least for now) one of the most free and dynamic. Businesses can make a profit in the United States serving more than 300 million relatively well-off consumers. Those companies can hire some of the world's best-educated and skilled workers, enjoy strong protections for tangible and intellectual property, and move goods and money in and out of the country more or less freely. Even during the current recession and financial turmoil, foreign capital has continued to flow into the United States in a "flight to quality."

Meanwhile, the amount of savings we set aside each year falls chronically short of investment. During that same period, 2004–08, gross savings in the U.S. economy averaged $1.8 trillion a year, an amount equal to about 14 percent of GDP.[6] The real engine of savings in our economy is the supposedly shortsighted corporate sector, which puts aside hundreds of billions of dollars each year in undistributed profits or "retained earnings." In the private household sector, as we are often reminded, savings have fallen to near zero in recent years, and the federal government runs large and now exploding fiscal deficits, which are a form of "dissavings" only partly offset by modest surpluses that state and local governments accumulate in normal years. The persistent gap between domestic savings and investment—roughly $700 billion a year, or 5 percent of GDP— suspiciously resembles the size of the chronic current account deficit.

Filling the gap so that investment in America can be fully funded are foreign savers. Each year, households, corporations, and governments abroad put aside a staggering pool of savings of $6 trillion or more. Those foreign savers have quite rationally decided to park 10 to 15 percent of their savings in the world's largest economy, the United States.[7] Foreign savings have become even more readily available in recent years because of falling government barriers to capital flows, a greater willingness of global savers to invest outside their home country—a decline in what is called "home bias"—and a "savings glut" in oil-exporting countries and emerging economies such as China. A telling sign that the world has been awash in savings is the recent decline in global real interest rates.[8]

Thus, the "global imbalances" that we are supposed to worry about in large part reflect a positive development in the global economy—the emergence of a vibrant cross-border market for assets. The liberalization of trade that began after World War II has finally

78

been matched by a liberalization of capital flows. When capital flows were restricted, the only way a nation could pay for imported goods and services was by exporting goods and services of equal value. Now people can trade for goods and services by offering assets in return, and vice versa.

Global trade is still balanced in a cosmic sense, but individual nations can now mix and match current transactions and capital flows to match their own internal level of savings and investment. Domestic savers and investors can now search abroad for better returns, whereas domestic borrowers, corporations, and entrepreneurs can seek financing beyond the limited pool of domestic savings.

The good news for Americans is that the U.S. trade deficit reflects a continued willingness of savers around the world to put their money to work in the U.S. economy. Foreigners still like to buy our stuff—we remain the world's top exporter of goods and services combined—but they love to buy our assets. U.S. real estate, U.S. Treasury bills, bank deposits, and corporate bonds and stocks have remained relatively attractive to world savers. In our globalized world, Americans enjoy a comparative advantage not just in a range of high-end services and products but also in offering attractive investment assets. Why is that such a bad thing?

The Trade Deficit and Jobs—The Real Story

For critics of trade, the deficit symbolizes everything that is wrong with free trade and U.S. trade policy. They claim with passionate intensity that the trade deficit is a drag on growth, that it destroys millions of good middle-class jobs, that it is mortgaging our future to foreign lenders, and that it will end in a messy "hard landing" for the economy. None of those charges can be made to stick.

One of the most persistent myths about the trade deficit is that it destroys jobs. Critics of trade rely on a simplistic formula that assumes that imports invariably displace U.S. jobs and that only exports create jobs, and therefore a trade deficit by definition will cause a net loss of employment. A union-backed organization in Washington called the Economic Policy Institute has raised this line of analysis to an art. It routinely publishes studies that supposedly show that our bilateral trade deficits with China, Mexico, and other trading partners have put millions of Americans out of work. Typical was an October 2007 report with the headline-grabbing title, "Costly Trade with China: Millions of U.S. jobs displaced with net job loss in every state."[9]

A major flaw of such studies is that they ignore the other channels through which trade and globalization create economic activity and employment opportunities in the U.S. economy. They focus on one column of our international accounts while ignoring the other. Foreign capital flowing into the United States—the flip side of the trade deficit—creates jobs through direct investment in U.S. companies and indirectly by lowering interest rates, which stimulates more domestic investment. Meanwhile, imports allow U.S. employers to expand production and consumers to shift their cost savings to buy other goods and services. Even when trade does displace workers, in a flexible and growing economy, new jobs will be created elsewhere.

By focusing on bilateral balances, the EPI studies offer a misleading picture of the overall impact of trade. Although the total trade balance is determined by our nation's underlying levels of savings and investment, our various bilateral deficits are allocated by comparative advantage and patterns of savings and investment in individual countries. We run a large bilateral trade deficit with China not because of currency manipulation or unfair trade but because China has a comparative advantage in making the kind of lower-end consumer products that millions of Americans love to buy.

The EPI studies exaggerate the number of American companies and workers who compete directly against those who produce Chinese imports. As we saw in the previous chapter, many of our main imports from China—shoes, clothing, toys, and consumer electronics—were being imported from other countries before China's emergence as a major supplier. In fact, as imports from China have risen since 2001 as a share of total imports, imports from other Asian countries have been in relative decline. So imports from China do not typically displace U.S. production but instead displace imports from other countries.

The actual experience of the U.S. economy provides a powerful rebuttal to the elaborate computer models that supposedly show that trade deficits destroy jobs. If the EPI model were accurate, a worsening trade deficit—imports rising faster than exports— would cause net job creation to slow and the unemployment rate to rise. But in the real U.S. economy, the one where we all live and work,

Table 5.2
AS THE TRADE DEFICIT GROWS, UNEMPLOYMENT FALLS

	Trade Deficit as % of GDP			Unemployment Rate		
Period	Beginning	End	Change	Beginning	End	Change
1982–87	0.5%	3.2%	2.7%	8.5%	5.7%	−2.8%
1988–91	3.2%	0.5%	−2.7%	5.7%	7.3%	1.6%
1992–00	0.5%	3.9%	3.3%	7.3%	3.9%	−3.4%
2001	3.9%	3.6%	−0.3%	3.9%	5.7%	1.8%
2002–06	3.6%	5.8%	2.2%	5.7%	4.4%	−1.3%
2007–08	5.8%	4.5%	−1.3%	4.4%	7.0%	2.6%

a rising trade deficit is typically accompanied by faster job growth, while a shrinking deficit usually accompanies slower job growth.

The reason for the surprising correlation is that imports and jobs typically rise together with expanding domestic demand. Confident consumers will spend more on domestic as well as imported goods. Businesses that are expanding production will not only hire more workers but also import more machinery, inputs, and raw materials. The same rising tide that lifts domestic demand and employment also whets the appetite of American consumers and businesses for imported as well as domestic goods and services.

The EPI computer model may tell us that a trade deficit means fewer jobs, but the real-world experience of the American economy and the American people tell us the opposite. Consider America's recent economic experience, as laid out in Table 5.2. From 1982 to 1987, the trade deficit exploded during the Reagan era of the "twin deficits," while at the same time the unemployment rate fell from 8.5 percent to 5.7 percent. From 1988 to 1991, critics of the trade deficit cheered as a weaker dollar helped shrink the deficit to almost zero, yet during that same time the unemployment rate rose to a recessionary 7.3 percent.[10]

During the Clinton-era expansion of 1992–2000, the trade deficit ballooned while employment surged and the unemployment rate dipped below 4 percent. During the Bush II years, the trade deficit shrank slightly during the recession of 2001 while unemployment jumped, then the deficit rose through 2006 as the recovery gained steam and the unemployment rate fell back below 5 percent. Since 2007 and the onset of recession, the trade deficit has predictably declined while the unemployment rate has climbed. If the EPI model reflected the real economy, its next report should be titled, "Declining Trade Deficit Costly: Millions of U.S. Jobs Lost as Imports Fall."

For all the same reasons, a trade deficit is not a drag on growth. The trade balance is more like a safety valve or ballast for the economy. When the economy is in danger of overheating, imports expand to meet increased domestic demand in a way that does not stoke inflationary pressures. When the domestic economy slows, exports will usually grow faster than imports, or at least decline more slowly as they have during the current recession, providing an external source of demand to keep American factories working more than they would otherwise.

Americans should be wary that the critics of trade might actually get their wish. According to their story line, we could create millions of new middle-class jobs if only we could find a way to reduce the inflow of imports. Yet whenever imports really do decline, the news is bad for American workers. In a 2007 study for the Progressive Policy Institute, author Doug Karmin found that, "Since 1960, imports have decreased in value only five times—in 1961, 1975, 1982, 1991, and 2001. These years happen to mark the last five major U.S. recessions—periods when the economy slowed and unemployment rose."[11] The year 2009 is on course to join that dubious list.

During the economic expansion of the 1990s, the Clinton administration's Council of Economic Advisers explained that "the trade balance is a deceptive indicator of the Nation's economic performance and of the benefit that the United States derives from trade."[12] The state of the economy exerts a strong influence on demand for imports, the council noted, causing the trade deficit to increase when the U.S. economy is growing rapidly and to diminish when the economy is weak. "An increasing trade deficit is therefore usually the result of a strong economy, not the cause of a weak one."[13]

America As a "Debtor Nation"

There is no evidence that the trade deficit hurts the U.S. economy in the short run, but what about the long run? Are we mortgaging our nation's future prosperity and independence by borrowing hundreds of billions of dollars every year from abroad?

By definition, the cumulative effect of chronic trade deficits is that foreign ownership of U.S. assets will grow faster than U.S. ownership of assets abroad. The difference in the stock of cross-border assets is called the Net International Investment Position. During most of the 20th century, Americans owned more assets abroad than the rest of the world owned in the United States. In the mid 1980s, however, as large current account deficits accumulated, our nation's net investment position turned negative. In the eyes of many, America became a "debtor nation."

Like the trade deficit itself, our net investment position means less than what it appears. At the end of 2007, foreign investors owned $20.1 trillion worth of assets in the United States, whereas Americans owned $17.6 trillion in assets abroad. The $2.5 trillion gap is what Americans supposedly "owe" the rest of the world. If direct investment is calculated according to its current market value, rather than its value when acquired, the gap shrinks to $1.7 trillion.[14]

America's net international investment position is large by any measure but not quite so intimidating when compared to the overall size of the U.S. economy and the stock of assets owned by Americans. America's negative investment position represents about 16 percent of GDP. By a more fitting "assets-to-assets" comparison, it represents less than 3 percent of the more than $100 trillion in total assets owned at the end of 2007 by U.S. households, nonprofits, and businesses.[15]

It is misleading to refer to America's negative net investment position entirely as debt. Debt is commonly understood to be a specific amount owed to another party, to be repaid with interest during a specified period. Most of the assets owned by foreigners are indeed debt instruments such as U.S. Treasury bills, corporate bonds, and bank deposits. But more than 40 percent are equity holdings, such as corporate stock, real estate, and direct investment.[16] Those holdings are not debt in any real sense. Americans are not obligated to repay anything. Although foreigners earn dividends and profits from those assets, they are not entitled to any fixed interest or repayment of principal. When foreign holders sell those equity assets, they will receive whatever the market price happens to be at the time of sale.

Yes, But Is the Trade Deficit Sustainable?

Economists have been debating since the 1980s whether large trade deficits are sustainable. Clearly, the United States cannot run ever-expanding trade deficits forever. At some point, foreign savers will have gobbled up all available U.S. assets. But we are far from that point, and if market signals—exchange rates, interest rates, and asset prices—are allowed to adjust, trade balances will also adjust to a sustainable equilibrium.

So far, Americans have invested their money abroad wisely—so wisely, in fact, that we continue to earn a net surplus on investment income. Since 1990, U.S. residents have earned an average return of 1.3 percentage points more on our investments abroad than foreigners have earned in the United States.[17] One reason our returns are higher is that the United States is considered a more secure home for investment than most other locations in the world, which means those who invest in the United States will demand a smaller "risk premium" for investing here.

As a result, even though foreigners own a couple trillion dollars' more of assets in the United States than Americans own abroad, Americans continue to earn more on our international investments than what foreigners earn here. In 2007, American investors earned $818 billion abroad in interest, dividends, and operating profits, while foreign investors earned $736 billion on their holdings in the United States. That means Americans earned a net $82 billion surplus on foreign investment. Far from being a net drain on our national income, foreign investment remains a modest net positive. This is a "burden" that we can sustain for years to come.

Persistently large trade deficits are not unique in the world or in our own history. Great Britain, Spain, and Australia are all developed nations that have recently run trade deficits of comparable magnitude as a share of their economies. Like the United States, all of them have enjoyed relatively good economic performance during the past 20 years compared to other advanced economies.

America's own history shows that persistent trade deficits can be sustainable for long periods of dynamic growth. For most of our first century as a nation, Americans imported more merchandise from the rest of the world than we exported. According to economic historian Robert Lipsey, "The United States began its existence as a net debtor and all through the 19th century and up to World War I it paid out more in interest on its debts then it earned on its foreign assets."[18] The trade deficits of that era made room for a steady inflow of foreign capital that "went to large, lumpy, social overhead capital projects, such as canals, railways, electrical utilities, and telephone and telegraph systems."[19]

Today's inflow of capital is not funding canals and railways, but as we will see in the next chapter, it is funding automobile and chemical plants, research and development (R&D) facilities, and the huge and growing federal budget deficit. The trade deficits of today, like those of the 19th century, allow the world to invest in expanding the productive capacity of the private-sector American economy. The net inflow of investment, then and now, makes American workers more productive than we would be otherwise, leading directly to better jobs and higher living standards.

A Hard or Soft Landing?

Another fear is that trade deficits will erode the confidence of foreign investors in the U.S. economy, spurring them to withdraw their funds and precipitating a "hard landing" for the U.S. economy. The often predicted scenario has become a standard feature of news stories and TV analysis: Big trade deficits spark worries abroad, foreign investors withdraw their funds, the dollar plunges, interest rates soar, and the U.S. economy stumbles into recession.

As much as the critics would try, the economic downturn that accelerated in 2008 cannot be blamed on the trade deficit. It was not precipitated by foreign investor jitters, a slumping dollar, rising interest rates, or any other element of the hard-landing scenario. It was sparked by the bursting of the domestic housing bubble, which was entirely a "made in America" phenomenon. If anything, America's relative attractiveness to foreign investors has been enhanced during the period of global economic uncertainty as global savers seek a "safe haven" for their investments. As a result, the dollar strengthened during 2008 as interest rates fell—just the opposite script from what the trade-deficit doomsayers have been predicting for years. We should be thankful that as our domestic credit markets stumbled, Americans have been able to borrow what we need from the rest of the world.

The most likely scenario for the unwinding of the trade deficit will not be a hard landing but a soft landing. At some point in the future, a critical mass of global investors will decide that the share of their portfolios invested in the U.S. economy has reached an optimum level. As interest in U.S. assets levels off, so too will demand for dollars to buy those assets. As the dollar adjusts downward, so too will the current account deficit, as a weaker dollar makes U.S. exports relatively more attractive in global markets. The key to a soft landing will be flexible and open markets that allow capital flows and exchange rates to adjust to changing fundamentals.

A trade-deficit-induced "hard landing" is unlikely as long as the United States maintains a hospitable climate for investment. If foreign investors lose confidence in the U.S. economy for whatever reason, we will be in for a rough ride. A current account deficit is not necessary for that scenario to happen. Even if the United States were to maintain a perfectly balanced current account and net international investment position, we would still be vulnerable to a loss of confidence and a withdrawal of foreign investment. Indeed, if Americans lose confidence in the economy and begin sending more of their savings abroad, the "hard landing" scenario would be just as plausible. In truth, any nation connected to the global economy is vulnerable to one degree or another to capital flight. Our response should not be to seek a smaller trade deficit or to slap controls on capital flows but to make every effort to maintain our attractiveness as a home for foreign investment.

Why Protectionism Won't Work

Raising trade barriers or devaluing the currency cannot "cure" the trade deficit because neither would do anything to alter our nation's underlying levels of savings and investment. If the central bank devalued the U.S. dollar, the result would be to pump more dollars into the global exchange markets. As those dollars found their way back to the U.S. economy, the overall inflation level would rise. Prices for U.S. exports would soon reflect higher domestic costs, offsetting the depreciation of the dollar and leaving U.S. exports no more competitive than before the depreciation.

If Congress were to impose new barriers on imports in a misguided effort to close the trade gap, the results would be equally self-defeating. In 2003, Omaha, Neb., billionaire Warren Buffett proposed an idea in *Fortune* magazine to eliminate the trade deficit by requiring tradable "import certificates," a kind of "cap and trade" scheme for the current account deficit. Under his plan, if a U.S. company wanted to import $100,000 worth of stuff, the company would need a certificate, which it could obtain only by exporting $100,000 worth—thus guaranteeing "balanced trade." The certificates would be tradable because the companies that export would not necessarily be the same companies wanting to import.[20] Buffett's proposal is really just an old and failed idea wrapped in a new gimmick. Countries such as India tried for decades to manage their balance of payments through import licensing schemes, only to give up after years of corruption, lagging trade, and slow growth.

Famous for his long-term outlook on investing, Mr. Buffett failed to think through even the most obvious and immediate implications of his plan. If Americans were forbidden to spend more on imports than we earn from exports, the world's foreign exchange markets would be deprived of the $700 billion that Americans currently spend annually on imports over and above what we earn for exports. The constricted supply of dollars would cause the price of the dollar to soar. A sharply appreciating dollar, in turn, would make U.S. exports less competitive in the global marketplace. The lethal combination of a soaring dollar and a major new restriction on imports would mean a drastic fall in trade overall, with exports falling and imports tumbling even further.

Meanwhile, an expensive dollar would make U.S. assets less attractive to foreign investors. The $700 billion in net foreign investment flowing into the U.S. economy each year (the flip side of the current account deficit) would dry up. Less demand for U.S. assets would force the federal government to pay a higher interest rate to finance its budget deficit. Homeowners would pay higher rates on their mortgages, aggravating the already high foreclosure rate. American companies would pay more to banks and bondholders to finance investment, and foreign companies would build fewer factories in the United States. The U.S. economy would slow even further.

Increase Savings, Not Trade Barriers

If our politicians are determined to do something about the trade deficit, the most constructive step they could take would be to promote a higher level of national savings. More domestic savings would reduce the need for foreign funds to finance domestic investment. A larger pool of domestic savings would cause domestic interest rates to fall, which would make U.S. interest-bearing assets less attractive to foreign investors, reducing foreign demand for dollars and causing the dollar to depreciate in the foreign exchange markets. A weaker dollar, in turn, would make U.S. exports more competitive and imports less so—shrinking the trade deficit without resorting to an artificially debased U.S. dollar, higher trade barriers, or wacky import licensing schemes.

How to spur greater domestic savings is both straightforward and challenging. The most direct approach would be to reduce or eliminate the federal budget deficit. If the federal government were to borrow a few hundred billion dollars less each year, the pool of domestic savings would rise, and more domestic funds would be available for investment. My Cato colleagues have provided a long list of ideas of where to cut the federal budget in a way that would put a huge dent in the deficit without raising taxes.[21] Politicians should not complain about the trade deficit unless they are willing to drastically reduce the federal government's gargantuan appetite for debt that contributes so much to the size of the trade deficit in the first place. Ironically, many members of Congress who complain loudest about the trade deficit have voted in the name of economic "stimulus" to plunge us ever deeper in debt.

Policies should also be implemented to encourage more savings among households. This encouragement could be done most effectively by eliminating the bias in the federal tax code that currently favors debt and discourages savings and investment. Taxing consumption rather than production and income would give individuals and companies an incentive to save more of their income for the future. The domestic pool of savings would grow, reducing the demand for foreign capital to fund domestic investment.

It would also be helpful if politicians and economic commentators would stop lecturing Americans that it is our patriotic duty to consume as much as we can, even if it means running up credit card debts and borrowing more against our home value than necessary. Rediscovering a "culture of thrift" would put more families on a firm financial footing while providing more domestic savings for the national economy. Our individual bank balances would be larger, and our nation's trade deficit smaller.

The greatest threat posed by the trade deficit is not anything inherent in its nature but the danger that politicians will seek to administer protectionist "cures" that would be far more damaging than the imagined harm caused by a macroeconomic statistic.

6. Foreign Investment: Paying Dividends for American Families

In late 2008, the CEOs of the "Big Three" Detroit-based automakers flew to Washington in their corporate jets to ask Congress for billions of dollars in emergency aid. Caught in a downward spiral of declining sales and stubbornly high costs, the CEOs predicted the virtual end of the American automobile industry if Congress denied them tens of billions in "bridge loans." At a November 19, 2008, hearing before the House Financial Services Committee, now-former General Motors chief Rick Wagoner warned members that "if the domestic industry were allowed fail, the societal cost would be catastrophic." His counterpart at Ford, Alan Mulally, predicted that "the collapse of the U.S. automotive industry would be a calamity for the entire economy."[1]

Both CEOs spoke as though they represented the "U.S. automotive industry," when in fact the Big Three are only a part, and a declining part, a rapidly changing U.S. motor vehicle market. More than half the new cars now bought by Americans each year are made by car companies headquartered outside the United States, bearing such foreign nameplates as Toyota, Honda, Nissan, Kia, Volkswagen, and BMW. Most of those "foreign" cars are made in the United States by workers who are just as American as employees of the Big Three. And two of the Big Three automakers—Ford and GM—now sell more of their own cars abroad than they do in the United States, with most of those cars made abroad. In short, the U.S. automobile market and industry have become globalized.

As a consequence, we can no longer neatly divide the auto industry into "us" versus "them." Toyota, Subaru, Isuzu, Mazda, Mitsubishi, Nissan, Honda, and Hino are all Japanese companies that produce motor vehicles in the United States. According to the Japanese Automobile Manufacturing Association, its members made 3.4 million vehicles in the United States in 2007 at 17 plants in 11 different states. Most cars now made in the United States are not made in

Michigan and Ohio, but in such places as San Antonio, Texas; Vance, Alabama; Georgetown, Kentucky; Smyrna and Decherd, Tennessee; West Point, Georgia; and Greer, South Carolina. Those and other factories owned by foreign producers now employ nearly a third of all automotive industry workers in the United States, and that share continues to grow.

Meanwhile, Ford and GM have gone global themselves. Nearly two-thirds of GM's vehicle sales in the first quarter of 2008 were outside the United States. Through a joint-production venture with Shanghai Automotive Industry Corp., the company supplies 10 percent of the cars sold in China, second only to Volkswagen in market share. GM sells twice as many Buicks in China as it does in the United States.[2] It builds cars and SUVs in South Africa for export to Europe and has become the biggest nondomestic carmaker in Russia, selling more than a quarter of a million vehicles there in 2007.[3] At Ford, international operations in 2007 accounted for 46 percent of its assets, 53 percent of its revenue, and 57 percent of its vehicles sold. Although Ford sales have been dropping in the U.S. market, they were up 19 percent in South America and 26 percent in China in 2007.[4] All three Detroit automakers have deeply integrated their North American operations with our NAFTA partners, Canada and Mexico.

Cross-border investment is not unique to the automobile industry. Across the American economic landscape, foreign investment is raising the productivity of American workers, injecting new competition into the consumer market, and opening opportunities for American companies to reach new customers and earn more profits in the world's fastest-growing markets. Fears about undue foreign influence in the United States or U.S. companies "shipping jobs overseas" or a global "race to the bottom" are overblown or unfounded.

Foreign investment flows are the deep undercurrent of the global economy. Trade in goods and services produces the waves and the froth, but like the mighty Gulf Stream, it is the trade in assets that determines the climate. The United States is by far the largest recipient and supplier of global foreign investment. At the end of 2007, Americans owned $17.6 trillion in assets abroad, whereas foreign investors owned $20.1 trillion in assets in the United States.[5] The stock of both inward and outward investment has grown exponentially in recent years, doubling since 2003 (see Figure 6.1).

90

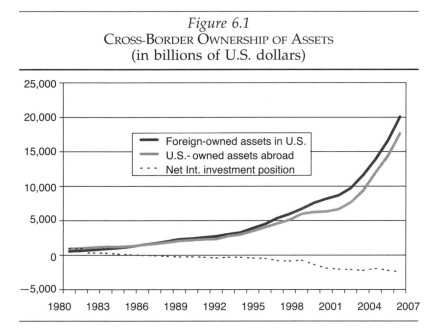

Figure 6.1
CROSS-BORDER OWNERSHIP OF ASSETS
(in billions of U.S. dollars)

Foreign investment flows through two channels: portfolio investment and direct investment. Portfolio investments are "passive," like buying shares in a mutual fund in which the investor has no influence over how the enterprises are run. Examples are bank deposits, bonds, or stock shares amounting to less than 10 percent of an individual company's value. Direct investments occur when a foreign investor buys 10 percent or more of the controlling shares of a company, or when it owns the foreign affiliate outright. When the foreign investor's share exceeds 50 percent, the company is known as a majority-owned foreign affiliate, or MOFA. Multinational companies are those that own controlling shares in at least one affiliate outside their home country.

Most of the investment flows worldwide are of the portfolio variety. Tens of billions of dollars can move across borders in an instant, with bonds, stocks, and other investment paper changing hands frequently. Direct investment tends to be more stable because it involves ownership and control of hard assets—factories, warehouses, real estate, and companies with office buildings and equipment.

91

Foreign investment has never been more important to the global economy. According to the U.N. Conference on Trade and Development, foreign-direct investment flows in 2007 reached a record $1.8 trillion. The United States was the largest recipient country, followed in order by the United Kingdom, France, Canada, and the Netherlands. (Notice that China is not on that list.) The global stock of foreign direct investment (FDI) has reached $15 trillion. An amazing 11 percent of global economic output is now produced by the nearly 800,000 foreign-owned affiliates operated by the world's 80,000 multinational companies.[6]

Foreign investment, like trade in goods and services, has brought broad benefits to millions of Americans—in two fundamental ways. When foreigners invest in the United States, the inflow of portfolio capital benefits the large majority of Americans with lower interest rates, whereas FDI injects new competition into the consumer market and creates better-paying jobs by upgrading our factories and machinery and introducing new technology and ways of doing business. And when Americans invest abroad, we earn higher returns on our savings, we diversify our investment portfolio to safeguard the future, and we reach new customers with American-brand goods and services.

The World Invests in America

In 2001, I spoke at a conference in an unusual venue—the auditorium of the sprawling BMW plant in Greer, South Carolina. I was invited there by then-Rep. and now-Sen. Jim DeMint, a South Carolina Republican who has successfully run for re-election in his district and state on a protrade platform. While there, I learned that the German-owned state-of-the art plant employed 4,000 workers, who at the time were making Z-3 Roadster convertibles. (I wasn't paid by BMW or anybody else for the trip, although I was half hoping that I could be compensated in-kind with the title to one of the new cars on the lot.) By 2007, employment at the facility had grown to 5,400 full-time workers producing 157,000 vehicles, two-thirds of them exported mostly through the port of Charleston. BMW announced in 2008 that it would be investing another $750 million to expand capacity to 240,000 vehicles per year.[7] Conveniently, the BMW plant is just down Interstate 85 from a French-owned Michelin tire factory. In fact, upstate South Carolina is home to hundreds of foreign-owned facilities attracted by the state's flexible workforce and friendly business climate. It is a success story that has been replicated in a number of other states.

The United States is a magnet for global savings. Year after year, hundreds of billions of dollars flow into the United States from abroad to invest in our economy. An important share of the inflow is FDI. From 2003 through 2007, inflows of FDI in the U.S. economy averaged $153 billion a year. Major investments flowed into the financial, insurance, and wholesale sectors, but by far the biggest single share flowed into U.S. manufacturing. During that period, foreign manufacturing companies invested an average of $59 billion a year in America's manufacturing base. Sectors that attracted the most foreign investment were chemicals, machinery, computers and electronics, and "other manufacturing."[8] It appears that foreign companies are also skeptical of America's rumored "deindustrialization."

A Foreign Boss, Five Million Good Jobs

Foreign-owned affiliates in the United States employed more than five million American workers in 2006, according to the Commerce Department's latest survey. That is 4.6 percent of the private workforce, up from 3.4 percent 20 years ago. States with the highest share of workers employed by foreign affiliates are Connecticut, South Carolina, Delaware, New Hampshire, and New Jersey. Two million workers are employed by manufacturing affiliates—more than one in eight U.S. factory workers. The highest shares of foreign-affiliate employment are in chemicals, mining, and motor vehicles and parts. In 2006, 325,000 Americans worked for foreign affiliates in the motor vehicle and parts sector alone, 278,000 in chemicals, and 180,000 in nonmetallic mineral products such as cement.[9]

Americans who work for foreign-owned affiliates typically have some of the best jobs available. On average, they earn $63,400 a year compared to the U.S. average of $48,200.[10] And the main reason why those affiliates pay so well is that they are among the most globally connected, productive, and innovative enterprises in America. Foreign-owned affiliates account for 19 percent of total U.S. exports and 26 percent of imports. Together, they spent $34 billion on R&D in 2006. As the Commerce Department noted, "U.S. affiliates accounted for 14 percent of the total R&D performed by all U.S. business, a share notably higher than the affiliate share of U.S. private industry value added or employment."[11] Three-quarters of the foreign-affiliate R&D was concentrated in manufacturing, especially chemicals, motor vehicles, and pharmaceuticals.

Americans should think of FDI in our country as a form of "insourcing." For years and on a large scale, foreign companies have been "shipping jobs overseas" to America. By acquiring affiliates in the United States, foreign multinational companies can deliver their products and services more directly to millions of middle-class and wealthy American consumers. They can more successfully research and develop new products for the American market if they are closer to their customers. They can hire skilled and motivated American workers. And they can enjoy the advantages of operating in a relatively free and open market with a transparent legal system and stable political environment. The continual inflow of foreign investment is, among other things, an expression of confidence in the American system.

A Matter of Interest to U.S. Borrowers

Even when foreign investors are not directly operating affiliates and employing Americans, we still benefit from their passive investment in the U.S. economy. The inflow of portfolio capital into U.S. stocks, bonds, and bank accounts leads to lower borrowing costs for Americans and more investment by Americans in our own economy. Of the $20 trillion in foreign-owned assets in the United States at the end of 2007, by far the biggest share was portfolio investment, including $6 trillion in corporate bonds and stocks, $4 trillion in bank deposits, $3.3 trillion in foreign official assets (mostly U.S. Treasury bills owned by foreign central banks), and $2 trillion in financial derivatives.

Those trillions in passive investment provide working capital for U.S. companies and help our profligate federal government finance its yawning budget deficit without devouring all of the nation's private seed corn. When foreigners buy a $1,000 Treasury bond, that is $1,000 the U.S. government does not need to borrow from the limited pool of domestic U.S. savings. Instead, we can use our savings to fund education, investment in plants and equipment, and research into new products. Foreign investment thus almost entirely eliminates the "crowding out" of domestic private investment by government borrowing.

94

Foreign investment in the U.S. economy has exerted measurable downward pressure on U.S. interest rates. Because Americans are free to tap into the global pool of savings, the "price" of borrowing—in other words, the rate of interest—is lower than it would be if we were limited to our own supply of domestic savings. In a 2006 study from the National Bureau of Economic Research, economists Francis E. Warnock and Veronica Cacdac Warnock calculated the impact of foreign investment just in U.S. Treasury bonds alone from 1984 to 2005. They found that "foreign inflows into U.S. bonds reduce the 10-year Treasury yield by 90 basis points"[12] That's almost a full percentage point lower than what rates would be without the inflows. Almost two-thirds of the reduction came from the purchase of bonds by East Asian sources, mostly the central banks of China and Japan.

Those lower rates translate into real savings for Americans. A homeowner with a $150,000, 30-year mortgage is saving more than $1,000 a year in interest payments. That can spell the difference between continued homeownership and foreclosure for a large number of American families. The federal government is saving more than $40 billion a year from lower interest payments on its outstanding public debt. Lower interest rates also mean lower costs for American farmers and small businesses who need to borrow for new equipment, buildings, and land. Those savings can be attributed directly to foreign investment in U.S. Treasury bills.

Through portfolio investment in the United States, anonymous foreign investors have done far more over the years to make housing more affordable for Americans than shell games and gimmicks by Fannie Mae and Freddie Mac. And the foreign investors did not distort the market with "subprime" loans misdirected and repackaged in mysterious ways that aggravated the housing bubble and crash. Instead, foreign investment has delivered a transparent and universal cut in long-term interest rates available equally to all Americans.

A Loss of Sovereignty, or a Stake in Our Prosperity?

Despite all the benefits of inward foreign investment, reasonable Americans worry that the cost is too high. One major concern is the loss of American sovereignty. When foreign investors own a $20 trillion share of U.S. assets, it raises the fear that our nation will be vulnerable to outside influence and even blackmail by hostile foreign powers. A foreign holder could threaten to withdraw large amounts of capital, driving up interest rates, driving down the value of the dollar, and disrupting the U.S. economy. Those worries focus on funds controlled by foreign governments, such as central bank reserves and government-directed "sovereign wealth funds" (SWFs). On February 28, 2007, after the stock market had dropped precipitously the day before, then-Sen. Hillary Clinton of New York took to the floor of the Senate to warn her colleagues, "And while our markets were reeling, alarm bells were ringing once again over the irresponsible fiscal and economic policies of this Administration that continue to surrender the economic sovereignty of our country to foreign banks, investors, and governments piece by piece."[13]

The worries expressed by Senator Clinton are possible in theory, but highly unlikely for several reasons.

One, despite the rapid growth of foreign investment in the United States, it remains modest compared to the total value of U.S. assets. At the end of the second quarter of 2008, the combined assets of households, nonprofits, and businesses in the United States was still a whopping $110 trillion.[14] Foreign investment is less than 20 percent of that total, and foreign investment directed by central banks and other foreign government agencies is only 3 percent. Foreign investment is too diversified to give any one investor much leverage. The central bank of China is the single biggest foreign holder of U.S. Treasury bills, with nearly $600 billion in its portfolio in 2008. But even those holdings represent only about 15 percent of the federal government's outstanding public debt and a tiny fraction of total U.S.-based assets. And when one foreign holder of U.S. assets sells, another foreign investor may be ready to buy.

Two, even if an outside investor such as the government of China could disrupt the U.S. economy by dumping U.S. Treasury bills, it would not be in the Chinese government's own interest to do so. An economic downturn in the United States, such as the one that hit the U.S. economy full force in 2008, also exacts a toll on our commercial partners. Countries such as China see their exports to the U.S. market slump along with the dollar value of their remaining U.S. assets. Investment in the United States gives foreigners a stake in America's prosperity.

Three, SWFs are still a small and unremarkable slice of global investment. These funds are often established by countries that have accumulated large foreign currency reserves, such as the oil-exporting countries of the Middle East. The funds seek higher returns by diversifying out of more conservative government bonds and into stock funds and real estate. According to testimony in February 2008 by then-Treasury Undersecretary David McCormick, the 40 SWFs in the world control $3 trillion in assets, compared to the $190 trillion stock of global financial assets and $62 trillion managed by private institutional investors.[15] SWFs do operate under different rules than private funds: They do not typically pay domestic taxes, and they can forgo profits for the sake of national objectives. But SWFs so far have not behaved much differently from other actors in global capital markets. Their managers want solid returns at low risk. At a time when our domestic credit markets are reluctant to lend, we should welcome foreign savers who want to put their money to work in America.

Concerns about sovereignty and foreign investment can sound like self-fulfilling prophesies. Out of fear that foreigners may remove or deny us investment funds, we are urged to take actions that in effect deny us what we fear losing. By this tortured logic, we must deprive ourselves of the immediate benefits of inflowing capital— namely, lower interest rates—to avoid the small risk of being partly deprived of the inflow in the future. We deny ourselves a benefit now at great and continuing expense, out of fear that someone else may remove some of the benefit in the future.

Other worries focus on specific direct investments by foreign companies in certain "strategic" U.S. assets. Those worries are multiplied when the enterprise is controlled by a foreign government. In the 1980s and early 1990s, fears focused on private Japanese investors buying U.S. technology companies and prominent real estate. More recently, firestorms have erupted over the proposed purchase of the American energy company UNOCAL by the China National Offshore Oil Corporation in 2005, and the proposed operation of six U.S. ports by Dubai Ports World in 2006. Public and congressional opposition scuttled both acquisitions. Fears in both cases were exaggerated. The CNOOC acquisition would have given the Chinese no leverage in domestic or global energy markets. The Dubai Ports World company is based in the Persian Gulf state of the United Arab Emirates, which is among the most modern, moderate, and globally connected of the Arab states. It operates port facilities around the world in a number of Western countries. The actual threat to U.S. port security would have been negligible.

Even if truly worrisome acquisitions were to surface, the U.S. government has established a review mechanism to ensure that U.S. security is not compromised. The Committee on Foreign Investment in the United States is an interagency committee that includes the Secretary of the Treasury and other top U.S. officials. The CFIUS has the power to screen and reject any foreign acquisition that in any way compromises U.S. national security. It would be foolish to sacrifice the benefits of foreign investment out of misguided fears that have already been reasonably and adequately addressed in a review process that Congress strengthened in 2006.

The greatest danger is not too much foreign investment in the U.S. economy but unwise policies that send investment elsewhere. Xenophobia, burdensome regulations, high corporate tax rates, an inadequately educated and trained workforce, and trade and immigration restrictions can discourage foreign investors from choosing to put their savings to work in the United States. If foreign investment inflows decline, American workers will be the losers.

Americans Invest in the World

The other side of the foreign investment coin is even more controversial but just as beneficial. Each year Americans spend hundreds of billions of our savings to buy assets in foreign countries. Our freedom to invest abroad allows American companies and businesses to reach new customers for their products and American citizens to earn higher returns on our savings.

Many of our fellow Americans take a darker view of outward foreign investment. Companies that establish and expand operations abroad stand accused of "outsourcing good American jobs." In 2004, Democratic presidential candidate John Kerry branded business executives who made such decisions "Benedict Arnold CEOs." In his nomination acceptance speech in Denver in 2008, Barack Obama pledged that, "Unlike John McCain, I will stop giving tax breaks to corporations that ship jobs overseas, and I will start giving them to companies that create good jobs right here in America."

To demonize U.S. companies that own production facilities abroad is to target virtually every major American company. At latest count, more than 2,500 U.S. corporations own and operate a total of 23,853 affiliates in other countries. In 2006, majority-owned foreign affiliates of U.S. companies posted $4.1 trillion in sales, created just under $1 trillion in value-added, employed 9.5 million foreign workers, and earned $644 billion in net income for their U.S.–based parent companies.[16]

In a global economy, it can make good sense for corporations to actually make and deliver some of their products outside their home country. It certainly makes sense for the foreign-owned companies that employ those five million Americans at their affiliates in the United States. American companies that operate affiliates abroad do so for similar reasons.

For individual Americans, investing in the world has been profitable. In 2007, Americans earned $818 billion on their investments abroad. That works out to a return on investment of 4.6 percent on the $17 trillion in U.S.–owned assets, a rate of return almost a full point higher than what foreign investors earned on average in the U.S. market. The freedom to invest abroad has allowed millions of Americans to earn higher rates at less risk through their 401(k) plans, pension funds, and mutual fund investments.

Reaching Billions of New Customers

The primary reason why U.S. companies acquire affiliates abroad is to sell more products to foreign customers. Certain services can only be delivered on the spot, where the company and the client must be in the same place. McDonald's cannot "export" Big Macs to Russia, nor can Wal-Mart export its retail services to Mexico. The provider must have a physical presence in the foreign market. U.S. companies also establish foreign affiliates because of certain advantages in the host country—lower-cost labor, ready access to raw materials and other inputs, reduced transportation costs, and proximity to their ultimate customers. Operating affiliates abroad allows U.S. companies to maintain control over their brand name and intellectual property such as trademarks, patents, and engineering expertise. Yes, the motivations can include access to "cheap labor," but labor costs are not the principal motivation for most U.S. direct investment abroad—as we will see in a moment.

Politicians focus most of their attention on comparing exports and imports, but the most common way American companies sell their goods and services in the global market today is through their overseas affiliates. In 2006, U.S. multinational companies sold $3,301 billion in goods through their majority-owned affiliates abroad and $677 billion in services. For every $1 billion in goods that U.S. multinational companies exported from the United States in 2006, those same companies sold $6.2 billion worth through their overseas operations.[17] For every $1 billion in service exports, U.S.–owned affiliates abroad sold $1.6 billion.[18]

Contrary to popular myth, U.S. multinational companies do not generally use their foreign operations as an "export platform" back to the United States. Close to 90 percent of the goods and services produced by U.S.–owned affiliates abroad are sold to customers either in the host country or exported to consumers in third countries outside the United States. Even in Mexico and China, where low-wage workers are supposedly too poor to buy American products, more than half of the production of new and existing U.S. affiliates is sold in their domestic markets and another third is exported to other countries, whereas customers in the United States accounted for only 17 percent of sales.[19] Think of General Motors in China or Ford in Europe: the primary focus of their overseas operations is to produce cars custom made for local markets, not to export back to the United States to displace production here.

More Jobs Abroad, More Jobs at Home

Investing abroad is not about "shipping jobs overseas." There is no evidence that expanding employment at U.S.–owned affiliates comes at the expense of overall employment by parent companies back home in the United States. In fact, the evidence and experience of U.S. multinational companies points in the opposite direction: Foreign and domestic operations tend to complement each other and expand together. A successful company operating in a favorable business climate will tend to expand employment at both its domestic and overseas operations. More activity and sales abroad usually require more managers, accountants, lawyers, engineers, and production workers at the parent company.

Consider Caterpillar Inc., the Peoria, Ill.–based company known for making giant earthmoving equipment. From 2005 through 2007, the company enjoyed booming global sales because of strong growth in overseas markets, especially those with resources extracted from the ground. According to the company's 2007 annual report, Caterpillar earned 63 percent of its sales revenue abroad, including $1 billion in sales in China alone. In response, Caterpillar ramped up its employment at its overseas affiliates during that time from 41,238 to 50,788, an increase of almost 10,000 workers. During that same three-year period, the company expanded its domestic employment from 43,878 to 50,545, a healthy increase of 6,667. As the current downturn took its toll on the company's sales, it has downsized its workforce abroad as it has downsized at home.

Caterpillar's experience is not unusual for U.S. multinational companies. A 2005 study from the National Bureau of Economic Research found that, during the 1980s and 1990s, there was "a strong positive correlation between domestic and foreign growth rates of multinational firms." After analyzing the operations of U.S. multinational companies at home and abroad, economists Mihir A. Desai, C. Fritz Foley, and James R. Hines Jr. found that a 10 percent increase in capital investment in existing foreign affiliates was associated with a 2.2 percent increase in domestic investment by the same company and a 4 percent increase in compensation for its domestic workforce. They also found a positive connection between foreign and domestic sales, assets, and numbers of employees.[20] "Foreign production requires inputs of tangible or intellectual property produced in the home country," the authors explained. "Greater foreign activity spurs higher exports from American parent companies to foreign affiliates and greater domestic R&D spending."[21]

The positive connection between foreign and domestic employment of U.S. multinational companies has continued into the current decade. As Figure 6.2 shows, parent and affiliate employment have tracked each other since the early 1980s. More recently, employment rose briskly for parents and affiliates alike in the boom of the late 1990s, fell for both during the downturn and slow recovery of 2001–2003, and then rose again for both from 2003 through 2006. Although the numbers have not been reported yet for 2007 and 2008, it's likely that the loss of net jobs in the domestic U.S. economy will be mirrored by much slower growth or outright decline in foreign affiliate employment.

The myth of jobs being shipped overseas endures on the campaign trail. In a primary debate in Texas in February 2008, then-Senator Obama said, "In Youngstown, Ohio, I've talked to workers who have seen their plants shipped overseas as a consequence of bad trade deals like NAFTA, literally seeing equipment unbolted from

Figure 6.2
U.S. MULTINATIONAL EMPLOYMENT
(thousands)

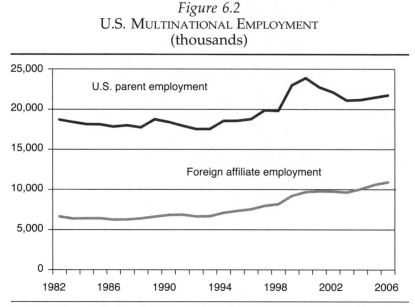

SOURCE: Raymond J. Mataloni Jr., "U.S. Multinational Companies: Operations in 2006," *Survey of Current Business* 88, no. 11 (November 2008): Table 1, p. 27.

the floors of factories and shipped to China."[22] That makes for a good sound bite in the heat of a campaign, but it does not reflect the broader reality of outward foreign investment by U.S. manufacturers.

Outflows of U.S. manufacturing investment to Mexico and China have been modest by any measure. Between 2003 and 2007, U.S. manufacturing companies sent an average of $2 billion a year in direct investment to China and $1.9 billion to Mexico. That pales in comparison to the $22 billion a year in manufacturing capital "shipped" to Europe, but talking about seeing equipment unbolted from the floors of U.S. factories and shipped to England just doesn't have the same effect. The modest annual outflow in investment to China and Mexico is positively dwarfed by the annual inflow of manufacturing investment to the United States and the average of $165 billion a year that U.S. manufacturers invest domestically in plant and equipment.[23]

The fear of manufacturing jobs being shipped to China and Mexico is not supported by the evidence. While U.S. factories were famously shedding those 3 million net jobs between 2000 and 2006, U.S.–

Table 6.1
EMPLOYMENT AT U.S.–OWNED AFFILIATES, 2000–06
(thousands)

	Total			Manufacturing		
	2000	2006	Change	2000	2006	Change
All countries	8,171	9,498	1,326	4,409	4,536	128
Rich economies	5,296	5,751	455	2,545	2,450	−96
Other economies	2,876	3,747	871	1,864	2,087	223
Mexico	823	890	67	642	545	−97
China	252	589	337	194	365	172
India	71	211	140	48	67	19
U.S. employment	131,785	136,174	4,389	17,263	14,197	−3,066

SOURCE: Mataloni Jr., "U.S. Multinational Companies: Operations in 2006," Bureau of Economic Analysis.

owned manufacturing affiliates abroad increased their employment by a mere 128,000 jobs. An increase in 172,000 jobs at U.S.–owned affiliates in China was offset by an actual decline in employment at affiliates in Mexico and Europe, where the number of manufacturing jobs decline by nearly 200,000 (see Table 6.1). As we saw in chapter 4, the large majority of factory jobs lost in the United States since 2000 were not shipped to China or anywhere else, but were lost to automation and other sources of increased efficiency in U.S. manufacturing.

U.S. investment in China remains modest compared to the huge investment that politicians and pundits have in making it an issue. U.S. direct investment in China remains a relatively small part of China's overall economy and a small part of America's total investments abroad. Of the nearly 10 million workers that U.S. affiliates employ abroad, fewer than 5 percent are Chinese. American-owned affiliates employ just as many manufacturing workers in high-wage Germany as they do in low-wage China.[24]

Politicians are not usually specific about exactly what "tax breaks" they are talking about. The biggest tax exemption for U.S. companies that invest abroad is the deferral of tax payments for "active" income. U.S. corporations are generally liable for tax on their worldwide income, whether it is earned in the United States or abroad. But the relatively high U.S. corporate tax rate is not applied to income earned abroad that is reinvested abroad in productive operations. U.S. multinationals are only taxed on foreign income when they repatriate the earnings to the United States. Not surprisingly, the deferral of active income gives U.S. companies a powerful incentive to reinvest what they earn abroad, but this is not a green light to "ship jobs overseas."

Such deferral may sound like an unjustified tax break to some, but every major industrial country offers at least as favorable treatment of foreign income to their multinational corporations. Indeed, numerous major countries exempt their companies from paying any tax on their foreign business operations. Foreign governments seem to more readily grasp the fact that when corporations have healthy and expanding foreign operations, it is good for the parent company and its workers back home.[25]

If President Obama and other leaders in Washington want to encourage more investment in the United States, they should lower the U.S. corporate tax rate, not seek to extend the high U.S. rate to the overseas activities of U.S. companies. Extending high U.S. tax rates to earnings abroad would put U.S. companies at a competitive disadvantage as they try to compete to sell their goods and services. Their French and German competitors in third-country markets would continue to pay the lower corporate tax rates applied by the host country, while U.S. companies would be burdened with paying the higher U.S. rate. The result would be lost sales, lower profits, and fewer employment opportunities in the parent company back on American soil.

Politicians who disparage investment in foreign operations are wedded to an outdated and misguided economic model that glorifies domestic production for export above all other ways for Americans to engage in the global economy. They would deny Americans access to hundreds of millions of foreign customers and access to lower-cost inputs through global supply chains. In short, they would cripple American companies that are trying to compete in global markets.

The Myth of the "Race to the Bottom"

Another common but unfounded fear of foreign investment is that it stokes a "race to the bottom." This dark theory of globalization contends that if multinational companies can move their capital freely around the world, they will gravitate to countries where wage costs are lowest and labor and environmental standards are the least

104

restrictive. Richer countries such as the United States will then be forced to reduce domestic wages and weaken standards in a "race to the bottom" to keep investment capital from fleeing. The push to insert labor and environmental standards into all trade agreements springs from just such fears. If we don't explicitly forbid our free-trade partners from trashing their own standards and suppressing their own workers' wages, so the theory goes, U.S. exporters and workers will face unfair pressure to denigrate our own standards to remain competitive.

The "race to the bottom" is yet another common myth about free trade and globalization that is refuted daily by what is actually happening in the world. If the theory were true—that a major driver of investment decisions for American multinational companies is a remorseless search for cheap labor and low standards abroad—then we should expect that most outward foreign investment from the United States would flow to low-wage, low-standard countries. The reality is quite the opposite. The large majority of U.S. outward investment flows to other rich, developed, high-wage, high-standard countries.

In the half decade from 2003 through 2007, of the $45 billion in manufacturing investment that U.S. companies sent abroad on average each year, 71 percent flowed to the rich, high-standard economies of Europe, Canada, Japan, Australia, and New Zealand. If we include the upper-middle-income economies of Hong Kong, Israel, Singapore, South Korea, and Taiwan, the share approaches 80 percent. The proportion of nonmanufacturing investment flowing to other relatively wealthy countries is even higher.[26] Far from racing to the bottom, U.S. multinational companies are racing to invest in the world's richest and most expensive places.

In a 2001 study on manufacturing investment, the consulting firm of Deloitte and Touche labeled this phenomenon the "high-wage paradox." Why would U.S. companies prefer to locate their overseas affiliates in countries where wages and standards are highest when hundreds of millions of workers are available in countries where wages and standards (and presumably business costs) are much lower? There is really no paradox at all. What companies ultimately seek is not lower costs, but higher profits. U.S. companies can operate just as profitably in a rich country as in a poor country, and often more so. After all, it is the rich countries where consumers have the most money to buy what U.S. companies make, where the workers have the education and skills to fill technical and well-paying jobs, where goods, services, and capital move freely across borders, where the utility and infrastructure systems work best, where the laws are transparent and the courts fair, and where the threat of political upheaval is minimal.

For most U.S. companies and industries, labor costs and environmental regulations are only two of many factors that determine where to locate new investment. Complying with environmental regulations typically accounts for less than 1 percent of production costs for industries in Western countries, ranging up to 2 percent for more pollution-intensive industries.[27] U.S. companies will gladly pay higher wages for more productive workers and comply with more stringent environmental regulations if the overall business climate is hospitable.

All that explains why more U.S. FDI flows to Ireland (population 4 million) in a typical year than to the entire continent of Africa (population 700 million). More U.S. manufacturing FDI flows to the tiny but rich European Low Countries of Belgium, the Netherlands, and Luxembourg (population 27.5 million) than to China, Mexico, and India combined (population 2.5 billion). Labor and regulatory costs are obviously higher, much higher, in the smaller European countries (higher even than in the United States), but those higher costs are more than offset by the huge advantages that companies enjoy by operating in a rich, open, and relatively free economy.

The expanding freedom of Americans to invest abroad has not compromised in any way our ability to maintain whatever environmental, safety, and labor regulations we choose. U.S. environmental regulations today are among the strictest in the world, and U.S. air and water standards have improved accordingly. As we saw in chapter 3, U.S. incomes and living standards have been rising decade after decade in the era of globalization—not racing to the bottom as the critics wrongly tell us. In developing countries, the spread of globalization has lifted living standards and reduced poverty and child labor, as we will see in chapter 8.

Foreign investment flowing into and out of the United States has put our economy on a sounder footing, further enriching us as consumers, workers, and investors, while allowing American companies to reach new markets around the world. America would be foolish to forfeit such rewarding dividends.

106

7. America in the Global Economy: Strong, Free, and Open for Business

American consumers, producers, borrowers, and investors—that is, just about all of us—benefit from our greater freedom to participate in the global marketplace, but so too does the American economy as a whole. Free trade has not just been good for Americans; it has been good for America.

The current recession cannot be blamed on our engagement in the global economy. Recessions have been a fact of life throughout our nation's history, during times when trade barriers were high and, more recently, when barriers have been low. Trade policy cannot repeal the business cycle.

Expanding trade and deeper commercial relations with the rest of the world have equipped our country to face the challenges and embrace the opportunities of a changing world. Free trade and globalization have raised the speed limit of our economy, allowing our domestic output to grow faster and at a more even pace than if we had been a more "self-sufficient" nation. And a healthier economy has come without sacrificing our national sovereignty and independence.

Critics of trade paint a far different picture, one that denigrates the recent performance of the economy and extols, even romanticizes, the virtues of previous eras when the United States was less open to the global economy. But a look back at our economic history during the "golden era" of protectionism reveals that we really are much better off today with America's more open, 21st-century economy, even as we struggle to emerge from a deep recession.

America's Protectionist Past

Opponents of trade have constructed a myth that America's economic and industrial might grew in the 19th century because of high tariffs that protected upstart American companies from European competition. That fable has been embraced by many conservatives and liberals alike, from Pat Buchanan to Sen. Sherrod Brown. The real story of our history is that America grew into a global economic power despite high tariffs, not because of them.

It is a simple historical fact that the U.S. government maintained high tariffs on a range of imports throughout the 19th and into the early 20th century. Alexander Hamilton, Treasury Secretary under George Washington and one of our nation's founders, championed the protective tariff as a way to boost American manufacturing. In his influential 1791 "Report on Manufactures," Hamilton argued that America needed a strong manufacturing base to compete with Europe. He urged subsidies and tariffs to counter European support for their own producers and to speed America's transition from an agricultural to an industrial economy. "In such a position of things," he wrote, "the United States cannot exchange with Europe on equal terms; and the want of reciprocity would render them the victim of the system which should induce them to confine their views to agriculture, and refrain from manufactures."[1]

For the next 140 years or so, with a few brief exceptions, Congress followed Hamilton's advice. From the beginning of our republic, tariffs were an important source of revenue for the federal government as well as a tool for protecting certain industries. Before the Civil War, high duties were imposed in part to help the government pay off its debts from the War of 1812, culminating in the 1828 "Tariff of Abominations." The overall level of tariffs fluctuated, depending on which party was in power in Washington. The cotton-exporting Southern states supported free trade with Great Britain, their best customer, whereas the more industrial northern states saw Britain as their chief competitor and wanted to keep British imports out. Import duties rose during the Civil War and remained high during most of the period of Republican, northern-state political dominance after the war. According to Dartmouth trade economist and historian Douglas Irwin, the average tariff-rate equivalent of trade barriers ranged from 30 percent to 49 percent during the half century between the Civil War and World War I.[2]

Those high tariffs coincided with the epic expansion of American industry, a coincidence that skeptics of trade have pounced on. They compare America's industrial expansion in the late 19th century to free-trade Britain, which lost its leadership in manufacturing to the United States during that period. They also compare the success of high-tariff America back then to the "deindustrializing" low-tariff

America today. But, of course, correlation does not necessarily mean causation. Just because American industry expanded behind high tariffs more than a century ago does not mean that the high tariffs were the key to the expansion. A closer look at that era shows that the tariffs were a drag on the U.S. economy. America in the 19th century grew despite the tariffs, not because of them.

The High-Tariff Fable Exposed

The biggest hole in the high-tariff fable is the fact that it was not the protected industries that led America's economic surge in the late 19th century. According to Douglas Irwin, the sectors with the fastest productivity growth were services such as transportation, distribution, utilities, communications, and construction. Productivity growth in those nontraded sectors was much more rapid after the Civil War than in manufacturing or agriculture. In contrast, protection of textiles, silk, and woolens did nothing to boost the overall output or competitiveness of the U.S. economy. It was not protected steel mills and textile factories that spearheaded America's emergence as a global economic power back then, but the railroads, the telegraph, the residential building trade, and electrical production and distribution.[3]

Although high tariffs on manufactured goods did nothing to promote America's overall growth, they did impose real costs and distortions on the U.S. economy. Tariffs on capital goods—machinery used to produce other goods—reached 40 percent by 1890, forcing American companies to pay artificially high prices for British machine tools, steam engines, steel rails, and precision instruments, reducing investment from what it would have been under free trade.[4] Lower investment in capital goods retarded the growth of knowledge and productivity among American manufacturers. Another economic historian, the University of California–Berkeley's Brad DeLong, writes that the lesson from that period in American history is that "a high tariff economy is a lower-investment economy, a lower capital stock economy, and a lower wage economy."[5]

High tariffs further aggravated the problem of industrial concentration and even monopolies. By shielding domestic producers from foreign competition, the tariff wall allowed them to exercise monopoly pricing power against consumers. In the late 19th century, about the time of the Sherman Act, a current saying was that "the tariff is the mother of the trust." Those who denounce the trusts and the concentration of wealth at the time should aim at least some of the blame at high tariffs.

America's industrial expansion in that era is less impressive in hindsight than the advocates of protection portray. What drove the expansion of U.S. manufacturing was not any great leap in competitiveness but a massive influx of capital and labor. In the language of economists, our industrial growth was "extensive" rather than "intensive." We produced more because inputs of labor and capital grew, not because labor and capital together became remarkably more productive. When we consider the combined productivity growth of capital and labor, or "total factor productivity" (TFP), America's record in the late 19th century was about the same as Great Britain's during the same period. "In the end, productivity growth in the 'protectionist' United States was roughly the same as that in the 'free trade' United Kingdom," concluded Dartmouth's Douglas Irwin.[6]

What allowed the United States to pull ahead of Great Britain in total output was the huge increase in the stock of both capital and labor. The capital came from domestic savings but also from abroad in the form of foreign investment, much of it from Britain itself. The steady inflow of capital from abroad was the main reason why the United States ran almost continuous trade deficits through the second half of the 19th century. Much of the expansion of labor came from the rest of Europe in the form of millions of immigrants, the "huddled masses" who arrived at Ellis Island from Scandinavia, Germany, Italy, Poland, Austria-Hungary, and Russia. In the half century from 1865 through 1914, the United States more or less welcomed 26.4 million legal immigrants.[7] As a share of the U.S. population, the immigration rate during that period was more than double the rate today.

Consider the irony: The same era that Pat Buchanan and other trade skeptics praise for its high tariffs was also an era of persistent trade deficits and mass immigration! And all the evidence shows that it was those trade deficits and the inflow of foreign capital they accommodated combined with large-scale immigration that did the most to transform America into an industrial giant, not self-damaging tariffs.

Smoot-Hawley's Colossal Failure

America's protectionist tradition culminated with passage of the Trade Act of 1930, forever etched in the nation's memory as Smoot-Hawley. It is worth spending a few moments recounting the story of what has become the most infamous piece of trade legislation in American history. Many of the same skeptics of trade who extol the virtues of high tariffs in the late 19th century also downplay the impact of the 1930 tariff law on the American economy. The bill was named after its two chief sponsors, Sen. Reed Smoot of Utah and Rep. Willis Hawley of Oregon, both Republicans. The bill was introduced in June 1929 and began as an attempt to protect American farmers (sound familiar?). During the next year, it devolved into a feeding frenzy of special interests all wanting protection from allegedly unfair foreign competition. In the end, it raised tariffs punitively on hundreds of manufacturing and agricultural products, some of them not even made or grown in the United States. Congress passed the final version of Smoot-Hawley on June 13, 1930, and President Herbert Hoover signed it into law soon thereafter.

It would be an exaggeration to say the Smoot-Hawley tariff bill caused the Great Depression, but it did aggravate the economic downturn and certainly did not deliver the tonic its supporters promised. From 1929 to 1932, imports to the United States plunged. As nominal prices fell, the per-item duties imposed by Smoot-Hawley rose sharply as a percentage of import value. Whether in response to the U.S. action or for other reasons, most foreign nations followed America's example by raising their own tariffs against American exports. Even formerly free-trade Great Britain jumped on the protectionist bandwagon. What followed was a downward spiral of global trade, the disintegration of national economies, and deepening international tensions. By 1938, the volume of trade among industrialized countries had fallen below what it had been in 1913.

Skeptics of trade are curiously quick to downplay what should have been one of their crowning achievements. Trade historian Alfred Eckes Jr., for example, argues that the Smoot-Hawley tariff law affected only a minority of import categories and could not have had the negative impact that critics of the bill claim. Although it is true that most imports continued to enter the United States duty free even after passage of the Trade Act of 1930, the duties that were imposed were so steep and strategically targeted that it was bound

111

to have a major impact on trade flows. After all, reducing import competition was the very purpose of the law. Doug Irwin estimates that Smoot-Hawley raised the effective average tariff rate on all imports from a range of 24 to 27 percent in the 1920s to a peak of 35 percent in 1933.[8] As a consequence of Smoot-Hawley, the height of America's tariff wall rose by a third, and imports fell by more than half. The architects of the tariff bill had accomplished their task all too well.

If the ultimate aim of the Smoot-Hawley tariff bill was to save American jobs and protect American industry, it was a colossal failure. Enactment of the tariff bill was followed by the most sickening economic free fall in our nation's history. From 1930 to 1933, not only did trade collapse, but real output of goods and services fell by one-third, unemployment soared to 25 percent of the workforce, and the stock market lost 89 percent of its value from its peak in 1929. If the Smoot-Hawley tariff bill had such a minimal impact on imports and the economy, as Alfred Eckes and others argue in hindsight, that begs the question of why Congress and their import-competing constituents worked for over a year to enact it. The answer, of course, is that advocates of protection, then as now, really thought they were protecting the U.S. economy when in fact they were compounding its misery.

Out of the Protectionist Wilderness

President Franklin D. Roosevelt and the new Democratic majority in Congress soon began to dismantle the damage of Smoot-Hawley. In 1934, Congress enacted the Reciprocal Trade Agreements Act, which empowered the secretary of state to negotiate agreements with U.S. trading partners to reduce tariffs by as much as 50 percent. FDR's visionary secretary of state, Cordell Hull, used the authority of RTAA to negotiate agreements with Belgium, Switzerland, Great Britain, and more than a dozen other countries covering 60 percent of U.S. trade. By the end of the 1930s, the average effective tariff rate had fallen back to the level of the 1920s, undoing the worst of Smoot-Hawley.[9]

In the aftermath of the 1930s and World War II, the United States joined with its postwar allies to drive a stake into the kind of "beggar thy neighbor" protection that had sown so much misery and discord. A major step was the signing in 1947 of the General Agreement on

Tariffs and Trade. The agreement committed the 23 original member nations to lower tariffs on a range of industrial goods and to apply tariffs in a nondiscriminatory manner, meaning that imports from any other GATT member would face the same tariff rate as that which applied to imports from the "most favored nation." GATT members also agreed to "national treatment" of imports from other members, meaning that domestic regulations would apply equally to all products regardless of origin. Members could not enforce one set of health and safety regulations on domestic products while imposing more stringent regulations on imports as a disguised form of protection.

Membership in the GATT codified America's historic turn away from its protectionist past. By the late 1940s, the average effective tariff rate on imports had fallen to 11 percent, the lowest level of protection for at least a century, perhaps since the days of Alexander Hamilton.[10] America's decisive turn in the direction of free trade and away from its protectionist past did not occur with NAFTA in 1993, the election of Ronald Reagan in 1980, the move to floating exchange rates in 1973, or the Kennedy Round trade agreement of 1967. It occurred in 1947 with America's entry into the GATT. By embracing lower tariffs and a global, rules-based trading system, the U.S. government erected an important pillar of America's postwar prosperity.

The turning point is important because the critics of trade assign the strong growth of the U.S. economy after World War II to the mythical pre-globalization past, when in fact it belongs squarely in the present era of globalization. The true golden era of America's growth, prosperity, and global influence began simultaneously with our nation's embrace of the global economy.

A More Open, Productive U.S. Economy

Through eight rounds of GATT negotiations and other trade agreements, the U.S. government lowered barriers to imports in the decades after World War II. America's openness to trade has not been a steady progression throughout the postwar period. Barriers to trade may have actually climbed somewhat in the 1970s and 1980s because of the U.S. government's trade distorting quotas—including "voluntary" export restraints—that restricted imports of automobiles, textiles and apparel, iron and steel, semiconductors, and other products. Quotas are especially damaging to the "protected" economy because the higher prices charged to consumers, the so-called quota rents, go directly into the pockets of the foreign producers who can still sell into the protected market rather than to the protecting government in the form of tariff revenue. Irwin calculates that the trade restrictiveness index actually rose to the 15 percent range by the early 1990s but has declined to an unprecedented low of 5 percent because of the elimination of the Multifiber Arrangement and other quota-based restrictions after conclusion of the Uruguay Round in 1994.[11]

Turning to free trade has been an important reason why the U.S. economy has grown strongly in postwar decades. Lower barriers at home have spurred innovation and productivity growth for American producers, while expanding markets abroad have opened new opportunities to export. The result has been faster and steadier growth.

Since the signing of the GATT, the U.S. economy has grown by an average of 3 percent per year. The growth record of the U.S. economy in an era of more open trade has been impressive—in two important ways more impressive than the era of protected industrialization that the critics of trade hold up as a superior model. One, growth today is driven more by productivity gains than by increases in labor and capital. Growth of TFP in the past half century has been far higher than TFP during the late 19th century. Because of new technology, human capital, and the invigorating breeze of global trade, Americans are working smarter. We can produce more from each hour worked and each unit of capital. This more intensive growth leads more directly to higher living standards.

Recessions Are Nothing New

The other way that growth in our more open era has outperformed growth in the protectionist path is its consistency. This argument may seem odd in the midst of a serious recession, which may prove to be one of the deepest and longest of the postwar era. But the recession that began in late 2007 came at the end of a quarter of a century in which the U.S. economy enjoyed strong growth, moderating inflation, and two relatively short and shallow recessions. Recessions are not a unique feature of our more globalized era. In fact, economic downturns were more frequent, deeper, and longer during past eras when barriers to trade were much higher.

The high-tariff golden age of the late 19th century so admired by skeptics of trade was also a time of wrenching and frequent boom-and-bust cycles. From 1854 to 1944, the U.S. economy suffered 21 recessions averaging 21 months in length. During that era, despite tremendous growth, the U.S. economy was contracting 41 percent of the time. A depression in the 1870s lasted six years. The "Gay Nineties" and the "Roaring Twenties" each witnessed four recessions. And, of course, let us not forget that the Great Depression of the 1930s occurred on the protectionists' watch.

In welcome contrast, the more globalized era since World War II has seen a moderation of the business cycle. According to the National Bureau of Economic Research, our nation suffered through nine recessions totaling 96 months in length between 1945 and 1985, representing 20 percent of the time. Since then, including the most recent recession that began in December 2007, our economy has been in recession about 12 percent of the time. Like a superior investment, our more globalized economy has delivered growth rates at least as good as past protectionist eras but with less volatility.

Evaluating the "NAFTA Era"

Perhaps no advancement of the trade agenda has been so reviled by the critics as the North American Free Trade Agreement. NAFTA has been blamed by critics of trade for a long list of economic ills, real or imagined, since it went into effect on January 1, 1994. But by virtually every measure, the U.S. economy in the NAFTA era has performed better than in the era leading up to it.

Consider Table 7.1, the "NAFTA Scorecard." It compares the 15 years since its enactment, including the recession year of 2008, to the 15 years that came immediately before NAFTA. The comparison is illuminating. Since NAFTA's passage, the U.S. economy has grown faster, inflation has been cut in half, the average unemployment rate has been lower by almost two full points, and manufacturing output accelerated. Labor productivity has jumped, and the annual growth in real compensation per hour has almost doubled. Median household income has grown by more than $6,000 in real dollars, compared to an almost negligible gain during the preceding period. The average poverty rate has fallen.

The only two measures that have not "improved" are total job creation and manufacturing employment. But a slight decline in

Table 7.1
NAFTA "SCORECARD"

Major Economic Indicators	Before NAFTA 1979–93	"NAFTA era" 1994–08
Real GDP growth (annual)	2.7%	3.0%
Inflation (average annual rate)	5.4%	2.7%
Job growth (millions)	25.6	24.0
Unemployment rate (average annual)	7.0%	5.1%
Manufacturing output (growth)	35%	58%
Manufacturing jobs lost (net, 1,000s)	2,158	3,278
Labor productivity (annual growth)	1.6%	2.3%
Real compensation (annual growth)	0.7%	1.3%
Median household income (change)	$206	$6,090
Poverty rate (average annual)	13.8%	12.8%
Misery Index (average annual)	12.4%	7.8%

SOURCES: Census Bureau, Labor Department, Commerce Department, Federal Reserve Board.

overall job growth occurred because of slower labor force growth. And falling manufacturing employment was entirely because of rising productivity, because actual output increased in the NAFTA era. Of course, NAFTA has not been the primary reason for the superior performance of the U.S. economy since its passage, but it has contributed to a more open and globalized American economy that has helped to propel our modern growth. And it has clearly not brought about the economic Armageddon that prominent opponents of NAFTA predicted.

Tapping into Global Markets

Like a more diversified stock portfolio, trade and globalization have given us a more resilient and flexible economy. Exports can take up slack when domestic demand sags, and imports can satisfy demand when domestic productive capacity is reaching its short-term limits. Access to foreign capital markets can allow domestic producers and consumers alike to more easily borrow to tide themselves over during difficult times.

Three-quarters of the world's buying power and 95 percent of the world's people exist outside the United States. The most rapidly growing major markets in the 21st century are not within our own borders but in Asia and other emerging markets. These countries represent a huge potential market for U.S. producers in general and hundreds of thousands of American small businesses in particular.

Exporting to the world has reached Main Street. A quarter of a million U.S. companies export to foreign markets, the large majority of them small and medium-sized enterprises (SMEs) that employ 500 or fewer workers. According to the U.S. Chamber of Commerce, more than 230,000 SMEs now account for nearly 30 percent of U.S. merchandise exports. The number of such companies exporting has more than doubled since 1992.[12]

This growth has been propelled by not only the expansion of global trade generally but also technological developments especially favorable to smaller exporters. On the cutting edge of this development has been the spread of the Internet and e-commerce. There are now more than 1.3 billion Internet users in the world today, and the number is growing rapidly. Of those, 85 percent shop online. With the assistance of delivery services such as FedEx and UPS, small businesses are able to reach global markets without the daunting expense of establishing sales teams and distribution networks in foreign countries. The Internet has also facilitated the slicing up of global supply chains, creating more opportunities for smaller U.S. companies to find profitable niches as suppliers for larger multinationals.

One of the most important and fastest growing markets for America's small-business exporters is China. In 2008, Americans exported $65 billion worth of goods to China, making it our fourth largest customer for U.S. goods in the world, behind only the European Union and our NAFTA partners, Canada and Mexico. Small and medium-sized U.S. companies are basking in this export success. In 2004 (according to the most recent figures we have), 19,210 SMEs in the United States were exporting to China. That is more than six times the number that were exporting in 1992. The share of U.S. companies exporting to China that are small or medium-sized enterprises has grown during that time from about three-quarters to more than 90 percent. SMEs accounted for 35 percent of U.S. merchandise exports to China in 2004, a higher share than their 29 percent share of exports overall.[13] Board any flight from the United States bound for China, and you will probably be sitting near somebody representing a small U.S. company heading off to buy and sell in the world's fastest growing major market.

Earnings from abroad have helped to keep the U.S. economy afloat during the recent turbulence. As the *Wall Street Journal* summarized in a front-page story in August 2007, "Economies in most other parts of the world—including China, Latin America and Europe—have grown faster than the U.S. over the past 18 months, providing a countercyclical balance for multinational companies. Overseas growth could provide further support for companies and investors if parts of the U.S. economy continue to worsen."[14]

American companies have been earning a larger and larger share of their profits overseas for decades now. According to economist Ed Yardeni, the share of their profits that U.S. companies earn abroad has increased steadily from about 5 percent in the 1960s to about a quarter of all profits today. Even the iconic Harley-Davidson motorcycle company in Milwaukee, Wis., has become a multinational company. The company that once came begging to Washington for protection from foreign competition is enjoying robust sales and profits abroad even as its domestic sales slump. In the second quarter of 2007, the company saw its profits jump by 19 percent, fueled by the double-digit growth in sales in Europe, Japan, and Canada even as its domestic sales fell 5.5 percent.[15]

The more moderate business cycle is no trivial development. Recessions mean real pain to real families—layoffs, extended unemployment, pay cuts, home foreclosures, and business bankruptcies. Although most people keep their jobs during a recession, the number of people suffering dislocation rises sharply. Moderation of the business cycle in recent decades is something to be thankful for, and expanding trade and globalization deserve a slice of the credit.

Exercising American Sovereignty

Critics of trade charge that the various trade-expanding agreements that the U.S. government has signed have compromised our national sovereignty. They claim that we have signed over our ability to determine not only our own trade policies but also our own health, safety, and environmental regulations. Dark warnings about surrendering our sovereignty to "secret tribunals" and shadowy "world government" conspiracies come from such sources as Ralph

Nader, the John Birch Society, and congressman and presidential candidate Ron Paul.

Tariffs are a tool of centralized government economic planning, whereas trade agreements help protect individual Americans from being manipulated by government planners. Agreements are not a transfer of sovereignty from the U.S. government to authorities outside the United States but from governments around the world to citizens. Political power is not transferred abroad but merely curtailed at home.

Signing trade agreements is not a surrender of American sovereignty but a prudent exercise of sovereignty. When the U.S. government enters a trade agreement such as NAFTA or the Uruguay Round, it is making a deal with other governments that it will grant American citizens greater freedom to buy goods and services provided by citizens of the other countries if those other countries will grant their citizens greater freedom to buy the goods and services we provide. The participating governments agree to curtail their own harmful economic policies, first for their own benefit, and also for the benefit of others. As trade economist Robert Lawrence concluded, "Just as individuals do not lose their liberty when they voluntarily sign beneficial contracts, so nations do not abridge their sovereignty when they sign trade agreements that advance their interests."[16]

Of course, trade agreements can be very complex documents that go beyond the reduction and elimination of tariffs. One reason agreements can be so detailed is because of numerous phase-out periods and exceptions demanded by noisy protected industries that do not want to surrender their privileged positions. A related reason is regulations on "rules of origin" to prevent countries outside the agreement from enjoying its benefits.

Why Ron Paul and Ralph Nader Are Both Wrong about the WTO

Some otherwise sensible free traders get confused on this point. Rep. Ron Paul (R-TX) supports free markets and espouses free trade, but he also opposes virtually all free trade agreements as unconstitutional infringements on the sovereignty of the U.S. government. He always votes against trade agreements and routinely sponsors resolutions to withdraw the United States from membership in the

WTO. While the congressman understands the benefits of free markets, he is as mistaken about trade agreements as the Naderites on the left and the John Birchers on the right.

Trade agreements do not limit our freedom as individual Americans. They are written to limit the power of governments to interfere in the peaceful commerce of their citizens. By limiting the scope of government action, trade agreements actually enhance the liberty and prosperity of the people living in the participating countries.

Ron Paul and Ralph Nader both demonize the WTO, but that modest institution poses no threat to American sovereignty. Membership in the WTO encourages the United States to keep its own markets open, for the benefit of U.S. consumers and import-using industries. It also promotes trade liberalization abroad, which opens markets and keeps them open for U.S. exporters. WTO agreements open foreign markets along with our own and put those commitments in writing, so there is less temptation for governments to backslide and re-impose damaging trade barriers under short-term political pressure.

Americans have witnessed the benefit of a global trading system during the recent downturn. A major reason why more governments have not raised barriers to U.S. exports is the existence of agreements they signed along with the U.S. government to reduce barriers and keep them down. Governments know that if they raise tariffs beyond the "bound" rates written in WTO agreements, or if they violate other provisions designed to keep markets open, they will be vulnerable to challenge in the WTO dispute settlement system. This is one of the huge advantages we enjoy today compared to the 1930s, when the race to raise trade barriers was unchecked by either economic sense or international agreements. Representative Paul rightly blames the government for causing the Great Depression but criticizes modern-day trade agreements that make those mistakes of the past less likely to occur again. Trade agreements have provided a rule of law for trade relations rather than the beggar-thy-neighbor rule of the jungle that prevailed so disastrously in the 1930s.

By its nature, the WTO is incapable of infringing on U.S. sovereignty. It lacks any tangible enforcement power other than the respect and credibility that its dispute settlement mechanism has built among its members. It is a contractual organization driven by the consensus of its membership. Unlike the International Monetary

Fund or the World Bank, the WTO dispenses no large amounts of money to foreign governments with strings attached. Unlike the United Nations, it dispatches no troops with "WTO" written on their helmets. Unlike the European Union, it writes no rules that are automatically enforceable in member countries.

The WTO's chief function is to facilitate negotiations among its members and then to render nonbinding opinions as to whether particular laws and regulations of its members are consistent with the WTO rules. Those rules are written by members through protracted negotiating rounds and are only adopted when all members finally agree.

A Firewall of Protection for U.S. Sovereignty

The sovereignty of the U.S. government is protected behind an insurmountable series of firewalls built into the WTO system. First, no trade rules become adopted within the WTO without the consensus agreement of every one of its members. This provision grants the U.S. government effective veto power over any change or expansion of WTO rules.

Second, the WTO's basic charter explicitly allows member countries to impose trade restrictions in the name of national security, public health and safety, and other areas where issues of sovereignty are most sensitive.

Third, any challenge to a U.S. trade–related law must be initiated by another WTO member and will proceed to a dispute settlement panel only after efforts to reach a compromise among the disputing members have failed. The WTO itself does not initiate any challenges to U.S. laws or regulations. It is not a regulatory cop prowling the global trade beat looking for offenders.

Fourth, if the U.S. government actually loses a case in dispute settlement, the WTO has no authority or power to do anything to enforce the decision. If the U.S. government decides to ignore a WTO decision against it, the WTO itself possesses no coercive power of any kind that could be used to enforce any outcome the U.S. government does not want to accept. The ultimate decision to impose retaliatory tariffs can only come from a WTO member government that filed the original complaint.

Finally, if the complaining member ultimately decides to impose sanctions against exports from the United States, the U.S. government retains exactly the same freedom of action it has always possessed in the face of foreign trade threats. Trade sanctions have been used and abused as a tool of commercial and foreign policy for decades, by the United States as well as by other nations. The WTO's "enforcement" mechanism has not conferred any new power on other countries that they would not have if the WTO system did not exist. In fact, by establishing a set procedure for settling trade disputes, WTO rules make it *less* likely that the United States will face the external pressure of sanctions.

Belonging to the WTO enhances the freedom and prosperity of Americans without surrendering an inch of national sovereignty.

Opening Markets Abroad

The U.S. government's membership in the WTO has yielded tangible benefits for American citizens. Successive rounds of negotiations through the GATT have lowered global trade barriers here in the United States and around the world. WTO agreements also restrict the ability of foreign governments to place quotas on imports, impose domestic regulations that unfairly discriminate against U.S. products, and subsidize domestic industries that compete against American firms. Those agreements don't just benefit large U.S. exporters. Small and medium-sized companies benefit from the more predictable rules and dispute settlement procedures. By providing transparency, trade agreements enhance the ability of smaller U.S. companies to cut through what can be the bewildering customs and regulatory red tape in foreign markets.

WTO membership allows the U.S. government to challenge the trade practices of other nations within the rule of law. If other members are violating their commitments, the United States can present its case before an impartial panel of trade experts. In the 14-plus years the WTO has been in operation, its dispute settlement mechanism has arbitrated hundreds of cases in what most observers agree to be a fair and restrained manner.

Of course, belonging to the WTO means U.S. laws can also be challenged by other countries. Between establishment of the WTO in 1995 and mid-2007, the U.S. government has brought 84 cases against other member governments and been the defendant in 94 cases against its own trade practices.[17] During that time, the U.S. government successfully used the WTO dispute settlement system to open foreign markets in 53 of those cases, 28 by winning a final judgment on the core issues of the complaint and 25 by settling favorably before completion of the case. Appealing through the WTO has helped the U.S. government to remove barriers to the sale of U.S. semiconductors in China (2004); beef and rice in Mexico (2003); genetically modified crops in the European Union (2003); apples in Japan (2002); milk in Canada (1997); 2,700 specific product categories in India, including high-technology products, petrochemical, textiles, and agricultural products (1997); and copyrighted sound recordings in Japan (1996).[18]

Even when the U.S. government loses a case brought against it in the WTO, the American people usually win. That's because the questionable trade barriers our own government is trying to defend often benefit the protected industry but at the expense of other U.S. companies and millions of American households (for all the reasons we shall see in chapter 9). WTO cases have resulted in the reduction or removal of U.S. barriers against imported underwear from Costa Rica, wool shirts from India, shrimp from Asia, computer chips from Korea, steel from a host of countries, lamb meat from Australia and New Zealand, and lumber from Canada.[19] Those "losses" in the WTO brought the U.S. government into closer compliance with its international commitments and delivered lower prices to domestic consumers and producers. When it comes to trade policy, the U.S. government is not always on the side of American consumers and families, so when it "loses" as a defendant in the WTO, we often win.

Confidently Embracing the World and the Future

We should think about trade policy not just for what it means for Industry X or Union Y but what it means for the United States of America. By engaging in the global economy, we have made our nation stronger and more influential in the world.

For a nation, free trade is like fresh air and exercise. It can be uncomfortable at first as the body adjusts to the new regime. We breathe hard, we sweat, and our muscles ache. But soon our aerobic capacity expands, and we discover that we can run faster and farther, we can lift more weight, and we can more quickly shake off the ups and downs of life. In contrast, protectionism is like lounging on the couch, watching reruns, and eating Cheetos in a stale room with the windows shuttered. It may feel comforting in the short run, but it leads to flabbiness, fatigue, and decline for the protected parts of the body.

123

The payoff to the American economy from its postwar trade liberalization has been measurable and immense. Scott C. Bradford, Paul L. E. Grieco, and Gary Clyde Hufbauer calculated the benefits to Americans from the postwar reduction in trade barriers and transportation and communication costs. Using several different models, they estimate that the benefits to Americans from increased consumption, variety gains, and increased productivity amounts to 7.3 percent of our total gross domestic product. That means "roughly $1 trillion of annual U.S. GDP is attributable to global integration,"[20] or $7,100 for a typical household. They also estimate that achieving global free trade would boost the U.S. economy by another $450 billion, potentially adding another $4,000 to a typical American family's income.[21] The only barriers standing between Americans and the final gains from trade liberalization are politicians and interest groups wedded to the status quo.

A vibrant economy connected to the world expands American influence. Other countries are more likely to pay attention to American interests when our economy carries more weight in the world rather than less. Foreign policy expert Joseph Nye referred to this as "soft power." A U.S. economy that is buying and selling more goods, services, and assets in the world will be a nation more able to influence other countries through means other than military force or other threats. We should not hide the light of our free and dynamic society under a bushel basket of trade and investment barriers.

Pursuing free trade offers a "two-fer" for U.S. policymakers: For the same reasons we pursued freer trade after World War II, free trade allows us to promote higher living standards at home while advancing our broader foreign policy interests. As we'll see in the next chapter, trade and globalization are making the world a more hospitable place for us, our nation, and our values.

8. More Like Us: The Growth of the Global Middle Class

A quiet revolution has changed the world for the better in the past three decades. The world is becoming more like us—more middle class, not just in what people wear and eat but in the way they live and think. Across a broad swath of what used to be called the Third World, incomes have been rising and poverty has been falling. Ownership of such middle-class tokens as a car, a refrigerator, and a computer are becoming more widespread. More kids are going to school, even college, leaving the farm for a better life in the city.

The impact of the emerging global middle class goes beyond daily living standards to shape the world in a way that is more hospitable for Americans today and for generations to come. An educated, property-owning middle class has become the backbone of democracy in a majority of the world's nations. Expanding commercial ties, coupled with representative government, have encouraged nations to live at peace with one another. The rising middle class has helped to spread middle-class, "bourgeois" virtues of thrift, industry, trustworthiness, and tolerance.

Trade and globalization have profoundly shaped the world we all live in today. Since 1980, according to the International Monetary Fund, world trade has grown five-fold in real terms. Trade expressed as a share of world GDP has risen from 36 percent to 55 percent, and that growth accelerated in the 1990s and into the new century. Financial globalization has also proceeded at an even more rapid pace. The total value of cross-border financial assets has more than doubled since 1990 relative to global GDP, from 58 percent to 131 percent in 2004.[1] Those trends took a hit as the global downturn deepened in 2009, but even so the world is still much more globalized than it was three decades ago, and the emerging economies that have participated in the latest wave of globalization have arguably benefited the most.

Plugging into globalization allows less developed countries to turbocharge their growth. Study after study has found that nations that are open to the global economy grow faster and achieve higher incomes than nations that remain closed, and this is especially true for poor countries that want to escape their poverty. Development economists call it the "late-comers' advantage." Farms and factories in poor countries can now produce for global markets rather than their own limited domestic customer base. They can enjoy the benefits of off-the-shelf technologies developed in rich countries—such as the Internet, computers, software, cell phones, pharmaceuticals, and scientific instruments—without paying the up-front cost of R&D. According to the World Bank, new technologies that took 50 years to spread to most countries in the world now reach less developed markets in one-third the time.[2]

The advanced economies, especially the United States, Canada, and western European countries, blazed a development trail starting with the Industrial Revolution two centuries ago. Now more and more of the world's people are following our path, taking advantage of the human knowledge, technologies, and prosperous markets that have been developed over decades and at great initial expense. In a recent study for the Copenhagen Consensus Project, international economists Kym Anderson and L. Alan Winters concluded that, "The past experience of successful reformers such as Korea, China, India, and Chile suggest trade opening immediately boosts GDP growth rates by several percentage points per year for many years."[3] When compounded over two or three decades, those faster growth rates allow dramatic gains during a single generation.

A Rising Middle Class, Falling Poverty

The global economic downturn that reared its head in 2008 should not obscure the unprecedented material progress that globalization has brought to the world in recent years. Beginning in the 1990s, growth began to accelerate in China, India, and other emerging markets. The growth has been broadly based, creating the greatest expansion of the global middle class in human history. For the first time ever, a majority of the world's people now live in cities, and more people work in the service economy than in agriculture— milestones that the United States passed decades ago.[4]

In sheer numbers, the World Bank calculates that 400 million people in less developed countries have already achieved an annual middle-class income of $16,800 to $72,000 per household. That number is on track to triple to 1.2 billion by 2030.[5] By 2030, per capita income in the developing world will reach $11,000 a year in real terms—approximately the living standard in today's Czech Republic in the European Union. In a separate study released in July 2008, Goldman Sachs researchers Dominic Wilson and Raluca Dragusanu defined the middle class somewhat differently but came to the same conclusion: "An astonishing 2 billion people could join the global middle class by 2030!"[6] They estimate the global middle class to be growing by about 70 million people a year, which is close to the annual growth in the world's population of 80 million. In other words, just about all of the world's net population growth is now occurring in the middle class.

The rise in the global middle class has gone hand in hand with a heartening drop in global poverty. The share of the world's population living in absolute poverty has been cut in half in the past 25 years. According to the World Bank, 52 percent of the world's population lived on the equivalent of $1.25 a day or less in 1981. By 2005, that share had dropped to 25 percent. For the first time in centuries, the total number of poor people living in the world has actually begun to decline in absolute numbers in the past two decades.[7] The current global downturn has put that progress on pause temporarily, but we can expect it to resume when global growth returns to its more recent trend.

Progress has been across continents, as we can see in Figure 8.1. Even in Sub-Saharan Africa, the poverty rate finally began to fall after 1996. In China alone, since its market reforms began 30 years ago, the number of people living in absolute poverty has dropped by more than 600 million. The number of people in China living on $2.50 per day or less has also fallen sharply.[8] This is the greatest anti-poverty program the world has ever seen. It has occurred primarily not because of foreign aid, internal redistribution, or threats to impose trade sanctions but because of market reforms and expanding trade.

The real news is not that more than a billion people in this world remain in desperate poverty but that so much rapid progress has been made in our globalized era. The poor have always been among

Figure 8.1
PROGRESS AGAINST GLOBAL POVERTY
(percent living in absolute poverty)

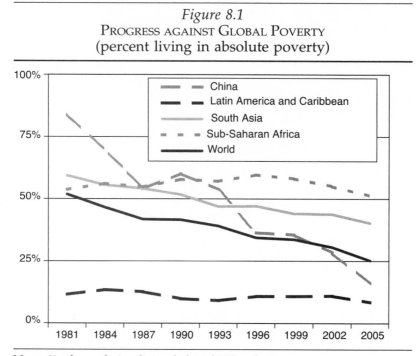

NOTE: % of population living below $1.25 a day.
SOURCE: World Bank.

us. In the early 1800s, an estimated 80 percent of the world's population lived on today's equivalent of $1.50 a day or less.[9] It took more than 150 years of spreading globalization, industrialization, and technology to cut that share in half. The miracle is that mankind has managed to cut the ranks of the poor in half again, this time in a mere 25 years. Simply put, globalization and free trade have done more to lift people out of poverty than all the government foreign aid programs that ever existed.

If that were the sum of the story, it would be good news enough. But all sorts of positive things start to happen when the average per capita income in a developing country surpasses about $5,000 a year. Freed from the specter of starvation, people turn their attention to the relative luxuries of sending their children to school; accessing electrical, water, and sewer utilities for their homes; acquiring a TV, cell phone, household appliances, and a car; buying more health care and travel; and demanding protection for their property, a cleaner environment, and a larger voice in their own government. By spurring faster growth and rising incomes, trade and globalization also promote a rising consumer class and social progress.

For any American who has traveled recently to emerging economies, those are not hollow numbers. In places as diverse as Seoul, South Korea; Beijing, China; Mumbai, India; and Monterrey, Mexico, I have seen with my own eyes how ubiquitous automobiles, cell phones, laptop computers, and other consumer goods have become. More than a billion people in the world continue to live in deep poverty, but the real story of our time is how many of them are escaping to a life that more closely resembles our own.

If we look beneath the headlines, we can find stories of the emerging middle class. In Brazil, the shantytowns around its major cities, known as *favelas*, are being transformed into something resembling middle-class suburbs. In the metropolis of São Paulo, new apartment buildings are going up, and electricity, piped water, and sewer systems are being rapidly extended. A 2005 study of households in four *favelas* in São Paulo found that virtually all owned refrigerators and color TVs (often more than one), nearly half owned cell phones, and almost a third owned DVD players and cars. In the words of the *Economist* magazine, "They are members of a new middle class that is emerging almost overnight across Brazil and much of Latin America. Tens of millions of such people are the main beneficiaries of the region's hard-won economic stability and recent economic growth. Having left poverty behind, their incipient prosperity is driving the rapid growth of a mass consumer market in the region long notorious for the searing contrast between a small privileged elite and a poor majority."[10]

More Customers and Business Partners

For Americans, the rise in the global middle class and the decline in global poverty have yielded direct and indirect benefits that will benefit our country and our children and grandchildren for decades to come. In the most direct way, a wealthier world means more potential customers and business partners for American producers and more suppliers competing to satisfy American consumers.

American companies are well positioned to sell their goods and services to a growing global market. American companies will increasingly find their best growth opportunities not in our mature domestic market but in rapidly expanding emerging economies. As hundreds of millions of people abroad join the global middle class, their appetite for and ability to buy the more sophisticated type of products and services offered by American producers will only grow. As the global middle class expands, the World Bank predicts that it "will participate actively in the global marketplace, demand world-class products, and aspire to international standards of higher education. That is, they would have the purchasing power to buy automobiles (perhaps second hand), purchase many consumer durables, and travel abroad."[11]

Increased travel will bring more Chinese, Indians, and Latin Americans to the United States to spend dollars at our restaurants, hotels, and tourist attractions. Demand for airliners, including the new Boeing 787 Dreamliner, will predictably increase. Demand for U.S.–based medical and educational services will climb. By 2017, pharmaceutical sales in the biggest emerging markets are predicted to reach $300 billion a year, equal to today's sales in the top five European markets and the United States combined. America's leading drug companies are well positioned to meet the growing demand for an expanding array of medications and designer drugs.[12] The Goldman Sachs study predicts rising global demand for meat, personal computers, financial services, insurance, and health care—sectors where American producers and brand names predominate.

The rising global middle class offers the best hope for America's automobile manufacturers. As we saw in chapter 6, Ford and General Motors are already selling more cars abroad than in the United States, and that trend will only grow. The Goldman Sachs team that has studied the emerging middle class notes that families in developing countries begin to buy automobiles when per capita income reaches $5,000, with the growth in demand peaking at $10,000 per capita. The number of cars on the road in the world is expected to climb from 600 million today to 2.9 billion by 2050. By 2030, there will be as many cars in China as there will be in the United States. If one out of ten cars is replaced each year, annual global car sales will also jump from just under 60 million in 2008 to nearly 300 million by 2050—a five-fold increase.[13]

In a more globalized world, our children will find more opportunities to work profitably with people around the world.

Rising Global Social Standards

The rise of a global middle class and the decline in poverty has not just been about higher incomes and more consumption. The rising global tide we have seen in the past two decades has allowed families in developing countries to acquire healthier lives.

The amazing progress of mankind during our era of globalization was summarized powerfully by Cato senior fellow Johan Norberg in a recent paper he delivered to the Swedish Globalization Council.[14] Rising living standards enabled by globalization are about more than cars and TVs. You probably won't hear these facts on the nightly news:

Life Expectancy. People in most poor countries are living longer than ever before, and the gap between rich and poor countries is closing. Since 1960, the average life expectancy in developing countries has jumped from 45 years to 65 years. The gap between life expectancy in the developing and advanced economies has been cut in that time from 24 years to 14 years. Most of the credit belongs to the growth of medical knowledge, but globalization has helped to develop and spread that knowledge. It has enabled people in poor countries to better afford the medicines, vaccinations, and public health improvements that put that knowledge into practice.

Infant Mortality. The global infant mortality rate, the share of children born alive who die before their first birthday, fell by 60 percent between 1960 and 2005. Again, the spread of modern medicine played the primary role, but rising levels of trade and income were its handmaidens. The share of children vaccinated against measles, diphtheria, tetanus, and whooping cough has jumped sharply to about three-quarters. Smallpox and polio, which were scourges as recently as the 1950s, have been virtually eliminated from the human race. As a result, the number of children dying each year in the world dropped by 2 million from 1990 to 2005. Only the most hardened critics of globalization can fail to be encouraged by such tangible progress.

Daily Bread. An adult human being needs 2,000 to 2,310 calories a day to perform everyday activities while preserving health and body weight. In 1961, the average daily per capita intake of calories in developing countries was 1,930, or just below the minimum. By 2002, after a "Green Revolution" on the farm, the average intake had risen to 2,666. The share of people living in developing countries who are undernourished was cut by more than half, from 37 percent to 17 percent. Famines caused by natural disasters such as crop failures have become a thing of the past.

Literacy. As recently as 1970, fewer than half of adults in developing countries could read or write. Today the proportion has risen to two thirds. Progress has been even more rapid among youth, especially young girls. Girls still lag boys in years of schooling for a host of cultural reasons, but the amount of schooling for girls compared to boys climbed from 56 percent in 1960 to 73 percent in 2000. The gap in East Asia and Latin America has been abolished entirely.

Child Labor. With more boys and girls in school learning to read and write, the share working has been falling. Worldwide, the proportion of children ages 10 to 14 who are working fell from 25 percent in 1960 to 10 percent in 2003, and it has continued to fall since then.

In February 2007, I was called upon to testify before a Senate subcommittee that was considering an anti-sweatshop bill supposedly designed to improve working conditions and reduce child labor in factories abroad. Presiding over the hearing was Senator Dorgan, a sponsor of the legislation and, as you may have gathered from preceding chapters, a critic of free trade and globalization. One of the witnesses before me told the story of Halima, an 11-year-old girl working long and exhausting hours in a garment export factory in the impoverished South Asian country of Bangladesh.

As heart wrenching as these stories can be, Halima is not a victim of free trade and globalization, but of her own government's failure to promote rapid and sustainable economic growth. Her story does not represent that of the 90 percent of children in the world today who are in school, and it does not even represent the declining minority of those who are working. As I told the committee in my own opening statement later in the hearing:

> By raising incomes in poor countries, free trade and globalization have helped pull millions of kids out of the workforce and helped them enroll in school, where they belong. The International Labor Organization recently reported that the number of children in the world ages 10 to 14 who are working rather than attending school has dropped by 11 percent

since their previous report in 2002. There are 20 million fewer Halimas today than there were just 4 or 5 years ago. And it's not because of [Congress wielding] a legislative billy-club, it's because of trade and growth in developing countries. . . .

Parents in poor countries love their children just as much as we love our own. When they rise above a subsistence income, the first thing they do is remove their children from the workforce and put them in school. Studies confirm that labor-force participation rates by children decline sharply with rising per capita GNP.

The overwhelming majority of child laborers toiling in poor countries work in sectors far removed from the global economy. More than 80 percent work without pay, usually for their family, and typically on subsistence farming. I notice we don't have any representative [at the hearing today] from a rural farming area, where most poor people live in the world and most child laborers toil. Most others work for small-scale domestic enterprises, typically non-traded services, such as shoe shining, newspaper delivery, and domestic service.[15]

If Congress were to enact anti-sweatshop legislation, it would hinder the very progress that its advocates claim they want to promote. Raising tariffs on goods imported from poor countries would eliminate the best paying jobs in those societies. When parents in poor countries suffer a loss of income, they will be more likely to remove their children from school and send them back to the field or the streets in a desperate attempt to make up for the loss.

How do we expect hundreds of millions of people to pull themselves out of poverty if we do not allow them access to global markets? It is morally and economically incoherent to denounce global poverty and sweatshops one moment and to denounce imports from and foreign investment to the very same countries where the poor people actually live.

Mexico Before and After NAFTA

One way that critics of trade have sought to undermine it is by painting a dark picture of Mexico in the NAFTA era. They claim that since the passage of NAFTA in 1993, real wages in Mexico have declined and poverty has increased. They even blame NAFTA for spurring more illegal immigration, arguing that lower tariffs have flooded the Mexican market with subsidized U.S. corn, displacing

Mexican corn farmers who have then migrated illegally to the United States.

Mexico is a country with its share of problems, and no one would confuse Tijuana with San Diego or Ciudad Juarez with El Paso. But its problems did not begin with the passage of NAFTA, and in fact its deepening commercial ties to the United States before and after enactment of NAFTA have helped Mexicans modernize their economy and political system. Mexico is a far better place than it was 20 or 30 years ago, and NAFTA is one of the reasons.

NAFTA codified a process of economic opening that had actually begun early in the 1980s in the wreckage of Mexico's old model of a closed economy dominated by a single party, the Institutional Revolutionary Party, or PRI. NAFTA reduced and eliminated Mexican trade barriers to U.S. exports during the 15 years after it went into effect.

In December 1994, within a year after enactment of the agreement, Mexico suffered an economic crisis. The government was unable to pay its short-term debts, its currency (the peso) plunged in value, prices and interest rates shot up, and the country suffered a sharp drop in output and employment. Real wages fell, and poverty increased. U.S. exports to Mexico fell, turning a small bilateral trade surplus with Mexico into a deficit.

Despite what the critics of trade claim, NAFTA was not the cause of the peso crisis. In fact, it would be more accurate to see the crisis as the last, dying gasp of the old Mexican order. Since the mid 1970s, Mexico had suffered various forms of economic crises related to its six-year election cycle. The PRI government would spend heavily on the eve of each election to enhance its re-election prospects, and then the bills would come due afterward, fomenting an economic crisis. The deepest and most prolonged was the 1982 banking crisis, which occurred a full decade before NAFTA and required most of the 1980s to undo.

Thanks to NAFTA, Mexico bounced back from the 1994 crisis far more quickly than it had recovered from the 1982 crisis. Although Mexico's economic growth has not been spectacular since NAFTA, it has been strong and steady enough that, despite the peso crisis, real wages are higher today than before NAFTA and the poverty rate is lower. Progress has been especially strong in those regions of the country that have been most closely tied to trade with the United States.[16]

The critics are wrong about corn, too. American farmers produce mostly yellow corn, which Mexicans import as feed for cattle. Mexican farmers grow mostly white corn, which they use domestically to make tortillas and other foods for human consumption. Although U.S. exports of corn to Mexico have indeed increased under NAFTA, Mexico's domestic corn production has also increased. According to a 2007 study by the Woodrow Wilson Center in Washington, D.C., Mexican farmers grew about 15 million metric tons of corn a year before NAFTA, compared to an average of 20 million tons a year from 2001 to 2006.[17] The U.S. government should not be subsidizing the production of corn in the United States, but that is not a fault of NAFTA, and the free trade in agriculture that NAFTA brought about has not devastated or even reduced Mexican corn production.

Those Mexicans who have migrated to the United States in recent years have not typically come from the corn growing regions, anyway, but from certain states in central Mexico with a tradition of sending migrants north. If the United States had spurned NAFTA, Mexican workers would have even fewer opportunities in their own country, and Mexico would be a less cooperative partner with the United States in dealing with illegal immigration and other border issues.

Democracy and Human Rights

Another way that people outside the United States are becoming more like us in our more globalized world is through the spread of civil liberties, human rights, and democracy. Along with the expansion of trade and foreign investment in the past three decades, the world has also become more hospitable to other realms of human freedom, and the two developments are related.

Political scientists since Aristotle have noted that an educated and property-owning middle class provides the most solid foundation for democracy. When citizens own homes, businesses, and financial assets, they are less likely to succumb to revolutionary appeals that have brought so much upheaval and misery to poor countries. When people are better educated, they are more able to exercise independent judgment in choosing their rulers and public policy. Economic independence nurtures the confidence to assert social and political independence from the government. Those traits have been the durable foundation of American freedom since our founding.

Consistent with those theories, our more globalized world has also become a more democratic world. According to the think tank Freedom House based in New York, the past 35 years of expanding global trade have also witnessed the blossoming of political and civil freedom around the world. Freedom House rates nearly 200 countries every year according to freedom of speech, assembly, and worship as well as the freedom to participate in open, competitive elections.

In its annual "Freedom in the World" report, the organization groups countries into three categories: "Free"—those countries in which citizens enjoy full civil and political freedoms of the kind that we Americans take for granted; "Partly Free"—those countries in which some freedom exists but is seriously curtailed; and "Not Free"— those countries in which basic political rights are absent and basic civil liberties are widely and systematically denied.

In the past 30 years, the number of countries that are "Not Free" declined by a third, whereas the number that are "Free" doubled. The share of nations that are democracies has jumped from 42 percent in 1989–90 to a plateau of 61 to 64 percent since 2000. In 1973, when the surveys began, Freedom House found that 35 percent of the world's population lived in countries that were classified as "Free." Today that share has grown to 46 percent. In that same time frame, the share living in countries classified as "Partly Free" has slipped from 18 to 17 percent, and the share living in countries classified as "Not Free" has dropped from 47 percent to 37 percent.[18] If the percentages were the same today as in 1973, there would be roughly 700 million fewer people living in the full sunlight of democracy and civil liberty, and 700 million more living in the darkness of tyranny.

How Free Trade Nurtures a Free Society

Expanding trade and globalization deserve a share of the credit. Economic freedom and development have spread the tools of communication. Hundreds of millions of people in developing countries now have access to cell phones, the Internet, and satellite TV. Increased foreign travel and foreign investment have exposed them to a world of new friendships, ideas, and lifestyles. A more open and less controlled economy fosters the growth of "civil society"—

including new businesses, independent labor unions, professional associations, and clubs, or what the great 18th-century British statesman Edmund Burke called society's "little platoons." People in a free and open market tend to see people outside their ethnic and religious group not as threats but as potential customers and business partners. People learn to practice tolerance and compromise in their everyday lives, essential public traits for a democracy.[19] Growth has also created a rising global middle class that is economically independent and politically aware. Freed from the daily shackles of toiling for subsistence, these middle-class families have turned their attention to such causes as securing property rights, improving the environment, and getting their kids through college. As people embrace the daily freedom of the marketplace and property ownership, they come to expect more freedom in the political sphere.

Nations open to the global economy are significantly more likely to enjoy greater political and civil freedoms than those countries that are relatively closed. Governments that grant their citizens a large measure of freedom to engage in international commerce find it increasingly difficult to deprive them of political and civil liberties, whereas governments that "protect" their citizens behind tariff walls and other barriers to international commerce find it much easier to deny those same liberties. A special panel commissioned by the WTO to survey the state of the world trading system on the WTO's 10th anniversary rightly observed, "Generally, the marks of closed economies are lack of democracy and a free media, political repression, and the absence of opportunity for individuals to improve their lives through education, innovation, honest hard work and commitment."[20]

If we compare the economic openness of individual countries to their civil and political freedom, we can see an unmistakable pattern: Citizens of the most economically open countries are far more likely to enjoy political and civil liberty than citizens of less open countries. The annual *Economic Freedom of the World Report*, by James Gwartney and Robert Lawson, measures the level of economic freedom in 140 countries around the world, including the freedom to engage in international transactions. Their study considers tariff rates and foreign exchange and capital controls. Among the 28 countries in the top quintile of openness, 22 are rated "Free" by Freedom House. Among the 28 countries in the bottom quintile of openness, only five are rated "Free." In fact, the number of "Free" countries rises in each quintile along with the freedom of citizens to engage in the global economy.

Globalization provides a double boost for democracy and human rights. Trade itself opens societies directly to more outside influences that promote freedom. And by enabling faster growth, trade and openness raise incomes and expand the middle class, which also reinforce the desire for broader freedoms in society. If we track civil and political freedom by income, we see the same powerful pattern as we did with economic openness. Wealthier countries tend to enjoy more political and civil freedoms than poor countries. Figure 8.2 shows the average political and civil freedom in the world among countries at a given income level. For each income level, the graph shows the average political and civil freedom ratings for countries in that "neighborhood"—the nearest 20 countries on either side of that income. With 193 countries represented, each neighborhood is a kind of floating quintile measuring the gradual changes in freedom as we move up the income ladder.

According to the graph, political and civil freedoms expand slowly from $1,000 to about $5,000 annual per capita income—the same significant threshold we mentioned earlier in the chapter. In this income neighborhood, political rights average 3.9 on the Freedom House scale and civil liberties 3.5, placing these nations squarely in the "Partly Free" category. From then on, the neighborhoods improve more rapidly. By $15,000 per capita, the average scores cross the threshold into the "Free" category, and by $34,000, government oppression of civil liberties and political rights is at a minimum. The ratings suffer slightly at incomes above that because of the presence of a few oil-rich but freedom-poor states such as Qatar, Brunei, Kuwait, and the United Arab Emirates.

The spread of economic freedom, trade, globalization, and middle-class incomes has helped to lay the foundation for the flowering of democracy in such formerly authoritarian countries as South Korea, Taiwan, and Chile. It is not a coincidence that within a decade after the passage of NAFTA, one-party rule in Mexico was broken with the election of Vicente Fox in 2000. NAFTA helped to break the grip of the long-ruling PRI over the economic life of the country. Now Mexico has become a vigorous multiparty democracy. In contrast, countries where political freedom and civil freedoms are in retreat,

138

Figure 8.2
WELCOME TO THE NEIGHBORHOOD

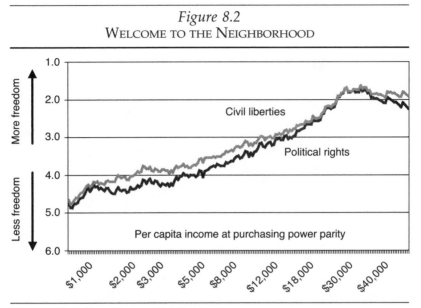

SOURCES: Freedom House, CIA Factbook.

such as Venezuela and Zimbabwe, are also countries where governments are busy curtailing economic freedom.

Promoting Freedom in China

The connection among economic freedom, growth, and political and civil freedom should encourage Americans who love liberty and strike a note of fear in the hearts of oppressive governments around the world. China's rapid economic rise has moved it into a mixed neighborhood where "Free" countries become more common than "Not Free" countries. If the experience of other countries offers a pattern, the communist rulers in Beijing will find it increasingly difficult to suppress the legitimate desires of their citizens to enjoy political rights and civil liberties commensurate with their citizens' expanding economic freedoms and middle-class incomes. The recent economic downturn and rising unemployment in China may provide a spark.

Another potential catalyst for political change in China could be environmental and land-use concerns. Chinese citizens have become more willing to challenge the government to provide cleaner air and water and to protect their homes from unjust takings by the government. During a visit to Shanghai in 2006, I read in the local English-language press that homeowners had successfully halted development of a second leg of a high-speed magnetic levitation train. In a scenario familiar to American homeowners, Chinese families feared the presence of the train would reduce the value of the homes they can now buy and own. More recently, the *International Herald Tribune* reported in January 2008, "Demonstrations against the maglev in downtown Shanghai over the weekend, the city's largest public protest since thousands took part in sometimes violent anti-Japanese demonstrations in 2005, present authorities with a new challenge: a growing middle class that wants a say in major decisions about development in the city."[21] Call it NIMBY—"Not in My Back Yard"—with Chinese characteristics.

The line connecting globalization to human rights and democracy is not always straight. The world is too complex a place. Culture and history influence the political order along with economic arrangements. The city-state of Singapore has one of the most open economies and highest standards of living in the world, but the civil and political freedoms of its citizens remain partly curtailed. Despite its economic reforms and rapid growth, the Chinese communist government refuses to allow much noneconomic freedom. Many oil-producing states in the Middle East have achieved relatively high incomes and have selectively opened their economies, but most of them remain stubbornly "Not Free." But these outliers do not disprove the dominant positive correlation between economic development and political and civil freedom.

The global advance of freedom has not followed a straight upward slope either. For reasons as varied as the countries, the past three years have witnessed a stall in the rising share of countries and people enjoying political and civil freedom. Arch Puddington, the head of Freedom House, noted in the most recent report that one-fifth of the world's countries have suffered major or incremental reversals of freedom in the past two years. But the world remains a far more hospitable place for basic civil liberties and representative government than it was 30, 20, or even 10 years ago, and expanding trade and globalization are a major part of the story.

Free Trade's "Peace Dividend"

Our more globalized world has also yielded a "peace dividend." It may not be obvious when our daily news cycles are dominated by horrific images from the Gaza Strip, Afghanistan, and Darfur, but our more globalized world has somehow become a more peaceful world. The number of civil and international wars has dropped sharply in the past 15 years along with battle deaths. The reasons behind the retreat of war are complex, but again the spread of trade and globalization have played a key role.

Trade has been seen as a friend of peace for centuries. In the 19th century, British statesman Richard Cobden pursued free trade as a way not only to bring more affordable bread to English workers but also to promote peace with Britain's neighbors. He negotiated the Cobden-Chevalier free trade agreement with France in 1860 that helped to cement an enduring alliance between two countries that had been bitter enemies for centuries. In the 20th century, President Franklin Roosevelt's secretary of state, Cordell Hull, championed lower trade barriers as a way to promote peaceful commerce and reduce international tensions. Hull had witnessed first-hand the economic nationalism and retribution after World War I. He believed that "unhampered trade dovetail[s] with peace; high tariffs, trade barriers and unfair economic competition, with war."[22] Hull was awarded the 1945 Nobel Prize for Peace, in part because of his work to promote global trade.

Free trade and globalization have promoted peace in three main ways. First, trade and globalization have reinforced the trend towards democracy, and democracies tend not to pick fights with each other. A second and even more potent way that trade has promoted peace is by raising the cost of war. As national economies become more intertwined, those nations have more to lose should war break out. War in a globalized world means not only the loss of human lives and tax dollars but also ruptured trade and investment ties that impose lasting damage on the economy. Trade and economic integration have helped to keep the peace in Europe for more than 60 years. More recently, deepening economic ties between China and Taiwan are drawing those two governments closer together and helping to keep the peace. Leaders on both sides of the Taiwan Strait seem to understand that reckless nationalism would jeopardize the dramatic economic progress that the region has enjoyed.

A third reason why free trade promotes peace is because it has reduced the spoils of war. Trade allows nations to acquire wealth through production and exchange rather than conquest of territory and resources. As economies develop, wealth is increasingly measured in terms of intellectual property, financial assets, and human capital. Such assets cannot be easily seized by armies. In contrast, hard assets such as minerals and farmland are becoming relatively less important in high-tech, service economies. If people need resources outside their national borders, say oil or timber or farm products, they can acquire them peacefully by freely trading what they can produce best at home.

The world today is harvesting the peaceful fruit of expanding trade. The first half of the 20th century was marred by two devastating wars among the great powers of Europe. In the ashes of World War II, the United States helped to found the General Agreement on Tariffs and Trade in 1947, the precursor to the WTO that helped to spur trade between the United States and its major trading partners. As a condition to Marshall Plan aid, the U.S. government also insisted that the continental European powers (France, Germany, and Italy) eliminate trade barriers between themselves in what was to become the European Common Market. One purpose of a common market was to spur economic development, of course, but just as importantly, it was meant to tie the Europeans together economically. With six decades of hindsight, the plan must be considered a spectacular success. The notion of another major war between France, Germany, and other Western European powers is unimaginable.

Compared to past eras, our time is one of relative world peace. According to the Stockholm International Peace Research Institute, the number of armed conflicts around the world has dropped sharply in the past two decades. Virtually all the conflicts today are civil and guerrilla wars. The spectacle of two governments sending armies off to fight in the battlefield has become rare. In the past decade, wars have been fought between the governments of Eritrea and Ethiopia in 1998–2000, and the United States and Iraq in 2003, but between 2004 through 2007, no two nations were at war with one another.[23] Civil wars have ended or at least ebbed in Aceh (in Indonesia), Angola, Burundi, Congo, Liberia, Nepal, Timor-Leste, and Sierra Leone.[24]

Coming to the same conclusion is the Human Security Centre at the University of British Colombia in Canada. In a 2005 report, it documented a sharp decline in the number of armed conflicts, genocides, and refugees during the past 20 years. The average number of deaths per conflict has fallen from 38,000 in 1950 to 600 in 2002. Most armed conflicts in the world now take place in Sub-Saharan Africa, and the only form of political violence that has worsened in recent years is international terrorism.[25]

All this helps explain why the world's two most conflict-prone regions—the Arab Middle East and Sub-Saharan Africa—are also the world's two least globally and economically integrated regions. Terrorism does not spring from poverty but from ideological fervor and political and economic frustration. If we want to blunt the appeal of radical Islam to the next generation of Muslim children coming of age, we can help create more economic opportunity in those societies by encouraging more trade and investment ties with the West. Enacting free trade agreements with certain Muslim countries, such as Morocco, Jordan, Bahrain, and Oman, represented small steps in the right direction. An even more effective policy would be to unilaterally open the U.S. market to products made and grown in Muslim countries. A young man or woman with a real job at an export-oriented factory making overcoats in Jordan or shorts in Egypt is less vulnerable to the appeal of an Al-Qaida recruiter.

Of course, free trade and globalization do not guarantee peace or inoculation against terrorism. Hot-blooded nationalism and ideological fervor can overwhelm economic calculations. Any relationship involving human beings will be messy and non-linear. There will always be exceptions and outliers in such complex relationships involving economies and governments. But deeper trade and investment ties among nations have made it less likely than for generations past that America's sons and daughters will be called upon to fight in a war.

The Moral Case for Trade

As if it were not enough to argue that free trade has lifted millions out of poverty, strengthened human rights and democracy, and spread peace, let me make one more bold claim: Free trade and globalization encourage individuals to behave in better ways. The same "invisible hand" that turns our personal drive for betterment to the public's benefit also shapes our characters. The commercial and personal interactions with people from other countries that have come with globalization teach us tolerance, sympathy, humility, prudence, trustworthiness, and a spirit of service to our fellow human beings.

Success in the global marketplace requires winning the trust of strangers, proving reliability, and cooperating with people of differing language, culture, ethnicity, and race. The late Pope John Paul II, in a 1991 encyclical called *Centesimus Annus*, described the global economy as a sphere of activity where "people work with each other, sharing in a 'community of work' which embraces ever widening circles."[26] In this expanding economic community, the pope observed, a market system encourages the virtues of "diligence, industriousness, prudence in undertaking reasonable risks, reliability and fidelity in interpersonal relationships, as well as courage in carrying out decisions which are difficult and painful but necessary, both for the overall working of a business and in meeting possible set-backs."[27] As markets expand across borders and into new regions of the world, those "bourgeois virtues" increase at the expense of such vices as sloth, mistrust, duplicity, prejudice, and xenophobic nationalism.

The expansion of global markets reinforces fair play and the rule of law. Citizens and officials are not exposed to the temptation to game the system and seek special favors. When imports are controlled by arbitrary tariffs, quotas, and licensing regimes, opportunities multiply for graft and bribery. In less developed countries, it is not uncommon that citizens who want a consumer good or need a spare part must seek the favor of someone in authority. Barriers to trade can also promote smuggling, underground supply chains, and criminal cartels. For all those reasons, studies show that nations that are more open economically tend to be less corrupt.[28]

Historically, those cities and countries at the forefront of international trade were also among the most open and tolerant societies of their day. Venice in the 1400s and the Dutch Republic in the 1600s were the leading commercial centers of their eras. They each provided freedom and legal protection to Jews and religious dissenters. Their citizens learned to welcome people of differing religions and races because intolerance was, among its other shortcomings, bad for business. Today, as we have seen, societies open to trade are more likely to be open to freedom of religion and speech and political pluralism.

In the end, the argument in favor of free trade comes down to one of basic justice. If an American wants to trade what he has produced for something a person or group of people in another country have produced, our government should not interfere. To use the power of government to forbid a transaction that is beneficial to the two parties involved is to violate the sovereignty of free individuals. Trade barriers rob people of the rightful fruits of their own labor, distributing the spoils to other people with no moral claim to the confiscated wealth other than political power.

Free trade gives to each person sovereign control over that which is his own. In his 1849 essay, "Protectionism and Communism," the French political economist Frederic Bastiat wrote,

> Every citizen who has produced or acquired a product should have the option of applying it immediately to his own use or of transferring it to whoever on the face of the earth agrees to give him in exchange the object of his desires. To deprive him of this option when he has committed no act contrary to public order and good morals, and solely to satisfy the convenience of another citizen, is to legitimize an act of plunder and to violate the law of justice.[29]

That should be reason enough for Americans to demand that the last fetters on our freedom to trade be removed.

9. The Protectionist Swindle: How Trade Barriers Cheat the Poor and the Middle Class

Our politicians love to say that the United States is "the most open economy in the world," and it's true that America's trade barriers are relatively low compared to most other countries. But we are not the most open economy in the world, not even close. Our generally low average tariff rate disguises high tariff "peaks" on certain goods and other barriers against a range of imports important to millions of American workers and families. Those remaining trade barriers slow our economy and cost American consumers and producers tens of billions of dollars a year.

If an Olympics were held for the most open economy, the United States would be out of medal contention. According to the most recent annual *Economic Freedom of the World Report*, people living in 26 other countries enjoy greater "freedom to trade internationally" than do Americans. The report considers not only tariffs on imports but regulatory barriers, exchange rate and capital controls, and actual levels of trade. Bragging rights for the most open economies belong to, in descending order, Hong Kong, Singapore, the United Arab Emirates, Chile, the Netherlands, Ireland, Hungary, Switzerland, the Slovak Republic, and Estonia. The United States lies back in the pack, in 27th place among the 140 ranked nations.[1]

Despite the claims of openness, our government imposes significant barriers against imported clothing, footwear, leather products, glassware, watches, clocks, table and kitchenware, costume jewelry, pens, mechanical pencils, musical instruments, cutlery, hand tools, ball and roller bearings, ceramic wall and floor tile, railway cars, processed fruits and vegetables, rice, cotton, sugar, milk, cheese, butter, and canned tuna. Through 232 separate antidumping measures, the government imposes tariffs as high as 280 percent on products from 39 different countries, mostly against imported steel and chemicals.[2] Federal law prohibits or restricts foreign competition in domestic airline service, broadcasting, intercoastal shipping, and government contracting. When it is not interfering in our freedom to trade, the government distorts trade with an array of export promotion programs and other subsidies to favored businesses and farm sectors.

Every one of those barriers and programs is backed by domestic special interests that benefit from restricted competition, but every one also extracts money from millions of consumers and taxpayers, leaving our economy weaker and American families poorer than we would be without the intervention.

Harmonized Tariff Nightmare

The first tip off that America is not a free trade country is the tariff code itself. The official Harmonized Tariff Schedule of the United States rivals the U.S. income tax code for random complexity. It fills 2,959 pages, encompasses 99 chapters, and features 10,253 separate tariff lines.[3] Each line is designated by an eight-digit tariff code and accompanied by three separate tariff rates. Column 1 "General" is the rate that applies to most countries, and Column 1 "Special" applies to countries with which we've signed free-trade agreements or to which we've extended unilateral preferences. Column 2 contains the highest tariff rates reserved for a handful of unsavory states that are on the U.S. government's black list, such as North Korea and Cuba.

General tariff rates in Column 1 apply uniformly to more than 90 percent of our trading partners, but there is nothing uniform about the rates. A bit more than a third of the lines are duty free, meaning the tariff is zero, but the rest are all over the map. One out of every twenty lines imposes a duty greater than 15 percent.[4] Rates vary even among products that appear similar. A reasonable person would be stumped to explain why one rate applies to one line of products, and another rate to the line above or below it.

Open the harmonized tariff schedule at random, and you will quickly confront the puzzling complexity of it all. Figure 9.1 displays a typical page. In chapter 10, "Cereals," the tariff for durum wheat is 0.65 cents per kilogram, for Canadian western extra strong hard red spring wheat, 0.35 cents per kilogram. Rye, oats, and yellow corn enter duty free, but importers of yellow dent corn must pay

0.05 cents per kilogram, popcorn 0.25 cents, rice in the husk 1.8 cents, husked brown rice 0.83 cents, grain sorghum 0.22 cents, canary seed 0.32 cents, barley for malting purposes 0.1 cents, and barley for other purposes 0.15 cents.

In chapter 61, "Articles of apparel and clothing accessories, knitted or crocheted," the tariff on men's or boys' overcoats of various kinds is 15.9 percent if made of cotton. If the coat is primarily of man-made fibers but contains 25 percent or more by weight of leather, the tariff is 5.6 percent; if 23 percent or more by weight of wool or fine animal hair, the tariff is 10 percent plus 38.6 cents per kilogram. Overcoats of wool or fine animal hair are assessed a tariff of 16 percent plus 61.7 cents per kilogram. If it contains 70 percent or more by weight of silk or silk waste, the tariff drops to 0.9 percent. Women's or girls' overcoats made of wool or fine animal hair face a slightly higher ad valorum (percentage) duty than their male counterparts, 16.4 percent, but a slightly lower per kilogram duty of 55.9 cents. (Perhaps our government wants women to wear coats that are heavier but less expensive than those worn by men.)

In chapter 72, covering "Iron and Steel," ferronickel enters duty free, but ferromolybdenum is charged 4.5 percent of value, ferro-tungsten and ferrosilicon tungsten 5.6 percent, ferrotitanium and ferrosilicon titanium 3.7 percent, ferrovanadium 4.2 percent, and ferroniobium 5 percent. In chapter 92, "Musical instruments; parts and accessories of such articles," upright and grand pianos face a general duty of 4.7 percent; other pianos 3.5 percent; guitars, violins, harps and other stringed musical instruments 3.2 percent; guitars valued under $100 (excluding the value of the case) 4.5 percent; brass-wind instruments 2.9 percent; drums 4.8 percent; while keyboard pipe organs, piano accordions, mouth organs, and cymbals enter duty free.

See the pattern? Me neither. Like the federal tax code, the tariff schedule has devolved into a mishmash of disconnected duties with varying rates that defy any rational explanation. The rates are arbitrary, discriminatory, and distortionary. They appear to be generated randomly by a computer, or by a roomful of protectionist monkeys pressing buttons for fun. Of course, each tariff rate has its own history, probably originating in a meeting years ago between congressional staffers and lobbyists for domestic producers seeking "protection" from foreign competitors, only to be lowered through protracted negotiations with other countries.

Figure 9.1
HARMONIZED TARIFF SCHEDULE OF THE UNITED STATES (2008) -
SUPPLEMENT 1
annotated for statistical reporting purposes

Heading/ Subheading	Stat Suffix	Article Description	Unit of Quantity	Rates of Duty		
				1		2
				General	Special	
6103		Men's or boys' suits, ensembles, suit-type jackets, blazers, trousers, bib and brace overalls, breeches and shorts (other than swimwear), knitted or crocheted:				
6103.10		Suits:				
6103.10.10	00	Of wool or fine animal hair (443)	No.......... kg	38.8¢kg + 10%	Free (BH, CA, CL, IL, JO, MX, P, SG) 12.7¢/kg + 3.3% (MA) 9.9% (AU)	77.2¢kg + 54.5%
		Of synthetic fibers:				
6103.10.20	00	Containing 23 percent or more by weight of wool or fine animal hair (443)	No.......... kg	60.3¢kg + 15.6%	Free (BH, CA, CL, IL, JO, MX, P, SG) 18.6¢kg + 4.8% (MA) 15.5% (AU)	77.2¢kg + 54.5%
6103.10.30	00	Other (643)	No.......... kg	28.2%	Free (BH, CA, CL, IL, MX, P, SG) 5.7% (JO) 8.5% (MA) 15.5% (AU)	72%

				General	Special	2
		Of other textile materials:				
		Of artificial fibers:				
		Containing 23 percent or more by weight of wool or fine animal hair (443)	No...... kg	Free		77.2¢kg + 54.5% 72%
6103.10.40	00					
		Other (643)	No...... kg	Free		
6103.10.50	00					
		Of cotton:		9.4%	Free (BH, CA, CL, IL, JO, MX, P, SG) 3% (MA) 8.4% (AU)	90%
6103.10.60						
	10	Jackets imported as parts of suits (333)	doz. kg			
	15	Trousers, breeches and shorts imported as parts of suits (347)	doz. kg			
	30	Waistcoats imported as parts of suits (359)	doz. kg			
		Containing 70 percent or more by weight of silk or silk waste (743)	No...... kg	0.9%	Free (AU, BH, CA, CL, E, IL, J, JO, MX, P, SG) 0.4% (MA)	45%
6103.10.70	00					

SOURCE: U.S. International Trade Commission, Harmonized Tariff Schedule of the United States.

And this is the tariff schedule we offer to our "most favored" friends. If a country is not granted the general duty rates in Column 1 "General" or the generally lower or duty-free rates in Column 1 "Special," it must face the prohibitive rates in Column 2. Those rates date back to the trade-killing Smoot-Hawley Tariff Act of 1930 and are punishingly higher than the general rates. The most common Smoot-Hawley tariff rates are 25 percent, 35 percent, 40 percent and higher, with spikes exceeding 100 percent. Per kilogram duties in Column 2 are commonly 5, 10, or 20 times the general Column 1 duties. When certain members of Congress threaten to repeal normal trade relations with China or another targeted country, the effect would be to shove them into Column 2 and impose prohibitive tariffs that would bar most of our trade with that country.

Declaring War on Consumers

American workers and families pay for those tariffs every day in the form of higher prices and fewer choices when we shop. The tariffs are really discriminatory sales taxes imposed on imports. Those taxes drive a wedge between prices received by producers abroad and those paid by consumers in the United States. A 20 percent tariff will typically mean U.S. consumers will be stuck paying a higher price for the good than they would under free trade, while the foreign producer of the good makes fewer sales and earns less revenue than they would under free trade. The U.S. government, of course, collects revenue from the tariff, but at the expense of less trade and a less efficient use of our own productive resources, leading to a "deadweight loss" to our economy.

Among the most damaging trade barriers for American families are those imposed on what we wear and what we eat.

Clothing

When Americans shop to clothe themselves and their children, they pay higher prices, sometimes much higher, than they would otherwise because of government trade barriers. According to the U.S. International Trade Commission (USITC), in its biannual study of significant U.S. import barriers, the trade-weighted average tariff on imported clothing in 2005 was 10.6 percent.[5] (A trade-weighted average takes into account the volume of trade, with more heavily traded items accounting for a proportionally larger share of the average.) That is a lot higher than the overall average trade-weighted applied tariff rate of 1.4 percent.[6] Congress imposes some of its highest tariff rates on items that are most popular with American consumers. For example, certain women's and girls' man-made fiber pants face a 28.2 percent tariff, blouses 32 percent, and man-made fiber sweaters 32 percent.[7] Men's and boys' woven shirts, man-made fiber knit shirts, man-made fiber trousers, and swimwear imported from China and Vietnam face tariffs of more than 20 percent. [8]

Our government artificially jacks up the cost of clothing for American families through tariffs, quotas, and complex "rules of origin" that require foreign apparel makers to use American-made textiles in order for their clothing exports to qualify for the lowest import duty rates. A 2004 "Memorandum of Understanding" with China limited clothing imports from 2005 through 2008 by imposing 21 quotas covering 34 categories of textile and apparel products. The MOU required China to hold shipments to no greater than 7.5 percent above the previous year.[9] The alleged purpose of the MOU was to avoid "market disruption" and promote the "orderly development of trade." The real purpose was to shield domestic producers from the full effects of liberalized trade with China, all at the expense of American consumers. The USITC calculates that restrictions on imported clothing and textiles are the most costly trade barriers of all.[10]

Footwear

When the government is not taxing the shirt on your back, it is taxing the shoes on your feet. Some of the highest rates in the tariff schedule are reserved for imported footwear, especially the less expensive shoes families buy at discount stores. The USITC reckons the average tariff on shoes and other imported leather products was 10.7 percent in 2005.[11] Again the average disguises tariff peaks as high as 67 percent aimed at the more popular, mass market footwear.

The anti-consumer nature of the shoe tariffs prompted a bipartisan group of more than 150 members of Congress to sponsor the Affordable Footwear Act of 2007. The bill would eliminate tariffs on more than half of shoe imports. The bill's preamble notes that the government collected $1.8 billion in duties on imported shoes in 2006, a tax burden that falls disproportionately on low- and moderate-income families because they spend a larger share of their disposable income on shoes and other necessities. Shoe tariffs don't even "save" a significant number of jobs. The American shoe sector is so uncompetitive

153

that even when hiding behind tariff walls, imports now account for 98 percent of domestic shoe sales. There are virtually no jobs left to save.[12]

Not content to tax our shoes, the government also taxes imported socks. In January 2008, the Bush administration imposed a temporary 13.5 percent tariff on the 8.3 percent of imported socks that come from Honduras. The tariff was meant to placate a certain Republican lawmaker in Alabama with several sock factories in his district and a few other, mostly southern, lawmakers whose votes were thought necessary for upcoming trade deals the administration wanted. The trade agreements never came to a vote, but 300 million Americans were socked with higher prices to keep their feet warm and dry. All this for the sake of a domestic sock industry that, by its own count, employs only 20,000 workers in jobs that are not well paid.[13]

Food

Americans who have struggled to pay rising food prices may be surprised to know that it is the explicit policy of the U.S. government to keep the domestic price of certain foods fixed well above prices paid on world markets. Our government conspires with producers to restrict domestic supply by imposing tariffs and tariff-rate quotas on imported sugar, rice, milk, butter, and canned tuna.

Tariff rate quotas, or TRQs, allow a certain amount of a good to enter from a designated country under a low or zero tariff, but any imports above the quota face prohibitively high rates. In all, 195 tariff lines are subject to TRQs, with in-quota rates averaging 9.1 percent and out-of-quota tariffs an intimidating 42 percent.[14] The intended result is to drive a wedge between the lower global prices and a higher domestic price. Domestic producers and our own government reap extra revenue from the higher prices, while American families and food-processing industries are stuck paying the difference.

One of the most protected commodities is sugar. Because of subsidies and tariff-rate quotas in place since 1981, Americans have been paying two to three times the world price for sugar. Higher sugar prices also drive up what we pay for candy, soft drinks, bakery goods, and other sugar-containing products. The federal government guarantees domestic producers a price of at least 22.9 cents per pound for beet sugar and 18 cents for cane sugar. To maintain those prices, it enforces a rigid system of quotas that virtually guarantees domestic producers 85 percent of the nation's sugar market. The government grudgingly allows the importation of specific amounts of sugar and sugar-containing products from certain countries to fill the remaining 15 percent. The Godfather himself could not have devised a more effective protection racket.

The sugar program redistributes money from the many sugar users to the few sugar producers. According to a 2000 study by the General Accounting Office, the higher prices engineered by the sugar program cost American households and sugar-consuming industries $1.9 billion a year. Of that, $1 billion goes into the pockets of a relatively small number of sugar producers—about 5,000 sugar-beet growers and fewer than 1,000 sugar-cane growers. Another $400 million goes to the favored sugar-producers abroad who are allowed to sell into the inflated domestic U.S. market, what economists call "quota rents." With tariffs, at least our own government collects the revenue, but with the quota system, the money goes to foreign exporters and their governments. And the other $500 million? It just disappears in lost efficiency, or "deadweight loss," to the U.S. economy.[15] A more recent study of the sugar program by the USITC found a similar negative impact.[16] The sugar program enriches a few thousand sugar producers by ripping off consumers and by making our nation poorer.

American families also pay more for their milk, butter, and cheese, thanks to federal dairy price supports and trade barriers. The federal government administers a Byzantine system of domestic price supports, marketing orders, tariff-rate quotas, export subsidies, and domestic and international giveaway programs. Federal policy blocks American consumers from buying lower-cost dairy products from more efficient producers in New Zealand and Australia. As the USITC staff concluded, "A consequence of government intervention has been to raise U.S. domestic [dairy] prices substantially above world market prices."[17] According to the USITC, between 2000 and 2002, the average U.S. domestic price of nonfat dry milk was 23 percent higher than the world price, U.S. cheese prices were 37 percent higher, and the price of U.S. butter was more than double the world price.[18]

Hungry for a bowl of rice with your glass of milk? The federal government protects domestic rice producers with an array of tariffs on various kinds of rice imports. According to the Harmonized Tariff Schedule of the United Sates, rice tariffs range from 0.44 cents per kilogram on lower quality, broken rice to 2.1 cents per kilogram on husked, brown rice. Imported white and parboiled rice face an ad valorem (or percentage) rate of 11.2 percent. U.S. tariffs are significantly lower than tariffs imposed by other developed countries, such as Japan and Korea, but existing U.S. tariffs of 3 to 24 percent still keep domestic rice prices higher than they would be otherwise if Americans could buy rice freely from producers abroad.[19]

Thinking of a tuna sandwich for lunch? The U.S. government limits imports of canned and pouch tuna through the familiar tariff-rate quota system. Tariffs average 17.7 percent on tuna packed in oil and 10.8 percent on the more common tuna packed in water. The TRQs take their biggest bite in the Pacific island of American Samoa, where three-quarters of the canned tuna for the U.S. market is processed. TRQs add 4 to 8 percent to the final cost of tuna (with producers paying the rest of the tariff) The amount of tuna that can be imported at the lower, in-quota rate is limited each year to 4.8 percent of domestic consumption during the previous year. This rule requires importers to stockpile large quantities of tuna in customs-bonded warehouses in late December while they wait for the quota to be determined for the New Year. Once the New Year arrives, they rush to import the tuna before the 4.8 percent quota is filled.[20]

On top of all those tariffs, the government imposes unnecessary regulations designed to advantage American producers at the expense of consumers. In the 2002 farm bill, Congress imposed a new "country-of-origin labeling" (COOL) requirement on beef, lamb, pork, fish, shellfish, and other perishable agricultural commodities. After understandable resistance from retailers, the government finally began in March 2009 to require that such food items must have the country of origin stamped on them. This is nothing but a form of regulatory harassment designed to play to antiforeign prejudices. COOL provides zero health or safety information; foreign meat and produce must conform to exactly the same health and safety standards that apply to domestic-made goods. The U.S. Department of Agriculture estimates the COOL regulations will cost $89 million to implement in the first year and $62 million annually even after 10 years of adjustment. Although the costs are significant, the USDA found the public benefits to be negligible. Country-of-origin labeling was not meant to serve the public but instead to provide yet another unfair advantage to domestic producers at the expense of the public.[21]

The cost of all those restrictions on imported food may sound like nickel and dime stuff, but it adds up to real money out of the pockets of American families. The Organisation for Economic Cooperation and Development, in its annual assessment of rich-country farm policies, estimates that U.S. agricultural trade barriers transferred $11.8 billion from American consumers to producers in 2007. That amounted to an annual "food tax" of $39 on every single American, or $155 for a family of four.[22]

Planes, Cars, Cutlery, and Clocks

Government tariffs hit us when we travel and when we stay at home. To make public transportation less economical, the government imposes a 14 percent tariff on imported railway or tramway passenger coaches.[23] Imported motor cars are assessed a 2.5 percent tariff, whereas motor vehicles designed for the transport of goods are socked with a 25 percent tariff. The latter category covers light trucks and at one time even applied to imported minivans.

If you choose to fly instead of drive, you will pay a higher airfare because of government restrictions on airline competition. Foreign-owned carriers are flatly banned from flying paying passengers from one U.S. city to another. Of course, there are legitimate security reasons for not allowing the national air carriers of Syria and Iran to fly across U.S. airspace, but such concerns are silly when applied to British Airways, Qantas, Air Japan, and other established carriers from friendly, developed nations. European Union officials rightly complain that American-owned airlines are free to make money flying paying passengers from London to Berlin or other internal routes in Europe while European carriers are forbidden from serving internal U.S. routes.[24]

Federal law also prohibits foreign investors from controlling more than 25 percent of the voting stock of a domestic airline. Those restrictions preclude entrepreneurs such as Britain's Richard Branson from starting and controlling a low-cost carrier to serve passengers within the United States—making it more expensive for low-income grandparents to visit their grandchildren. The result of those restrictions is less investment in our domestic airline capacity and less competition for service and airfares. On top of airline restrictions, the U.S. government sticks the flying public with high tariffs on imported luggage.

If you decide to stay at home and build your household nest, the U.S. customs service will not leave you alone. The tariff code imposes an average, trade-weighted tariff of 7.9 percent on ceramic tile, a 6.4 percent on costume jewelry, 4.6 percent on cutlery and hand tools, 4.5 percent on glassware, 3.9 percent on musical instruments, 5.1 percent on pens and mechanical pencils, 5.4 percent on tableware, earthenware, and pottery products, and 5.1 percent on watches, clocks, and parts.[25] As with most other categories, average tariffs mask much higher duties on particular products that are often the less glamorous, mass-market items middle- and lower-income Americans buy.

Taxing Imports, Taxing the Poor

Import taxes on food, clothing, and shoes fall especially hard on the poor and middle class. The lower a family's income, the more it will spend proportionately on basic necessities. As the Organisation for Economic Cooperation and Development concluded in its study on rich-country farm programs, tariffs on imported food "can bear heavily on low-income consumer households, for whom food constitutes a larger share of their total expenditures."[26] In this way, U.S. trade barriers against farm products act as a regressive tax. Higher prices at the grocery store negate some or all of the income support the government seeks to deliver to low-income households through such programs as food stamps. What the government gives with one hand, it takes away with the other.

In the same way, U.S. tariffs on clothing and shoes fall disproportionately on the poor. Edward Gresser of the Democratic-leaning Progressive Policy Institute has done more than anyone to expose the anti-poor bias of the U.S. tariff code. Poring over those 3,000 pages and 10,000 lines, Gresser has discovered a disturbing pattern: More expensive, higher-end items enter under the lowest or zero tariffs, while the highest rates fall on the less expensive product lines most likely to land in the shopping cart of a poor, single mother.

For example, synthetic fiber men's shirts prompt a 32.5 percent tariff, cotton shirts 20 percent, and silk shirts 1.9 percent. Ladies' polyester underwear is assessed a 16 percent tariff, silk underwear 1.9 percent. Men's dress leather shoes, the kind worn in Wall Street brokerage houses and Washington think tanks, are charged an 8.5 percent duty, sneakers of more than $20 a pair 20 percent, and sneakers under $3 a pair a whopping 48 percent.[27] As Gresser concludes:

> In general, American tariffs are low or zero on high-technology products and heavy industry goods. They are zero or trivial on natural resources and industry goods, and also low on luxury goods. But they are very high on a narrow but important set of products: the cheap and simple clothes, shoes, and food that poor people buy and poor countries make and grow. . . . Without any particular intention, therefore, the United States has created a system that is open and kind to wealthy countries and rich people, but wildly harsh for the poor.[28]

According to Gresser, a recent welfare system graduate earning $15,000 a year as a maid in a hotel will forfeit about a week's worth of salary in a year to the U.S. tariff system, while the hotel's $100,000-a-year manager will give up only two or three hours' pay. And the defenders of the status quo can't even argue they are saving jobs, since so few American workers are still employed making cheap shoes and clothing.

This is the status quo that so many "progressives" in America, from the Public Citizen Naderites to AFL-CIO labor leaders, are expending millions of dollars to defend. They reflexively oppose any trade agreements that would reduce those regressive tariffs. Their trade policy boils down to keeping barriers high on goods made and grown by poor people abroad and consumed by poor people here at home.

Trade barriers are a costly and regressive form of income redistribution. They take from the many and the disproportionately poor, and give the spoils to the politically connected few. What is fair about that?

Crippling American Producers

Consumers are not the only losers from America's remaining trade barriers. Duties and restrictions on trade impose damaging costs on American companies, hobbling their ability to compete and forcing them to downsize, outsource, or even relocate abroad.

159

When government intervention raises the domestic price for raw materials and other commodities, it imposes higher costs on "downstream" users in the supply chain. Higher costs can mean higher prices for consumers, reduced competitiveness for U.S. exporters in global markets, lower sales, less investment, and ultimately fewer employment opportunities and lower pay in the affected industries. If domestic prices for a key commodity become too expensive, domestic producers may be forced to go out of business or to move production to other countries where they can buy the commodities at lower prices. Import restrictions can also disrupt deliveries, just-in-time inventory management, and production cycles by forcing domestic users to rely on a smaller number of suppliers.

A Sour Deal for Candy Makers

Consider the poster boy for self-damaging protectionism, the U.S. sugar program. When the program is not raising prices for consumers at the store, it is savaging the bottom line for American companies. Artificially high domestic sugar prices raise the cost of production for refined sugar, candy, and other confectionary products, chocolate and cocoa products, chewing gum, bread and other bakery products, cookies and crackers, and frozen bakery goods. Higher costs cut into profits and competitiveness, putting thousands of jobs in jeopardy.

In a report issued on Valentine's Day 2006, the U.S. Commerce Department found that the sugar program is not such a sweetheart deal for the U.S. food manufacturing industry. When U.S. companies are forced to pay two to three times the world price for wholesale refined sugar, as they have for the past 25 years, it erodes their competitiveness and profitability. For makers of confectionary products and breakfast cereals, for example, sugar accounts for 20 to 30 percent of the total cost of production. As a consequence, "Many U.S. [sugar-containing product] manufacturers have closed or relocated to Canada, where sugar prices average less than half of U.S. prices, and Mexico, where sugar prices average about two-thirds of U.S. prices."[29]

The Commerce report surveys the damage: Ferrara Pan Candy in Forest Park, Ill., closed its domestic facilities and eliminated 500 jobs while opening one plant in Mexico and two in Canada. Hershey Foods closed plants in Pennsylvania, Colorado, and California while moving production to Canada. The Chicago area, long a hub for the confectionary industry, has been especially hard hit. The city lost 4,000 jobs in the industry from 1991 to 2001, including 1,000 jobs at Brachs facilities.[30] In 2002, Kraft Inc. announced that it was closing a Life Savers candy factory in Holland, Mich., in order to relocate production to Canada, where the company could buy sugar at world-market prices.[31] The number of sugar refineries in the United States has dropped from 23 to 8, in large part because of the high costs of domestic raw sugar.[32]

In each of those cases, company representatives cited the high price of domestic sugar as a major reason for the exodus of productive capacity and employment from the United States. In all, 6,400 workers in the sugar-processing industry have lost their jobs because of their own government's deliberate policy to drive up the cost of their major input. According to the USITC, the sugar program "saves" only 2,200 jobs in the sugar growing and harvesting industry. So our sugar policy eliminates three jobs for every one it saves. The Commerce report concluded that "eliminating sugar quotas and tariff rate quotas and allowing sugar to freely enter the United States duty free would result in economic gains in the form of increased domestic food manufacturing production and U.S. exports, gains for consumers, taxpayer savings, and a net positive effect on U.S. employment."[33] Now that would be a nice Valentine present to the country.

I've participated in many a panel discussion where I have heard lobbyists for the sugar growers complain that other countries "dump" sugar on global markets. They claim with a straight face that sugar quotas are a "no-cost" program because they do not typically require direct tax expenditures. They warn against allowing more imports into what is already "a chronically oversupplied U.S. market."[34] But dumping is not the real issue. The American Sugar Alliance also opposes increased imports from Australia, a country that offers minimal support to its farmers. Most tropical countries where cane sugar is grown are too poor to lavish government tax subsidies on their growers. And even if subsidized sugar has worked its way into global markets, our government should not deprive domestic consumers and workers from reaping the benefits of lower prices. It is laughable to claim the sugar program is "no cost" when it forces American families and factories to pay more than a billion dollars a year in higher prices. And if the domestic U.S. market is "chronically oversupplied," that is because the sugar program itself encourages domestic overproduction. A lower, world-market price would curb the most inefficient domestic production while stimulating greater consumption, bringing supply and demand into a sustainable balance.

Steel Tariffs and Quotas

Another way trade barriers damage American producers is by restricting access to steel on global markets. The domestic U.S. steel industry has been among the most protected sectors of the economy for decades. The domestic industry hid behind quotas during most of the 1980s. In 2002, President Bush unwisely imposed restrictions on imported steel to fulfill an implied promise during the 2000 campaign and to win over additional votes for Trade Promotion Authority. The quotas lasted for 20 months, restricting imports from a number of our trading partners. The tariffs were finally lifted after the U.S. government lost a challenge in the WTO brought by a dozen countries that justifiably complained that the restrictions violated our commitments to international trade rules our government had agreed to follow.

In this case, our trading partners did us a favor. Steel tariffs may keep a few aging steel mills running, but they impose costs on U.S. industry. When our own government restricts imports of steel, it results in a higher domestic price for steel, driving up production costs for steel-using industries such as automobile manufacturing, machine tool makers, metal fabrication plants, and construction. During a congressional debate on steel tariffs in 1999, my Cato colleagues and I calculated that for every one American working in the steel industry, there were 40 Americans working in those industries that must buy steel to make their final products.[35] Once again, protectionism favors the few at the expense of the many.

Driving Up Shipping Costs

Congress adds to the cost of doing business in the United States by driving up the cost of moving goods by ship. American producers who want to move goods from one U.S. port to another must pay artificially high rates due to Section 27 of the Merchant Marine Act of 1920. Known more commonly as the Jones Act, it requires that any ship carrying goods between U.S. ports must be U.S. built, U.S.

registered, U.S. owned, and staffed by a crew made up predominantly of U.S. citizens. No foreign-owned shipping companies need apply. This outright ban on any international competition in intercoastal shipping imposes a heavy price on U.S. industry and our entire domestic transportation infrastructure.

Under the Jones Act, a foreign-flagged ship can enter a U.S. port with cargo from just about any port in the world except another U.S. port. A foreign-flagged ship can carry cargo from Miami to the Bahamas, and then from the Bahamas to Charleston, S.C., but not directly from Miami to Charleston. Under similar restrictions in the Passenger Vessel Services Act of 1886, a foreign-owned cruise ship can carry passengers from Seattle, Wash., to Vancouver, Canada, but not from Seattle to Juneau, Ala. The result is the same: American tourists, like American business owners, pay more than they should to travel between U.S. ports.

Building and operating ships is much more costly in the United States than in most other countries. The daily cost of operating a U.S.–flagged container ship is $34,260 compared to $22,190 to operate a foreign-flagged ship. Operating a U.S.-flagged tanker costs $27,900 per day compared to $16,600 to operate a foreign-flagged tanker.[36] By mandating the use of U.S. ships, the Jones Act drives up the cost of moving goods between U.S. ports, forcing more goods to be shipped by rail or truck, which adds to costs and congestion on America's railways and roadways.

Defenders of the Jones Act claim it promotes national security by maintaining a merchant marine fleet in case of war. But Jones Act ships tend to be old and of limited use in times of real emergencies. In fact, during the 1991 Gulf War, only one Jones Act ship actually went to war; President George H. W. Bush suspended the law because it was interfering in the efficient transfer of goods. President George W. Bush again suspended the law in 2005 so that fuel and other needed supplies could more quickly reach New Orleans after Hurricane Katrina.[37] What is an expensive indulgence for domestic shippers during peacetime becomes an intolerable liability for the nation during times of emergency.

More recently, in the name of combating terrorism, the U.S. Congress voted to impose sweeping new costs on ships bound for the United States. A provision in the SAFE Port Act of 2006 requires that, by mid 2012, 100 percent of all containers must be scanned for radioactive material before being loaded on a U.S.-bound vessel. No American wants to leave a door open for terrorists to smuggle a nuclear device into the country, but this provision is overkill. It treats the most secure, supervised, and low-risk containers the same as those that pose a higher risk. The result will be millions of dollars of additional costs with no additional security.

The U.S. Customs and Border Patrol agency estimates the SAFE Ports provision will impose $380 million to $640 million annually in additional filing requirements alone. The head of the CBP warned Congress that the 100 percent screening requirement will have an "enormous" impact on trade, resulting in "lower profits and higher transportation costs for U.S. importers."[38] That fear has been seconded by our trading partners in Europe, who warned in a 2008 EU study that the screening requirement will have a "potentially devastating economic impact." A pilot program in the port of Southampton, Great Britain, revealed the steep costs of full implementation. "This measure is unilateral and would disrupt trade and cost legitimate EU and U.S. businesses a lot of time and money while no real benefit is proved when it comes to improving security," the EU report concluded.[39]

So why was the 100 percent screening requirement approved by Congress? Because it allows members to impose a regulatory tax on imports while sounding tough on national security. Never mind that it will not actually make us any more secure and that the costs of this unfunded mandate will ultimately be imposed on not just foreign producers and shippers but also on American consumers and businesses.

Our Unfair "Unfair Trade" Laws

America's antidumping law is considered holy writ by members of Congress. They express horror at the thought that American companies would be left to the mercy of global competition without being able to use the antidumping law to defend themselves against "unfair" trade. But the antidumping law itself is unfair and has no connection to fairness or sound economics.

American trade law defines dumping as selling imports in the U.S. market at "less than fair value"—at a price below the average total cost of production or below the price in the exporter's home market. If the U.S. Department of Commerce determines that dumping exists, and if the U.S. International Trade Commission determines that dumping has caused "material injury" to the domestic industry, then duties are imposed on the targeted category of imports to offset the alleged dumping.

At first glance, the law sounds reasonable. Why would a foreign producer sell something at a loss or a price lower than they could get in their home market unless they had some devious purpose such as putting their rivals out of business so they can charge monopoly prices? In reality, foreign producers have plenty of legitimate reasons to do both.

U.S. companies sell at below-average total cost every day in the domestic market. In fact, all businesses that are losing money, which is typically half of all businesses in operation (and even more during a recession), are by definition selling at below average total cost. They keep selling because the additional ("marginal") cost of producing each new item is lower than what they receive for the sale of each item, but still not enough to also cover the firm's fixed costs. By the law's definition, the money-losing Big Three U.S. automakers have been "dumping" their cars on the U.S. market for years.

U.S. companies also sell at different prices in different markets in order to meet the local competition or establish a presence in a new market. The company may sell its products at a higher price in Connecticut than in rural Mississippi. It's called "price discrimination," and it is perfectly legal. There is nothing predatory about the practice. Thus the antidumping law unfairly punishes foreign producers for engaging in practices that are normal and perfectly legal among domestic U.S. producers.

By design, the antidumping law is stacked against foreign producers and their American customers. When a domestic company petitions the Commerce Department for relief against alleged unfair trade, the targeted foreign producers must fill out long and complex forms that require teams of specialized lawyers to decipher. The law is written in such a way that "dumping" is almost always found, and the dumping margins tend to be high. One reason is a technique called "zeroing," in which the Commerce Department ignores sales of imported products at prices above "fair value," while counting only those priced below. This technique inflates the dumping margins in cases where dumping would exist without zeroing. Not surprisingly, zeroing has been repeatedly and successfully challenged in the WTO by our major trading partners.

Once the Commerce Department finds dumping, the USITC determines whether the "unfairly traded" goods have caused "material injury" or threaten to cause such injury to the domestic industry. Here, too, the threshold is low and stacked against foreign producers and their U.S. customers. Most existing businesses are better off with less competition, so allowing more price-competitive imports to be sold in the U.S. market will probably inflict some injury on domestic producers. The right question should be whether any injury has been inflicted on the U.S. economy as a whole, including consumers and import-using industries, and there the answer would almost always be "no." Although domestic producers of a product will suffer from lower prices, the more numerous domestic consumers will gain.

The antidumping law has been heavily used by the steel industry to selectively cripple its foreign competition. Of the 232 antidumping measures in force at end of 2007, 51 percent were aimed at steel and iron products. Antidumping duties can range as high as 280 percent and can all but eliminate imports in the targeted category. Once in place, antidumping orders typically remain in place for years. Forty percent of the current measures have been in place for more than a decade, with the oldest dating back to 1973.[40] The United States has agreed to submit its antidumping measures to five-year sunset reviews, but most duties are kept in place even though there is nothing inherently wrong with "dumping" as legally defined. If our government cared about our welfare, it would welcome rather than punish healthy price competition.

"Rip-Off America" Provisions

Along with the many barriers it maintains against imports, the federal government has rigged its own procurement system against foreign providers and the U.S. taxpayer. The Buy American Act and other provisions require the U.S. military and other agencies to buy from American suppliers even if it means paying a lot more for the same or an inferior products and services. The $787 billion American Recovery and Reinvestment Act of 2009, signed in February by President Obama, contained its own "Buy American" provisions.

The Buy American Act of 1933 requires federal agencies to do just that: Buy American. The law steers federal procurement spending to supplies, construction material, and "domestic end-products" manufactured in the United States in which more than half of their components are also made in the United States. The "Buy American" requirement can be waived if it is deemed "inconsistent with the public interest," if the product is not available domestically, or if it is not available at a "reasonable" cost. The requirement can also be waived if an imported alternative can be procured for a price that is 6 percent less, including import duties, than the price of a domestic good. If the domestic provider is a small business or located in an area of high unemployment, the import must be available at a 12 percent discount, and if the purchase is for national defense, the import must be at least 50 percent cheaper.[41]

For the benefit of taxpayers and our military, the Buy American Act has been modified in recent decades. The WTO Agreement on Government Procurement allows U.S. companies to bid on foreign government contracts on a reciprocal basis with major trading partners. Certain information technology hardware and software goods are exempt from the rules. But for most government contracts, the Buy American Act gives domestic producers the license to overcharge the government 6 to 12 percent on routine contracts and up to 50 percent on military contracts.

Cargo preference laws require that U.S.–flagged ships must transport at least half of all government-owned cargo and virtually all military cargo. All exports funded by the Export-Import Bank must be transported on U.S. ships unless a waiver allows shipment by the recipient country. The Fly America Act requires that government-financed transport of passengers or cargo must take place on a U.S.-flag air carrier or on a code-sharing foreign airline. The Food Security Act of 1985 requires that U.S.–flagged ships be used for 75 percent of food shipments by the U.S. Department of Agriculture and U.S. Agency for International Development.[42] Thanks to those requirements, we as taxpayers must pay more to fly officials to their meetings, transport subsidized U.S. exports, and deliver food to hungry people.

State and local governments also discriminate against foreign producers at the expense of their own taxpayers. The European Union cites 10 states that require that local construction projects use only

U.S.–made steel, even if steel can be purchased at a lower price on international markets.[43] As our European friends see it, "In the field of procurement, the main U.S. trade barriers are contained in a wide array of clauses in federal, state and local legislation and regulation giving preference to domestic suppliers or products, or excluding foreign bidders or products altogether."[44]

When our government is not excluding foreign competitors, it is subsidizing U.S. companies directly. The Export-Import Bank provides loans, loan guarantees, and subsidized insurance rates to some of America's largest exporters, especially the aircraft sector. (There is good reason why the Ex-Im Bank is known as "Boeing's Bank.").[45]

The Market Access Program subsidizes overseas advertising promotion for companies using U.S. farm products to the jingle of $254 million in 2005. The Dairy Export Incentive Program subsidizes the export of milk powder, butterfat, and cheese. Through the Export Enhancement Program, the Department of Agriculture offers cash bonuses to exporters, allowing them to sell abroad at below cost (an act that in other circumstances our government might call "dumping"). In all, 19 federal agencies oversee 100 separate export promotion programs.[46] Hundreds of other direct government subsidies on a state and local level are channeled to companies trying to compete in global markets, with taxpayers footing the bill.

The mandate to "buy American" sounds patriotic, especially on matters of national defense, but the true impact of these laws is to weaken our security. The federal government does not have a bottomless pot of money to spend. Buy American provisions mean we get less bang for the buck. We either pay more for the same amount of national defense, or we buy less defense with the same dollars. In the 2009 "stimulus bill," the Buy American provisions mean taxpayers will see fewer bridges, roads, and buildings built, whereas more debt will be passed on to our children.

There is nothing patriotic about wasting tax dollars or sending our troops into battle without the best possible equipment our money can buy. If a foreign power tried to deny us the ability to buy the defense-related products we need in global markets, we would consider it an act of war. Yet in the name of a misguided patriotism, we seem ready to inflict a global embargo on ourselves.

How Trade Barriers Weaken America

Every one of the trade barriers and subsidies maintained by the U.S. government imposes a drag on the U.S. economy. For the benefit

168

of a few small, concentrated special interests, millions of Americans pay higher prices, import-using producers and their workers suffer, and our economy grows more slowly than it would if trade were free.

When the government imposes tariffs on a category of imported goods, it starts a damaging chain reaction through the whole economy. Import prices rise for consumers and the volume of imports falls for the targeted products, as intended, which allows domestic producers to raise their own prices. Demand will shift to domestically made products, spurring more output and employment in the protected domestic sector, but overall demand will fall as consumers are put off by the higher prices. Meanwhile, U.S. exports in the liberalized sector fall because our domestic producers become even less price competitive in global markets. Output and employment in nonprotected sectors will decline, the overall economy will shrink slightly, and total employment will remain unchanged.

Shrinking and Re-Slicing the Pie

Trade barriers impose more costs on our economy than any benefits produced. When we import more of a certain category of good than we export, say shoes or shirts, by definition we are buying and consuming more of that type of good than we produce. More Americans have more money at stake as consumers of the good than as producers. So when a tariff raises the domestic price of an item, we have more to lose collectively as consumers than we have to gain as producers.

Trade barriers are portrayed as a way to protect "our" producers against "their" producers, our jobs against their jobs. But in practice as well as theory, trade barriers are really about protecting some American producers at the expense of other American producers, some American workers as the expense of other American workers. Protection is worse than a zero sum game. As we learned from the example of sugar quotas, protection redistributes wealth from one group of citizens to another while destroying wealth in the process by making our overall economy less productive. It re-divides and shrinks the pie at the same time.

Trade barriers are also sold as a way to protect jobs, an especially appealing pitch during times of recession and high unemployment. But again, the real impact of higher barriers is to save some jobs and destroy others, usually in equal numbers. The U.S. International

169

Trade Commission determined in its study that "about 60,000 workers would move from contracting sectors to expanding sectors as a result of liberalization."[47] In other words, keeping those trade barriers in place suppresses trade and output while protecting a small number of jobs, while preventing the creation of the same number of jobs in other, more productive and sustainable sectors of the economy.

A Tax on Imports Is a Tax on Exports

Trade barriers impose further damage on the economy by making it harder for America's most competitive companies to export to foreign markets. When tariffs, quotas, and regulations make it difficult for foreign producers to sell in the U.S. market, those producers earn fewer dollars. Fewer dollars flowing into global currency markets drives up the price of dollars, making U.S. exports relatively more expensive. How can foreigners buy our exports if we deny them the opportunity to earn dollars by selling in our market? Fewer goods sold in the U.S. market quickly translate into fewer U.S. goods sold on global markets. A tax on imports becomes a tax on exports.

America's trade barriers also impede our exports by complicating efforts to negotiate lower trade barriers abroad. Our remaining barriers to imported agricultural products, for example, make poor countries less likely to open their markets to U.S. goods and services. The Doha Round negotiations in the WTO foundered in part on the reluctance of the United States and other rich nations to open our protected markets to farm goods grown in poor countries. The protected domestic sugar industry opposed the Central American Free Trade Agreement because it contained a modest increase in the amount of sugar Americans can buy from our small neighboring democracies.

In a February 2008 letter, major U.S. business groups complained to the Bush administration that the sugar quotas in the farm bill will hurt their ability to compete in global markets. In the letter, the National Association of Manufacturers, the U.S. Chamber of Commerce, the American Beverage Association, Grocery Manufacturers Association, National Retail Federation, and 11 other key trade groups highlighted the direct cost to the U.S. economy of quotas on imported sugar:

> The sugar industry is the most highly protected U.S. agricultural industry and has already won major additional protection in the pending farm bill, as well as an increase in their

> government-guaranteed price. . . . Our trading partners will
> be reluctant to enter into agreements if they see the U.S.
> Congress passing legislation that invalidates key provisions
> of one of our most important trade agreements. . . . reopening
> NAFTA's sugar provisions could put in jeopardy the market
> access achieved not only for U.S. farmers, but for U.S. manu-
> facturers and service providers as well.[48]

Remaining trade barriers make America look hypocritical in the
eyes of the rest of the world. Our politicians demand more open
markets abroad while clinging to our own politically sacrosanct
trade barriers at home. We fail to set a good example for other
countries to follow. "Do as I say, not as I do" is as unconvincing on
an international level as it is on a personal level.

"Dumbing Down" the U.S. Economy

Protectionism wastes time and energy by encouraging special
interests to seek favors from the government. Millions of dollars of
industry resources that could be spent on research, product development, investment in new plants and equipment, and employee training are instead diverted to lobbying for or against trade protection.
The American Sugar Alliance, USA Rice Federation, the American
Iron and Steel Institute, the National Textile Association, as well as
certain trade unions all maintain Washington offices staffed with
well-paid lobbyists charged with the mission of maintaining and
raising barriers against their foreign competition—at the expense of
the general American public. Those trade groups, in turn, raise and
contribute millions of dollars to political activities to win influence
on Capitol Hill.

Hiding behind trade barriers has not even proven to be good for
the protected industries in the longer run. Protected sectors tend to
grow weaker and less competitive when shielded from competition.
High trade barriers have not "saved" the domestic textile, apparel,
footwear, and other low-end manufacturing sectors from long-term
decline and job losses. Higher domestic prices forced on consumers
also dampen demand and promote substitutes, shrinking the domestic market. The protected sugar industry has seen its share of the
domestic sweetener market cut in half since 1967,[49] while protected
U.S. rice growers have seen their share of global exports steadily
decline since the 1970s, when the United States was the world's

leading exporter.[50] For protected sectors, trade barriers are a kind of devil's bargain. The industries have sold out their long-term viability for short-term dominance over shrinking markets.

Trade barriers "dumb down" our economy by undoing the good work of our best engineers, scientists, and entrepreneurs. The most creative and best-trained minds in America developed the jet engines, the containerization technology, and the Internet and global telecommunications that have done so much to promote the growth of global trade and output. In contrast, trade barriers are a kind of anti-technology. The mind-numbing columns of arbitrary tariff rates in the Harmonized Tariff Schedule and the tangled regulations that limit trade and investment stand in opposition to decades of technological advancement. We find a way to move goods, services, and capital around the world faster, more efficiently, and at lower cost, only to watch the politicians in Washington throw sand into the gears by erecting artificial barriers to commerce.

Think about it: If one of our children grows up to invent a way to move goods and bits of information even more rapidly around the world, we rightly call that "progress"; if another child grows up to become a populist politician who advocates raising trade barriers to slow the movement of those same goods and data across borders, we perversely call that "progressive."

Even if you are convinced that American companies need protection from foreign competition, how confident can we be that Congress will enact the right policies? Once we open that door, Congress needs to decide which industries deserve protection, which imported products need to be subject to tariffs or TRQs, and how high the tariffs should be. How confident can we be that Congress will impose such tariffs in a way that serves the public interest and not the special parochial interest of a small minority of producers? This is the same Congress, after all, that earlier in 2009 passed an omnibus appropriations bill riddled with 8,000 earmarks for pet spending projects. This is the same Congress that presides over an income tax code stuffed with deductions and credits aimed at social engineering. Predictably, the same institution has given us a tariff code that defies rational explanation.

"A Conspiracy Against the Public"

Americans instinctively understand that competitive and open markets are healthy. When producers must compete openly for the consumer's dollar, prices tend to come down, and quality and choices improve. But that same competition can make life uncomfortable for established producers, who would rather carve up markets among themselves and stifle new competitors. Adam Smith exposed the problem two centuries ago in *The Wealth of Nations* when he warned, "People of the same trade seldom meet together, even for merriment and diversion, but the conversation ends in a conspiracy against the public, or in some contrivance to raise prices."[51]

In 1890, the U.S. Congress enacted the Sherman Act in an effort to prevent just those kinds of conspiracies. As the cornerstone of U.S. antitrust law, the statute prohibits "every contract, combination . . . or conspiracy in restraint of trade."[52] Over the decades, U.S. courts have interpreted the law to forbid such anticompetitive acts as price fixing, division of markets among competitors, and bid rigging. The Supreme Court has embraced a "quick-look" test that defines a violation as when "an observer with even a rudimentary understanding of economics could conclude that the arrangements in question could have an anticompetitive effect on customers and markets."[53]

All the trade barriers described in this chapter fail the "quick-look" test. They trample on the spirit if not the letter of U.S. antitrust law. The overriding purpose of tariffs and price supports is to fix prices for the benefit of a cabal of producers at the expense of "customers and markets." TRQs by definition allocate market share among producers to maximize their profits at the expense of buyers. (We'll let those foreigners have 4.8 percent of the domestic tuna market, not one can more!) Buy American provisions are nothing more than bid rigging wrapped in patriotic clothing.

Free trade is not just a matter of sound economics, although it is certainly that. Free trade is also a matter of justice, fairness, and social equity. In contrast, protectionism is a conspiracy against liberty and the public good, a conspiracy encouraged, enabled and joined by our own government.

10. A Trade Agenda for a Free People

U.S. trade policy should enhance the freedom of individual Americans, promote economic growth and prosperity, and advance our broader national interest in a more hospitable, peaceful world.

In more reflective moments away from the campaign trail, most of our nation's political leaders understand all that well enough. In the middle of a best-selling book, an aspiring American politician wrote a passage that would have fit comfortably in this book (had I been able to write as well):

> There is no doubt that globalization has brought significant benefits to American consumers. It's lowered prices on goods once considered luxuries, from big-screen TVs to peaches in winter, and increased the purchasing power of low-income Americans. It's helped keep inflation in check, boosted returns for the millions of Americans now invested in the stock market, provided new markets for U.S. goods and services, and allowed countries like China and India to dramatically reduce poverty, which over the long term makes for a more stable world.[1]

The author is Barack Obama; the book is *The Audacity of Hope.*

Our new president and members of Congress from both parties should pursue a trade policy that reflects "the better angels of our nature," as President Abraham Lincoln expressed it at the end of his first inaugural address. They should work together to systematically eliminate the last vestiges of an old trade policy rooted in mercantilist thinking of the 17th century and the politics of America's 19th century. Here are eight policy proposals that would bring U.S. trade policy into the 21st century:

1. Eliminate All Tariffs on Products of Special Interest to the Poor at Home and Abroad. Eliminating tariffs on products disproportionately consumed by low-income families would immediately put money in the pockets of Americans who would gain the most from the additional income. It would eliminate the most regressive form of taxation our federal government imposes. For those looking for a way to stimulate consumer spending, eliminating those tariffs would increase the spending power of the segment of society with the highest propensity to spend extra income on consumption. The loss of $25 billion in federal revenue now collected by the customs service represents a mere 1 percent of federal revenue projected for Fiscal Year 2009. It could easily be "paid for" through spending cuts or a small upward adjustment in other revenue sources less biased against the poor. Congress could consider a single bill for an up-or-down vote that would eliminate all trade barriers on food, clothing, shoes, and any other consumer items that millions of American families buy and consume every day.

2. *Repeal All Tariffs and Other Trade Restrictions That Raise the Cost of Production for U.S.–Based Companies.* The federal government should not impose unnecessary costs on U.S. companies trying to compete in global markets. Congress should repeal all tariffs and other trade restrictions that arbitrarily raise the cost to American companies for raw materials, intermediate inputs, capital machinery, and the transportation of goods. If Congress wants to promote the United States as a base for global manufacturing, it could give special attention to current restrictions that inhibit the competitiveness of U.S.–based manufacturers, such as restrictions on imported sugar and steel and intercoastal shipping. All those reductions could be consolidated into a single bill to be voted on by Congress without the threat of crippling or compromising amendments.

3. *Rebase the U.S. Antidumping Law on the Traditional Yardstick of "Predatory Pricing."* Selling at below "fair value" should be redefined to mean predatory pricing—selling at a cost intended to drive competitors from the market and thereby gain monopoly pricing power. If markets are kept open, this scenario will virtually never happen. Our "unfair trade laws" should be reformed so that they are no longer unfair to foreign producers but treat foreign producers the same as we do domestic competitors. A reformed law should require the Commerce Department and U.S. International Trade Commission to consider consumer and downstream producer interests alongside the interests of producers seeking protection. Lower import prices by definition will make life more difficult for domestic competitors; the real question is whether lower prices serve the

national interest, and the answer is almost always yes. In sum, the antidumping law should be rewritten to serve the nation, not special interests.

4. Direct the U.S. International Trade Commission to Analyze the Income-Transfer Effects of Existing and Proposed U.S. Tariffs. The commission's biannual report on "Significant Import Barriers" provides a useful catalog of the major remaining barriers to trade, but the reports are silent on the deepest impact of those barriers. The real but relatively small net negative impact of those barriers on the overall economy disguises their much larger effect on income redistribution. Barriers on food, clothing, and shoes benefit a small slice of American producers at the expense of tens of millions of American households. The USITC model should be able to tell us who pays the cost of those barriers and how much they pay.

5. Consolidate All Unemployment, Job Retraining, and Wage Insurance Programs to Apply Equally to All American Workers, Not Just Those Displaced By Trade. The federal program of "Trade Adjustment Assistance" fails to help the vast majority of American workers displaced from their jobs and seeking a new line of work for reasons that have nothing to do with trade. A worker displaced by technology, domestic competition, or changing consumer wants is no less deserving of consideration when lawmakers craft public policy. Potential ideas include tax-exempt job retraining accounts that would allow adult workers to deduct payments for technical and professional retraining. A private-sector system of unemployment insurance should be encouraged so all workers can afford the option of insurance against prolonged unemployment. Health care benefits should also be divorced from employment through universal deductibility of insurance premiums and the expansion of health savings accounts so workers do not face losing their health insurance when they lose their jobs. This proposal would benefit all displaced workers, not just the relatively small minority who lose their jobs because of import competition.

6. Improve the Education System to Prepare Americans for the Workplace Opportunities of the Future. As technology and globalization shift our economy up the value chain, skills and education will become even more important for American workers. It is simply a fact of life that the ability of our children to earn a middle-class income in tomorrow's economy will increasingly depend on their human capital—the skills and knowledge they possess. The shortcomings of the American public education system and what to do about them are beyond the scope of this book, but the answer to anxieties about the future lies in preparing our children for the higher-skilled jobs of today and tomorrow, not raising trade barriers further to preserve the lower-skilled jobs of the past.

7. Promote Domestic Savings By Cutting the Federal Budget and Reforming the Tax Code. Both of these policy proposals are far removed from trade, but they would directly address political concerns about the U.S. current account deficit. Reducing, with the goal of eliminating, the federal budget deficit would free capital for other private-sector uses, reducing the demand for foreign savings to pay the current costs of our government. Our national pool of private savings can be increased by reducing the bias in the federal tax code against savings. One approach would be to shift federal taxes from income to consumption. The federal income tax could be repealed and replaced with a national sales or value-added tax. The current income-tax code could be reformed by creating a new individual savings account that would allow taxpayers to defer income taxes indefinitely on all saved income, paying taxes only when it is actually spent on consumption. Expanded 401(k)s and individual retirement accounts would also increase incentives to save for the future, providing more domestic savings for investment. A larger pool of domestically generated savings would reduce demand for foreign capital and incrementally encourage a smaller current account deficit.

8. Talk about the Benefits of Import Competition at the Highest Levels of Our National Trade Discussion. The president of the United States and the president's economic team have a unique responsibility to safeguard the economic interests of the entire nation, not the noisiest producer groups. In speeches, in the annual Economic Report of the President, in veto warnings to Congress, and in trade negotiations with other countries, the president should exercise leadership in guarding the interests of all Americans in an open and competitive American economy. The president has a special obligation to give voice to the single largest economic constituency group in the country—consumers. Members of Congress should do the same, standing up for the large majority of constituents in their states and districts who have much more to gain from free trade than from erecting and maintaining anti-competitive trade barriers. As the face of U.S. foreign policy, the president also has the greatest responsibility to use trade policy as a tool not just to promote economic development and fairness but also to encourage the spread of freedom and peace abroad.

For Main Street America, free trade is the trifecta of trade policy. Simply and effectively, it enhances our liberty, promotes prosperity, and advances peace. It reduces the role of government in our daily lives. It says "No" to the special interests and "Yes" to our national interest. Free trade confidently embraces the future. It affirms that Americans have much to offer the world and much to gain from collaborating with people in other countries as customers, suppliers, business partners, and friends. Free trade unites us with other people in an ever-widening "community of work" that provides a powerful alternative to conflict and war. Free trade embodies a policy of hope rather than fear.

Notes

Chapter 1

1. U.S. Maritime Administration, "U.S. Waterborne Container Imports by Trading Partner," 2007, Maritime Statistics, www.marad.dot.gov.

2. For trade figures before 1960, see U.S. Census Bureau, *Historical Statistics of the United States, Colonial Times to 1970*, Bicentennial Edition, Part 2 (Washington: U.S. Census Bureau, 1975), International Transactions, Series U 1-25, Balance of International Payments, 1790–1970, p. 864; for 1960 through 2007, see Council of Economic Advisers, *Economic Report of the President 2009* (Washington: Government Printing Office, 2009), Table 103, U.S. International Transactions 1946–2008, p. 402.

3. U.S. Department of Commerce, "U.S. Net International Investment Position at Yearend 2007," Press Release, Bureau of Economic Analysis, June 27, 2008, www.bea.gov/international/index.htm#iip.

4. Bank of International Settlements, "Triennial Central Bank Survey of Foreign Exchange and Derivatives Market Activity in 2007—Final Results," Press Release, December 19, 2007, www.bis.org/press/p071219.htm.

5. David Hummels, "Transportation Costs and International Trade in the Second Era of Globalization," *Journal of Economic Perspectives* 21, no. 3 (Summer 2007): 138.

6. Ibid., p. 133.

7. Ibid., p. 136.

8. Ibid., p. 152.

9. Anne Kim, John Lageson, and Jim Kessler, "Why Lou Dobbs Is Winning," in *The Economic Program* (Washington: Third Way, 2007), pp. 7 and 19.

Chapter 2

1. W. Michael Cox and Richard Alm, *The Best of All Worlds: Globalizing the Knowledge Economy—2006 Annual Report* (Dallas: Federal Reserve Bank of Dallas, 2006), p. 21.

2. Adam Smith, *An Inquiry into the Nature and Causes of the Wealth of Nations* (New York: Random House, 1776, 1937), p. 625.

3. Lou Dobbs, *Exporting America: Why Corporate Greed Is Shipping American Jobs Overseas* (New York: Warner Business Books, 2004), p. 124.

4. AFL-CIO, "2007 AFL-CIO Democratic Primary Forum," August 8, 2007, www.ontheissues.org/2007_AFL-CIO_Dems.htm.

5. Ibid.

6. U.S. Department of Commerce, Economics and Statistics Administration, and U.S. Census Bureau, "Current Industrial Reports: Apparel: 2006," June 2007, Table 5.

7. U.S. Department of Labor, Bureau of Labor Statistics, "Occupational Employment and Wages, 2006," Press Release, May 17, 2007, www.bls.gov/OES.

8. U.S. Department of Labor, Bureau of Labor Statistics, "Consumer Price Index," various tables, www.bls.gov/cpi/#tables.

9. Kenneth S. Rogoff, "Disinflation: An Unsung Benefit of Globalization?" *Finance & Development* 40, no. 4 (December 2003): 54–55.

10. W. Michael Cox and Richard Alm, *The Best of All Worlds: Globalizing the Knowledge Economy—2006 Annual Report* (Dallas: Federal Reserve of Dallas, 2006), p. 10.

11. Christian Broda and David E. Weinstein, "Globalization and the Gains from Variety," National Bureau of Economic Research Working Paper no. 10314, February 2004, p. 1.

12. Ibid., p. 15.

13. Ibid., p. 3.

14. Japanese Automobile Manufacturers Association, "Driving a New Generation of American Mobility," November 2008, p. 2, www.jama.org/library/brochure_Nov2008.htm.

15. U.S. Maritime Administration, "U.S. Waterborne Container Imports," 2007.

16. U.S. Census Bureau, "Country and Product Trade Data, U.S. Imports from All Countries from 2003 to 2007 by 5-Digit End-Use Code," Foreign Trade Statistics, www.census.gov/foreign-trade/statistics/product/index.html.

17. Author's calculation from U.S. Census Bureau, "Country and Product Trade Data," Foreign Trade Statistics, www.census.gov/foreign-trade/country/index.html.

18. Christian Broda and John Romalis, "Inequality and Prices: Does China Benefit the Poor in America?" University of Chicago, March 26, 2008, p. 1.

19. See U.S. Department of Commerce, "U.S. Trade in Goods (Imports, Exports, and Balance) by Country," www.census.gov/foreign-trade/balance/index.html#W. Monthly imports from each trading partner were compared to average imports over a 12-month period that includes the five months before and the six months after the month being compared.

20. Terry J. Fitzgerald and Ronald A. Wirtz, "The Wal-Mart Effect: Poison or Antidote for Local Communities," *Fedgazette* (Federal Reserve Bank of Minneapolis) 20, no. 1 (January 2008), http://www.minneapolisfed.org/publications_papers/fedgazette/issue_index.cfm.

21. Marsha Salisbury, "Special Report: Top 100 Importers and Exporters," *Journal of Commerce* 8, no. 21 (May 28, 2007): 16A–24A.

22. Charles Fishman, *The Wal-Mart Effect: How the World's Most Powerful Company Really Works—and How It's Transforming the American Economy* (New York: Penguin Press, 2006), p. 15.

23. Ibid., p. 16.

24. Jerry Hausman and Ephraim Leibtag, "Consumer Benefits from Increased Competition in Shopping Outlets: Measuring the Effect of Wal-Mart," original paper presented at EC² Conference, Marseille, France, December 2004, revised draft October 2005, http://econ-www.mit.edu/files/1036.

25. Ibid., p. 26.

26. Miguel L. Bustillo and Ann Zimmerman, "Wal-Mart Flourishes as Economy Turns Sour," *Wall Street Journal*, November 14, 2008.

27. Center for American Progress, "Debating Wal-Mart's Impact on American Workers," Panel Discussion, November 16, 2005, www.americanprogress.org/kf/walmart_transcript.pdf.

Chapter 3

1. Council of Economic Advisers, *Economic Report of the President 2009* (Washington: Government Printing Office, 2009), Table B-36.

2. For 1965–2006 employment and labor force figures, see Council of Economic Advisers, *Economic Report of the President 2007* (Washington: Government Printing Office, 2007), Table B-35, pp. 272–273; for July 2007 figures, see Economic Indicators, Government Printing Office, July 2007, p. 11, http://origin.www.gpoaccess.gov/indicators/.

3. Council of Economic Advisers, *Economic Report of the President 2009* (Washington: Government Printing Office, 2009), Table B-43, pp. 335.

4. Robert E. Scott, "Phony Accounting and U.S. Trade Policy: Is Bush Using Enron-like Tactics to Sell Trade Deals to the Public?" Economic Policy Institute Issue Brief no. 184, October 23, 2002.

5. Robert E. Scott, "Costly Trade with China: Millions of U.S. Jobs Displaced with Net Job Loss in Every State," Economic Policy Institute Briefing Paper no. 188, May 2, 2007.

6. Lori G. Kletzer, *Job Loss from Imports: Measuring the Costs* (Washington: Institute for International Economics, 2001), pp. 18–19.

7. U.S. Department of Labor, Bureau of Labor Statistics, "Business Employment Dynamics," Economics News Release, Table 1. Private Sector Gross Job Gains and Losses, Seasonally Adjusted, www.bls.gov/news.release/cewbd.toc.htm.

8. Ben S. Bernanke, "Trade and Jobs," speech at Duke University, Durham, North Carolina, March 30, 2004, www.federalreserve.gov/boarddocs/speeches/2004/20040330/default.htm.

9. David Lieberman, "Extra! Extra! Are Newspapers Dying?" *USA Today*, March 18, 2009, p. 2B.

10. Council of Economic Advisers, *Economic Report of the President 2009* (Washington: Government Printing Office, 2009), Table B-47.

11. Ibid., Table B-49.

12. W. Michael Cox and Richard Alm, *Myths of Rich & Poor: Why We're Better Off Than We Think* (New York: Basic Books, 1999), pp. 18–21.

13. Ibid., p. 26.

14. See U.S. Department of Labor, Bureau of Labor Statistics, "Current Employment Statistics," BLS, Tables B1 and B2, http://www.bls.gov/ces; U.S. Department of Labor, Bureau of Labor Statistics, "Employment, Hours, and Earnings from the Current Employment Statistics Survey (National)," Tables B-1 (employment) and B-4 (average hourly earnings), www.bls.gov/webapps/legacy/cesbtab1.htm.

15. Bureau of Economic Analysis, International Economic Accounts, "U.S. International Transactions Accounts Data: Private Services Transactions," Table 3a, www.bea.gov/international/bp_web/list.cfm?anon=75516&registered=0.

16. See U.S. Department of Labor, Bureau of Labor Statistics, "Occupational Employment Statistics," http://www.bls.gov/oes/home.htm.

17. U.S. Census Bureau, "Income, Poverty, and Health Insurance Coverage in the United States: 2007," August 26, 2008, Table A-1, p. 31.

18. Ibid., Table A-1, p. 29.

19. Ibid.

20. W. Michael Cox and Richard Alm, *Myths of Rich & Poor: Why We're Better Off Than We Think* (New York: Basic Books, 1999), p. 63.

21. Jacob Hacker, Testimony before the House Committee on Education and Labor, January 31, 2007, p. 15.

22. Federal Reserve Board, "Flow of Funds Accounts of the United States," March 12, 2009, http://www.federalreserve.gov/releases/z1/

23. Brian K. Bucks, Arthur B. Kennickell, Traci L. Mach, and Kevin B. Moore, "Changes in U.S. Family Finances from 2004 to 2007: Evidence from the Survey of Consumer Finances," *Federal Reserve Bulletin* 95 (February 2009): A1–A55.

24. Ibid., Tables 16 and 17, p. A48.

25. Ibid., p. A45.

26. Ibid., p. A41.

27. Ibid., p. A50.

Chapter 4

1. Bruce Springsteen, "Born in the USA," Columbia Records, 1984.

2. Patrick J. Buchanan, "Death of Manufacturing: The Rise of Free Trade Has Eroded America's Industrial Base and with It Our Sovereignty," *The American Conservative*, August 11, 2003, www.amconmag.com/issue/2003/aug/11/.

3. Byron L. Dorgan, *Take This Job and Ship It: How Corporate Greed and Brain-Dead Politics Are Selling Out America* (New York: St. Martin's Press, 2006), pp. 10, 24, and 241.

4. U.S. Census Bureau, "U.S. International Trade in Goods and Services: Exhibit 1, Exports, Imports, and Balance of Goods by Selected NAICS-Based Product Code," Press Release FT-900, U.S. Department of Commerce, February 11, 2009, www.census.gov/foreign-trade/Press-Release/current_press_release/press.html.

5. Unless otherwise noted, figures in the bulleted items are from the U.S. Department of Commerce, Economics and Statistics Administration, and U.S. Census Bureau, "Current Industrial Reports," www.census.gov/cir/www/alpha.html.

6. U.S. Department of Commerce, Economics and Statistics Administration, and U.S. Census Bureau, "Current Industrial Reports: Civil Aircraft and Aircraft Engines; and Aerospace Industry: 2007," June 2008, Table 1.

7. U.S. Department of Commerce, Economics and Statistics Administration, and U.S. Census Bureau, "Current Industrial Reports: Steel Mill Products: 2007," July 2008.

8. Federal Reserve Board, "Industrial Production and Capacity Utilization," G-17 Series, Table 3, www.federalreserve.gov/releases/g17/download.htm.

9. U.S. Department of Commerce, Economics and Statistics Administration, and U.S. Census Bureau, "Current Industrial Reports: Computers and Peripheral Equipment: 2007," July 2008, Table 3.

10. U.S. Department of Commerce, Economics and Statistics Administration, and U.S. Census Bureau, "Current Industrial Reports: Major Household Appliances: 2007," April 2008, Table 2.

11. U.S. Department of Commerce, Economics and Statistics Administration, and U.S. Census Bureau, "Current Industrial Reports: Refrigeration, Air-Conditioning, and Warm Air Heating Equipment: 2006," July 2007, Table 2

12. U.S. Department of Commerce, Economics and Statistics Administration, and U.S. Census Bureau, "Current Industrial Reports: Electric Housewares and Fans: 2007," May 2008, Table 2.

13. U.S. Department of Commerce, Economics and Statistics Administration, and U.S. Census Bureau, "Current Industrial Reports: Carpet and Rugs: 2007," May 2008. The average house size was 2,349 square feet in 2006, as reported by Margot Adler, "Behind the Ever Expanding American Dream House," *All Things Considered*, National Public Radio, July 4, 2006, www.npr.org/templates/story/story.php?storyId = 5525283#email.

14. U.S. Department of Commerce, Economics and Statistics Administration, and U.S. Census Bureau, "Current Industrial Reports: Inorganic Chemicals: 2007," June 2008.

15. U.S. Department of Commerce, Economics and Statistics Administration, and U.S. Census Bureau, "Current Industrial Reports: Paints and Allied Products: 2007," February 2008, Table 2.

16. U.S. Department of Commerce, Economics and Statistics Administration, and U.S. Census Bureau, "Current Industrial Reports: Pharmaceutical Preparations, Except Biologicals: 2007," June 2008, Table 1.

17. Motoko Rich, "Potter Was Still Magical, But Not All Books Rose," *New York Times*, May 30, 2008.

18. Daniel Ikenson, "Thriving in the Global Economy: The Truth about U.S. Manufacturing and Trade," Cato Institute Trade Policy Analysis no. 35, August 28, 2007, p. 5.

19. Ibid., p. 9.

20. Ibid., p. 8.

21. Council of Economic Advisers, *Economic Report of the President 2004* (Washington: Government Printing Office, 2004), p. 60.

22. John R. MacArthur, *The Selling of "Free Trade": NAFTA, Washington, and the Subversion of American Democracy* (Los Angeles: University of California Press, 2000), pp. 3–57.

23. Ibid., p. 8.

24. U.S. Federal Reserve Board, "Industrial Production and Capacity Utilization: Data from January 1986 to Present (Tables 1, 2, and 10), Industrial Production, Seasonally Adjusted," Series B00004, www.federalreserve.gov/releases/g17/table1_2.htm.

25. Representative Brad Sherman, "Trade, Foreign Policy, and the American Worker," Opening Statement, House Foreign Affairs Committee, Hearing, March 28, 2007.

26. Frederick W. Smith, "Deregulation and the Global Market Revolution," *Cato's Letter* 4, no. 4 (Fall 2006): 3.

27. U.S. Census Bureau, "Country and Product Trade Data, U.S. Imports from All Countries from 2003 to 2007 by 5-Digit End-Use Code," Foreign Trade Statistics, www.census.gov/foreign-trade/statistics/product/index.html.

28. Harmonized U.S. Tariff Schedule, U.S. International Trade Commission, "Section xv: Base Metals and Articles of Base Metal," Heading 7204 for scrap metal and "Section X: Pulp of Wood or of Other Fibrous Cellulosic Material; Waste and Scrap of Paper or Paperboard; Paper and Paperboard and Articles Thereof," Heading 4707 for Recovered (Waste and Scrap) Paper and Paper Board, http://www.usitc.gov/tata/hts/bychapter/index.htm.

29. Byron L. Dorgan, *Take This Job and Ship It: How Corporate Greed and Brain-Dead Politics Are Selling Out America* (New York: St. Martin's Press, 2006), pp. 25–38.

30. Council of Economic Advisers, *Economic Report of the President 2004* (Washington: Government Printing Office, 2004), p. 66.

31. U.S. Department of Commerce, "U.S. Trade in Goods (Imports, Exports, and Balance) by Country," www.census.gov/foreign-trade/balance/index.html#C.

32. "Foreign Firms Dominate China's Exports," *Asia Times*, June 30, 2006.

33. "China's Exports, Imports of Electronic Products Slow Down," *China People's Daily*, October 2, 2007.

34. C. Fred Bergsten, Bates Gill, Nicholas R. Lardy, and Derek Mitchell, *China: The Balance Sheet: What the World Needs to Know Now about the Emerging Superpower*, Center for Strategic and International Studies and Institute for International Economics (New York: Public Affairs, 2006), p. 107.

35. Ibid., p. 90.

36. James Fallows, "Why China's Rise Is Good for Us," *The Atlantic Monthly*, July/August 2007, p. 68.

37. Ibid., p. 69.

38. Greg Linden, Kenneth L. Kraemer, and Jason Dedrick, "Who Captures Value in a Global Innovation System? The Case of Apple's iPod," Personsal Computing Industry Center, June 2007, p. 10.

39. Ibid., p. 8.

40. Apple Inc. "100 Million iPods Sold," Press Release, April 9, 2007, www.apple.com/pr/library/2007/04/09ipod.html.

41. U.S.–China Economic and Security Review Commission, *2005 Report to Congress of the U.S.–China Economic and Security Review Commission* (Washington: Government Printing Office, 2005), p. 4, www.uscc.gov/annual_report/2005/05annual_report_contents.htm.

42. C. Fred Bergsten, Bates Gill, Nicholas R. Lardy, and Derek Mitchell, *China: The Balance Sheet: What the World Needs to Know Now about the Emerging Superpower*, Center for Strategic and International Studies and Institute for International Economics (New York: Public Affairs, 2006), pp. 104–5.

43. Office of the U.S. Trade Representative, "U.S.–China Trade Relations: Entering a New Phase of Greater Accountability and Enforcement: Top to Bottom Review," February 2006, p. 9.

44. U.S. Department of Commerce. "U.S. Trade in Goods (Imports, Exports, and Balance) by Country," http://www.census.gov/foreign-trade/balance/index.html#C.

45. U.S. Department of Commerce, "U.S. International Trade in Goods and Services," Press Release FT-900, Exhibit 14a, http://www.census.gov/foreign-trade/Press-Release/current_press_release/press.html#current

46. U.S. Department of Commerce, "U.S. Exports to All Countries from 2002 to 2006 by 5-Digit End-Use Code," http://www.census.gov/foreign-trade/statistics/product/enduse/exports/index.html.

47. U.S. Department of Commerce, Bureau of Economic Analysis, "National Income and Product Accounts: Exports and Imports of Goods and Services by Type of Product," Table 4.2.5, http://www.bea.gov/national/nipaweb/SelectTable.asp?Selected = N.

48. U.S. Department of Commerce, "National Income and Product Accounts," Real Exports and Imports of Goods and Services by Type of Product, Chained Dollars, Table 4.2.6, http://www.federalreserve.gov/releases/G17/download.htm.

49. U.S. Federal Reserve Board, "Industrial Production and Capacity Utilization: Historical Data," Industrial Production, Seasonally Adjusted, Tables 1 and 2, http://www.federalreserve.gov/releases/G17/download.htm.

50. U.S.–China Economic and Security Review Commission, *2005 Report to Congress of the U.S.–China Economic and Security Review Commission* (Washington: Government Printing Office, 2005), p. 14.

51. Daniel Ikenson, "Thriving in the Global Economy: The Truth about U.S. Manufacturing and Trade," Cato Institute Trade Policy Analysis no. 35, August 28, 2007, p. 4.

52. William H. Lash III, *U.S. International Trade Regulation: A Primer* (Washington: American Enterprise Institute, 1998), p. 83.

53. U.S. Department of Commerce, "Department Concludes Study on Effect of Imports of Iron Ore and Semi-finished Steel on U.S. National Security," Press Release, January 9, 2002, www.commerce.gov/opa/press/Secretary_Evans/2002_Releases/Jan_09_DOC_Iron_Steel.html.

54. Byron L. Dorgan, *Take This Job and Ship It: How Corporate Greed and Brain-Dead Politics Are Selling Out America* (New York: St. Martin's Press, 2006), p. 24.

55. Daniel Ikenson, "Thriving in the Global Economy: The Truth about U.S. Manufacturing and Trade," Cato Institute Trade Policy Analysis no. 35, August 28, 2007, p. 8.

56. U.S. Census Bureau, *Historical Statistics of the United States, Colonial Times to 1970*, Bicentennial Edition (Washington: U.S. Census Bureau, 1975), Labor Force and Employment, by Industry, Series D 167-181, www2.census.gov/prod2/statcomp/documents/CT1970p1-05.pdf; and Council of Economic Advisers, *Economic Report of the President 2008* (Washington: Government Printing Office, 2008), Tables B-35 and B-46, www.gpoaccess.gov/eop/tables08.html#erp2.

57. Council of Economic Advisers, *Economic Report of the President 2004* (Washington: Government Printing Office, 2004), pp. 76–77.

58. Robert Rowthorn and Ramana Ramaswamy, "Deindustrialization—Its Causes and Implications," International Monetary Fund Economic Issues no. 10, September 1997, p. 2.

59. International Monetary Fund, "The Boom in Non-Fuel Commodity Prices: Can It Last?" in *World Economic Outlook* (Washington: International Monetary Fund, 2006), p. 10.

60. U.S. Department of Commerce, Bureau of Economic Analysis, "National Income and Product Accounts," Table 2.4.5. Personal Consumption Expenditures by Type of Product, www.bea.doc.gov/bea/dn/nipaweb/index.asp.

61. Council of Economic Advisers, *Economic Report of the President 2004* (Washington: Government Printing Office, 2004), pp. 77–78.

Chapter 5

1. Nancy Pelosi, Charles B. Rangel, John B. Lewis, Michael R. McNulty, Stephanie Tubbs Jones, Rahm Emanuel, and Kendrick Meek, "Congressional Leaders Urge Bush to Act as 2006 Annual Trade Deficit Breaks All-Time Record," letter to President George W. Bush from the House Committee on Ways and Means, February 13, 2007, http://waysandmeans.house.gov/news.asp?formmode = release&id = 479.

2. U.S. Department of Commerce, Bureau of Economic Analysis, "U.S. International Transactions Accounts Data."

3. Paul Krugman, *The Age of Diminished Expectations* (Washington: Washington Post Co., 1994), p. 51.

4. U.S. Department of the Treasury, Treasury International Capital (TIC) Data, "TIC Monthly Reports on Cross-Border Financial Flows," Press Release, November 18, 2008.

5. U.S. Department of Commerce, Bureau of Economic Analysis, "National Income and Products Accounts of the United States: Saving and Investment," Table 5.1, and "Gross Domestic Product," Table 1.1.5, http://www.bea.gov/national/nipaweb/SelectTable.asp?Selected = N.

6. Ibid.

7. Richard Cooper, "Living with Global Imbalances: A Contrarian View," Institute for International Economics Policy Brief no. PB05-3, November 2005.

8. Ben S. Bernanke, "Global Imbalances: Recent Developments and Prospects," speech at the Bundesbank Lecture, Berlin, Germany, September 11, 2007.

9. Robert E. Scott, "Costly Trade with China: Millions of U.S. Jobs Displaced with Net Job Loss in Every State," Economic Policy Institute Briefing Paper no. 188, October 7, 2007.

10. Council of Economic Advisers, *Economic Report of the President 2009* (Washington: Government Printing Office, 2009), Tables B-1, B-42, and B-103.

11. Doug Karmin, "The Facts on Trade Deficits and Jobs," Progressive Policy Institute Policy Report, October 2007.

12. Council of Economic Advisers, *Economic Report of the President 1996* (Washington: Government Printing Office), p. 250.

13. Ibid., p. 252.

14. Elena L. Nguyen, "The International Investment Position of the United States at Yearend 2007," *Survey of Current Business* 88, no. 7 (July 2008): Table 1, p. 17.

15. Federal Reserve Board, "Flow of Funds Accounts of the United States," March 12, 2009. http://www.federalreserve.gov/releases/z1/.

16. Elena L. Nguyen, "The International Investment Position of the United States at Yearend 2007," *Survey of Current Business* 88, no. 7 (July 2008).

17. Diana Farrell, Susan Lund, Alexander Maasry, and Sebastian Roemer, "The US Imbalancing Act: Can the Current Account Deficit Continue?" McKinsey Global Institute, June 2007.

18. Robert E. Lipsey, "U.S. Foreign Trade and the Balance of Payments, 1800–1913," National Bureau of Economic Research Working Paper no. 4710, April 1994, p. 11.

19. Ibid., p. 17.

20. Warren E. Buffett, "America's Growing Trade Deficit Is Selling the Nation Out from Under Us," *Fortune*, October 26, 2003.

21. Chris Edwards, *Downsizing the Federal Government* (Washington: Cato Institute, 2005).

Chapter 6

1. Barney Frank, "Stabilizing the Financial Condition of the American Automobile Industry," House Financial Services Committee, Full Committee Hearing, November 19, 2008, www.house.gov/apps/list/hearing/financialsvcs_dem/hr111908.shtml.

2. Matthew Symonds, "A Global Love Affair: A Special Report on Cars in Emerging Markets," *The Economist*, November 15, 2008, pp. 4–6.

3. General Motors, *General Motors Corporate 2007 Annual Report* (Detroit: General Motors, 2008), www.gm.com.

4. Ford Motor Company, *2007 Annual Report* (Dearborn, MI: Ford Motor Company, 2008).

5. Elena L. Nguyen, "The International Investment Position of the United States at Yearend 2007," *Survey of Current Business* 88, no. 7 (July 2008): 17.

6. U.N. Conference on Trade and Development, *World Investment Report 2008* (New York: U.N. Conference on Trade and Development, 2008), p. 3.

7. Douglas P. Woodward and Paul Guimarães, "BMW in South Carolina: The Economic Impact of a Leading Sustainable Enterprise," Moore School of Business, University of South Carolina, September 2008, p. 1.

8. U.S. Department of Commerce, Bureau of Economic Analysis, "Foreign Direct Investment in the U.S.: Balance of Payments and Direct Investment Position Data," International Economic Accounts, www.bea.gov/International/Index.htm.

9. Thomas Anderson, "U.S. Affiliates of Foreign Companies: Operations in 2006," in *Survey of Current Business* 88, no. 8 (August 2008): 183–204.

10. Council of Economic Advisers, *Economic Report of the President 2007* (Washington: Government Printing Office, 2007), p. 178.

11. Thomas Anderson, "U.S. Affiliates of Foreign Companies: Operations in 2006," in *Survey of Current Business* 88, no. 8 (August 2008): 198.

12. Francis E. Warnock and Veronica Cacdac Warnock, "International Capital Flows and U.S. Interest Rates," National Bureau of Economic Research Working Paper no. 12560, October 2006, p. 4.

13. Hillary Clinton, "In Remarks on Senate Floor, Senator Clinton Urges Action to Address U.S. Foreign Debt and Trade Imbalance," Press Release, February 28, 2007, clinton.senate.gov/news/statements/details.cfm?id = 269893&&.

14. Federal Reserve Board "Flow of Funds Accounts of the United States," March 12, 2009. http://www.federalreserve.gov/releases/z1/.

15. David H. McCormick, "Do Sovereign Wealth Funds Make the U.S. Economy Stronger or Pose National Security Risks?" Testimony before the Joint Economic Committee of Congress, Hearing, February 13, 2008.

16. Raymond J. Mataloni Jr., "U.S. Multinational Companies: Operations in 2006," in *Survey of Current Business* 88, no. 11 (November 2008): Table 17.2, p. 43.

17. Ibid., Table 3 and Table 17.2.

18. Ibid., Table 17.2; for services exports in 2006, Council of Economic Advisers, *Economic Report of the President 2008* (Washington: Government Printing Office, 2008), Table B-106.

19. Ibid., Mataloni. p. 35.

20. Mihir A. Desai, C. Fritz Foley, and James R. Hines Jr., "Foreign Direct Investment and Domestic Economic Activity," National Bureau of Economic Research Working Paper no. 11717, October 2005, p. 1.

21. Ibid., p. 3.

22. Steve Chapman, "Why Are These People So Ashamed of NAFTA?" *Reason Online*, February 28, 2008, http://www.reason.com/news/show/125218.html.

23. U.S. Census Bureau, "U.S. Capital Spending Patterns: 1999–2006," October 7, 2008, www.census.gov/csd/ace/.

24. Raymond J. Mataloni Jr., "U.S. Multinational Companies: Operations in 2006," *Survey of Current Business* 88, no. 11 (November 2008): p. 45.

25. For a more detailed discussion of the impact of U.S. corporate taxation on the activities of U.S. multinationals, see Chris Edwards and Daniel J. Mitchell, *Global Tax Revolution: The Rise of Tax Competition and the Battle to Defend It* (Washington: Cato Institute, 2008), esp. Chapter 6.

26. U.S. Department of Commerce, Bureau of Economic Analysis, "U.S. Direct Investment Abroad: Capital Outflows Without Current-Cost Adjustment, 2007," International Economic Accounts, www.bea.gov/International/Index.htm.

27. Hakan Nordstrom and Scott Vaughan, *Special Studies: Trade and Environment* (Geneva: World Trade Oraganization, 1999), p. 4.

Chapter 7

1. Alexander Hamilton, "Report on Manufactures," 1791, reprinted in Daniel J. Boorstin, ed., *An American Primer* (Chicago: University of Chicago Press, 1966), p. 181.

2. Douglas A. Irwin, "Trade Restrictiveness and Deadweight Losses from U.S. Tariffs, 1859–1961," National Bureau of Economic Research Working Paper no. 13450, September 2007, data appendix, pp. 29–31.

3. Douglas A. Irwin, "Tariffs and Growth in Late Nineteenth-Century America," National Bureau of Economic Research Working Paper no. W7639, April 2000, pp. 16–17.

4. J. Bradford DeLong, "Trade Policy and America's Standard of Living: A Historical Perspective," in *Imports, Exports, and the American Worker*, ed. Susan M. Collins (Washington: Brookings Institution, 1998), p. 369.

5. Ibid., p. 351.

6. Douglas A. Irwin, "Tariffs and Growth in Late Nineteenth-Century America," National Bureau of Economic Research Working Paper no. W7639, April 2000, p. 7.

7. U.S. Department of Homeland Security, *Yearbook of Immigration Statistics: 2007* (Washington: Citizenship and Immigration Services, 2008), Table 1, www.dhs.gov/ximgtn/statistics/publications/LPR07.shtm.

8. Douglas A. Irwin, "Trade Restrictiveness and Deadweight Losses from U.S. Tariffs, 1859–1961," National Bureau of Economic Research Working Paper no. 13450, September 2007, data appendix, pp. 29–31.

9. Ibid., pp. 29–31.

10. Ibid., pp. 29–31.

11. Ibid., p. x and p. 16.

12. Israel Hernandez, "U.S. Trade Policy and Small Business," Testimony before the House Committee on Small Business, June 13, 2007.

13. Ibid.

14. Timothy Aeppel, "Overseas Profits Provide Shelter for U.S. Firms," *Wall Street Journal*, August 9, 2007, p. A1.

15. Ibid.

16. Robert Z. Lawrence, "The United States and the WTO Dispute Settlement System," Council of Foreign Relations, CSR no. 25, March 2007, p. 14.

17. Ibid., p. 19.

18. Ibid., Table 1.

19. Office of the United States Trade Representative, "Snapshot of WTO Cases Involving the United States," updated: February 17, 2009, http://www.ustr.gov/WTO/WTO_Fact_Sheets/Section_Index.html?ht=

20. Scott C. Bradford, Paul L. E. Grieco, and Gary Clyde Hufbauer, "The Payoff to America from Global Integration," in *The United States and the World Economy*, ed. C. Fred Bergsten (Washington: Institute for International Economics, 2005), p. 86.

21. Ibid., p. 95.

Chapter 8

1. International Monetary Fund, "Globalization and Inequality," in *World Economic Outlook* (Washington: International Monetary Fund, 2007), p. 33.

2. World Bank, "Developing Countries Must Improve Capacity to Absorb and Use Technology, says World Bank," Press Release, January 9, 2008.

3. Kym Anderson and L. Alan Winters, "The Challenge of Reducing International Trade and Migration Barriers," Copenhagen Consensus Project, February 29, 2008, p. 17.

4. See United Nations Population Fund, "Linking Population, Poverty and Development Urbanization: A Majority in Cities," accessed May 6, 2009, http://www.unfpa.org/pds/urbanization.htm; and International Labor Organization, "Global Employment Trends," Brief, January 2007. Table 5, p. 12, http://www.ilo.org/public/english/employment/strat/download/getb07en.pdf.

5. World Bank, *Global Economic Prospects 2007: Managing the Next Wave of Globalization* (Washington: World Bank, 2006), p. xvi.

6. Dominic Wilson and Raluca Dragusanu, "The Expanding Middle: The Exploding World Middle Class and Falling Global Inequality," Goldman Sachs Global Economics Paper no. 170, July 7, 2008, p. 3.

7. Shaohua Chen and Martin Ravallion, "The Developing World is Poorer Than We Thought, But No Less Successful in the Fight against Poverty," The World Bank, Policy Research Working Paper no. 4703, August 2008, p. 33.

8. Ibid., pp. 35–36.

9. Johan Norberg, "Four Decades That Changed Our Planet," Swedish Globalization Council Background Report no. 1, 2007, p. 18, www.regeringen.se/globaliseringsradet.

10. "Adios to Poverty, Hola to Consumption," *The Economist*, August 16, 2007.

11. World Bank, *Global Economic Prospects 2007: Managing the Next Wave of Globalization* (Washington: World Bank, 2006), p. xvi.

12. "Pharmaceuticals: Racing Down the Pyramid," *The Economist*, November 15, 2008, p. 76.

13. "Survey: A Global Love Affair: A Special Report on Cars in Emerging Markets," *The Economist*, November 15, 2008.

14. The paragraphs that follow are based on Johan Norberg, "Four Decades That Changed Our Planet," Swedish Globalization Council Background Report no. 1, 2007, www.regeringen.se/globaliseringsradet.

15. Daniel Griswold, "The Best 'Anti-Sweatshop' Policy: Expanding U.S. Trade with Developing Countries," Testimony before the Trade, Tourism, and Economic Development Subcommittee of the Senate Commerce, Science, and Transportation Committee, Hearing on "Overseas Sweatshop Abuses, Their Impact on U.S. Workers, and the Need for Anti-Sweatshop Legislation," February 14, 2007, www.freetrade.org.

16. See International Monetary Fund, *World Economic Outlook* (Washington: International Monetary Fund, 2007), p. 42; Daniel Lederman, William F. Maloney, and Luis Serven, "Lessons from NAFTA for Latin America and the Caribbean Countries: A Summary of Research Findings," World Bank, Washington, December 2003.

17. John Burstein, "U.S.–Mexico Agricultural Trade and Rural Poverty in Mexico," report from a task force convened by the Woodrow Wilson International Center for Scholars and Funación IDEA, April 13, 2007.

18. For the 2008 figures, see Arch Puddington, "Findings of Freedom in the World 2008—Freedom in Retreat: Is the Tide Turning?" in *Freedom in the World 2008*, Freedom House, http://www.freedomhouse.org/template.cfm?page=130&year=2008; for the 1973 figures, see Adrian Karatnycky, "Liberty's Expansion in a Turbulent World: Thirty Years of the Survey of Freedom," in *Freedom in the World 2003*, Survey Population, Freedom House, http://www.freedomhouse.org/template.cfm?page=130&year=2003.

19. Michael Mandelbaum, "Democracy without America: The Spontaneous Spread of Freedom," *Foreign Affairs* 86, no. 5 (September/October 2007): 123–25.

20. Peter Sutherland, Jagdish Bhagwati, Kwesi Botchwey, Niall FitzGerald, Koichi Hamada, John H. Jackson, Celso Lafer, and Theirry de Montbrial, *The Future of the WTO* (Geneva: World Trade Organization, 2004), p. 10.

21. Andrew Torchia, "Maglev Train Fuels Fundamental Change for Chinese Protests," *International Herald Tribune*, January 15, 2008.

22. Quoted in Douglas Irwin, "GATT Turns 60," *Wall Street Journal*, April 9, 2007.

23. Stockholm International Peace Research Institute, *SIPRI Yearbook 2008: Armaments, Disarmament and International Security* (Solna, Sweden: Stockholm International Peace Research Institute, 2008).

24. "Somewhere Over the Rainbow: The World's Silver Lining," *The Economist*, January 24, 2008.

25. Human Security Centre, *Human Security Report 2005: War and Peace in the 21st Century* (New York: Oxford University Press, 2005), pp. 1–2.

26. Pope John Paul II, *Centesimus Annus* (Rome: The Vatican, May 1, 1991), Section 32.

27. Ibid., Section 32.

28. See, for example, Felipe Larraín and José Tavares, "Does Foreign Direct Investment Decrease Corruption?" *Cuadernos de Economia* 41 (August 2004): 217–230.

29. Frederic Bastiat, *Selected Essays in Political Economy* (Irvington-on-Hudson, NY: Foundation for Economic Education, 1995), p. 197.

Chapter 9

1. James Gwartney and Robert Lawson, *Economic Freedom of the World: 2008 Annual Report* (Vancouver, BC, Canada: Fraser Institute, 2008), pp. 9–12.

2. World Trade Organization, "Trade Policy Review Report of the Secretariat: United States," May 5, 2008, p. 39, www.wto.org.

3. U.S. International Trade Commission, Harmonized Tariff Schedule of the United States, www.usitc.gov/tata/hts/bychapter/index.htm.

4. World Trade Organization, "Trade Policy Review Report of the Secretariat: United States," May 5, 2008, p. 32.

5. U.S. International Trade Commission, "The Economic Effects of Significant U.S. Import Restraints: Fifth Update 2007," Investigation no. 332-325, February 2007, p. 64.

6. Ibid., p. xvii.

7. Ibid., p. 64.

8. Ibid., p. 68.

9. Ibid., p. 62.

10. Ibid., p. 58.

11. Ibid., p. 87.

12. See H.R. 3934, "The Affordable Footwear Act," 110th Congress, Section 2, "Findings."

13. Greg Hitt, "Socks Burden Bush's Trade Goals: Curb on Imports to Sustain Agenda Remains Possibility," *Wall Street Journal*, January 17, 2008.

14. World Trade Organization, "Trade Policy Review Report of the Secretariat: United States," May 5, 2008, p. 82.

15. U.S. General Accounting Office, "Sugar Program: Supporting Sugar Prices Has Increased Users' Cost While Benefiting Producers," GAO/RCED-00-126, June 2000, pp. 6–7.

16. U.S. International Trade Commission, "The Economic Effects of Significant U.S. Import Restraints: Fifth Update 2007," Investigation no. 332-325, February 2007, p. 20.

17. U.S. International Trade Commission, "The Economic Effects of Significant U.S. Import Restraints: Fourth Update 2004," Investigation no. 332-325, June 2004, p. 25.

18. Ibid., p. 25, n. 57.

19. U.S. International Trade Commission, Harmonized Tariff Schedule of the United States, Chapter 10.

20. U.S. International Trade Commission, "The Economic Effects of Significant U.S. Import Restraints: Fifth Update 2007," Investigation no. 332-325, February 2007, pp. 36–40.

21. World Trade Organization, "Trade Policy Review Report of the Secretariat: United States," May 5, 2008, p. 89.

22. Organization for Economic Cooperation and Development, *Agricultural Policies in OECD Countries: At a Glance 2008* (Paris: Organization for Economic Cooperation and Development, 2008), pp. 84–85.

23. U.S. International Trade Commission, Harmonized Tariff Schedule of the United States, "Railway or Tramway Passenger Coaches and Special Purpose Railway or Tramway Coaches, Not Self-propelled," Chapter 86, Line 8605.00.00 www.usitc.gov/tata/hts/bychapter/index.htm.

24. European Commission, "United States Barriers to Trade and Investment: Report for 2007," April 2008, p. 80, http://www.eurunion.org/eu/index.php?option = com_content&task = view&id = 1731.

25. U.S. International Trade Commission, "The Economic Effects of Significant U.S. Import Restraints: Fifth Update 2007," Investigation no. 332-325, February 2007, pp. 85–89.

26. Organization for Economic Cooperation and Development, *Agricultural Policies in OECD Countries: At a Glance 2008* (Paris: Organization for Economic Cooperation and Development, 2008), p. 37.

27. Edward Gresser, *Freedom from Want: American Liberalism and the Global Economy* (Brooklyn, NY: Soft Skull Press, 2007), p. 167.

28. Ibid., pp. 166 and 168.

29. U.S. Department of Commerce, International Trade Administration, "Employment Changes in U.S. Food Manufacturing: The Impact of Sugar Prices." February 14, 2006, p. 3.

30. Ibid.

31. Tim Jones, "Life Savers Takes Business to Canada over Sugar Costs," *Chicago Tribune*, January 30, 2002.

32. "Food and Beverage Jobs Disappearing Due to Sugar Program," Promar International, December 2003, p. 1, www.promarinternationa.com.

33. U.S. Department of Commerce, International Trade Administration, "Employment Changes in U.S. Food Manufacturing: The Impact of Sugar Prices," p. 11.

34. Remy Jurenas, "Background on Sugar Policy Issues," Congressional Research Service Report RL33541, updated July 26, 2007, p. 16.

35. Brink Lindsey, Daniel Griswold, and Aaron Lukas, "The Steel 'Crisis' and the Costs of Protectionism," Cato Trade Briefing Paper no. 4, April 16, 1999, p. 8.

36. U.S. International Trade Commission, "The Economic Effects of Significant U.S. Import Restraints: Fifth Update 2007," Investigation no. 332-325, February 2007, p. 98.

37. Richard Karp, "Katrina and Oil Prices," Council on Foreign Relations, September 7, 2005, www.cfr.org/publication/8834/katrina_and_oil_prices.html.

38. World Trade Organization, "Trade Policy Review Report of the Secretariat: United States," May 5, 2008, p. 28.

39. European Commission, "United States Barriers to Trade and Investment: Report for 2007," April 2008, p. 7, http://www.eurunion.org/eu/index.php?option = com_content&task = view&id = 1731.

40. World Trade Organization, "Trade Policy Review Report of the Secretariat: United States," May 5, 2008, p. 39.

41. Ibid., pp. 70–71.

42. Ibid., p. 121.

43. European Commission, "United States Barriers to Trade and Investment: Report for 2007," April 2008, p. 41, http://www.eurunion.org/eu/index/php?option = com-content&task = view&id = 1731. The 10 states are Connecticut, Illinois, Louisiana, Maine, Maryland, Michigan, New York, Pennsylvania, Rhode Island, and West Virginia.

44. Ibid., p. 12.

45. World Trade Organization, "Trade Policy Review Report of the Secretariat: United States," May 5, 2008, p. 59.

46. Ibid., p. 60.

47. U.S. International Trade Commission, "The Economic Effects of Significant U.S. Import Restraints: Fifth Update 2007," Investigation no. 332-325, February 2007, p. xvii.

48. U.S. Chamber of Commerce, Emergency Committee for American Trade, National Association of Manufacturers, et al., "ECAT Opposes Unraveling of NAFTA," Letter to Nancy Pelosi and Leaders Reid, Boehner and McConnell. February 4, 2008, www.ecattrade.com/press/content.asp?ID = 726.

49. Sugar accounted for 86 percent of total U.S. consumption of sweeteners in 1967 and 43 percent in 2002. See U.S. International Trade Commission, "The Economic Effects of Significant U.S. Import Restraints: Fourth Update 2004," Investigation no. 332-325, June 2004, p. 12.

50. Nathan Childs, "Rice Situation and Outlook Yearbook," U.S. Department of Agriculture, Economic Research Service, November 2005, p. 53.

51. Adam Smith, *An Inquiry into the Nature and Causes of the Wealth of Nations* (New York: Random House, 1776, 1937), p. 128.

52. J. Eugene Marans, John H. Shenefield, Joseph E. Pattison, and John T. Byam, *Manual of Foreign Investment in the United States*, 3rd ed. (Eagan, MN: Thomson West, 2004), p. 53.

53. Ibid., p. 54.

Chapter 10

1. Barack Obama, *The Audacity of Hope* (New York: Random House, 2006), pp. 145–46.

Index

195

About the Author

Daniel Griswold directs the Center for Trade Policy Studies at the Cato Institute in Washington, D.C., where he has authored numerous studies on trade and immigration policy. He has written for major newspapers such as the *Wall Street Journal* and the *Los Angeles Times*, appeared on CNN, PBS, C-SPAN, Fox News and other national TV and radio networks, and testified before congressional committees. Earlier in his career, he served as a congressional press secretary and the editorial page editor of the *Colorado Springs Gazette*. After growing up in a small town in the Midwest, he earned a bachelor's degree in journalism from the University of Wisconsin at Madison and a diploma in economics and a master's degree in the Politics of the World Economy from the London School of Economics.

Cato Institute

Founded in 1977, the Cato Institute is a public policy research foundation dedicated to broadening the parameters of policy debate to allow consideration of more options that are consistent with the traditional American principles of limited government, individual liberty, and peace. To that end, the Institute strives to achieve greater involvement of the intelligent, concerned lay public in questions of policy and the proper role of government.

The Institute is named for *Cato's Letters*, libertarian pamphlets that were widely read in the American Colonies in the early 18th century and played a major role in laying the philosophical foundation for the American Revolution.

Despite the achievement of the nation's Founders, today virtually no aspect of life is free from government encroachment. A pervasive intolerance for individual rights is shown by government's arbitrary intrusions into private economic transactions and its disregard for civil liberties.

To counter that trend, the Cato Institute undertakes an extensive publications program that addresses the complete spectrum of policy issues. Books, monographs, and shorter studies are commissioned to examine the federal budget, Social Security, regulation, military spending, international trade, and myriad other issues. Major policy conferences are held throughout the year, from which papers are published thrice yearly in the *Cato Journal*. The Institute also publishes the quarterly magazine *Regulation*.

In order to maintain its independence, the Cato Institute accepts no government funding. Contributions are received from foundations, corporations, and individuals, and other revenue is generated from the sale of publications. The Institute is a nonprofit, tax-exempt, educational foundation under Section 501(c)3 of the Internal Revenue Code.

CATO INSTITUTE
1000 Massachusetts Ave., N.W.
Washington, D.C. 20001
www.cato.org

In the Shadow of Denali

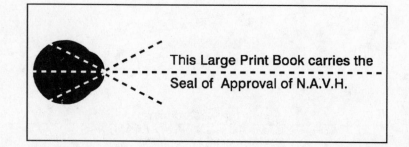

This Large Print Book carries the
Seal of Approval of N.A.V.H.

THE HEART OF ALASKA, BOOK 1

IN THE SHADOW
OF DENALI

TRACIE PETERSON
AND KIMBERLEY WOODHOUSE

THORNDIKE PRESS
A part of Gale, Cengage Learning

GALE
CENGAGE Learning·

Farmington Hills, Mich • San Francisco • New York • Waterville, Maine
Meriden, Conn • Mason, Ohio • Chicago

GALE
CENGAGE Learning®

Copyright © 2017 by Peterson Ink, Inc. and Kimberley Woodhouse.
The Hearts of Alaska #1.
Scripture quotations are from the King James Version of the Bible.
Thorndike Press, a part of Gale, Cengage Learning.

ALL RIGHTS RESERVED
This is a work of historical reconstruction; the appearances of certain historical figures are therefore inevitable. All other characters, however, are products of the authors' imagination, and any resemblance to actual persons, living or dead, is coincidental.
Thorndike Press® Large Print Christian Fiction.
The text of this Large Print edition is unabridged.
Other aspects of the book may vary from the original edition.
Set in 16 pt. Plantin.

LIBRARY OF CONGRESS CATALOGING-IN-PUBLICATION DATA

Names: Peterson, Tracie, author. | Woodhouse, Kimberley, 1973- author.
Title: In the shadow of Denali / Tracie Peterson and Kimberley Woodhouse.
Description: Large print edition. | Waterville, Maine : Thorndike Press, 2017. |
    Series: The heart of Alaska; 1 | Series: Thorndike Press large print Christian
    fiction
Identifiers: LCCN 2016045908 | ISBN 9781410496256 (hardback) | ISBN 1410496252
    (hardcover)
Subjects: LCSH: Large type books. | BISAC: FICTION / Christian / Historical. |
    FICTION / Christian / Romance. | GSAFD: Love stories. | Christian fiction. |
    Historical fiction.
Classification: LCC PS3566.E7717 I5 2017b | DDC 813/.54—dc23
LC record available at https://lccn.loc.gov/2016045908

Published in 2017 by arrangement with Bethany House Publishers, a division of Baker Publishing Group

Printed in the United States of America
1 2 3 4 5 6 7 21 20 19 18 17

This book is lovingly dedicated in
memory and honor of:

Cassidy Faith Hale

(March 14, 2000 —
September 16, 2015)

So young. So vibrant. So fun.

I wish I'd had more time with you.
More hugs. More laughter.

The past few months without
you have been so very
hard as we've walked with
your family through this
journey. But even through the
heartache, there is joy.

Joy in the memories.

Joy in the knowledge of where you
are—
No more tears. No more pain.

Joy in the anticipation of
seeing you again —
and praising our Lord forever.

Joy in the lives touched and changed
on this earth
by you — because you dared
to shine your light.

You've inspired us all.

Your light — *His light* — is still shining.

I'm gonna let it shine . . .

A NOTE FROM THE AUTHORS

We are overjoyed that you have chosen to join us for yet another journey into our great country's history. Again — as with our other collaborations — we'd like to reiterate that while this novel is rich with historical detail about Curry, Alaska, its incredible Curry Hotel, the Alaska Railroad, Talkeetna, Denali (Mount McKinley), and the people who lived and breathed this little bit of history — please remember that this is a work of fiction. While many real people are used in the story, their personalities and dialogue are from our imaginations. Please see the Dear Reader letter at the conclusion of the book to find out more details about the amazing research for this series and the author liberties that were taken.

We (Kimberley and Tracie) are passionate about Alaska. Kim's family lived there for many years and Tracie has spent oodles of time in that great state as well. On our last book tour together, our readers told us over and over how excited they were for another Alaska book. So here it is.

Curry, Alaska, and the grand Curry Hotel were very real indeed, although now the only way to see it is through the lens of historical photographs. At mile 248 on the Alaska Railroad today there are interpretive signs and a few lost remnants of Curry. The historic Curry Lookout is the only remaining piece still standing of this fascinating part of Alaska's history.

To give you a glimpse into this time and setting, we'd like to share an excerpt from the Preface of a book written by one of the team that was the very first to summit the tallest mountain in North America, Denali, back in 1913. Hudson Stuck's passion for Alaska, its peoples, its lands, and its mountains is commendable to this day. And one hundred years after the publication of his book, we would see the author's wish and desire come to fruition as the Great Mountain was rightly given back his true name: *Denali.*

From *The Ascent of Denali* by Hudson Stuck (Scribner, 1914):

Forefront in this book, because forefront in the author's heart and desire, must stand a plea for the restoration to the greatest mountain in North America of its immemorial native name. If there be any prestige or authority in such matter from the accomplishment of a first complete ascent, "if there be any virtue, if there be any praise," the author values it chiefly as it may give weight to this plea.

It is now little more than seventeen years ago that a prospector penetrated from the south into the neighborhood of this mountain, guessed its height with remarkable accuracy at twenty thousand feet, and, ignorant of any name that it already bore, placed upon it the name of the Republican candidate for President of the United States at the approaching election — William McKinley . . .

. . . The author would add, perhaps quite unnecessarily, yet lest any should mistake, a final personal note. He is no professed explorer or climber or "scientist," but a missionary, and of these matters an amateur only. The vivid recollection of a back bent down with burdens and lungs at the limit of their function makes him hesitate to describe this enterprise as recreation. It was the most laborious undertaking with which he was ever connected; yet it was done for the pleasure of doing it, and the pleasure far outweighed the pain. But he is concerned much more with men than mountains, and would say, since "out of the fullness of the heart the mouth speaketh," that his especial and growing concern, these ten years past, is with the native people of Alaska, a gentle and kindly race, now threatened with a wanton and senseless extermination, and sadly in need of generous champions if that threat is to be averted.

And so, dear friends, we take you back a century to the dawn of a new era for Alaska. A new national park, the first successful attempt to climb Denali, the people who loved the land, the pioneers who blazed the trails, the railroad that connected it all, and the incredible Curry Hotel in the remote Alaska Territory.

We give you: *In the Shadow of Denali.*

Kim and Tracie

PROLOGUE

1917

Henry Brennan — the insufferable man — should've been dead.

But he wasn't.

Frank Irving cursed his luck. His partner was still very much alive.

It was all the fault of that too-good, overzealous guide.

It wouldn't be so bad if Frank hadn't been the one to hire John Ivanoff. But he had.

How was he to know the man was a native Alaskan who'd climbed around Mount McKinley so many times he had private nicknames for certain parts? He'd thought John sounded so normal, and *Ivanoff* was Russian.

He'd certainly seemed perfect on paper. Solid reputation as a guide — which Henry required — but no actual full-ascent experience, so he could be blamed for any fatal accident — which Frank required.

"Gentlemen, we need to take advantage of this good weather," the guide called from outside the tent. "Be ready to leave in ten minutes."

Fighting the urge to lose his breakfast, a sign of the altitude sickness he and Henry both shared, Frank began to shove everything into his pack. John Ivanoff was nothing but a tyrant.

Who knew the man would end up being such a conscientious guide, especially after he agreed to shorten the preparation schedule from six months to eight weeks? Such a man should be easy to buy, especially because John dreamed of opening his own mountaineering guided tour business. But no! He was another of those churchy Bible-thumpers like Henry. It made Frank twitch.

The side walls of the tent shifted with another gust of frigid mountain wind. Frank and Henry had made a fortune the past twenty years selling these very same tents to all the gold-rush-fever idiots who stopped in their Seattle store before heading to Alaska. It had been Frank's idea to make a killing off of all the crazies who thought dashing off to the frozen north to dig for gold would be their pot at the end of the rainbow. But he hadn't planned to stay in a tent himself. Ever. Especially not at the top of a mountain. And definitely not for this many weeks.

But desperate times called for desperate measures. And he was desperate.

Desperate to call the profits his own.

Not just half. *All.*

That's why he'd cooked up this hare-brained plan to climb Mount McKinley. He was tired of sharing with his partner. And they'd signed an agreement when they started the company. So if he eliminated Henry . . .

It'd all be his.

So here he was. On the side of this stupid mountain. They'd trained for months on lesser mountains and talked of all the equipment they would try out and then advertise to sell.

Henry had been thrilled. The do-gooder. Always an outdoorsman, he didn't want to give up his own exploring for a job in the office at the factory.

So the opportunity was born. New national park. Big, treacherous mountain.

It was remote. And bound to be a place where a tragic mishap could occur and nothing could be done about it.

It all seemed so easy.

But then John Ivanoff happened. The man was everywhere, constantly watching. And

— unfortunately — prepared for any possible scenario.

It should not have taken this long to find a way to get rid of Henry, but Frank couldn't do it when the native haulers were with them — too many witnesses — and he definitely couldn't finagle it with all the sled dogs around. They'd find the body for sure. So he'd waited.

As the helpers, sleds, and dogs stayed behind, the paths got steeper and the air got thinner. And his patience thinned right along with it. But he'd come this far. He might as well finish the climb. Perhaps it would even be good for business to make it to the top and then have tragedy befall them. He'd have the acclaim of the press for his success *and* the sympathy of the public for his loss.

Frank swept the tent flap aside, stepped into the frigid wind, and grimaced.

John coiled a rope, a sappy smile on his face. "We have to cross Cassidy Lane today. It's dangerous, but one of my favorite places on Denali."

The native name for Mount McKinley rolled off John's tongue with ease and some sort of weird reverence. Frank found it annoying. Since the President of the United States had signed something called the

14

Mount McKinley Park Bill, that's what the mountain should be called. Not that Frank cared two nickels about the name. But, as Henry pointed out, it meant he and Frank could claim to be the first climbers to reach the peak *in* Mount McKinley National Park. Some team back in 1913 had a documented ascent, but that was before the new national park bill had been signed into effect. Not that it mattered. Frank only cared about the opportunity this afforded to be rid of his partner. He was tired of this wretched mountain.

"Cassidy Lane?" Henry poked his head out of the second tent he'd shared with the guide, since Frank hated to share and was adamant that he wanted privacy. "Named for your daughter?" He emerged with his pack, a knitted cap in hand and a fur hat dangling over one arm.

"Sure is." John kept winding the rope like it was as natural to him as breathing. "It's a dangerous, narrow path along a cliff. I almost fell off it once."

Frank's heart rate perked up. This was promising. "How long ago?"

"Many years." John's face sobered. "The weather changed on us instantly. What had been a calm, bright day like this one sud-denly turned fierce."

15

Another gust of wind almost lifted Frank off his feet. This was calm?

"I didn't think I was going to make it." John reached the end of the rope, the loops perfectly matched. "But I kept thinking of my Cassidy, recalling every memory from the time she was born up to then, until I made it home."

Henry put down his pack, then pulled on the black knitted cap over his graying hair. Just the night before he'd told Frank they needed to experiment with different materials to find or create something that would be better at holding in body heat. Especially at these temperatures. He'd even tried to convince Frank that one tent would be better than two — less to carry, and they could share body heat. But Frank would have none of it. It was just one more reason he hated his partner. The man always came up with the most marvelous ideas and of course was given all the credit.

"When I told Cassidy — much later, of course — she made light of it and said that if I ever got here again, I would just have to take another trip down Cassidy Lane and I'd be sure to make it home."

"Instead of Memory Lane? How delightful." Henry slapped the guide's shoulder, the same sentimental smile on his face as the one John had worn a minute ago.

Frank wanted to lose the contents of his stomach right then and there. This time, however, it had nothing to do with altitude sickness. Fatherhood made saps of even the strongest men. Henry had been all but worthless since his brats had come along. Rushing home to be with his family instead of shouldering his fair share. Talking to customers about his son or one of the girls. How many did they have? Two? Three? Didn't matter. Because Henry's repellent brood wouldn't inherit any part of The Brennan/Irving Company. The business contract Henry and Frank signed when they first opened stipulated that should one partner die, the other partner inherited full control.

Which was why this plan worked.

He'd make a show of supporting the grieving family — with everything but actual money. Martha Brennan was a comely enough woman. She'd remarry, move away, and The Brennan/Irving Company would become The Irving Company.

No more sharing profits. No more running each and every idea by Henry. No more of the honesty-at-all-times practice. No more faking he actually liked these people.

Stupid Henry. Didn't he know how much money they could make now that they'd established a reputation for selling the best ropes, tents, and climbing attire in the Pacific Northwest? Now was the time to *cut* quality and boost profits.

Henry gave John another hearty pat on the back, then donned the fur hat and tied it. "What say you, expert guide? We still a go for the summit today?"

John nodded, glancing upward. "Yes, but as you can see, the clouds are draping him today. Once we reach the top, you'll have a beautiful view of the clouds below."

It bugged Frank that John called the mountain "he" and "him" all the time, but to be fair, everything about John Ivanoff, Henry Brennan, and this blasted mountain made Frank furious.

"Any danger of storms?"

"There's always that danger here. I don't see any immediate threat, but remember, storms roll in fast." John threw the heavy rope over his shoulder. "If you two are ready to go, I think we should head up. I've already done my tests on the ropes and ice climbs for today."

"We're already at 18,500 feet." Frank huffed for breath. "There's less than two thousand feet to reach the summit."

John nodded. "Two thousand feet that will take us at least six hours."

"Both ways?" Frank felt all the energy leave him. Would it never end?

Chuckling, John shook his head. "Well, we could always let gravity work with us on the trip down — if you'd like to go faster."

Henry pulled on his pack with what appeared little effort. "Well, I say let's go. I'm anxious to finish this climb, and I must say that sleeping in a warm bed in front of a roaring fire sounds awfully good after four long weeks trudging and climbing in the ice and snow. I'd like to have full feeling back in my hands and feet." He shook his head and patted his partner's back. "But that's why we're doing it, right? To experience the thrill for our customers?"

Reminding himself to play along, Frank tried to sound excited and supportive. "Lots and lots of customers. Yes. That's the plan. If the government would just get the road built into this area, we could bring more customers than we could ever imagine. All with John as our guide. We just won't tell the customers about not feeling their fingers and toes." He laughed too loud for his own ears.

"Of course." John's smile looked a little uneasy.

"Lead on, then." Frank ducked his head and adjusted his thick gloves over a thinner pair. No use giving away that John's dream of being their business partner for guided tours was as doomed as Henry's of a warm bed.

Henry carried a long walking stick — one carved with their names and the date — that they planned to drive into the snow at the top later that day. His eagerness shone in his eyes as he nodded to John. "I'm ready. Let's go!"

By two in the afternoon, their weary troop reached the southern peak of Mount McKinley. Even as the wind tried to knock him off his feet and the air was too thin for a decent breath, Frank couldn't help feeling a little euphoric. "We did it, boys . . . We're the first ones . . . to climb Mount . . . McKinley in the new . . . Mount McKinley National Park." His sentences were punctured by the many breaths he had to take.

Henry handed John the wooden pole. "The honor . . . should go . . . to you."

No it shouldn't!

But the guide grinned and plunged the marker into the snow. "Success!"

Hardly, but there was always hope. A hearty gale from the west brought his attention up. The clouds moved in at a rapid clip and were tinged an ominous gray.

"We need to get down, and quickly," John yelled and waved a hand at the clouds. "That doesn't bode well."

They hurried to take a few pictures. Henry and John wanted to have a visual record of the trip, and Henry thought it would make for great advertising. Of course he was right, but it only made Frank's hatred grow. And all he really cared about was getting rid of the man and getting off the wretched mountain.

With the pictures taken, Henry went to repack the camera.

"Here, let me . . . put it in mine," Frank said. "You need . . . to get your pack on . . . and your hands are shaking." No sense losing the camera and photographs if he had any success eliminating his problem.

"Thanks." Henry nodded. "A man never had a better partner." He slipped his backpack on again and moved to John's side as snow began to fall. "Do we have . . . time to get to safety?"

"Yes, if we . . . move fast. But stay sure of . . . your footing. Going down is often . . . more dangerous and . . . time-consuming. Be prepared for the gusts of wind . . . that may try to knock you off your feet, and

21

blowing snow . . . can disorient you, so hold tight to the rope between us." John looked back to the clouds above. "We should try to get to camp. If that's not possible, we'll make a shelter on the way and ride out the storm." The building clouds blocked out the sun that only minutes ago had been quite intense. John handed a rope to Henry. "Secure it around you. This doesn't look good at all."

"I have a bad feeling . . ." Henry's words were lost in a swirl of wind and snow.

Frank took as deep a breath as he could at twenty thousand feet. Fear lurked behind John's eyes, which didn't bode well for the plan. Only one person was supposed to die up here. Not him, not even John.

Just Henry.

1

Curry, Alaska — Mile 248 on the Alaska
  Railroad

Cassidy Faith Ivanoff walked up the stairs from the basement of the Curry Hotel with a massive tray in her hands. The staff was all abuzz. The railroad was finally about to be completed, and there were hushed whispers about the President of the United States coming to stay in their hotel as well. Imagine that. The President himself! Here, in Alaska. As far as she knew, no other President had ever visited the territory. It would bring Alaska to the attention of the rest of the country.

With the completion of the railroad connecting Seward to Fairbanks, the Curry Hotel was the ideal mid-journey stopping point. It had been built by the railroad not only for guests and tourists, but also for workers. Rumor had it a large town was sure to develop around the beautiful hotel. But right now there were only a few buildings from when the community had been called Deadhorse — a water tower, a roundhouse, and a power plant to generate electricity.

But Cassidy could imagine the growth and it excited her. The months had flown by since she'd first been hired as the cook's assistant at the spacious and luxurious hotel. Born and raised in Alaska, Cassidy and her father had been quite familiar with the area. Dad signed on to lead guests on guided tours, while Cassidy's passion for cooking made her a natural for the kitchen.

Unfortunately, cooking wasn't always the focus of her duties. In fact, she spent what felt like half of her time climbing up and down the stairs between the basement kitchen, provision rooms, and the main-level kitchen. Why they ever built the provisions rooms downstairs was beyond her. Must've been a man who designed it. Who never had to work in a big hotel like this.

"Cassidy, when you finish with the pickled onions, I need you to start on the crab salad." Margaret Johnson's voice prevailed across the room.

"Yes, Mrs. Johnson." The woman amazed Cassidy day in and day out. A hard woman, she was the hotel's head cook and Cassidy's boss. Rumor had it that she'd beaten out some big chef from San Francisco for the job. The manager insisted on calling Mrs. Johnson "Chef," but she still labeled herself as the cook. She ran the kitchen from 5:00 a.m. until 9:00 p.m. when the night cook took over. But he couldn't tie his shoes without her approval. Even off duty, she ran that kitchen. Day or night. And everyone knew it.

Cassidy smiled as she set the tray down and filled the elegant serving dishes with the pungent hors d'oeuvres.

No-nonsense and a little rough around the edges, Mrs. Johnson kept Cassidy on her toes. And Cassidy loved it. There had been few women in her life, but those who had been part of her upbringing were in many ways just like Mrs. Johnson. Blunt and to the point, without beating around the bush. It allowed for no doubt as to what was expected. But it tended to make Cassidy feel a little . . . lonely.

Setting the tray off to the side to be chilled, Cassidy reached for the crab legs and peeked at the woman barking orders to the kitchen hands. True, everyone else feared — even dreaded — the head cook, but beneath that gruff exterior, there was a glimmer of something deep and soothing.

Cassidy already had a soft spot in her heart for her.

Never having a memory of her mother, Cassidy found she often craved the company of older women, and she liked and respected Margaret Johnson. Maybe over time . . . they could be friends.

"Quit your day-dreaming, Cassidy Faith. We have hundreds of mouths to feed a fancy dinner to and I won't allow you to mess up the schedule."

And maybe not.

The two girls washing dishes giggled at the sink. Everyone knew that if Cook used your middle name, she was more than serious.

"Sorry, Mrs. Johnson." She couldn't keep from smiling to herself — she could always try, right? She donned her protective gloves, broke the shell of the first crab leg before her, and started pulling out the thick pink-and-white meat. Sweet and rich, it was one of Cassidy's favorites. She had lived off the land and sea of Alaska her entire twenty-three years.

Her father, John, was half-Athabaskan and had met and fallen in love with an Irish missionary's daughter. When the missionary couple heard of seventeen-year-old Eliza's plans to marry this native man, they were appalled at the "mixing of races" and demanded Eliza turn her back on John. But Eliza defied her parents and married him anyway.

Only a year passed before she died right after childbirth, and her parents left Alaska and told John it was God's punishment. They wouldn't even see Cassidy or acknowledge her existence.

Cassidy grew up knowing that she had been named after a family surname on her maternal grandparents' side, but she hated that she would never know them or know where her name came from. How could anyone turn their back on family? It baffled her to no end. Even after all these years. Strangely she felt as if it were all her fault — that she'd done something wrong without having had any say in the matter whatsoever. Dad assured her that this wasn't the case, that pain had driven her grandparents to make the choice they'd made. Still, it haunted Cassidy. She'd tried for years to imagine how she might go about contacting her grandparents and healing the division between them and her father, but there never seemed to be even a hint of what might work. She had no idea of where her grandparents had gone or even if they were still alive.

The shells piled up as she made swift work of the crab. The thoughts and memories kept her mind spinning and her hands busy.

Her middle name, Faith, was the last gift she'd been given by her mother. Over the years Dad had told Cassidy how Eliza Ivanoff prayed over her baby, blessed her with her name, and took her last breath. He'd challenged Cassidy to live up to her name on more than one occasion.

Just recently, in fact. A few months ago, when they'd left their home of Tanana — the only place she'd ever called home — to come work in Curry, Dad said it would be a grand step of faith. And so it was.

Cassidy would never have guessed the blessings that would come by taking that step. But she was indeed blessed.

She loved it here.

The Curry Hotel was more magnificent than any building Cassidy had ever seen. From the rich red carpets, the dark woods, and the deep leather chairs in the lobby, all the way to the gleaming kitchen with its Duparquet range and shiny aluminum and copper pots. There were even electric lights and hot water. Such things were never seen in most of Alaska, and yet they were here in Curry. The Alaska Railroad had outdone itself. And the enormous number of visitors proved its success.

She hadn't understood at the time that her Dad needed something different. After the successful summit of Mount McKinley in 1917, he'd changed. Maybe because he'd always wanted to open a guide service and that wouldn't be happening anytime soon — especially since the park still wasn't easily accessible — and maybe because having lost one of his climbers weighed him down. He'd probably never get over the loss, even though he'd told Cassidy that the man loved the Lord and was certain to be in heaven.

Their faith in God was also the Ivanoffs' foundation for living, and her father preferred to work with people who were of like mind. She'd only been seventeen when her father made that climb, but she knew that he blamed himself for the death of the climber. He took responsibility for getting the men up the mountain and returning them safely back down. Losing one of his clients had devastated her strong father, and she wasn't at all certain he would ever fully recover. It had stolen a good deal of his joy and brought plans for his own business to a rather abrupt halt. So he'd been working for the railroad all these years as an expert on the land and game. He'd supplied the workers with food and had been useful to the company in plotting out the best route. Highly esteemed by all who knew him, John Ivanoff was the best man she'd ever known. But even with that and the railroad's success, Cassidy knew her dad maintained a sense of failure.

"When you're done with that box, there's a second one waiting," Mrs. Johnson reminded her of the present task.

"Yes, Mrs. Johnson." Cassidy heard the agitation in the older woman's voice. Mrs. Johnson always worried about the clock and whether everything would be done in a timely manner. So far they had never missed serving a meal on time or in the finest presentation, but still the woman worried, so Cassidy did her best to speed up her actions. She wanted to please Mrs. Johnson for many reasons, not the least of which was her desire to earn the woman's respect and friendship. Even with all of her efforts, however, the task proved difficult. Mrs. Johnson wasn't one for frivolities, which apparently included friendships. The woman had little to do with anyone during the working hours — except of course to command her staff into perfect order. Then, when the workday concluded, Mrs. Johnson went off to her quarters to be alone. She seldom was seen at all in her off-hours. But

Cassidy wasn't going to be deterred. She had faith that if she pursued the friendship with Mrs. Johnson, it would eventually come about.

Cassidy's hands worked through more than a hundred crab legs from the first box and started in on the next. The scent of Mrs. Johnson's famous Parker House rolls filled the kitchen and made Cassidy smile. She and Dad had many challenges to face in their duties, but taking their place among the Curry Hotel staff seemed right. Yes, this had been a good step of faith for them both. And the excitement and challenge of the Curry Hotel made her happier than she could've dreamed. It made her father happy that they could work in a capacity that allowed him to keep an eye on her. The Alaska Territory was still more than seventy-five percent male, and she liked the protectiveness of her father. It also didn't hurt that she found comfort in being able to keep a closer eye on him as well.

As the resident recreational guide, John Ivanoff led hiking and fishing tours for the guests. He taught them all about Alaska's incredible wild flowers, berries, and plants, and helped them reel in large trophy fish to take pictures of and show their families back home. Then there were the truly adventurous groups that would travel by boat across the river and hike for miles up the ridge to gain the spectacular view of the High One and the surrounding mountains. He'd been kept very busy, and Cassidy was thankful that he was soon to have a full-time assistant to help.

"Thomas!" Mrs. Johnson's shrill tone made everyone jump, and all work clattered to an abrupt halt.

Cassidy laid a hand on her chest. That certainly jolted her out of day-dreaming. As she looked around the room, she spotted the seventeen-year-old kitchen boy, a wobbling stack of pots behind him. His face was ashen as he quaked in his boots. Oh bother, what had he done this time to rile the cook? A resounding crash behind the boy gave everyone the answer. He closed his eyes in resignation.

Several of the kitchen maids giggled.

"Kindly remember, Thomas, that you cannot haphazardly stack the large pots. There is a system, and everything must be in its place." Mrs. Johnson's tone was at least a tad softer than her initial screech.

More giggles.

"And there will be no laughter at Thomas's plight." Their boss rounded on the young women, hands on her hips. "Or I will have you scrub the floor by hand."

Straight faces and nods answered as they rushed back to their duties.

The bustle of the kitchen began again, but Thomas stood anchored to the floor, his cap in his hand.

"Cassidy, please assist Thomas in the proper placement of the kitchenware."

"Yes, Mrs. Johnson." Cassidy smiled at the young man as the older woman walked away. "Let's get this sorted, shall we? I must hurry and get back to the crab salad."

He nodded. And his stomach rumbled loud enough for Cassidy to hear.

She tried to cover for his embarrassment. "If you look closely, each shelf is labeled with the size of the pot that sits there. Only two in each stack. But once you learn it, it's not hard. They really just go in order of size from the smallest to the largest of big stock-pots. All the other pots hang from the ceiling over there, but you probably can see that for yourself. Just don't forget to line these handles up. She can't stand for any of them to be crooked on the shelves. She always says it's for ease of picking them up."

Grabbing the huge cauldrons from the floor, Thomas sighed. "I'm sorry I was in too big of a hurry to notice." Another big sigh as he fumbled with a large pot that probably outweighed him. "Seems I can't do anything right. If I'm too slow, I get hollered at, and if I try to speed up, things aren't done properly and I *still* get hollered at."

"You're learning, Thomas. And that's what matters. Mrs. Johnson may be tough, but she's fair. Pay attention and do your best. Besides, she knows you're still growing and all of us were clumsy in those stages." Cassidy stepped back to let him settle the items in their places. "And you know what? Next time you feel you're being 'hollered' at, why don't you just remember that they're doing it to teach you the correct way."

"You're always so positive." Thomas smiled down at her as he placed the last pot in its place. He stood back, looked at his work, and then reached forward, straightening the handles. "Thank you for always being so nice to me, and for your help."

"Oh, we were all your age at one time and have had to learn new jobs. The hotel only opened in March, so we'll keep learning together." Cassidy turned and wiped down her apron. Then she threw over her shoulder, "And I like being positive — makes the world a bit sunnier, don't you agree?"

"But it's so embarrassing to fall down and drop things. I admit it's been nice to finally grow taller 'cause I was always the shortest in my class. But my brain doesn't seem to know the difference, and my feet keep getting in the way." He followed her back through the kitchen.

"Everyone has to go through growing pangs. Give it time. You're doing just fine." She grabbed a roll off the cooling rack. "Here, eat this quick. It should help you through the next hour." Looking at Thomas broke her heart. He seemed so down. "You know what? I have an idea."

"Will it help me not be such an oaf around here?" He downed the roll in two bites.

Poor Thomas. She nodded. "Like I said, we all go through that stage. But I was an exceptionally clumsy child. I tripped over everything — even nothing at all — and fell down constantly. My dad always had a funny saying for me after he'd picked me up and brushed me off. It made me smile and maybe it will help you." She looked down at the pile of crab meat and the crab legs left to shell.

"What'd he say?"

Cassidy bit her lip. Maybe it was a bit silly for this boy who was almost a man. "Well . . . I'm a bit embarrassed to say it."

"Go on."

"It'll have to be our little secret." She

35

leaned closer and winked.

He cracked a half smile and the twinkle in his eyes was back. "I promise."

"Well, you see, I loved to give hugs. Always have, really. And not just people. I hugged our dogs, the pigs, chickens — I even tried to hug a squirrel once. That one didn't go over too well with the squirrel, I'm sorry to say."

He snickered and covered his mouth. "Sorry, I was just picturing it."

She gave him a smile and gathered the celery and onions she needed for the salad. "Anyway, after I would fall down, my dad would say, 'I guess the floor needed a hug.' " Cassidy couldn't help but laugh at the memory now. "I can't tell you how many times I hugged the floor . . . or the stairs . . . or a rock, a log, or the grass."

He laughed out loud.

Mrs. Johnson cleared her throat across the kitchen.

Thomas straightened. "I best get back to work. Thanks again, Miss Ivanoff. I'll never look at falling down the same way again." His smile was as big as his face.

"You're welcome. Now off you go. I'm sure you have quite a list to accomplish, as do I." She handed him another roll.

Thomas tucked the roll in his apron

pocket and walked out of the kitchen.

Mrs. Johnson joined Cassidy. "I suppose he did a decent job. At least the handles are straight."

"He really wants to please you." Cassidy pulled her gloves back out of her apron. "He's such a good young man."

Her boss shook her head. "I appreciate you encouraging him, but it seems he makes double the work for everyone."

"He's young and learning to handle himself." Cassidy hoped Mrs. Johnson wasn't thinking of having him fired. "I'm sure he'll improve."

Mrs. Johnson looked less than convinced. "Perhaps with any luck at all. Now. If we could just keep him from catastrophe for a whole day . . ."

Cassidy patted her arm and smiled. "But then we wouldn't know what to do with ourselves. He keeps us alert, doesn't he?"

The head cook huffed. "But what I wouldn't give for just one *dull* day around here."

A hush fell over the kitchen and Cassidy turned around.

"I'm sorry, Chef Johnson, but that won't be happening today." The hotel manager's eyes glowed with mirth. And since he rarely visited the kitchen — normally just sent a messenger — his presence meant big news.

Mrs. Johnson sauntered forward with her hands clasped in front. "Well, you could have at least let me dream it for a moment, Mr. Bradley."

He raised an eyebrow and kept smiling at their head cook. Not many people could get away with teasing the woman. "I shall remember that for future notice." He cleared his throat. "We have a fancy group with the *Brooklyn Daily Eagle* coming up for a formal dedication of the Mount McKinley National Park. It is a large group of about seventy, and we have been asked to help host and provide food for the ceremony. A number of staff will be asked to go along as well to assist and serve."

Mrs. Johnson didn't even flinch at the news. "We are up to the task, Mr. Bradley. Just let me know when."

He grinned and turned partially back to the stairs. "Just as I knew you would be. And as to the *when* — it's tomorrow."

2

A large cloud of steam escaped from the engine as Allan Brennan boarded the train. Finally. He'd made it to the Alaska Territory.

Claiming a seat by the window, Allan nodded at the conductor.

"Ticket?" the man asked as a dozen or so men poured into the car. Their boisterous voices all but drowned out the older man's voice. He punched the ticket and handed it back to Allan before moving on down the aisle.

With his bag stowed, Allan settled in to enjoy the scenery. The journey by Alaska Steamship from Seattle to Seward had been rough as far as the seas were concerned, but the beauty had been far beyond what he could ever imagine. All the tales his father told him were true.

Alaska truly was God's glorious display. There was nothing he'd ever seen that could compare. The men around him must have been used to the sight as more than one of them pulled their cap down over their eyes and settled in to sleep.

The weariness of travel was upon him, but Allan never could sleep sitting up. Besides, there were too many memories and thoughts of the future barreling through his mind to allow sleep to claim him. No matter how tired his body.

As the train gained speed, the swaying and rocking steadied into a constant rhythm. Leaning his head back, he wished his father could be with him. He'd spent his whole life following Henry Brennan around. Hiking, climbing, fishing, hunting. It didn't matter; if it was outdoors, they'd done it together.

Until it was time for college.

Then his father insisted he get a good education. But Allan wanted nothing more than to work by his father's side in the family company.

"The time for that will come, son. There will be plenty of work for you to do once you've finished college."

And with that insistence, Allan headed for the university. No sooner had he finished his schooling than the United States joined the war in Europe. His father and his business partner, Frank, were planning a grand expedition to scale Mount McKinley and Allan had planned to go with them, but the government needed men to fight in Europe and so he went to war instead. If only he could turn back the clock.

The last time he'd seen his father was a farewell at the train depot in Seattle as Allan headed off to become Captain Brennan and serve his country.

"I'm very proud of you, son," his father had said. "You will be in my prayers constantly. Just remember that even in this turn of events, God has a plan. And don't worry about climbing McKinley. The mountain will still be there when the war is over."

But his father wouldn't. Allan learned only a few months later that his father successfully summited Mount McKinley but had not survived the descent. The letter from his mother had found Allan at the front.

In the middle of a horrific battle, he learned he no longer had a father. And the thought threatened to crush him. He'd tried to harden himself to the news as grief clawed its way up his throat and almost overpowered him, but the war raged on around him and reminded him all too often of his loss. The more men he lost on the battlefield, the more he worked to bury his own sorrow. Life would never be the same again.

Returning home to Seattle and his father's company after the war didn't help. Henry Brennan was everywhere — which soothed and hurt all at the same time. Even though Frank Irving was a longtime family friend, he'd changed since Henry's death and angrily placed the blame on their expedition guide.

Allan inherited half of his father's share of the business as the only son, while the rest went to his father's partner. But it didn't change the fact that he had no desire to work in the factory. It was just too much after the loss of his father and the devastating effects of the war. So putting the entire company in Frank's capable hands in the meantime, he left his mother, Seattle, his sisters and their husbands, and headed off to learn more about mountain climbing. The only real connection he felt he had left with his father was Mount McKinley in Alaska.

And now he was on his way. After all these years.

The train slowed.

"Anchorage!" the conductor announced as he passed through the car. "Next stop, Anchorage!"

Some of the men moved toward the exit even while the train was still moving. The sound of metal on metal could be heard as the brakes brought the train to a stop. Allan cast a quick glance out the window. It didn't look like much of a town.

Several men disembarked with large duffel bags, no doubt workers for the railroad. Some of the remaining appeared to be sleeping, while a few at the end of the aisle were engaged in a heated argument. Just when Allan thought things might get out of hand, one of the men burst into laughter and slapped another on the back. The others joined in the merriment and things settled back down.

Two men entered Allan's car. The first was a young lad with nothing but a flour sack stuffed with what must be his belongings. He slipped into a seat beside one of the sleeping passengers. The second, an older gentleman, nodded to the seat across from Allan.

"This seat taken?"

"No. You're welcome to it." Allan offered a smile.

"Name's John." The newcomer removed his black fedora and held out his hand.

He shook it. "Allan. Nice to meet you."

"All aboard," the conductor called from

outside the window. He'd no sooner given the call than the train lurched forward and chugged slowly out of the station.

Stowing his hat above him, John ran a hand through his hair. "I love train travel." The man sat and looked out the window. "These puffer-belly steam locomotives sure are amazing, aren't they?"

"Indeed they are." Allan hadn't thought too much on the subject, but agreed anyway. "Do you live in Anchorage?"

"No, no. I was just there on some business for the railroad. How about you?"

"It's my first time in Alaska."

"Oh? Well, let me congratulate you on your choice to visit God's country! I hope you love it. My homeland is a little bit of heaven — even if it is much removed from the rest of the world."

Allan chuckled. "Thank you. It definitely is far removed — I didn't realize *how* far until this journey. I've heard stories all my life, but haven't made it until now." He felt his smile diminish. "The war held me up for a bit and then . . ." This poor stranger didn't deserve his melancholy memories. "It doesn't matter. I'm glad to be here."

"So what brings you up here?"

"A number of things." Allan paused, uncertain how much he wanted to say. "I'd

44

heard so much about it that I wanted to see Alaska for myself. I also took a job. That's why I want to know everything I can." The conversation focused all on him made him uncomfortable. Time to change the subject. "What do you know about Mount McKinley?"

"Oh, more than we have time for on this train ride." John leaned forward, his eagerness apparent. "In fact, up until the age of twelve, I lived just north of the High One — er . . . Mount McKinley. Then when my father died, we moved to Tanana. I've lived there until recently." John smiled. "What would you like to know about the mountain?"

"Is it really as massive and dangerous as the stories I've heard?"

"Yes, indeed. It's over twenty thousand feet and a treacherous beast to climb. The weather is unpredictable, and an earthquake a few years back changed the landscape of the mountain and its glaciers. Oh, but what a view."

Allan leaned forward too. "Does this mean you've climbed it?" A thrill started in his toes and raced up his spine. There were only a handful of men who had climbed the king of the Alaska Range.

"I have." The man's face fell and he

looked out the window and leaned back. "But that's a story for another day."

Maybe the man never made it to the summit. Precious few had. "So you must know a lot about the other mountains in the Alaska Range as well?"

He nodded but kept his gaze toward the window. Several moments passed with only the *clackety-clack* of the train to fill the space around them. "They are the most beautiful sight in all the world. Sultana — Denali's . . . McKinley's Wife, stands just to the west and south of him. Beautiful and even more dangerous, she's incredibly steep — much more so than the High One."

"Why do you call it Denali and the High One?"

John's dark eyes twinkled. "Because that's his name. I'm part native Alaskan — Ahtna-Athabaskan, to be precise. The native peoples of this great land named the mountains centuries ago. Denali means the High One. Sultana — or Mount Foraker, as you may know it — means the Wife."

Allan pulled a notepad and pencil out of his coat pocket. This would be good to take note of. "So who decided to call it McKinley?"

John chuckled. "That's a sore subject up here. It's only been in the last couple

46

decades, and many Alaskans aren't too keen on it. Let's just say a gold prospector did and leave it at that."

The story intrigued him, but he respected the man's reserve. He seemed so knowledgeable and yet something seemed to hold him back. There was so much to learn. Maybe the gentleman thought it best to not overwhelm him. But Allan pushed on with his questions. He simply couldn't resist. "What about bear and moose? I've heard they're abundant and that gold prospectors had a lot of trouble with them."

John looked at him with his smile back in place. "There's a lot of them, yes — also caribou, dall sheep, and wolves — but some of the prospectors' stories are a bit exaggerated. Besides, those prospectors invaded the natural habitat of the creatures, wouldn't you say?"

Allan thought about that for a moment and nodded. "You're right. In fact, isn't that why the President made it a national park to begin with — to protect the wild game?"

"Yes, he did. But they didn't have a superintendent to manage it until two years ago."

"How do you protect a national park with no one up here?"

"Exactly. There was a lot of poaching going on. But thankfully, they brought on Harry Karstens as superintendent. It's a huge job, but he's up for the challenge."

Allan leaned forward again. He knew that name. "Wait. The same Harry Karstens that was part of the first complete ascent of Mount McKinley? I read the book put out by his partner, Hudson Stuck."

"One and the same."

Guess there couldn't be a better choice than a man who knew and understood the mountain so well. "Does he have any help in his role as superintendent?"

"Not really. At least from what I hear, he's the only one paid for the job. And it's a big one."

"I can only imagine. There're still no roads in or out?"

"No. But the railroad does provide the access that will be needed for roads to be built farther into the park."

Writing down the facts he wanted to remember, Allan let the conversation die down. To think he was so close to where his father had last walked. Maybe there was some other explanation for what happened to Dad. He could only hope. His father's body had never been recovered, so maybe there was a clue on the mountain somewhere. But what chance did he have at climbing it? He'd been hired to do a job. He'd best focus on that first. One day, he would make it up the mountain. One day.

His mind filled with questions and he realized he had the perfect opportunity in front of him. "John, do you mind if I ask you more questions? If I'm going to be working up here, I'd like to learn everything I possibly can."

"I'm happy to help. It's always nice to pass the time with good conversation."

"I've read incredible stories about the gold rush up here. Is there really gold for everyone?"

John chuckled. "If only that were true. Well, I take that back. I would venture to say there's enough gold for the world up here, but it sure would take a lot of men, a lot of work, and hundreds of years to bring it out."

As the train passed through thick trees and brush, Allan realized how true that statement had been. There wasn't much "civilization" in Alaska yet and from what he could tell, there wouldn't be for quite a while. "So what about the stories that talk of huge berries, and salmon that can be pulled out of the streams with your bare hands?"

"Those are true. You just have to know

where to find them." John crossed his legs and rested his hand on one knee. "My favorite are the salmonberries."

For some reason that didn't sound appetizing. "There's a berry that tastes like fish?"

"Heavens, no!" John's laughter filled the car, causing several of the men to momentarily glance their way. "They're just *called* salmonberries. Look like giant raspberries and can be orange, white, or pink."

The rest of the afternoon passed in good conversation and Allan filling his notepad with scribbled notes. It was easy to forget his exhaustion while conversing with John. The man was a consummate storyteller and walking encyclopaedia.

Eventually, the train began a steady deceleration.

John stretched. "Well, we should be getting close to Curry. That's our stop. If you're continuing on, you'll spend the night there."

"Curry is my final stop as well." Allan reached a hand forward. "It was a pleasure, John. Thank you for your abundant insight. I'm sure my new boss will appreciate the crash course you gave me."

"It was *my* pleasure. You are most welcome. I hope we will see much more of one another." John clasped Allan's hand and shook it.

The train puffed and squealed as it pulled into Curry. Chaos ensued as soon as the train came to a stop. Allan grabbed his belongings and his hat and followed John out of the car.

They stepped onto the platform, and in the crowd a young lady with dark hair smiled and waved. Her eyes seemed to twinkle. "Dad!"

A massive two-story structure dominated his view. A couple of bay windows framed the lower level on either side of the canopy denoting the Curry Hotel Depot. The broad wooden platform stretched from one end of the hotel to the other and beyond. And all this. In the middle of nowhere.

"Dad!" The waving young beauty drew closer.

John chuckled and turned to him. "That's my daughter. It's nice to have a welcoming party, isn't it? Let me know if you need anything. Just ask anyone at the hotel for John Ivanoff and they'll find me." He walked away and toward his daughter.

Everything seemed to stop. Allan felt his pulse pounding in his ears. Ivanoff? John Ivanoff?

The noise of the platform died away.

51

Looking from side to side, Allan tried to shake the feeling. But the world blurred around him instead. Several moments passed before he could see straight. Then his hearing returned. The engine behind him gave a huge huff. People were talking. Laughing. Milling about.

Off in the distance, the dark-haired lady held on to John's elbow as they walked into the hotel.

But how could this be?

Had he really just spent the day with the man responsible for his father's death?

3

Mr. Bradley claimed Cassidy's father as soon as they walked in the door.

"John, good to see you!" The men shook hands. "Your new trainee should have been on that train as well. Did you meet him?" Mr. Bradley rarely took time to wait for a response, much less breathe. Always too much to do. Too much to say. "The summer schedule is getting overly full, so you'll need to get him in shape as quick as possible." He turned to walk away. "Go find him. His name's Brennan. Allan Brennan." And with that, he headed for the main desk in the lobby, talking all the way. "Mrs. McGovern, I am in need of the books for today."

"He always needs something." Mrs. McGovern elbowed Cassidy.

Cassidy laughed. "He never stops, does he? Sometimes I don't even hear the words — they just seem to all meld together. Isn't that right, Dad?" Turning toward her father, she gasped. "Dad! You're pale as a sheet." Grabbing his arms, she steered him toward a leather chair by the fireplace. "What is it? Are you sick?"

He shook his head and sat. "Brennan. I had no idea." The words whispered on an exhale.

"What? That his last name was Brennan? I'm so confused." She lowered herself to look into his eyes. "Please tell me what's wrong."

"I'm fine."

"You don't seem fine."

Her father shook his head again and looked at her with a stiff smile. The light in his eyes when he greeted her off the train was gone. "Nothing to worry about." He stood up. "But I do need a favor. Would you mind finding the young man I was with on the train? You probably noticed us shaking hands when you were waving to me. He'll need to get settled and then I'll meet with him in an hour in the baggage room." His face was stern. "Can you do that?"

"Of course. I'm afraid I wasn't listening to Mr. Bradley's announcement all that close. What is the man's name?"

"Brennan," he whispered. "Allan Brennan."

Something wasn't right. Her dad had looked forward to the hiring of an assistant for weeks, so his sudden turn couldn't be in regard to that. And no matter what he said, she *was* worried. Something bothered him.

"Did you eat today?" She knew her father was given to overlooking that simple need when he was pressed with work.

Again he shook his head, but this time his voice was less strained. "I forgot."

Relief washed over her. "Well, you need to go to the kitchen right now and have Mrs. Johnson give you something to eat. Tell her you've had a spell."

Patting her hand, he nodded. "I'll take care of it in a few minutes."

Watching her father walk to the railroad agent's office, Cassidy puzzled over it.

He turned and looked at her. "Hurry! I'm fine and I promise I'll get something to eat."

Stuffing her hands into the pockets of her apron, she went in search of Mr. Allan Brennan.

Outside on the platform, it wasn't hard to find him. He stood in the same place. Case beside him, hat in his hands. What was that all about?

Cassidy walked the last few steps to him and cleared her throat. His blond hair picked up the sunlight. "Mr. Brennan, I presume?" As he looked up at her, she couldn't help but notice the pain etched across his face and in his green eyes. Pain and something else. Was it anger? Surely not. No doubt it was just the confusion of his new setting.

She reached out to him. "Are you all right?" Goodness, first Dad and now his new assistant.

Her touch appeared to break through his state. "I apologize." He straightened his shoulders and looked directly into her eyes. "Yes, I'm Allan Brennan. But how did you know my name?"

Cassidy laughed. "Mr. Bradley — the hotel manager — just told me." She stuck out her hand in greeting. "You'll find up here in Curry that we all know everyone pretty quickly. I'm Cassidy Ivanoff. You'll be working with my father."

He took her hand and shook it. But the longer he shook it, the firmer his grip became. "So your father is John Ivanoff?"

"Yes."

"He'll be training me?"

"Yes."

"And you're his daughter?" He stopped shaking her hand but continued to hold it.

"Yes, we've established that." She smiled and looked down at their hands. "Would you mind if I have my hand back?" Even though he acted a bit odd, Cassidy felt sympathy for him. She'd never get over the pain she'd seen in his eyes.

He released her hand. "Pardon me, Miss Ivanoff. I believe all the travel has gotten to me. I'm not at all myself." His tone took on a more formal sound.

"All's forgiven. Exhaustion and busyness take their toll on all of us. Even my father forgot to eat today. Why don't you get your things? I'm to help get you settled. You have a meeting with my father in . . ." She glanced down at the watch attached to her apron. "Fifty minutes in the baggage room."

He picked up his large case. "This is all I have. Lead the way."

As they entered the lobby, Cassidy pointed to the left. "The dining room and main-level kitchen are over there. And to the right are the agent's office, the baggage room, and several other rooms. Up the stairs are guest rooms, as well as straight ahead beyond the stairs. Downstairs is the section gang bunkroom, provisions rooms, down-stairs kitchen, storage, and the laundry facilities." She walked to the main desk in the lobby to the left of the grand staircase. "The manager's office is behind here, and Mrs. McGovern is the head housekeeper.

We'll check in with her about your accommodations."

Cassidy stepped back as the housekeeper gave swift instructions to Allan. While she waited, she studied him, wondering where he was from, why he was in Curry, and what troubled him so much.

"Cassidy." Mrs. McGovern's voice always sounded pinched when she was in a hurry. "Your father said you would show Mr. Brennan around."

Cassidy nodded. "Yes, ma'am. I have a few minutes, but then I'll need to get back to the kitchen." Turning to Allan, she smiled. "Follow me, please. If you haven't noticed, we're quite efficient around here. The Curry Hotel is a busy place."

Allan followed her out the front door and to the north of the hotel. "I can see that." His tone was rather gruff.

Cassidy couldn't help but feel she'd done something to annoy the man. They walked in silence for a few seconds.

"I met your father on the train. He seems very knowledgeable."

Forgetting Allan's mood, Cassidy couldn't help laughing. If only this man really knew. Her father had more knowledge in his pinky finger than most men could hope for in a lifetime. "He is at that. He knows every plant, tree, shrub, hill, mountain, and beast in the interior of Alaska. If you want to know anything about hiking, climbing, or even what plants *not* to eat — he's the expert."

"Is he a tough man to work for?"

"Heavens, no." Cassidy stepped around a hole. "He's a wonderful man. Kind and patient. But I will say that he'll expect absolute perfection because Alaska demands it. This part of the world is most unforgiving."

They reached the staff housing and Cassidy checked her watch again. "Gracious. I must be going. We have a delegation coming through tomorrow to dedicate the national park. Don't forget about your meeting with my father. He's a stickler for being on time."

Removing his hat again, Allan half smiled. The anger seemed to leave his voice. "Thank you. I'll make sure I'm there." He extended his hand.

Cassidy placed her hand in his, fully expecting to end their tour on a shake. Instead, Allan held her hand again and gazed into her eyes. His eyebrows furrowed. For a moment, the intensity unnerved her. Pulling her hand away, a little flutter started in her stomach. "I must be . . . I have to go." She hated the way she stumbled over her words, but kept moving. No need to further her embarrassment. She honestly didn't know what had gotten into her.

The man was handsome, but so were many of the fellas who came through Curry. It certainly didn't give her a reason to swoon as soon as he smiled. Foolishness. That's what it was. Besides, she just met the man. Granted, he looked pretty depressed when she first saw him, and the smile did amazing things to his strong face. . . .

Gracious, she wasn't a ridiculous female. She refused to be like the other girls. Always trying to shorten their hems, wear more makeup, and try cigarettes. No. Not her. Cassidy Faith Ivanoff vowed to never try to impress a man.

If God had someone for her, He'd have to bring him all the way to Curry and love her exactly the way she was.

So what if God had brought Allan Brennan here to Curry? That didn't mean that He brought him here for *her.* She'd never be the *bee's knees* all dolled up in *glad rags* to go out on the town like all the young kitchen maids. It wasn't like any of them even had a town to "go out" on. There wasn't anything in Curry or even Talkeetna for that matter. But oh, to be young. They looked at the future with such bright and starry eyes.

Which made her feel ancient at only twenty-three. No. She didn't feel ancient. Well, maybe a little. But it wasn't like she didn't love her life. She loved the hotel. Loved her job. Loved to cook. Loved to meet all the people who came through their neck of the woods.

But for the first time, maybe she *did* want someone other than her father to love *her.*

Allan sat waiting for John Ivanoff to appear, wondering the entire time how he should handle the situation. He had enjoyed speaking to the man on the train, but then he hadn't known who John was. Hard to imagine that he could act as though nothing had changed between them when everything had.

"Glad to see you're punctual, Mr. Brennan, but I could have surmised as much after meeting you on the train." John gave a half smile and motioned to the man behind him. "This is Mr. Bradley, the manager of this wonderful establishment, and our boss."

"Pleased to finally meet you, sir." Allan shook hands with the manager, then turned back to John. "Your daughter told me that punctuality was important to you — it's always been important to me as well." Allan thought the man looked weary — almost like he had the weight of the world on his shoulders. Perhaps something had happened, some bad bit of news had come his way. Was that why Mr. Bradley was here?

"You won't be heading out on any guided tours tomorrow." The manager crossed the small room and looked out the window. "We have people coming to officially dedicate the park. We'll have to take supplies to the park entrance — it's just a short distance by train from here. A party of sorts has been planned with a barbecue. Your job is to be the muscle for the event, and to assist Mr. Karstens in every way possible."

John nodded.

"Yes, sir." Allan wrestled with his feelings. He could see John was upset about something, but Allan wanted answers.

Mr. Bradley left the room and closed the door.

Silence stretched as John shuffled some papers on the desk.

Allan had come all this way from Seattle to learn the truth about what happened on that fateful day back in 1917. Still, he wasn't cruel. He didn't want to make things worse for John. The man might never give him the answers if Allan offended him first thing. He might even get himself fired, and then he'd never know. But why didn't John bring it up? Maybe he didn't recognize Allan's last name. Had John forgotten his father — Henry Brennan — so quickly?

John took a seat behind the small desk. "Then there's going to be the event on the fifteenth of July with President Harding. That group will be coming in on the fourteenth, and I'm still uncertain as to whether there will be time for anything more than the actual event. We will need to be prepared for almost anything."

Allan nodded. "I understand." But he didn't.

"I know from our conversation on the train that you have a keen mind and a desire to learn. I also know from the information you supplied Mr. Bradley before he decided to hire you that you already know a great deal about vegetation and wildlife. That's definitely to your benefit."

"I've spent much of my life outdoors and have made it my habit to learn." Why wouldn't John acknowledge the obvious conversation that needed to be addressed? Was Mr. Bradley coming back?

"Well, while it will be to your benefit, Alaska is unlike any place else you've probably been. The isolation alone makes it almost impossible to easily recover from mistakes."

Like the mistake that cost Allan's father his life? It was all Allan could do to keep from voicing the question aloud. Now just didn't seem the right time to get into the matter. Especially if their boss was set to return.

John didn't appear to notice his discomfort, however, and continued talking. "The isolation is one strike against you. The unpredictability of the elements is strike two. I've lived here all my life. I've learned from the best and most knowledgeable about the weather signs and such, but the truth is everything can change up in the twinkling of an eye. Whether it's the weather or a grizzly bear charging you from out of nowhere — you can't let your guard down for even a moment. Do you understand?"

Allan nodded, his mind racing with accusations. But somebody let their guard down and his father died.

"A man can seem to have touched all the bases and still fail."

Was this his way of apologizing for what happened? Did John even remember his father and what happened six years ago?

"So does this proverbial baseball game

have a strike three?" Allan fought to keep his voice steady.

John looked at him strangely for a moment, then nodded. "Strike three is around every bush — every tree — every river. A man's own arrogant self-assurance is the worst enemy of all. I've seen men come here so certain they knew what they were getting themselves into — so boastful and full of themselves. They were unwilling to listen to instruction or to receive correction. They thought they knew it all."

Allan stiffened. He couldn't help but wonder if John was implying this was the case with his father and Frank. He gripped the arms of the chair. "And what happened?"

John looked up. "Strike three. They were out. The game was over."

Thomas Smith hauled the last bit of scraps out to the animal feed shack. Mrs. Johnson had been barking ongoing commands since Mr. Bradley told her about the fancy people coming through tomorrow. Thomas felt like he couldn't keep up. But he had to keep trying.

If he could just hang on to this job long enough and prove to Mr. Bradley that he was a hard worker, maybe he could be trained for another position. Maybe one day, he could make something out of himself working for the Curry Hotel.

Most seventeen-year-old orphans never had a chance like this. So he'd best not mess it up. Taking a deep breath, he emptied the huge tub of its scraps and went to the pump to clean it out. Cook would never allow him to bring it back dirty. And he wanted her to be happy with him. His future depended on it.

Granted, he didn't have a lot of book learning. But he could read and write and do simple arithmetic. The missionaries at the orphanage had seen to that. Maybe he could learn more if he needed to. He'd always been told that God would give him knowledge if he asked. Thomas wondered if God would give him better balance and less clumsiness if he asked.

"If You could" — he glanced heavenward — "I'd appreciate it."

A rudimentary education in the Christian faith along with his book learning were things he was thankful for. The missionaries felt it was their duty to save the souls of the native children at the orphanage, and although Thomas was white, he was often told that without accepting Jesus as Savior, his soul would be doomed. It sounded like a terrible thing to be doomed, so Thomas had quickly agreed to repent from his sins — although he wasn't exactly sure at the time what those sins were, since he was just a very little boy. But over the years, he'd repented to God every time he missed the mark. He'd learned that much. And he knew that Jesus was his only hope.

That became all too clear when the missionaries kicked him out, along with several other boys, when they'd reached their teen years. Overcrowding at the orphanage made it necessary, even though they provided free labor to the missionaries. Still, the missionaries had taught him to pray and believe in God, and sometimes that was all that got Thomas through the day. He didn't have earthly parents who loved him, but he knew there was a heavenly Father who did.

Now if he could just keep from dropping or spilling anything tonight, he could breathe a sigh of relief.

As he walked back to the hotel, Thomas thought of Cassidy's help earlier. She was so nice to him. Even when he messed up.

And there was something about her eyes. They were always . . . shining. Like she was — what was the word Mrs. Johnson used? — *delighted* about something.

He could imagine making it through each

day if he could just hear her laugh or see her smile.

The bustle of the kitchen greeted him as he walked back in and put the tub under the worktable where it was supposed to go. Making sure it was stable and the handles were straight, he took a moment to catch his breath. As he looked up, he spotted Cassidy coming up the stairs with a large tray.

"Lily, we need to make sure the hollandaise is done in precise timing, so please have the egg yolks and butter ready for me in five minutes." Even when giving an order as the cook's assistant, her voice singsonged through the air.

The kitchen maid nodded — "Yes, Miss Ivanoff" — and scurried off.

Thomas took that opportunity to move forward. "Let me take that tray for you, Miss Ivanoff."

"Why, thank you, Thomas!" She relinquished her hold on it and pushed her hair back into place. "It was getting quite heavy."

"Where do you need it?"

"Over there at my workstation by the stove. That hollandaise won't make itself." The most glorious smile lit her face as she beamed directly at him.

It took the words right from his mouth. All he could do was nod.

"Thomas!" Mrs. Johnson's voice made him jump. "I need you to refill the flour bins and fetch some more cream from the creamery."

"Yes, ma'am." With a look back at Cassidy, Thomas was sad to see she was already back to work. But what he wouldn't give to see her smile again.

He raced to the creamery and hefted one of the huge crocks. Even if he was clumsy, at least he was strong. The younger kitchen boys couldn't lift these.

In record time, he made it back to the kitchen and earned an eyebrow lift and nod from Mrs. Johnson, which was no small feat. Feeling sure of himself, he grabbed the two large flour bins and ran down the stairs to the provisions rooms. He filled both to the brim and headed back to the stairs, taking them two at a time.

When he reached the main kitchen, Mrs. Johnson had a hint of a smile on her face. "Good job, Thomas, right when I needed —"

Before he realized what was happening, he tripped over his own foot. Determined not to drop anything, he held fast to the metal bins.

But the flour had other ideas. The fine white powder flew up as he tumbled down.

Landing with a thud and *poof* of white dust, Thomas found himself on his back holding two metal bins with a shower of white descending over the whole kitchen.

4

John walked toward the manager's office, hoping for a few minutes with Mr. Bradley. It had been a long day and tomorrow would be even longer. Seeing young Brennan had turned his world upside down. For years, he'd been able to push aside the horrible loss of Henry Brennan, but the appearance of Allan brought it all front and center.

Their meeting had taken a great strain on John. It was apparent the young man was agitated — even angry. And who could blame him? No doubt there were unanswered questions, and the only man he'd had to talk to was Frank Irving — a man John knew to be nothing but trouble. John thought to put the matter out there for discussion, but Allan didn't seem willing. At least not yet. Sooner or later, they'd *have* to discuss it. As to how he would deal with it . . . John didn't have a clue. Maybe Bradley could give him some guidance. This situation affected him as well, since they were both employees, and John had never lied to the man.

Voices echoed out of the office. Apparently his planned conversation wouldn't be happening right now.

"The hollandaise was completely ruined, the meringue inedible, and the fried fish had to be refried to get the raw flour off. Our poor dinner patrons had to wait an extra three minutes for the next course! Three minutes, Mr. Bradley. As you know, that is completely unacceptable."

John entered the office and saw their manager appearing grim.

Mrs. Johnson stood on the other side of the room with her hands on her hips, Cassidy to her right with her hands folded in front, and Thomas to the right of her, his head down. "Mr. Bradley, I'm just asking for a reprieve. I'm no longer vexed about the flour incident — although it will probably take days to clean that dust out of everything — but with the city paper people coming through, I need perfection to —"

Thomas sniffed but kept his head bowed.

The head cook lowered her arms to her side and sighed. "I just could use a few days without a mishap. The kitchen is no place for trial and error, so either he goes or I do."

Bradley looked over at Cassidy. "Miss Ivanoff, are you able to provide the help our chef needs in the absence of Thomas?"

Cassidy nodded at the manager. "While I can't fill Thomas's shoes or lift the heavy items he hauls for us each day, I am willing to help in any way I can." She cleared her throat. "But Thomas *is* very valuable to us, sir, and is a good worker."

The gangly orphan boy lifted his head a little at that.

"Thomas . . ." Mr. Bradley came around his desk. "I know — we all know — that you are working very hard here for us. But I also understand that Mrs. Johnson has a valid plea. It's not completely fair to burden the assistant cook with extra work either."

The young man nodded.

"Your timing couldn't be more inconvenient, Chef Johnson, but —"

John moved forward. "I'm sorry to intrude, Mr. Bradley, but perhaps I could be of assistance."

Bradley extended an arm to him. "Certainly, John. What ideas do you have?"

"Well, I'm not quite sure I understand all that has happened" — he'd definitely have to ask Cassidy about the flour incident later

73

— "but I do know that Mr. Brennan just arrived, and while he will no doubt be a big help the next couple days with the dedication of the park, we could also use extra hands on our trip. There's quite a lot of equipment to be hauled and set up. Perhaps young Thomas could assist *me* for a few days?"

Relief washed over the young man's face. He closed his eyes, as if waiting for the judge to rule.

Mr. Bradley nodded. "Mm-hmm. I like the idea." He walked back around his desk. "Yes. I think that will be a good solution." He looked up at his head cook. "Is that satisfactory, Chef Johnson?"

Mrs. Johnson gave a curt nod. "Yes, Mr. Bradley. Thank you."

The boss looked at Cassidy again. John watched several expressions go across her face as the manager spoke to her. "Do you have anything else to say, Miss Ivanoff?"

"Only that" — she turned and smiled at the woman beside her — "I believe Mrs. Johnson and I agree in saying that Thomas hasn't done anything on purpose to upset the kitchen; neither has he done anything with malicious intent. He's just had a few . . . accidents. But we appreciate his work."

Always the peacemaker and looking out for those less fortunate. His Cassidy. She had a heart of gold.

Mrs. Johnson stiffened. "I don't need anyone to speak on my behalf. Thomas is loved by all the staff, but a kitchen isn't run on sentiment. I need proficiency and order."

"But you will allow him to come back to work for you?" Mr. Bradley asked with a raised brow.

The older lady harrumphed. "I'm not unreasonable. After a few days, yes, I'm sure we will all be right as rain."

"Good, then, it's settled. Don't let me keep you from your duties in the kitchen." Mr. Bradley sat in his chair. "I'd like a few moments to speak with Thomas and Mr. Ivanoff."

John caught Cassidy's eye and winked at his daughter before she followed Mrs. Johnson out. That girl had her hands full with the harsh woman, but if anyone could handle Mrs. Johnson, it was Cassidy.

Mr. Bradley waved John closer. "John, thank you for stepping in." He got up and walked over to Thomas. "I'm sure Thomas will work hard for you the next few days. He's a good listener. Just make sure he keeps his feet under him at all times." The boss patted the young man's shoulder and walked out to the front desk.

Long arms and legs didn't hide the hunch in the boy's shoulders. What had he gotten himself into? First, he'd have to keep Thomas busy, but he'd also have to keep him out of trouble as well. And if he'd learned anything from his daughter's stories, it was that his work had been cut out for him. "It's all right, son. I won't bite."

"Yes, sir." He toed the floor with his boot.

"You do know that I'm Cassidy's father, right?"

The boy looked up. Just as tall as John himself, the boy — no, the young man — finally looked him straight in the eye. "No, sir. I didn't."

"Well, she's told me a lot about you. And it's all good."

"Thank you, sir. Miss Ivanoff has been very good to me since Mr. Bradley hired me on."

"Glad to hear it." He gripped the young man's shoulder. "Now, why don't we discuss how you can help me tomorrow?"

"Yes, sir." The boy relaxed.

"The original plan was for this large delegation to go to the entrance of the park via the railroad and then travel twelve miles on horseback to the Savage River camp for the ceremony. But we heard last night by

76

telegram that because of a late-arriving train, they will not be able to travel that far. They've changed their plans, and Superintendent Karstens is working frantically to move all the equipment back from the Savage River. Now the event will take place at the park entrance right off the railroad. That's why they've asked for our assistance. We're not only taking up food and additional items that are needed, but we'll be helping to set up the chairs, tables, and anything else. Do you understand?"

"Yes, sir."

John walked over to the window and peered to the north. "This will be a huge boon to the national park, this territory, and the railroad, Thomas. Did you know that last year only thirty-four people visited the national park? The year before that, it was only seven." He turned and pulled out his pocket watch. "And now we will have the largest group ever to come through to dedicate the park, followed by the President to complete the railroad. These are exciting times."

"Yes, sir. I'm ready to help, sir."

John stuck his right hand into his vest pocket. "That's good to hear. But let's go over a few things, all right?"

Thomas nodded.

"First, don't hesitate to ask me questions if you don't understand what I've instructed you to do. Second, Mr. Brennan will also be in charge of you, so listen to him well." John watched for wariness in the boy. "Third, let's slow everything down. Take a bit more time to do things. The terrain will be much rougher, and you'll need to take your steps carefully. Work hard, and together with prayer, we will get through this."

"Yes, sir." There was a light in the young man's eyes that hadn't been there before. He stood a little taller and straightened his shoulders. "I'm a man of prayer too."

John smiled. "I'm glad to hear it, Thomas."

"I'm not real good at praying with a lot of fancy words, but I pray a lot."

"Fancy words aren't necessary. If they were, God wouldn't listen to most of us."

Thomas seemed to consider this a moment. "When would you like me to report to you in the morning?"

"Let's get started at five."

"Yes, sir." Thomas smiled. "I'll do my very best, sir."

"I'm sure you will."

He turned and headed toward the door but tripped and dropped his hat. As he went to pick it up, he fell on his face. After a brief moan, the boy stood again and found his voice. "I'm sorry, sir. It won't happen again, sir." Redness crept up his neck and face.

"It's quite all right, Thomas. Like I said, just take your time." He had to work to keep from chuckling out loud. No wonder poor Mrs. Johnson was beside herself with exasperation. "Say, you know what I used to tell my daughter when she was constantly tripping over her own feet?"

"Yes, sir, I know." The young man gave a lopsided grin. "I guess the floor just needed a hug."

As the train pulled into the McKinley National Park station early the next morning, Allan was surprised at how little had been built here. Wasn't this the glorious and grand entrance to the national park he'd longed to see for six years?

But instead, he was greeted by a few small shacks, and what appeared to be some hastily erected tents. The park headquarters was no more than a shanty, and the only structure of any size was a log roadhouse. Curry had been tiny compared to the great cities of the United States, but the Curry Hotel hadn't been lacking in anything. Even in the middle of nowhere. But here? It seemed a bit of a letdown to Allan's high hopes. He wondered if his father had felt much the same when he came through. None of these buildings were even here at that time. Neither was the railroad.

The group from the *Brooklyn Daily Eagle* might be a tad disappointed. But Allan kept his thoughts to himself. They couldn't even see the mountain from here — why didn't they have the ceremony at another location? There had been some spectacular views from the train. But maybe that's why originally they were going to the Savage River to have the ceremony. He looked back to the west. He knew off in the distance stood a most magnificent sight — Mount McKinley. And he was missing it.

John carried several large baskets, followed by Thomas, who hauled chairs.

Thomas gave him a wide grin. "Did you see McKinley? Isn't it huge?" He didn't stop to get Allan's answer.

And Allan could only nod. The mountain was incredible. The massiveness of it — its sheer presence was intimidating. He'd climbed mountains in the States and yet nothing could even compare.

"I need you to help Thomas get these chairs assembled," John said as he passed Allan with another load. "The mountain isn't going anywhere. You'll get to see it again."

The words hit Allan hard. His father had said the same thing. In fact, it was one of the last things he'd said to Allan.

John continued. "The delegation should be here by eleven, and I don't need to remind you that we need to make a good impression."

Allan could only nod. He hadn't expected this to be so hard. Why hadn't he just gotten everything off his chest yesterday when he'd had the chance? Now he'd had too much time to mull it over, and all that had accomplished was to make him angry. He needed this job. But would he be able to keep it after he confronted John?

Through the hours of the morning they worked, and the heat became more intense.

Watches were checked as anticipation grew. The group had been known to dedicate several national parks in the great nation of the United States, so to have them come to Alaska was indeed an honor.

Out of the corner of his eye, Allan saw Cassidy Ivanoff speaking with Mr. Karstens and her father. It appeared the two men had great respect for each other, but why wouldn't they? They were two of the few men to ever successfully climb to the summit of the mountain for which this great park had been named.

A slight breeze kicked up a whirl of dirt and Cassidy reached up to secure her hat, her dark hair coiled in a knot at the base of it. While he'd only known her a day, something tugged at Allan when he looked at her. But he couldn't put a name to it. The Ivanoffs were a fascination and fear for him all rolled into one. Perhaps he only felt that tug because she was the daughter of the man who'd left his father to die on Denali. Allan felt bile rise in his throat and forced it back down. If he didn't confront John soon, he'd explode.

"John Ivanoff should be jailed for murder. The man left your father to die on that mountain. He didn't even care enough to search for him." Frank's words haunted him.

What if Frank's story was true and John was completely responsible for his father's death? What if it *wasn't* true? Over the years, Frank's story had changed and he'd gotten more livid to the point of refusing to speak of it. And if the storm that hit them was as bad as he implied, how did he even know what happened? Could his father have still been alive when the others left him?

That thought was even more horrifying. Containing his emotions became the hardest battle of all. Allan felt like he was in a fog, not able to discern reality from nightmare.

The only bright spot in this horrid dream was Cassidy. Her sunny, positive disposition had a brilliant effect on everyone around her. Even though he didn't want it to. Could she really be the daughter of a murderer?

Allan shook his head. John didn't actually murder his father. But from what he understood, the man did leave his father to die on that mountain. And what role did Frank truly play in all this? As soon as the thoughts entered his mind, his gaze was pulled back to the Alaska Range and beyond that, its tallest peak. Would he ever know the truth?

"Allan!" John waved. "Come join us, I want you to meet the Seventymile Kid before the delegates detrain."

He had little choice but to put his thoughts aside and do what John bid. Approaching the trio, Allan admitted a sense of awe in meeting Harry Karstens. The man was a legend. He'd participated in the Yukon gold rush, making big money carrying supplies up the ice staircase carved out for those going north to seek their fortunes. He'd earned the nickname "Seventymile Kid" after spending time on the Seventymile River searching for gold. But more impressive, Karstens had been part of the very first successful ascent of McKinley.

"It's an honor to meet you." Allan extended his hand.

John interjected. "I apologize. If you'll excuse us, Cassidy and I have something to attend to."

"Of course, we can talk later." Karstens tipped his hat. "Cassidy, it's always a pleasure."

Once they were gone, the clean-shaven Karstens grasped Allan's hand in a firm grip. "I'm more than pleased to meet you. I knew your father. Good man."

The comment took Allan by surprise. "You did?"

"Indeed. Met him on more than one occasion, in fact. First ran into him at the store in Seattle. Then we met in Anchorage a couple times. We shared a lot of common interests." Karstens' expression sobered. "I was very sorry to hear about his death."

Allan swallowed hard. "Father loved it here. We wanted to one day make the climb together — after I returned from the war."

"It's a grueling climb and definitely not for the faint of heart, but you would have enjoyed it together. Your father loved a challenge." Karstens shook his head. "When our team made that first ascent, we had more than our share of trouble."

"I'd love to hear about it sometime. Frank never told me any details of the actual climb, and while I did read about your expedition with Hudson Stuck, I'd love to hear about it from you."

"I'd forgotten about Frank." A frown etched the man's face. "I can't say I had the same experience with him that I did with your father." He cleared his throat. "So . . . John tells me you're up here to assist him. It'll test your mettle to be sure, but if you stick it out, I think you'll never want to leave."

"I'm already quite besotted, sir." Allan looked in the direction of the great mountain. "In fact, I hope to follow in my father's footsteps and climb Denali one day. So I'll need all the advice and stories you have time to share."

Karstens slapped him on the back and his mood seemed to lighten. "I'll do what I can. You don't smoke a pipe, do you?" His eyes twinkled.

The question took Allan by surprise. He cocked his head slightly. "A pipe?"

The park superintendent chuckled. "My carelessness with a pipe started a fire that destroyed a good portion of our supplies. Burned our baking powder and sugar, and let me tell you what — when you're up there at fifteen thousand feet, it's not like you can just go buy some more."

The train let out a whistle as it approached, stealing everyone's focus.

"Well, it looks like the important folks are here." He gave Allan another pat on the back. "We'll talk some more later."

As the train puffed its way up the line to the station, everyone gathered at the platform to greet their prestigious guests. Allan tried to put aside Karstens' comment about Frank, but it was hard. What had he meant in saying that he didn't have the same experience with Frank that he'd had with Allan's father? Karstens wasn't keen on the man — that much was clear.

The delegates began to emerge and the real work began. Greetings went round and round as the people stretched their legs, commented on the beauty of the mountains, and spoke of the events of the day.

After refreshments were served by Cassidy and her staff, a rotund gentleman worked to hush the crowd. "Thank you, yes, thank you, ladies and gentlemen." He held up his hands until all was quiet. "I'd like to introduce our speaker for the dedication of the park today, Mr. William Hester, Jr. — the son of our esteemed president of the *Eagle*."

The applause was exuberant as Mr. Hester took the primitive stage. His words were eloquent, and Allan found himself greatly moved that this group of people would care so much to come all this way. He hoped they could look beyond the rustic conditions to the beauty around them. He watched the people listen and offer polite encouragement.

One particular reporter with a camera seemed focused on Cassidy. She appeared completely unaware of the man taking pictures; instead her attention was focused on Mr. Hester. As Allan studied her, he understood why the photo fellow was so enraptured. Cassidy had such stunning features. Dark hair and dark eyes, the lines of her face were elegant . . . noble even. His shock upon first arrival had obviously rendered his senses useless.

All too soon, applause brought his attention back, and Allan realized he'd missed the entire speech as Mr. Hester cleared his voice and spoke louder. "I'd like to conclude by stating that on this date, the ninth of July, in the year of our Lord, 1923, I declare that Mount McKinley National Park be formally dedicated to its rightful owners, the people of the United States."

Everyone stood and offered hearty applause.

Mr. Karstens, attired in his superintendent's uniform, addressed the crowd next. "Thank you all for coming. We'd now like to invite you to a mountain sheep barbecue to conclude our ceremony today."

Allan applauded with the rest of the group and then felt a tug on his elbow. Turning, he realized it was John. "I'm sorry, sir. I didn't realize you needed me."

"Nothing to apologize about. I just wanted to let you know that after the meal, the delegation will be boarding the train and heading to Fairbanks. After we help Karstens and the rest of the staff to disassemble the tents, he's allowing us to use a few horses and head into the park for a bit. This time of year, it will be light on into the night. It would be good for you and Thomas to see all of this for future reference."

"Yes, sir."

John walked toward the press delegates and then shook hands with many of them. Allan watched with mixed emotions. The man before him seemed nothing like the man Frank had described to him all these years.

His thoughts warred with each other. Last night, Allan hadn't gotten a lick of sleep because of it. Morning came all too early, but he put a façade in place, determined to do his best for the day. But behind it, a seething anger wanted to build over the death of his father. And yet John wasn't a man Allan wanted to hate. Quite the contrary.

Frank had declared John to be inept and callous. But nothing could be further from the truth. In fact, those qualities seemed more likely to fit Frank than John. All of his adult life, Allan had been wary of Frank, yet he chalked it up to some sort of displaced frustration that Frank survived when his father hadn't. Still, the ruthlessness about Frank always left a sour taste. Another reason why he couldn't stand to be at the factory working with the man.

In contrast, John seemed more like his father . . . Henry.

But even so, how could he ever respect and learn from the man who'd taken everything from his family? It seemed like just another of God's cruel jokes.

5

Frank Irving's secretary, Lucy, opened his office door. "Excuse me. This just came by messenger." She left it on his desk and scurried out.

Brennan was embossed on the outside. Good grief, what did that woman want now?

Opening the note with his gold letter opener, Frank hoped it was news that Allan Brennan had met some terrible demise.

The few lines of script jumped off the page. "No!" He crumpled the note in his hands.

Lucy rushed back in. "Did you call for something, sir?"

"No, and get out!" Frank leapt to his feet and locked the door behind his retreating secretary.

He stomped back to his desk and picked up the phone. "Get me my lawyer. Now."

The line rang back. "Cyrus, we need to talk."

"Frank, I have to be in court in an hour."

"Well, you better get here in the next two minutes, then."

Click. At least the man knew where his bread was buttered.

Pacing his office, he counted to 207 before Cyrus walked in, his shiny shoes squeaking on the floor. "Well, what is it this time? I've already told you I can't you help you with —"

"I've just had word that Allan is in Alaska."

"What?" Cyrus stopped preening in front of the mirror. "Why?"

"Probably because he wants to climb the stupid mountain where his father died."

Cyrus sat in a chair and crossed his arms. "So why is it so urgent that I'm here?"

"If you would have done your job properly ten years ago, I wouldn't be in this mess, so don't take that tone with me."

His lawyer leaned forward. "Pardon me, Frank. But I couldn't control your partner any more than you could. The document was legal and out of my hands."

"But you could have at least warned me before I risked my life climbing a twenty-thousand-foot mountain."

A heavy sigh left the man's lips. He squeezed them together. Several seconds passed before he spoke again. "I'm going to remind you one *last time,* Frank. *You* asked for the documents to be prepared. I prepared them. *You* signed them. Before Henry ever saw them or consulted his own attorney — and, might I add, *against* my advice. Henry had his own lawyer look at the papers before he signed them. Had Henry not written an addendum to his will — perfectly legal, I might add — *yes,* you would have gained control of everything. But he did. I truly hate repeating myself, but it seems you aren't willing to let it through your thick skull that I had *nothing* to do with the legal addendum to his will that he had drawn up, and I didn't have any power whatsoever to change anything that was in signed and legal documents. You argued with the judge and lost. You'd already gained half of Henry's holdings, so you now own seventy-five percent of the company. Please let it go."

Frank turned on him. "You fool. This isn't something to just 'let go.' The agreement was for the surviving partner to receive *all* the holdings of the company!"

"Ah, but that's where you're not above the law, Frank. In your case, if you had been the one to die, yes, everything would have reverted back to Henry. Because you have no children. But as you well know, Henry left half of his holdings to his son, Allan, while the other half did indeed come back to you."

"But that's not good enough." He couldn't admit that it had been bad choices on his part. He had invested and was losing. A lot.

Cyrus stood. "Thank you for wasting my time today so that I could explain once again why you didn't inherit *everything*. Next time you call me, it'd better be important." He walked to the door, but Frank slapped his hand on it and kept him from opening it.

"Don't tell me what to do. You work for *me*! Remember? I know where every penny you've made came from and I can bring you down." His anger boiled inside him. "Do not cross me." Frank stood back and straightened his jacket. "I need to discuss how much time I have to bring more capital in to cover the investments I've made. And what legal measures I have to prolong that time."

Eyes narrowed and arms crossed, Cyrus stayed put. "I'll be glad to help you with that, Frank. As long as you don't bring up the Brennan mess again."

"Fine." He slicked his hair back. "I just needed to vent and lost my temper."

"Good." Cyrus walked back to the chair.

"And, of course, I'll be charging my regular fees."

Frank seethed. Everyone wanted his money. "Of course." He pasted on his business smile. But as soon as he got his hands on the rest of the company, he'd change even more things around here. Greedy lawyers and annoying secretaries could easily be replaced.

Cassidy walked out of the roadhouse wearing her favorite pair of riding pants and the soft, brown leather boots her father had given her for her birthday last year. Every once in a while it sure was nice to not be in a dress and apron. Slinging her bag with her other clothes and water canteen over her shoulder, she looked forward to a bit of time away from the hustle and bustle of the hotel. Quiet. Mountains. And lots of fresh air. Just like what they used to have all the time. Before they joined the staff at the Curry. And exactly what she needed after the hectic busyness of the past few weeks, and especially the last few days.

Her father seemed changed since his return from Anchorage. She'd tried to talk to him about it last night, but he only told her it would work itself out. Then there was Allan. Friendly one minute and sullen the next. Almost as if the man fought some unseen war and the Curry Hotel was the battlefield. But why? She'd been praying for him and knew her father needed the help, but Allan Brennan was a conundrum.

As she made her way to the horses, Cassidy shook her head of the worrisome thoughts, let her hair out of its tight updo, and braided it. Much better. And much more conducive to trail riding in the park. Maybe they'd see some caribou. But hopefully not any grizzlies. She plumb didn't have the energy to deal with that today.

Her father rode up next to her. "I'm glad Fitzgerald cleared you to go with us today. You looked like you needed it."

"I look that bad, huh?" Cassidy winked at her father. "As the agent for the railroad, Mr. Fitzgerald knew it was best to listen to Mrs. Johnson's advice. After all, she usually gets what she wants. And after Mr. Bradley's surprise announcement yesterday about this event, I must admit it has been grueling. But I love what I do."

"I know, dear." He looked off into the distance. "And I'm glad for it."

"What about you?" Cassidy eyed him seriously. "You know I'm worried about you."

"I'm fine. There's a matter that needs my attention, but doesn't need to worry you. I promise it will be resolved and everything will be fine."

"I wish you'd confide in me." She touched his arm. "We've always talked through our troubles in the past."

Her father patted her hand. "And we will continue to do so, but this is something I have to do alone. At least for now."

She pasted on a smile. Stubborn man. "So Thomas and Allan will be joining us today?"

Her father looked solemn and nodded.

"What kind of expedition do you have planned?" Over the years, his work for the railroad had taken him many places along the line from Seward to Fairbanks. He'd been known as the resident expert since the president of the railroad hired him to take him out surveying before the national park was in place. Dad always loved this kind of thing. But perhaps he hadn't been feeling well. What if he'd seen a doctor in Anchorage and received bad news? After all, he'd just commented on having to do this alone. If it was something physical, he would naturally feel that way.

They rode in quiet silence for a few seconds. "I just need to show Allan what it's really like out here, what the railroad's plans are for eventual expeditions into the park from the hotel and from McKinley

Park. And Thomas . . . well, he has a lot to learn about everything. But I can tell he loves the outdoors. He might make a very handy assistant one day."

"Isn't Allan your assistant right now?"

"Yes. But he was hired on to apprentice under me so that eventually there would be another full-time guide. We'll both need adequate assistants if we are to fulfill all the plans the board has for us."

Their horses meandered to the stream where Dad had instructed the others to meet them. Dismounting, he picked up the gear that awaited them and settled some on Cassidy's horse, and the other supplies to his own.

She breathed in deep. Oh, how she loved the mountain air. And from here, there was nothing to intrude on the fresh scent. No trains, laundry, ovens, or even smelly kitchen boys. Glorious. Just glorious.

Closing her eyes, Cassidy let it all wash over her. It was here in the shadow of Denali that she felt God's presence so strongly. She could almost hear Him speak in the rustling trees and the rippling streams. His power in the majesty and glory of the panoramic beauty spread out before her.

"Thank You, Lord." She barely breathed aloud. She wanted nothing more than to spend the day in praise and worship. But hoofbeats behind her broke her reverie and she opened her eyes. No need for Allan to think she was a silly female who daydreamed all the time.

"All right. Looks like we have everyone." Her father moved to her left as Allan and Thomas rode up. "We're going to head west over some rough terrain, so take your time. The horses — as long as they aren't pushed — will secure their footing. I'd like both of you men to take note of your surroundings at all times, including the plant life and animals you see. I'll answer any questions you have."

"What about Miss Cassidy, sir?" Thomas's voice squeaked a bit on the end.

Her father patted the young man's shoulder. "Thank you for worrying about my daughter, but she knows almost as much as I do about Alaska. She can handle herself."

"Well, I don't know about knowing almost as much as you, but I did have a good teacher." Even with her banter, she couldn't seem to persuade her father to truly smile.

"Does everyone know how to use the rifle attached to your saddle?" Dad asked, then continued, "Prayerfully, we won't need them, but just in case we come across some aggressive wildlife, it's best to be prepared."

Manipulating the lever action of the Winchester, Allan checked to see if the weapon was loaded. Cassidy knew his response would meet with her father's approval. From the time she was little, Dad had always said the first thing to do when handling a firearm was to check to see whether or not it was loaded.

Thomas shook his head. "I've never fired any gun, Mr. Ivanoff."

"Thanks for your honesty, Thomas. I'll be sure to teach you the proper handling of weapons. Stick close to me and you'll be fine."

"I'm good to go." Allan sheathed his rifle.

"All right, then. Cassidy, you go ahead and take the lead on this first section. Thomas, you follow her, then Allan, and I will bring up the rear. Keep your eyes open."

Cassidy didn't need any more encouragement. With the wind at her back, she prodded her horse over the stream and into a steady walk. Thomas was full of questions for her father, so she listened to the men's voices behind her and enjoyed the beauty of the day and the mountains before her.

"Are you a fisherman, Thomas?" Dad's question filled the air.

Cassidy didn't bother to hear the young man's answer. They had emerged from a thicket of spruce into the open moraine, where a lush green carpet of vegetation was brightened considerably by the first fuchsia blossoms of fireweed. Not far away, an Arctic fox skittered for cover while several young caribou danced across the field under the watchful eye of the High One. The view took her breath. It must have done the same for the others because everyone went silent.

They rode on in awe. Cassidy remembered other trips she'd made with her father. Over the years they'd camped in places just like this, enduring all seasons in order for her to learn everything she could about surviving off the land. It was on those trips Dad shared stories about their Athabaskan ancestors and some of the lore they had handed down from generation to genera-tion. It was in a setting just like this that Cassidy learned that falling in love for the first time didn't necessarily require another person.

When she looked down at her watch, an hour had passed. Dad and the others were in an intense conversation about the various species of trees and vegetation. Thomas didn't know what any of the plant life was called, but Allan proved he'd studied before coming to Alaska. As they neared another, larger stream, Cassidy pulled her horse to a stop and turned to glance at the men.

"Are we ready for a rest?"

"I think so." Dad looked at the others and nodded.

The guys all dismounted at the stream.

"I need to stretch." Allan reached high. "I haven't been on a horse for a while."

Thomas wandered off a ways. "Mr. Ivanoff, what is this?"

Cassidy's feet hadn't even touched the ground when she turned. Gasping, she realized what Thomas was reaching for and jumped. "Thomas! Don't touch it!" She took off racing toward him, her father not far behind.

Their young charge yanked his hands back and held them aloft as if someone were holding a gun up to him. "I'm sorry!"

Cassidy smiled as she reached him and sucked in big gulps of air. "Don't apologize. It's all right. But did you touch it?"

"I . . . I don't know."

"Let's go rinse it off in the stream just to be safe." She grabbed Thomas by the shoulder and dragged the poor lad over to the water. "That's pushki — cow parsnip. And while it can be eaten once it's peeled and has lovely flowers, if you touch the hairy stem, it emits a chemical in the sap that will burn you in the sunlight and will itch like

101

the dickens. You'll be miserable for days. And we don't want that, now, do we?"

He shook his head.

"Why don't you wash up real good in the stream and we'll take a break."

Dad and Allan had followed them to the stream, and both men nodded in agreement.

"I'd actually like to speak with you privately, sir, if you don't mind." Allan clasped his hands behind his back.

Her father nodded, but his face was serious indeed. "I had a feeling you would." He extended an arm. "Why don't we head upstream?" He turned toward her. "Cassidy, would you save me some of that wonderful lemonade?" He stepped closer and lowered his voice. "And keep Thomas out of trouble."

"Of course, Dad." She plastered a big smile on her face, hoping to convince him that she didn't suspect a thing. Which, of course, was far from the truth.

As she brought items out of the saddlebags, she wondered what Allan Brennan could possibly have to speak to her father about. In private, no less.

Allan Brennan. Brennan. Hmm. Dad had been upset after hearing the last name *Brennan.* What could have troubled him so?

Laying out the leftover tea cakes and cream, it all came back to her. The man who died on her father's expedition up Mount McKinley had been named Henry. Henry *Brennan.* She covered her mouth and tried to think. What should she do? She remembered her father telling her that Henry's business partner blamed him for Brennan's death. In fact, he vowed to ruin John. Was that why Allan had come? Was the job merely a ruse to get close to his enemy? To think she thought him handsome — gracious, what had come over her? The questions poured out one on top of the other like a waterfall. Would Allan try to hurt her father? No. He didn't seem to be bent on revenge. But she didn't really know him, did she? And that look. When he was standing on the platform. Was that why he was here? How could she have been so taken in?

"Thomas, I need you to keep an eye on the horses. I'll be right back."

"Yes, ma'am."

Grabbing the jug of lemonade for an excuse to intrude in case she needed one, Cassidy raced off to find her father.

Hopefully before it was too late.

6

"Why didn't you tell me who you were on the train?" Allan couldn't hold it in any longer.

John sat on a large boulder at the edge of the stream. "I didn't know who *you* were. As far as I remember, we didn't exchange surnames."

It wasn't until they'd shaken hands in front of the hotel that Allan had first heard John's last name. He was right. There was no reason for either one of them to know who the other was.

"I'm sure you want to know more about the 1917 expedition up Denali." John gazed at the water.

"And the death of my father, yes." He didn't mean to sound so angry, but his patience was gone, his voice tight and thick. Every negative thing Frank ever told him about the expedition came back to haunt him now. Pleasantries would get them nowhere — Allan simply had to know. To-day.

John seemed in no hurry to speak, but he at least had the decency to offer an uncomfortable expression as he shifted his weight.

"Well?"

"Your father was one of the most intriguing men I've ever met. We became good friends over the weeks of our journey. Unlike his partner, Frank, Henry and I loved everything about the expedition — being outdoors, climbing . . ." He turned his head completely away.

"What?"

"We had some incredible theological conversations as well. Your father really knew his stuff. He helped me to overcome some anger and resentment toward my wife's parents that I'd long since buried."

"I'm sure he did." Allan grimaced. His faith had waned after the death of his father, leaving in its wake resentment toward God. God, who could have kept his father alive, but didn't. Allan knew his father would have reprimanded him for his attitude — had he been alive. But he was dead and that was why they were here having this conversation in the first place.

"John, I need to know what happened to my father. And I need to know now. I don't want to discuss politics or religion or any other nonsense." He knew he sounded like a child having a tantrum.

The man ducked his head, gave a heavy sigh, and then looked him square in the eye. "Son, I can tell you're hurting, but your father had a deep faith. He hardly thought it nonsense."

"Perhaps he was a fool for his beliefs." Allan didn't know where that had come from. He'd never thought of his father in that way.

As if reading his mind, John countered, "Your father was a better man than most I've known, and I don't appreciate you disrespecting him in such a way."

"How dare you!" Disrespect? And this man claimed to know his father after a few measly weeks? "What about the disrespect you are showing by not being honest with me?"

John stood. "I don't mean any disrespect, son."

"Stop calling me son! My father was the only one with that right." He hadn't meant to sound so harsh, but now that things had taken that turn, he was hard-pressed to contain his agitation. "I need answers, John."

"I know . . . Allan." He sighed long and hard. "Because I needed them too. I think I still do. The day your father died was one of the worst of my life. Made even more so because of the circumstances."

Allan couldn't take it any longer. "What exactly *were* those circumstances? Because Frank told me it was all your fault. Was it? Are you to blame for my father's death?"

"Now, you wait just a minute, Mr. Brennan!" Cassidy's voice came from behind him.

He turned and narrowed his eyes, watching her stomp through the thick tundra grass.

"I am so sorry that you lost your father" — she set a jug of something down on a rock and planted her hands on her hips — "but I can't believe you would stoop to blaming *my* father! Your father knew the risk he took when he hired Dad to take him up the mountain. Dad would have made those dangers very clear."

"Cassidy, please." John straightened, his stance wide and imposing. "If you're going to stay, I need you to be quiet and listen." His voice was firm.

She huffed and crossed her arms.

Allan calmed a bit. Something about Cassidy's indignation shamed him. Where had all this ugliness and anger come from? Would that make his father proud? He removed his hat and ran a hand through his hair. "I just want to know the truth." He stopped short of apologizing for his tirade.

"I wish I knew, Allan. I wish I knew." John walked closer and stood only a yard away, staring at the mountain. "The trip up was fairly good. We had a few problems here and there, but otherwise it was uneventful. The weather held — surprisingly so. We summited the southern peak around 2:00 p.m. that day. Your father was so proud and all smiles. After we placed the marker in the snow, I noticed the weather was turning rapidly." He rubbed a hand down his face. "So we started our descent immediately. There was a rope between all of us so we couldn't lose each other in the blinding snow. I *watched* him secure it around his waist. By now there was no need to double-check his work." Several moments passed as he clenched and unclenched his jaw. "The wind picked up — light at first and then it became fierce and turned into a whiteout. As the seasoned climber I went first, to make certain the footing would be sure. Frank followed and then Henry."

"Why was my father last?"

"Because he was more experienced than Frank. Simple as that. Frank didn't seem to care; he just wanted down. I think he knew

108

how out of place he was compared to your father and me."

Allan nodded. "Go on."

"We didn't stop moving. Just worked our way down in the storm. The stronger the wind grew, the more I gave serious thought to stopping and putting up shelter, but I felt confident we could make our high camp. We pressed on with very little visibility, and I felt a great sense of relief when we reached the camp. That is, until I discovered Henry was no longer behind Frank. And the rope was intact."

Allan felt a chill go through him. "So what are you saying?"

"I don't *know* what happened to him. The only way for the rope to be intact was if Henry untied it himself."

"Why would he untie the rope? Wouldn't he have told Frank if he did that?"

"The storm was too much — you couldn't hear anything above the wind's roar. And you couldn't see anything — not even your hand in front of your face."

"So you just left him there?" Allan's anger mixed with his sorrow.

A silent tear traced a path down the older man's face. "No. I would never abandon a man." He came closer and laid a hand on Allan's shoulder. Allan wanted to move away but found he couldn't. It was as if an invisible force held him in place.

"We had to wait the storm out at the camp, but I told Frank I wasn't going on without Henry. He balked at the idea, but I think it was because he was coming down with something. He had a terrible fever once the storm was past. So I left him in a tent and went in search of your father."

Allan closed his eyes. "You went back for him?" Frank never mentioned that.

"I searched for two days, Allan. Up and down the same path we had taken. The only conclusion I could come to is that he lost his breath and couldn't keep up, so he must have untied the rope to take a break rather than get dragged and fall. It's not unusual when a man is oxygen deprived and disoriented for him to make poor decisions. We were all suffering a bit of altitude sickness, but your father seemed the best out of all of us. He'd been completely rational and able to maneuver on top of the summit. Still the storm could have caused him to panic. Once he was detached from us, he could have gotten lost, fallen into a crevasse, or any number of things. I searched for hours on end, but at the conclusion of two days, I knew it was pointless. Frank was worse and I had an obligation to get him safely down before I lost another man on the mountain."

Allan's eyes snapped open. "Frank has always blamed you for what happened."

"No more than I blame myself. I was responsible for that expedition. I was the one with experience. I was the one who signed on to take them. It was . . . *my* fault."

The man was more than willing to accept his part in what happened, but what *had* happened? Allan felt no closer to the answer than when they'd begun the conversation. Worse still, there was no sense of satisfaction in John's declaration and acceptance of responsibility.

Anger radiated throughout him, even more than before. All these years . . . he'd believed everything Frank told him. But maybe that's why Frank blamed John — because he couldn't bear his own guilt over not knowing what happened to his partner.

Cassidy gave Allan a look he couldn't decipher and went to her father. "Dad, I'm so sorry. I didn't know you went back to try to find him. Is that how you lost those toes? When you went searching?"

John looked down at his daughter. "It was easier for me to keep it to myself. I didn't handle the loss of Henry very well, and you were only seventeen. You didn't need any more burdens to carry. And a little frostbite

111

for me was nothing compared to the loss of a friend."

Allan couldn't bear the conversation between father and daughter. No one else should be hurting! He was the one who lost his father. "If you'll excuse me. I need a few moments."

Walking away from the Ivanoffs, he tried to make sense of all he'd just heard. What happened? If John saved Frank's life by getting him down the mountain, then why did Frank blame John for Henry's death? Was Frank even lucid at that point? Or was that how Frank coped with the loss of his lifelong friend?

The emotions roiling inside him were more than he could manage.

Why did Dad untie his rope?

Tuesday's staff meeting in the downstairs kitchen was packed. Cassidy squeezed through a group of the maids to be near Mrs. Johnson.

"How was the dedication service yesterday?" the older lady whispered to her as others continued to gather.

The staff had gotten back to the hotel at such a late hour there hadn't been time to talk about the service and then this morning there had been so much to catch up on,

Cassidy hadn't had a chance to fill Mrs. Johnson in on the details.

"The dedication was lovely." Cassidy smiled. "We weren't as close to Mount McKinley as I would have liked, but it was very nice regardless."

"I'm glad it went well. And your trek into the park?"

"It could've been better."

"Oh, really?" She straightened as Mr. Bradley entered the room and softened her voice. "Well, you can tell me about it later. Today will be busy. We have chocolate mousse on the menu as well as lemon soufflé. I'll put you in charge of the mousse."

Mr. Bradley cleared his throat and silence descended on the room. "The reason this morning's staff meeting includes everyone is because we need to reiterate how important it is that the President of the United States will visit our hotel. The Curry Hotel is the prize jewel of the Alaska Railroad, and what better way to welcome our country's leader than to show him the very best Alaska has to offer."

Murmurs and whispered words grew through the room.

"I know you are all excited about the President's visit, but let me continue please."

113

Everyone hushed.

"Thank you. We've had word that the presidential party has reached Alaska via *The Henderson.*" Their manager held a telegram aloft and glanced at it. "In a few days, they should reach Seward. And from there, they will take the Presidential Special — a collection of elegantly appointed cars designed by our railroad for this auspicious occasion — all the way to Fairbanks. The ceremony for the completion of the railroad will be in Nenana." He lowered the paper and pulled out his pocket watch. "Now, considering today is the tenth of July, we have roughly four and a half days to prepare for the President's group of approximately seventy people."

A few gasps erupted.

"Mrs. Johnson, I'd like to see your plans for the menus by three o'clock this afternoon."

"Yes, Mr. Bradley. Miss Ivanoff and I will be in your office as scheduled." Margaret Johnson never seemed to fear a challenge.

Cassidy felt her palms beginning to sweat. Was she up for the challenge as well?

"Mrs. McGovern, I will need a detailed schedule of the laundry and the tallies for all pieces that come through our facility. The President wishes to have an update,

114

since we service not only the railroad and this facility, but the hospitals as well. He mentioned something about a congressional delegation, so make sure you have every detail. You will also need to have room designations." He looked down again. "Let's meet at three thirty."

"Yes, sir." There was that pinched tone again from the head housekeeper.

"Mr. Ivanoff and Mr. Brennan . . ." Mr. Bradley turned to the men on the side. "There will not be time for a lengthy expedition, but they have requested a short nature walk from our best guide to show them the splendors of Alaska."

"Yes, sir. We will plan for such an event." Cassidy's dad nodded.

"Good, good. Bring your plans tomorrow." The manager looked down at his papers again. "I believe that is all for now, but let me say again that there will be absolutely no tolerance of shenanigans in the coming days. This visit needs to be perfect. Our reputation is on the line."

"Yes, Mr. Bradley." The voices of the staff echoed in the room.

And off he went. Up the stairs and on to some other important task, Cassidy was sure.

Wiping her hands on her apron, she

turned to Mrs. Johnson. "Do you think . . ." Maybe this wasn't such a good idea. She chewed on her lip. She needed to vent some frustration, and the very best way was trying something new. Besides, she'd wanted to ask for weeks now.

"Well? Do I think what?" The cook raised her eyebrows.

She'd never know if she didn't try. "Do you think I could help with the soufflés tonight?"

Her boss sighed. "Hmmm . . . I know you've been wanting to learn, but there's an awful lot to accomplish today. And soufflés can be very tricky, since they have to be served immediately." Mrs. Johnson squinted. "We will be having the same two desserts on Friday. Let's wait until then. Do you think you can get the mousses done before luncheon so they can chill? Then you'd have time to practice."

"Yes, ma'am." More sweat covered her palms, but she wiped it away on her apron again.

"All right, if you think you can get everything else done, you can help with them. And after our meeting with Mr. Bradley today, you can watch how I make them step by step."

"I know I can do it. Even if I don't take a

lunch break on Friday, it will be worth it."

Mrs. Johnson laughed. "I do love your enthusiasm, Cassidy. If only everyone could see the world through your eyes."

If only more people really *could* see through Cassidy's eyes. John's daughter had a way of cheering everyone up — of offering help where she could. And he desperately needed help right now, but this kind of help wasn't going to come from Cassidy.

Lord, tell me what to say.

John waited for the other staff to leave the room. Allan stood beside him, apparently waiting for instruction. The rest of their journey into the park yesterday had been — from Allan's part — silent. Thomas asked lots of questions, John and Cassidy gave information, but the tension had been fierce as Allan refused to speak any more about the expedition.

Cassidy hugged John as they returned, and even though she didn't say it, he knew she was struggling with anger toward Allan. Fiercely loyal, Cassidy would try to protect him from attack.

But in this case, he deserved it.

When the last person retreated up the stairs, John turned to his apprentice. "I can only imagine that this is very difficult for you, Allan. I know how much it has affected me personally. But I do feel you are a good man. Your father was a very good man, so I'm sure he raised you to follow in his footsteps."

Allan's jaw tensed but he said nothing.

"The best I can do is apologize again for the tragedy of losing your father. And to say to you that I take full responsibility. I was the guide. It was my job to bring them up and down that mountain safely." John held out his hand. "I pray that one day you will be able to forgive me."

Allan stared back at him and then looked down at the offered hand. "I appreciate that, John. As you know, this was quite a shock for me, and I am asking for your patience in this matter as I work through the facts."

"If you feel that you can't work with me, I'll find you another position."

Allan appeared surprised by this. "No, that's not necessary." The younger man reached out and took John's hand. "In the short time since my arrival in Alaska, I have already come to respect you." He sighed. "And I owe you an apology as well. It was wrong of me to accuse you in such a way."

"It was understandable, son. I don't blame you for it. As to your respect, I will seek to earn it every day." John released his hand.

"But this will be a demanding summer for you, I'm afraid. There is a lot to learn, and we need to trust one another."

Allan nodded. "I came here to learn everything I can, to follow in my father's footsteps, and to finish what he started. I will work hard."

"And you'll be able to do as I instruct? You were very angry yesterday. And with good reason, but I need to know that you'll answer to me and heed my instruction." John hated pressing the issue, but it had to be voiced. There wouldn't be room for grudges. They needed trust. And a lot of it. "Will you be able to trust me?"

For a moment Allan said nothing, but then he gave a curt nod. "I will do whatever is required of me. You have my word."

Cassidy sat outside enjoying a few idle hours. Despite their complicated schedule, the work was well in hand. Mr. Bradley had agreed to let Thomas continue helping Cassidy's father and Allan, much to Mrs. Johnson's relief. Cassidy had to admit that Thomas's absence had made things in the kitchen run much smoother. Poor Thomas.

She flipped through a magazine that had been left behind by one of the guests and soaked in the sun's warmth after a few chilly days of rain. The magazine featured advertisements for cosmetics and modern time-saving appliances — efforts to entice old-fashioned women to throw off their shackles of nineteenth-century thinking, Cassidy mused. Inside the back was an ad for "The Eden — The Supreme Achievement in Electric Washing Machines." A smiling woman stood beside her new washing machine, looking for all the world as if this were the only place in the world she wanted to be. Further perusal revealed ads for various other appliances, foods, and clothing.

A giggle escaped her as Cassidy read about the latest in undergarments, designed to free women from the damaging effects of corsets. The new formless styles required wrapping one's chest to make it as flat as possible. Camisoles and step-ins were the rage, the latter being a one-piece article of clothing that took the place of bloomers and chemises. Silk was the fashionable material of the day for everything from undergarments to outer wear. Macy's advertisement showed dresses with hems that nearly touched the floor, all in the straight, formless style that the modern woman was supposedly delighted to wear.

"What's so funny?"

Cassidy snapped the magazine shut at the

sound of Allan's voice. She felt her cheeks grow hot. What was he doing here? "Nothing really." She pushed the magazine aside. "I was just amused by some of the advertisements." At least that much was true without explaining exactly what had caught her attention.

Allan glanced down at the magazine. "So are you going to bob your hair?"

Cassidy's gaze went to the cover and the model whose hair was clipped to a length just above her collar. She shook her head. "Not me. I can't imagine how much work that would be. It's a lot easier to brush mine out and braid it without worrying about putting in pin curls or slicking it up with whatever it is they use to plaster it into place."

"I'm glad. I'd hate to see you cut it."

She didn't like being the focus of his attention, especially after yesterday. He'd been so angry. Of course, if her father had died on the mountain and she didn't have answers, she'd probably be angry too. But it made her wary of Allan, since she didn't know him.

The silence stretched.

"You lived in Seattle before coming here, didn't you?" Best to offer an olive branch if possible.

"I did." He took the chair beside her. "Why do you ask?"

"No reason in particular. I just remember Dad saying something about that."

Allan frowned. "I see."

Cassidy heard the tone of his voice change. "So you still blame my father for your father's death?"

The question surprised her almost as much as it obviously surprised Allan. What had gotten into her? She hadn't meant to be confrontational — in fact, she thought she'd been trying to be neutral — but it was too late to take back the words now.

"No. But I don't know what I think." He looked out across the lawn. "It's hard to figure out what one should think or feel when the information given is in conflict."

"My father is a good man. I'm not just saying that because I'm his daughter. You can ask anyone who has known him for any length of time. He was devastated when your father was lost. He thinks he hid it well, and in truth he probably did better than most men, but I could see how much it ate at him."

She paused only a moment to let the words sink in. "I once overheard him discuss that climb with Superintendent Karstens. Dad told him that he kept going over and over all the details of the climb, trying to figure out if he'd somehow been neglectful or blind to the dangers. Mr. Karstens told him he could second-guess himself until the end of his days and it wouldn't change anything. Dad said he'd give just about anything if he could go back in time and do things different. Mr. Karstens asked him what he'd do differently and Dad said, 'Whatever it would take to bring Henry Brennan out alive.' "

For several long minutes neither one said a word. Cassidy hoped Allan would believe her father's sincerity. Her father would have traded places with Brennan, even knowing it would have left her orphaned. That was just how Dad was — how he would always be. The needs of others were more important than his own.

"My father's business partner, Frank Irving, said your father was cavalier in his attitude about the risks and that the weather had been threatening before they even made the summit climb."

Cassidy felt a surge of anger. "My father would never put people in danger. It would serve no purpose. And if he were as cavalier as your Mr. Irving suggests, why would he risk his own life? Perhaps Mr. Irving is the one who was negligent. After all, as I recall, he was on the rope between your father and mine. If it was such an easy thing to keep track of your father in the storm, then why didn't Mr. Irving realize he was gone?"

"You think I haven't asked myself those questions?" Allan fixed her with a look that betrayed his frustration. "I have looked for answers ever since learning of what happened. I owe it to my father to learn the truth and I can't rest until I do."

"And what if you never get those answers?" Cassidy forced herself to hold his gaze. "What if there aren't any?"

He shook his head. "I don't know."

"Is it truly so important to blame someone for what happened? It won't bring your father back."

"No, but it might make someone account for what happened."

"How?" She shook her head. "People come up here and get hurt or die all the time. Your father knew the risk of climbing the mountain before he went. He knew that my father couldn't guarantee his safety — that he had no control over the weather or ice fields or any other part of the mountain. He accepted that — so why can't you?" She got to her feet, afraid that if she didn't leave, she might say something she'd regret. "I hope you find peace of mind. I truly do.

124

But it's been my experience that such peace only comes through God."

A turmoil of emotions rocked her insides as she walked away. Why did it matter so much that he came to terms with this? Was it just because her father was the object of his doubt? Or was it something entirely different?

She cared about Allan — just as she did everyone who worked at the Curry Hotel, but perhaps she cared too much. She found herself thinking about him — looking for him at various times. At first she thought it was simply out of concern for her father, but now . . . now she wasn't at all certain that was all there was to it.

Shaking her head, Cassidy did her best to put the matter behind her. There was no way for her to make matters right between Allan and her father — they were going to have to settle this between them. So why did she feel so cold?

A wave of loneliness washed over her. Dad was dealing with this incredible loss all over again and was shutting her out. And then there was Allan.

She barely knew the man. But that look in his eyes when they'd met told her that he understood pain and heartache. Maybe even a touch of loneliness. Like her.

There seemed to be a connection. But what if she had just imagined it? Had longed for it? She shook her head. Losing her heart to Allan, a man who would accuse her father like that, would do nothing but complicate the matter further.

7

John laid his copious notes on Bradley's desk. "Here are all the details for the nature walk we plan to take the presidential party on Saturday evening."

Another day had flown past with details, planning, meetings, and of course the constant guests to attend to in the hotel.

The manager studied the page. "This looks outstanding, John. Thank you." He scribbled something on the paper. "How is Brennan working out?"

"Fine, sir. He's a hard worker."

"Did you know that he's part owner of an outdoor equipment company?"

"Yes, sir. I did." Would there come a time when Allan would share with the manager about John's failings? Of course it wasn't like Bradley didn't know about the death of Allan's father.

"A very enterprising young man. He even mentioned the possibility of speaking to the railroad about selling some of his gear here in Curry."

John nodded, a knot forming in his throat. "If you don't need anything else, I'd better get moving. We are taking a group fishing this afternoon."

"Well, I hope they catch the big one."

"Thank you." John headed out the side door of the office. The biggest problem he seemed to have right now was not the full schedule, not the training of his apprentice, and not even the fact that Thomas had a tendency to bumble up even the simplest of tasks.

Right now, he battled himself.

With Allan's appearance in Curry, the confrontation up at the park, and their conversation in the basement yesterday — John couldn't get past the one glaring issue.

He couldn't forgive himself.

The circumstances around the death of Henry Brennan haunted him. He thought he'd put the situation behind him. But all of Allan's questions brought it back to the forefront of his mind.

Had there been anything else he could have done to save Henry?

And now, Henry's son was here. Flesh and blood. Seeking answers.

While John knew what Allan sought could

only be found in God, he still felt responsible. Even more than that.

He felt guilty.

For failing Henry.

And for failing Henry's family.

Taking the stairs down to the basement, John prayed for wisdom. Cassidy had noticed he wasn't himself and had questioned him. No sense in worrying anyone else with his problems.

Boom!

The stairs shook. John rounded the corner into the section gang dining room. "Hello! Everyone all right?"

"Mr. Ivanoff — help! Over here!" Thomas's voice came from the laundry on the other side of the basement.

A cloud of white smoke billowed out of the door.

John raced over. "What's happened?"

"One of the pipes burst. I had just brought a load down from the train and fell. I thought it was my own clumsiness, but when I looked up, the ladies were on the floor."

It hit him. This wasn't smoke. It was steam. John looked at the south wall where Thomas pointed. Mrs. McGovern and two maids lay crumpled in the corner. Hissing came from the burst pipe.

"Thomas, you've got to get help. Everyone you can."

Allan collided with Thomas as the young man raced up the stairs. "Whoa, what's your hurry?"

"Mr. Ivanoff said to get everyone I could to help. A pipe burst in the laundry."

Allan nodded. "I'll go down. You grab everyone you find."

"Yes, sir."

He'd felt a jolt as he'd stood on the train platform. But since the train was leaving, he didn't give much thought to it.

The whole laundry was steam powered. That meant if a pipe burst, then boiling hot steam was flooding that area. The initial pressure would be abated, but the pumps would keep sending it until they could shut it off.

At the base of the stairs, Allan slipped. The floor was already wet from the water vapor and mist from the cooled steam, and the humid air almost choked him. As he reached the laundry, sweat poured down his face.

He found John carrying Mrs. McGovern out of the room. "Any more?"

"There's at least two more maids huddled in the southwest corner."

130

Taking a closer look at Mrs. McGovern, he noticed that her face was very red. Had she been burned by the steam? Allan didn't have time to think about the condition of the others. He plunged into the simmering room and went down to his hands and knees. He'd be more apt to find them that way.

Steam filled the room in a great white fog. Allan reached out and found hands grabbing for him.

"It's so hot! Help us, please!"

Allan latched on to an arm and pulled. A young maid's head hit his shoulder.

"Please help Marie. She's not talking anymore."

He carried the maid out and passed John on the way. "There's another maid unconscious in that corner. Her name's Marie."

The steam filled the basement of the hotel quickly. Allan set down the young girl as thunderous footsteps were heard on the stairs. "The floor's slippery. Be careful!" He only hoped they'd heed his warning.

He followed more men back into the laundry as John carried the other maid out.

John shoved her into Thomas's arms. "Get her out of here." He ripped off his jacket and vest and threw them down the hallway.

The suffocating heat had to be taking its

131

effect on his boss. But Allan followed his lead and ran once more back to the laundry. Several men were turning the giant valve to shut off the steam supply. John stood in front of the busted pipe with towels to keep the steam at bay. Allan grabbed more towels and went to help. The heat was almost unbearable. But if John could sacrifice himself to help the men, then so could he.

It took several minutes, but the room began to clear. Every man was soaked from head to toe. Two maintenance workers came in with large wrenches and clamps.

Mr. Bradley slipped as he came around the corner, and he grabbed on to the doorjamb. "Oh, thank goodness, you got it stopped!" The manager looked around the room at each man. "Thank you all."

The men all nodded, each gasping for air. "It took too many of us to get that wheel turned. Too hot and too slick," one of the men said. "That needs to be fixed. Coulda been a disaster."

"Do we know what happened?" Mr. Bradley asked.

"No, not exactly," the same man replied. "Must have been a weakness in the pipe. We'll get it repaired right away."

"It's a tragedy to be sure. Do we know how badly the women were hurt?"

"Not yet," John replied. "We just managed to get the last one to safety."

Allan breathed heavily, his hands on his hips. "It was John and Thomas who rescued the women, sir."

Mr. Bradley went over and shook John's hand.

Allan left the room and walked slowly to the dining room. Chaos ensued as everyone started cleaning up. Water was everywhere.

But his thoughts kept going back to John. He'd risked his own life over and over again to save someone else. Even blocking the boiling steam so the other men could shut it off. How many men would put themselves in harm's way like that?

But then an even more troubling question seared his heart — if Allan hadn't had an example to follow, would *he* have done the same?

The individual crystal dishes filled with luscious chocolate mousse sat in the large icebox chilling. Cassidy couldn't be prouder. They were her best yet.

"They turned out lovely. The texture is simply divine." Mrs. Johnson licked her lips. A sure sign of her satisfaction and pleasure.

Cassidy bounced on the balls of her feet. She kept her hands clasped in front of her to keep from hugging the older woman for the praise. "Thank you, Mrs. Johnson."

"I pity the men and women who've never tasted a mousse like this."

Wow. Three compliments in a row. She wasn't sure she was *that* deserving.

"All right. Well, we seem to be ahead of schedule." The head cook checked her watch and then wiped her hands on her apron. "Let's try a single batch of soufflé for the staff to enjoy. And if it turns out properly, we can do them together for the dinner guests."

What a challenge! Mrs. Johnson's lemon soufflés were famous. Cassidy had longed to make them since she'd arrived. And how incredible would it be to serve them to the wealthy crowd at dinner?

They gathered the ingredients together and set it all out on Cassidy's station. The older woman gave the eggs to Cassidy. "Separate them."

"Yes, ma'am." This was a job she could do in her sleep. Well, almost. Cassidy giggled to herself.

"What on earth has struck you as funny this time?"

"Nothing. Sorry." She worked very hard to look serious but feared she looked more like a fish.

Mrs. Johnson smiled and shook her head. "No one could ever accuse you of being melancholy, that's for sure." She grabbed a whisk and a clean bowl, and went right back to business. "Wipe the bowl down with a drop of vinegar. Only a drop, mind you."

"Yes, ma'am."

"It's time to whip the egg whites. Now one of the most important things is to make sure you do *not* overbeat them. They need to hold a stiff peak but not be dry."

The recipe really wasn't that difficult. Whipping the yolks with sugar and lemon zest, gradually adding hot cream, and cooking until it was pudding-like. Then folding the fluffy egg whites with lemon into the mixture. In no time, Cassidy felt she'd have it down to a perfectly timed routine.

As she gently set the tray in the oven, she said a little prayer.

Mrs. Johnson wiped her hands on a towel and headed toward her desk in the opposite corner. "Let me know when they're done. I need to check the list for the night cook and then must speak to Mr. Bradley. I shouldn't be long."

"Yes, Cook." Cassidy stared at the oven with her hand on her watch. Mrs. Johnson said it was a precise amount of time. But what if she messed it up in some way?

135

Several minutes passed as Cassidy cleaned up her worktable, glancing at her watch every ten or fifteen seconds. Time would never pass at this rate. The rest of the staff moved in steady rhythm, preparing their parts of the sumptuous feast for tonight. But she couldn't stand it any longer. Maybe if she just peeked in the oven it would set her mind at ease.

Mrs. Johnson spoke with two of the kitchen maids and headed toward the dining room. Now was Cassidy's chance. She pulled on the handle of the massive door and gently opened it a few inches.

Well, they didn't look like they were supposed to. In fact, they were all a touch lopsided. She closed the door. Maybe they rose up one side and then the other?

Trying to hide her disappointment, Cassidy checked her watch. Three and a half more minutes to go. She stomped her foot. The job of assistant cook hadn't just been handed to her. She'd worked really hard for this position and had studied and cooked and cooked and studied some more. Why, of all the kitchen workers, she could make the best hollandaise. Mrs. Johnson even said so, and that's why the job was always hers. Everything from demitasse to the perfect poached egg, chocolate mousse to roast lamb, Cassidy could cook it.

She just needed confidence in herself. The soufflés would be fine. She knew what she was doing.

One more glance at her watch told her it was time. Opening the oven door with towels in hand to grab the soufflés, she hoped for success.

But when she set them down, disappointment crept up her spine. They were all still crooked.

One by one, the individual soufflés deflated into their cups like turtles into their shells.

She wouldn't cry. She refused.

A couple of the kitchen maids walked by. One frowned and *tsk*ed at her. "Those don't look like the chef's."

The other whispered. "It's because it's Friday the thirteenth, don'tcha know? Nothing can go right today. Just look at the mess down in the basement."

Mrs. Johnson chose that moment to reappear, and Cassidy wanted to hide under the table. Instead, she placed her hands on her hips and studied her creations. Like a good student would do. Learn from her mistakes.

Without a word, the head cook grabbed a spoon. Dipping it into a cup, she filled her spoon with a bite. She blew on the hot morsel before popping it into her mouth. "Delicious, Cassidy."

She frowned. "But they collapsed."

"Yes, they did. But at least they taste like they are supposed to. Now we need to figure out what went wrong. And it had nothing to do with Friday the thirteenth. Such foolishness." The older woman scowled at the young help, and handed Cassidy another spoon. "Try it yourself."

Not wasting a moment, Cassidy did just that. And while the pleasing flavor and texture made her feel a sense of accomplishment, that didn't make up for the fact that they didn't look like they were supposed to.

"Before they collapsed, I noticed they were a little uneven."

"Yes, ma'am."

"So I'm guessing you forgot to run your finger around the edge of each cup to ensure they were clean of batter?"

"Um . . ." Had she? "I probably did forget."

"And did you use upward strokes with the butter when you prepared the dishes before sprinkling them with sugar?"

"Hmm, maybe not upward strokes."

"Did you perchance open the oven while they were baking?"

138

She winced. "Yes, I did."

"I had a feeling." Mrs. Johnson almost smiled. "I did that my first time too. Opening the oven will make them collapse almost every time. And while all soufflés will still go down after a few minutes, you want them done, not soupy, and nice and high for the presentation. That's why they are served immediately."

Cassidy nodded. She'd wanted to impress her boss, and now she'd made classic mistakes. All because she was in too big of a hurry — not wanting to be patient.

"There's a lot to learn, Cassidy. But you need to remind yourself that you are the assistant cook here! That's a hefty position." The woman waved for the staff to come over. "Now, while everyone tastes your delicious first efforts, you can work on the second."

A little bit of shock rolled through her limbs. "Truly, you want me to make them again?"

"As my father always used to say, when you fall off the horse, you must get right back on." The woman grabbed another spoonful. "And Cassidy?"

"Yes, ma'am?"

"Yum."

8

The temperature at nine in the evening still held the heat of the day as Allan walked along the train tracks. So many thoughts battled for attention — maybe the bright sunlight could help to burn them all away. The long daylight hours of summer in Alaska still baffled him. Hands in his pockets, he meandered along.

Off in the distance, Cassidy sat on a log. He hadn't meant to follow her outside, but he did. Would she want to talk to him?

His footsteps on the gravel caught her attention.

"Hi."

"Hello." She gave him a small smile. "What brings you out here?"

He shrugged. "Just needed a stroll, I guess." Hesitation brought him up short. Might as well be honest. "Actually, I saw you come out here."

"Oh?" Was that reluctance behind her eyes?

He pointed to the log. "May I?"

"Certainly."

Allan sat and kicked some rocks with his shoe. "I need to apologize to you."

Her shoulders lifted and she straightened. Gone was the smile.

"I was unfair to your father. And I'm sorry."

She looked back to the west. "While I appreciate your apology to me, I'm wondering if you've apologized to him as well — since he's the one you were unfair to." There was no malice in her tone. In fact, he heard — and almost felt — kindness and compassion in her voice.

"I have. He's been very patient and understanding."

She looked at him then and folded her hands in her lap. "I wasn't very considerate of your feelings either. All I heard was the pain in your voice and the accusations. I only wanted to protect my father. I'm sorry for jumping in where I shouldn't have."

He nodded. "It's perfectly understandable on your part, Cassidy." Turning toward her, he removed his hat. "Just as I am seeking to understand my father's death and want to defend him and his actions, I know you are

141

doing the same. And I respect that."

With a nod, she turned her face back to the west — the sunlight making her dark hair shine. "So you're no longer angry?"

Tough question. He sighed. "I'm trying to work on my anger over my dad's death. I know it's wrong. But no, I'm not angry at your father. He's a good man." He leaned closer to her, trying to catch her eye. "And I'd really like for us to be friends."

"Oh, Dad already thinks very highly of you. You're friends." She turned her head and gazed at him.

He smiled. "I meant" — he waved his hand between them — "that I'd really like for you and me — Cassidy and Allan — to be friends."

She tilted her head to one side and studied him, then shook her head and gave him a brilliant smile. "I already thought we were, so of course we can be friends."

"Well, I did wonder, because I had made you pretty mad — and rightfully so."

"I have moments of anger, Allan. Even with friends. And we *are* friends."

"Wonderful." If only his anger was just moments . . . one of these days, he'd have to tackle it. But he couldn't bear the thought of not having Cassidy as his friend. Best to change the subject. "Now, I was wondering if you could help me with some of the wild flowers around here."

She stood and he followed. Easy conversation flowed between them as they walked up and down the train tracks. Allan hadn't felt comfort like this in a long time. If only he could rewrite the past, he might have a chance for a happy future.

Thomas carried the last load of heavy equipment into the lobby. His arms ached from all the hauling.

"Put it over there by the fireplace," Mr. Bradley directed and pointed while writing on a paper with his other hand.

In all his seventeen years, Thomas had never seen anything quite so grand as all the preparations for the President of the United States. Of course, he'd never seen electric lights or running water until coming to work at the Curry Hotel a few weeks ago. The orphanage he grew up in didn't have either. In fact, most people in remote parts of Alaska didn't.

It was a thrill to get to use an indoor water closet rather than racing out in the cold to use a drafty privy. But he guessed the President wouldn't know about such things.

The maids set up a table with a fancy

tablecloth as Thomas began unloading the crates.

The manager walked up behind him and laid a hand on his shoulder. "You're doing a good job, son."

"Thank you, sir." Thomas reminded himself of John's wise words every day, to take a bit more time so he wouldn't drop anything or trip. "But do ya mind me asking what all this is for?"

"Why, it's a radio!" Mr. Bradley tucked his thumbs into his vest.

Thomas stood next to him and looked back at the jumble of pieces. "What's a radio?"

He chuckled. "Son, I think you'll have to experience it to understand. Radios make it possible for us to hear music, concerts, speeches, news, and all kinds of things from many miles away. In fact, they are installing an up-to-date long-wave receiver in Seward as we speak. We've been told that with the increase in power, they've been able to hear broadcasting from Long Island, New York, all the way in New Zealand. And that's nine thousand miles away."

"Well, ain't that ducky." He had no idea what it meant, but it obviously was a big deal to the manager. Especially to rush to get it installed, since they were expecting the presidential train at any moment.

Mr. Bradley laughed. "Yes, Thomas, it is. It will make it easier for us to stay connected up here. And we wanted the President's group to see that here at the Curry, we are up to the very best standards on everything."

Two men joined them and went to work on all the pieces. Wood and wires and round mesh-covered things. It was an odd puzzle to put together.

Thomas stood transfixed. Even though he had no idea what a radio did, the idea of it fascinated him.

The next moment, hissing emanated from the boxes.

"The static will get worse at certain times of day because of the long hours of sun in the summer." One of the men spoke to the manager. "We'll find a station to test today, but you'll have to look for others once the receiver is fully functional."

With a turn of the knob, everything changed. All of a sudden, the lobby was filled with voices. Speaking at quite a clip, the voices weren't anything Thomas could understand.

"Sir, what is that?" He stepped forward, mesmerized by the machine in front of him.

The one turning the knob stuck his ear

up to the side of it. "I believe that's Russian."

Unable to find anything else but the hissing, the man turned it off. "Well, at least we know it works."

"Yes," Mr. Bradley nodded. "But it's probably not best to be playing Russian radio for the President when he arrives."

The man packed up his bag of tools as red crept up his neck and ears. "I apologize. I can't control the reception. But in a few days, you should be able to hear more variety." He placed his hat on his head and rushed out the front door of the hotel, followed by the other man.

Mr. Bradley paced in front of the fire. "Well, I guess we will just have to keep trying it."

A long whistle sounded in the distance, followed by two short ones, and then another long.

A smile broke across Mr. Bradley's face. "Thomas, it's time to meet the President."

Staff members flooded the lobby from belowstairs, abovestairs, the dining room, and kitchen. Everywhere Thomas looked, someone was straightening a tie, brushing off an apron, or fixing their hair.

The maids and kitchen staff lined up in the lobby at brisk attention while the agent and his men, Mr. Bradley, Mrs. McGovern, Mr. Ivanoff, and Mr. Brennan all went outside.

"Thomas!" Mr. Bradley waved at him. "Come with me, just in case we need your help."

"Me, sir?" His voice squeaked.

"Hurry up."

Cassidy caught his elbow as he headed for the door. "Straighten your hair, Thomas, and put your cap on." She wiggled his tie tighter around his neck. "Stay still." She gave him a quick smile. "Now go."

He wiped down his apron just to be safe. Straightening his shoulders, he headed out the door and onto the platform.

The train had puffed to a stop, and several men checked around the platform and train.

Thomas watched all the other staff. Ramrod straight. Shoulders back. Everyone waited in anticipation.

A door finally opened and people began to disembark. Several more men looked around the platform and went into the hotel. When they came back out, one of the men went straight to a car in the back, one that looked just a bit spiffier than the others. He opened the door and a few elegant people emerged.

Flash lamps from several photographers

147

popped and sizzled as Thomas realized they were capturing this moment in history. And he was a part of it.

And then . . . there he was. An older gentleman with piercing eyes, silver hair, and bushy black eyebrows. The President of the United States of America. Standing in front of him.

Mr. Bradley extended a hand. "Mr. President, it's an honor to have you here in Curry, Alaska. I'm Alexander Bradley, the manager of the hotel."

"Why, yes, Mr. Bradley. How good to meet you. And who is this tall young man?"

The President was smiling at him. Mr. Bradley nudged him with an elbow. Thomas wasn't sure what to do, so he stuck out his hand. "I'm Thomas Smith, sir."

A flash lamp went off near his face and he had to close his eyes against the brilliance. When he opened his eyes, the party had moved down the platform.

He couldn't help but smile. What a gift Mr. Bradley had given him. He'd have this story to tell for the rest of his life. He, Thomas Smith, orphan — had just met the President and shaken his hand.

The dining room was decked out in its finest. A smile split Cassidy's lips. How exciting to be part of something so important as feeding the President and First Lady. She did a final check over all the serving dishes to ensure nothing had spilt on any of the edges. They were ready.

George, the head waiter, approached her, his white embroidered towel hanging over his left arm, the crispness of his black jacket in stark contrast. "I would like to go over the details of the menu with you."

"Of course." Cassidy pointed to a dish. "We will start with the grapefruit cocktail, olives, salted peanuts, and fresh salmonberries with cream. Then we will move to the cream of tomato. It will come out in the white-and-gold soup tureen." She watched for his nod of approval. "The next course will be boiled king salmon à la Seward, crab in shell, and the tasting spoon of smoked salmon. Following that, roast turkey with sage dressing, sweet potatoes, garden peas, and then a light salad." She went round to the other side to gather serving dishes and spoons. "Dessert will be baked Alaska and will be followed by Roquefort cheese and crackers and demitasse."

"Wonderful. Thank you, Miss Ivanoff." George turned and walked toward the other black-and-white-suited waiters.

She checked her watch. Their guests

would arrive at any moment. Scurrying back into the kitchen, she checked on the sponge cakes for the base of their dessert. Everything was as it should be. As she glanced around, she realized the noise level was much lower than normal. Everyone moved quickly and without a word. Spoons scraped on bowls, an occasional pot clanged, but the importance of their guests seemed to have glued everyone's lips shut. The thought made her want to giggle, but she thought better of it. Best not to provoke Mrs. Johnson yet again.

Mrs. Johnson marched through the kitchen, arms behind her back. She glanced at Cassidy. "I take it we are ready?"

"Yes, ma'am."

No sooner were the words out of her mouth than the booming voice of Mr. Bradley welcomed their guests into the dining room.

Time moved at a doubled pace after that. Each serving platter had to be perfect, the food the exact temperature, and each course precisely timed. When the roast turkey went out of the kitchen, Cassidy was already hard at work on the meringue for the baked Alaska.

Exhausted after beating the shiny peaks, she wiped her brow before assembling the individual desserts.

Mrs. Johnson headed her way. "Seems I have my hands free for a few moments. Let me help with that."

"That would be lovely. Thank you." Cassidy scurried to the icebox for the pre-molded rounds of ice cream. They worked together as if one were the right hand and the other the left. Cassidy had observed Mrs. Johnson for so long now, she could almost guess what she would do next. The baked Alaska took shape as they stacked ice cream on the cakes, and then smothered them in meringue. With this done, the trays went into the hot oven to bake the meringue around the luscious dessert.

While Mrs. Johnson crossed the room to instruct one of the maids, Cassidy carefully watched the clock. The meringue would brown in less than four minutes at the high temperature and she wanted to make certain it didn't burn. The time flew by.

"Beautiful!" Mrs. Johnson said as Cassidy pulled the tray from the oven. "A dessert fitting of the President, don't you agree?"

"Most assuredly, yes!" Cassidy grinned and began plating the desserts onto their serving platters.

"Wow." Thomas walked over to the table where the mountains of baked Alaska sat.

"What is it?" A stream of waiters entered and snatched up the trays.

Cassidy wasn't certain why Thomas was in the kitchen and could only hope that Mrs. Johnson wouldn't become riled. But to her surprise the head cook handed him a small bowl. "Baked Alaska. Try it." So the woman had a soft spot for the young man after all, didn't she? "It's cake and ice cream baked with a meringue around it."

His eyes grew wide. "I can eat this?"

"You sure can. But be quick about it, you'll be needed to help clear the tables." Mrs. Johnson pulled the last tray from the oven. "And the rest of you may have one as well. You've all earned it."

The kitchen staff all flocked to the table where Mrs. Johnson handed out dessert. It didn't take long for everyone to have a mouthful of the creamy dish.

Cassidy gave Thomas a nudge. "What do you think?"

"It's . . . amazing. You're amazing . . . I mean . . . well, you made this, right?"

She laughed. "I did."

He nodded. "You did a real good job." He continued to look at her as if he might say something else.

Mr. Bradley rushed in, and plates and spoons clattered to the table as everyone stood at attention. "Mrs. Johnson, I'd like you and Miss Ivanoff to accompany me into the dining room."

"Yes, sir." At least the older woman had the clarity of mind to respond. "Is something wrong?"

Cassidy blinked and looked around the room. All eyes were on her.

Mr. Bradley just motioned to them. "Come on, hurry."

"Let's go, dear." Mrs. Johnson grabbed her arm and Cassidy forced herself to swallow the ice cream in her mouth. She looked down at her apron and quickly swiped her mouth with her hand. It wouldn't do to meet the President with food on her lips.

Quiet conversation filled the room as all the dinner guests smiled and ate and drank from little coffee cups. In the center of it all sat a distinguished man and smiling lady.

Mr. Bradley held out an arm. "Mr. President, might I introduce to you our head chef, Margaret Johnson, and her assistant, Cassidy Ivanoff."

The gentleman stood and bowed to them. Goodness, no one had ever bowed to Cassidy before. Was this how the well-to-do greeted one another?

"I can't tell you what a privilege it is to meet you ladies. This meal has been one of the finest I've ever had, and I asked your manager here to allow me to say it to you in person."

"Why . . . thank you, Mr. President." Mrs. Johnson curtsied.

Cassidy just stood there. She didn't even know how to curtsy. Was she supposed to? She bent her knees a little and nodded.

The President came closer and smiled at her. "I take it your father is the knowledgeable guide who is to take us all on a hike later this evening."

"Yes, sir. Thank you, sir. It should be a beautiful night for it. There are still hours of daylight left."

"Is there anything in particular that the delegation and I shouldn't miss?"

"The fireweed, sir." Cassidy cleared her throat. "It's my favorite and is spectacular up the ridge."

Several of the women murmured to one another.

Mrs. Harding came a little closer and put her hand on her husband's arm. "Did I hear that we would have fireweed honey in the morning at breakfast?"

"Yes, ma'am. You did." Mrs. Johnson patted Cassidy's shoulder. "In fact, it's harvested right here by our own Miss Ivanoff."

"How lovely. I can't wait to try it." The

First Lady put a hand to her waist. "But I'm in need of a strenuous walk after that feast. Or I won't be able to eat for days."

The President moved forward again. "Thank you, ladies, for your time. The meal was delicious."

As the prestigious couple turned and walked toward other guests, Cassidy and Mrs. Johnson both exhaled at the same time. It elicited an "almost" chuckle out of Mrs. Johnson. "That wasn't so bad now, was it?"

Cassidy shook her head. But she didn't think she'd ever forget how nervous she felt. Mrs. Johnson didn't look completely un-moved by the experience. The woman had a way about her that always seemed indiffer-ent and reserved, but Cassidy could see by the gleam in the older woman's eyes that she was pleased.

Crash!

The sound of broken crystal and china hitting the floor filled the room. Cassidy closed her eyes, afraid to look, but knew she must. Peeking through one open eyelid, she looked toward the noise. Sure enough. Thomas was sprawled on the floor, an empty tray beside him. An unbroken china cup still rattled as it rocked on the floor. Looking back to Mrs. Johnson, Cassidy could see the expression of mortification on the older woman's face. Thomas was sure to be fired.

Cassidy raced over to his side, hoping to diffuse the situation before Mr. Bradley or Mrs. Johnson had a chance to blow up at the poor kid. Photographers readied their flash lamps.

But Mrs. Florence Harding beat her to him. The First Lady reached down a hand and helped Thomas up. "I'm so sorry, young man. I stepped directly into your path, didn't I?"

"No . . . no . . . no . . . ma'am. Not at all." His head shook back and forth at a rapid pace and cast a glance in the direction of the manager. He straightened his shoulders. "I'm sorry, ma'am. I was at fault."

"Nonsense. And don't try to coddle me just because I'm the First Lady. I take full responsibility." The woman was a genius. She had the whole room hanging on every word. Even Mr. Bradley was smiling, and no one would dare contradict her, even though they all knew it hadn't been her fault.

She reached a hand up and laid it on Thomas's shoulder. "You know, it reminds me of when I ran the *Marion Star* years ago.

I had all those newsboys trained to move so quick" — she snapped her fingers — "that I often got in the way and tripped them up when they'd pick up their papers because I wasn't moving fast enough. Again, please accept my apology." The woman beamed a smile at Thomas while a photographer took another shot.

"You're . . . you're . . ." Thomas couldn't seem to stop stuttering, but Mrs. Harding only smiled and gave him another pat on the shoulder.

"You are a very capable young man, and if I had a son, I would want him to be just like you." After one more pat she elegantly walked away.

If Cassidy had been on regular speaking terms with Mrs. Harding, she would've thanked her profusely later and then asked to learn her skills. The woman could smooth over a disturbance like no one Cassidy had ever seen.

It must take a lot of practice being a politician's wife.

The thing that mattered right now? Thomas was out of trouble. At least for the next few minutes.

9

Allan walked through the crowd checking to make sure everyone who needed a walking stick had one. Some of the women's footwear was questionable, but he'd already discovered with one woman's scathing glance that it wasn't a topic up for discussion if he wanted to live to see another day.

Biting his tongue, he handed out walking sticks instead.

John was up at the front being quizzed by the President. Hopefully he was having more luck than Allan had with the women. While it was wonderful their country's leader showed such an interest in this territory, Allan almost wished that this land could remain more of a secret. He'd only been here a week and he wanted to stay forever. No wonder his father loved this place.

Thoughts of his father brought his gaze back to John. For years, he'd blamed the man for his father's death. But the truth wasn't so easily found. Their conversations from the train — before they knew who the other was — haunted him day and night. His boss was consistent. Understanding. Even trustworthy. And the more he learned from John, the more he questioned the details from Frank. And the more he thought about the stories Frank told, the more he realized they didn't pan out. There were discrepancies. All over the place. Not just in the McKinley expedition.

His father once told him that gut instincts were good to heed. He thought of it as divine guidance — the Holy Ghost. Allan never gave it much credence. In fact, he thought his own gut instincts weren't all that accurate. It often seemed his feelings about people were complicated by the events that surrounded them. Father would have said to judge the fruit of the individual — the overall outcome of the person's life and treatment of others. Allan, however, tended to jump to conclusions. Momentary lapses of judgment became reasons to distrust and a single poor choice marked a man as incompetent.

One thing had always been clear — Frank never loved the outdoors like the Brennan men. Granted, he was very business-minded and successful, but he'd rather stay in his office and have meetings than go exploring himself. That in and of itself didn't make the man unworthy of trust, but Allan had to admit there were times when Frank grated on him. Frank was quick with a harsh admonishment for underlings. Allan had seen him fire a man for nothing more than misplacing an invoice. And if he were honest with himself, Allan knew he'd just as soon not work with Frank at all.

But how could Allan turn his back on his father's lifelong friend? Didn't he owe him . . . something?

With Frank and the rest of his family back in Seattle, Allan found it easy to focus on Alaska. He'd written to let them know that he'd arrived safely and what he was doing. His mother would be more than proud that he was following his father's footsteps. What he left unmentioned was his growing confusion over John Ivanoff and the accident that had claimed his father's life. He'd come here hoping for answers, but it seemed he'd only managed to unearth more questions.

"Allan" — John's voice broke through his reverie — "I believe we are ready."

He glanced up at the salt-and-pepper-haired man. "Yes, sir, we are."

John led the way down a path that he and

Allan had trampled down in the days prior. At this time of year the tundra grass was thigh-high, so to make it easier for the guests, they'd widened the path from a one-person walkway to about a four-person width. John had also been quite observant to remove any obstacles from the path. Could a man so conscientious as that have been less so when dealing with a climbing expedition? One that pivoted on life and death in the best of circumstances? Of course that had been years ago. Allan had heard that John was forty-five years old, so that would have made him just thirty-nine when he'd led the expedition in 1917. A man's character was surely set into place by that age, so it seemed unlikely he would have changed all that much. Not only that, but Allan had heard others talk about John. People who'd known him for many years. They all thought highly of him.

"Oh my. Just look at the flowers!" Mrs. Harding exclaimed.

Her statement started the ladies' comments on the brilliant colors, while the men asked about the area's wild animals. Their first planned stopping point was about a third of a mile down the path, but they'd gained about five hundred feet in elevation and already some of the ladies were struggling.

Looking down on a brilliant field of wild flowers, John stopped to explain which ones were which. Allan couldn't help smiling. John understood the abilities and inabilities of his clients. He was accommodating them without bringing it to their attention.

One of the ladies came forward with a flower. "What is this lovely blue one?"

"This is arctic lupine, one of my favorites to look at, but be careful, lupine is extremely poisonous." He took a small sketchbook out of his pocket. "Now, if you compare it to this one" — he pointed to a page — "this is the Nootka lupine, and it is my favorite of the lupine. I've seen them in the Chugach Mountains south of here and in the Aleutian Islands. Fields and fields of them. Their shape is fuller and almost like a Christmas tree, wouldn't you say?"

"Oh, yes. Beautiful." The lady set the flower in a basket she carried over her arm and went to inspect others.

John pointed to another group of flowers. "See the yellow ones in this grouping? Those are Alaska poppies. And those purple ones are purple mountain saxifrage."

Mrs. Harding carried two similar dark pink flowers. "Mr. Ivanoff, what can you tell me about these two? I thought they were the same, but now I don't believe so."

He smiled at the First Lady.

Allan studied the flowers. They indeed looked awfully similar, so he moved closer to listen.

His boss lifted the first one. "This one is called Eskimo potato."

The group around him laughed. One of the men hollered out, "Now, why would they call a pink flower a potato?"

"That's a good question. The natives have been known to eat the root of this plant for centuries — thus the potato name." John picked up the other flower. "While this one is called a wild sweet pea. If you look at the leaves of both, see how much they look alike? But the sweet pea has larger flowers and the roots are thought to be poisonous on this one." John handed them both back to the President's wife. "Legend says that many lives have been lost confusing the two. That was very astute of you to see the difference, Mrs. Harding."

"Are you an Eskimo?" One of the men interjected. He fixed John with an intense gaze.

"I'm part Athabaskan. That's one of the native peoples in this part of Alaska. There are many groups — tribes, if you would.

Those normally thought of as Eskimo are actually Inuit, Inupiat, and Yuit."

One woman stepped closer. "Do they really live in igloos — those houses made of ice?"

John smiled. "An igloo isn't just a house of ice. It can reference any house. But yes, there are those who out of necessity build houses of ice blocks. I've made similar shelters myself."

This created a sensation of murmurs amongst the tourists, while also stirring additional questions.

"Is it true that Eskimos don't feel the cold?" This question came from the same man who'd asked if John was an Eskimo. He eyed John as if he were some kind of strange specimen just discovered.

"People are people no matter the color of their skin or origin of their birth, and they acclimate the same," John replied. His expression was congenial and his tone suggested endless patience. "We who are native to Alaska get cold just like everyone else. It might be just at a considerably different temperature than you because of the climate we live in."

Mrs. Harding seemed to take pity on their guide. "I'd really like to see some fireweed now — if we may."

"Hear, hear," voiced the President.

"Then let's continue on." John smiled. "There's a beautiful view of it ahead."

Allan brought up the rear and watched a few of the women bobble in their crazy shoes, but said nothing. He knew the next stop would be a grand place to view the fireweed, and that is where they planned to turn around and head back. The President looked weary.

Hadn't he heard in the news that they'd been on a countrywide trip by train before they headed to Alaska? No wonder the man was tired.

As they reached the next point, *oohs* and *aahs* were heard throughout the group. Not only were the mountains of the Alaska Range visible over the ridgeline across the river, but an unending field of vibrant pink fireweed could be seen on the other side of the ridge where they stood.

John spoke in a loud voice. "As you can see, the flowers open from the bottom of the plant and over time will bloom all the way to the top. The legend of the fireweed is that when all of the blooms reach the top, winter will be on its way in six weeks. And I can tell you that for all of my life, the fireweed has been correct in its prediction." The group laughed.

The President gathered his entourage closer with a wave of his arms. "I've asked John to tell us a little more about Curry and his Athabaskan heritage while we take a rest."

The ladies sat on many low-lying rocks, while the men situated themselves on the ground.

Allan passed around the water canteens and then set his walking stick in front of him and rested both arms on it.

The history of the native people in this vast land was fascinating, but John only shared about them for a couple of minutes. He moved quickly into talk of Denali — now Mount McKinley — and how the new national park could change the face of Alaska and its tourism. From there, he praised the Alaska Railroad. "As you will see tomorrow, the railroad is finished. From Seward to Fairbanks, this land is now opened up for the world to see God's handiwork. It's a land rich in wild game, fish, and even gold." He pointed to the Curry Hotel below them. "And our government had the ingenuity to build at this incredible location, right here on the river and on the railroad, in the middle of the rail line, so that we could share this with the world. Although, I don't know about you, but I'm glad they changed the name from Deadhorse to Curry."

Chuckles resounded from the group.

"And I'm sure it doesn't take much of an imagination to know where the first name came from."

After some more chatter and questions, a man next to the President raised his hand. "I don't know about the rest of you, but I'd like to climb a little higher to get a better view of that twenty-thousand-footer."

Others nodded and murmured agreement.

"Mr. President, wouldn't it be a good idea to build a shelter people could hike to so they could see this spectacular view?"

"Indeed it would." He sat on a boulder.

John moved forward. "Whoever would like to climb a little higher is welcome to join us, but make sure you have sturdy shoes. There's not a direct path."

A few men stayed with a number of the ladies while the President and the rest of the group followed John up the side of the steep hill. Allan brought up the rear, assisting where he could.

"Aahhhh!" One of the younger men cried out and fell to the ground. He rolled to a sitting position and took hold of his ankle. "I stepped in a hole. I think I might have broken my ankle."

John was at his side almost immediately and assessed the injury. He ran his hands along the man's ankle. Allan noted the man was wearing shoes rather than the recommended boots. Had he the proper footgear, he probably wouldn't be in this kind of trouble now.

"I'm no doctor, but I'd say it's a sprain." John sighed. "However, we need to get you down the path quickly before the swelling gets too bad and we can't get that shoe off." He looked to Allan and waved him closer, speaking in a quieter tone. "I need you to finish the walk and get everyone back safely."

Allan nodded.

"I'll need another man to help me get Mr. . . ."

"Brown." The injured man cringed as John lifted him to stand on his good foot.

"To help me get Mr. Brown down to the hotel."

An older but fit gentleman raised his hand. "I'll be glad to help."

Allan moved forward to the President as they watched John and the other man work their way back down the path. It all happened so fast.

"Mr. Brennan, lead on."

He nodded and moved forward, his

thoughts all over the place. Why didn't John just ask *him* to take the injured man down? Allan was, after all, the junior man. He couldn't lead an expedition, much less one of this magnitude. With the President, for goodness' sake!

Several minutes passed in silence as they trudged up the hill. What struck him the most was John's servant attitude. It didn't make a difference to the man about whether it was the President or some man of no rank whatsoever. He went to him immediately to take care of him. Now, what did that truly say about this man that Allan called boss?

"Tell me more about this great mountain and Mr. Ivanoff." The President interrupted his thoughts.

Allan turned to see the President and First Lady smiling expectantly. Looking out at what he could see of the top of Mount McKinley, Allan stopped. "I'm afraid I must admit that I'm merely an apprentice. John is the expert, and I'm an inadequate replacement for him."

"But he must believe in you and trust you if he's asked you to carry on with us."

Allan considered all that he knew. "Mount McKinley is called Denali or The Great One by the native people here. That's the original name. It's over twenty thousand feet high and is highly glaciated granite."

The President laid a hand on Allan's shoulder as he took another big step and turned. "It's quite the view. Have you ever climbed it?"

"No. John has, but you'd have to speak to him." Allan hoped his tone didn't sound too dismissive.

"I can only imagine that would be an arduous journey and would take quite a man to accomplish such a feat."

"Yes. My father climbed it, and he was quite a man. He made the trip with John." Allan hadn't meant to mention his father and immediately regretted it.

"He must have told you wondrous stories."

"I'm sure he would have, but he died up there." Allan looked again at the mountain. "The stories I've heard have all come from other sources." He looked back at the President. "If you get the chance, you should talk to the park's superintendent, Harry Karstens. He was one of the very first to summit the mountain."

The older man frowned. "I am sorry about your father. What happened, if you don't mind my asking?"

Allan shook his head. "I don't mind, but I have no answers. My father's business partner was also along on the trip and he told me a terrible storm came up just after they reached the summit. My father was lost in the storm. They never found him."

"That must have been very hard for you. I'm sure it was hard on John and your father's partner as well. John doesn't strike me as the kind of man who would easily leave a comrade behind."

Allan didn't know what to say. The President's words seemed to pierce his heart. No. John didn't seem like the kind of man to leave someone behind.

"Well" — President Harding exhaled loudly — "I believe it's about time to head back to the hotel. Tomorrow will be a busy day and I'd like to check on Mr. Brown."

Allan stood for several moments thinking about the President's words.

Maybe it was time he put aside the anger that had been born out of Frank's rage and allow that perhaps John was truly the good man he appeared to be. The kind of man who wouldn't have left his father on the mountain had there been any other choice. He'd already told Cassidy that he wasn't angry. But had he meant it? Or had he just longed for her friendship? He hated how his emotions seemed to rock back and forth like a ship at high seas. What kind of man was he?

The kind to sacrifice himself to rescue people from a disaster? The kind to put one injured man's needs ahead of his own desires?

Those were things that described John. But not Allan. The thought struck him hard. He wanted to be that kind of man. The kind of man who was like his . . . father.

And his father had believed and trusted in John.

It was time he believed and trusted in John as well.

Even with all the profits of The Irving/Brennan Company, the money was running out. And Frank didn't like that one bit. He needed more of it — not less. Especially to keep funding his new investments that weren't doing so well right now. But they would.

They had to.

He'd always been brilliant at the business side of things. So why were his choices and his investments failing? He didn't like feeling . . . desperate.

He swirled the last bit of golden bourbon in his glass, then lifted it to his lips and gulped. Prohibition didn't help matters any.

He had to pay exorbitant prices to get the good stuff. Pity he couldn't get in on that scheme. There were millions to be made in bootlegging, but so far his queries into such matters had been met only with suspicion.

Walking over to the window, he cursed Henry Brennan.

For decades they'd been friends. Even though Henry was always the good one, the friendly one, the popular one — he'd never excluded Frank and his melancholy, pessimistic ways. But then they went into business together. All of Henry's ideas ended up successful. It got to the point where Frank's ideas were barely heard — except by Henry. When the company became even more successful, the board always looked to Henry, not Frank — as if the outdoorsman was the brains, even though he was *never* in the office.

Still, Frank stuck it out. He showed up day after day and became quite a savvy businessman. Before long, he learned how to skim profits off the top, and money became the ultimate prize.

Who cared that Henry had a wonderful marriage, the idyllic family life, and everyone thought he was the driving force behind the company? That all would change. With enough money, Frank figured he could buy his position of prestige.

Then Frank's wife left him, with a contemptuous letter spewing her hatred toward him, his lack of love for anyone or anything but money, and his fault at not being able to give them children.

The anger and hurt of that time pushed him over the edge — beyond a line he'd thought of crossing, but never thought possible.

So he'd plotted and planned and found a way to rid himself of Henry. If he couldn't have the idyllic life, then neither should his partner. Besides, Frank needed the money.

The plan worked, but not completely. Somehow he'd missed the loophole that Henry could write an addendum to his will and add that Allan would inherit half of his father's share. But three-quarters of the company wasn't enough for Frank.

It was time for something more drastic. The Brennan family was nothing but a drain on *his* company. The stupid son-in-law worked for him, Allan took his quarter share, and who knows what else he'd lost to them over the years.

No more.

There had to be a way to get rid of Allan. After that, it would be easy enough to get rid of Henry's son-in-law and any other

Brennan connection.

Frank walked back to his desk and sat down. Drumming his fingers on the mahogany top, he thought of a different plan. Murder wasn't necessarily needed. What if . . . a family member was found to be the one embezzling? And they were all in cahoots?

He smacked the desk with the palm of his hand and smiled. Yes. That would work. He could start with blaming Henry's son-in-law, Louis. And then through the investigation, he could frame them all for scheming against him — stating they were unhappy that Frank received so much of the company when Henry died. There were already two sets of books, and it would be easy enough to create a third that would indict Louis.

Now it would all play into Frank's hand. He would prove that Louis had been stealing profits to line his own pockets. It was their fault. They weren't happy with the will, so the sad little Brennan family had cheated poor Frank all these years.

Ah yes. Poor Frank.

To avoid a scandal that would bring shame upon his name, Allan would agree to sign over the whole company to Frank. He would have no other choice. Frank would be sympathetic but firm. Once Frank pointed out that if charged, Louis would go to prison for a very long time, Allan would agree to most anything. He wouldn't want to see his sister and her children left destitute and shamed.

Frank steepled his fingers together and leaned back in his chair. He could rescue his teetering investments and make even more money.

He would have it all, and this time nothing would go wrong.

10

Cassidy breathed in the crisp morning air. The Curry Hotel sat in the valley created by the Susitna River between two small ridge lines outside of the Alaska Range. The ridge across the river and to the west was about twenty-five hundred feet, and the ridge behind the hotel was somewhere around three thousand feet. She loved the safe and sheltered way it made her feel, encircled by these crests and hills. As if surrounded by family. It was . . . cozy.

But the thing she didn't like was the obstruction of the view of the full Alaska Range. If she wanted to see it, she had to climb. Most mornings she had neither the time nor the energy. But today had been different. She'd been wide awake at 4:00 a.m. and couldn't do a thing about it.

So she donned long pants and boots and headed up the steepest trail on Deadhorse Hill with her satchel and rifle slung over her back. It was the harder way to go, but it was a good deal shorter. And today, she wanted to get there as soon as possible. The summer daylight was nice this early in the morning, but she knew it would end up being a scorcher later, when she'd be working in the kitchen.

The events of the past couple weeks flew through her mind. It wasn't every day they dedicated a national park and posed for pictures in the paper, or had a visit from the President. On the fifteenth of July, after the President and all his people left, life went on at the Curry. Even though they were all completely worn out, they still had plenty of guests to take care of — the train didn't stop running just because the President came to Alaska. But oh, what fun they'd had listening to Mr. Bradley read the telegrams from his friends in Nenana.

Apparently, the President had missed the golden spike the first time he swung, and then he decided to just tap it in, since he had to hammer in the iron one that would stay in its place. But even this close to the actual location, the stories had already been changed and rearranged to fit the storyteller. And the heat had been so bad that day that several people passed out. Of course, the people of Nenana heard through the grapevine that many of the visitors had worn extra layers of undergarments since an "Alaska expert" had told them how cold it would be.

Cassidy shook her head. People's fascination with the Alaska Territory was growing, and so, she assumed, would the stories. She was thankful for the press and the advertising — she really was. Alaska would develop and be known. But she already missed the quietness and solitude of the way it had been.

Before so many new people came to work at the Curry, there'd been much more solitude. Yet she'd never felt lonely. The difference now was . . . what? She'd tried to make friends among the staff, and although everyone treated her well and seemed to like and respect her, there weren't *real* friends to be had. Not friends she could discuss anything of depth with. They were all caught up in the shallow frivolities of the day.

Except maybe . . . Allan. They were friends now. She'd noticed that he took time to find her and speak with her at least a few minutes each day. He was very nice . . . but . . .

She shook her head. She liked Allan a bit too much, perhaps. Still found herself looking for him and thinking about him. Was that normal?

Best to get her thoughts off the intriguing Mr. Allan Brennan.

But she did long for a true friend. Someone to share her thoughts and dreams with. Someone to discuss faith and questions she had in her study of God's Word.

What an odd feeling to be constantly surrounded by people in the hustle and bustle of life and yet feel so very alone.

As she reached the top of the ridge, she made her way to her favorite rock. She plopped down and put the rifle beside her. She hugged the satchel close, not bothering to take it from her shoulder, and looked out at the mountains she knew so well. What would the future hold for her? Now that the railroad was done, the national park was in place, and people were coming. Even though the Curry was lavish and beautiful with amazing amenities, the rest of Alaska was still harsh and wild. It's not like she'd have the chance to meet a lot of men her age. At least not men who would meet her criteria. She wanted a good man like her father. A God-fearing man who paid more than lip service to his faith. Sometimes it seemed like those men didn't exist — that her father was the last of them. Pulling her knees to her chest, she wondered about the plans God had for her. Was it just to be a cook at the Curry Hotel?

Or would she get to have a family of her own one day?

Cassidy laughed out loud. That wasn't exactly modern-girl thinking. Most women her age were caught up in rights for women, since they could now vote, keeping up with the men, changing their hairstyles and their clothes to rebel against the labels of the fragile female. And heavens, the new young maids were always talking about liquor, cigarettes, and things between men and women they shouldn't know about.

Getting a job at the Curry had been educational to say the least. Her sheltered little world quickly changed as everyone sought to educate her in the times. But after the shock wore off, she realized these things had been happening since the beginning of time. She was perfectly fine with keeping her dress hems at a modest length and didn't need to learn all the new lingo of the day. Nor did she care to try liquor or cigarettes, much less even speak of girls who wanted to be known as flappers.

So where did she fit? There weren't any cities around. And she certainly couldn't leave Alaska or her father to travel to the overcrowded and modern cities of the States — this was her home.

Pulling her Bible out of the satchel, Cassidy opened it to the book of Daniel. She'd been studying it with her dad for many months now — trying to decipher all the difficult passages in the later chapters. But her favorites were still the stories in the first six chapters.

Starting at the beginning, she read through chapter three without pause. As she looked up to the sky, she wondered if she'd be strong enough to make the same choices as Daniel and his friends, Shadrach, Meshach, and Abednego. Would she stand firm should the test arise?

A rustling sound from somewhere behind her made Cassidy reach for her rifle.

"Cassidy? Hello?"

The male voice jolted her from her spot. No one had ever disturbed her up here.

Thomas's head came over the ridge and she breathed a sigh of relief. "Thomas, I'm so glad it's you." She set the rifle back at her side.

He smiled at her and leaned over to catch his breath. "That's a hike up here. How often do you do it?"

"Now, you're not going to give my secret away, are you?" She placed her hands on her hips.

"Nah, I just saw you climbing up here

when I was down at the creek, so I thought I'd follow you." He stood up straight. "Make sure you're all right and all."

She worked to keep the smile to herself. "I'm perfectly fine. Thank you."

"Oh, good." He sat on the grass. "Whatcha reading?"

"The Bible."

"Oh."

"Have you read the Bible?"

"Sure, Miss Cassidy. The orphanage was run by missionaries and we had to read the Bible. If you didn't read it, the preacher would smack you over the head with it. He swore he'd get God's Word into us one way or the other." He smiled at his joke.

She couldn't help it. The picture his words conjured up in her mind made her laugh. She struggled to gain her composure. "That's not very nice. I'm so sorry that man hit you with the Good Book."

"Well, it packed a wallop to be sure, and I guess it motivated us to read our assigned verses." Thomas smiled. "Hey, at least I got you to laugh."

"That you did, Thomas." She shook her head and opened her Bible back up to Daniel. "Did you have a favorite book in the Bible?"

Thomas shook his head. "No, I guess I

183

liked the New Testament better than the Old. The Old Testament made God sound mean and overbearing. Like the preacher."

"Not all of the Old Testament is that way." Cassidy scooted over a bit and patted the rock. "Why don't you join me and I'll tell you what I've been reading. It's in the Old Testament and it's really quite amazing."

"Sure, why not?" He jumped up and made a beeline for the place beside her.

"I've been reading in the book of Daniel. Do you remember any of the stories about him?"

"He was the one in the lion's den, right?" When Cassidy nodded, Thomas took on a look of pride. "I guess that's all I know about him."

"Well, there's so much more. And by the time we get to the story of the lions' den, Daniel was an old man. But he was a very young man when the book begins. A little younger than you, in fact."

"Really?"

"Yes. And he was very handsome and smart. It even says, 'well favoured, and skillful in all wisdom,' but the problem was he was taken from his family — kidnapped — to a foreign land in order to serve a pagan king who didn't believe in the God of all creation." Cassidy realized maybe she needed to ask a really important question. "Do you believe in God, Thomas?"

"Of course I do."

"And you believe in Jesus?"

"Why, sure, He's God's son. He died on the cross for us. And that's why we have Easter."

"That's right." At least he had some basics. "Well, here he is — Daniel with three of his friends — all taken from their homes and forced to live in this foreign land. You see, they were taken because they were 'the best,' and the king wanted to collect them, kind of like trophies. Good-looking, wise young men. Anyway, in this land, they were to be trained for three years and would eat and drink the king's meat and wine. This wasn't slave food — this was the good stuff. But guess what Daniel did?"

"What?"

"It says that he chose not to 'defile himself' with the king's food — he wouldn't take it! This made the man in charge of them upset because it was his job to make these good-looking young men look even better and get even smarter. So Daniel asked the man — his name was Melzar — to allow them only to eat pulse and water for ten days and then to compare them to the rest so that he could prove to him they weren't going to starve or look worse. But they didn't want to disobey God."

"What is pulse?"

"Seeds and vegetables."

"That's not much to keep them going, is it?"

Cassidy thought about that for a moment. "I guess I never really thought about it that way, but you're right. Melzar agreed to do as Daniel asked and when the ten days were up, guess what happened?"

Thomas was intently focused on the story. "What?"

"Verse fifteen says, 'And at the end of ten days their countenances appeared fairer and fatter in flesh than all the children which did eat the portion of the king's meat.' So Daniel and his three friends looked better than all the others, and then verse twenty tells us that at the end of the three years of their training and supposed great fattening up from the king's good food, 'the king found them ten times better than all the magicians and astrologers that were in all his realm.' So they were smarter and wiser too, and they were only probably around eighteen or nineteen years old at this point."

"Huh." Thomas frowned. "How'd they do it?"

"*They* didn't do it. God did. And they

simply obeyed."

"You like that story?" His brow crinkled even more.

"I do."

"Why?"

That was a question she'd never been asked. "Well, I guess because it makes me want to be like Daniel."

"You want to be kidnapped and taken away?"

"No, but it makes me wonder how I would fare if something like that happened to me. My life has been easy, full of love and fun. I've never had any hard challenges come my way, and I want to be willing to stand firm when they do." Saying it out loud made her thoughts more real. Her life had been just about perfect. And definitely easy. Here, she'd been wallowing in thoughts of loneliness and longing for things the Good Lord hadn't blessed her with yet. It was shameful how selfish she'd been.

"Is that why you're so positive all the time?"

Another question that nudged her to think. Was it? Was it easy to be positive and encouraging and happy when things were good because that's pretty much all she'd known? "I don't really know, Thomas. I like to be an encourager, yes, but I want to be more than that."

"I think you're pretty perfect just the way you are, Cassidy."

"Oh, but I'm not." The more she examined her heart, the more she wanted to learn. A sudden and new craving for the Word overwhelmed her. "Thank you, Thomas. For helping me to see so clearly today."

"I didn't do nothing." A blush crept up his cheeks.

"Yes, you did." Cassidy stood up and straightened her shoulders. "No matter what, I want to dare to be a Daniel. And I don't think I've been doing a very good job. But that's going to change."

The two days since Thomas had talked to Cassidy passed way too fast. And there hadn't been much chance to speak with her since. But he'd thought about her. A lot.

And what she'd said. About Daniel. Thomas couldn't get those thoughts out of his mind. He had a lot of questions. More than anything, he longed to make something of himself. Not always be labeled as an orphan. But how?

Could Cassidy's Bible have more answers in it? He never knew there was a story of a boy his age doing anything significant. Now he wanted to learn more.

He wanted to be a man. And an honorable one. One people respected. And one who didn't drop things or stumble over things. Daniel had been well respected by the king himself when he was only eighteen. Could Thomas learn that much in a year?

As he carried another tub of scraps out to the feed shed, Thomas spotted Mr. Ivanoff. He wanted to be like Cassidy's father. The older man knew so much about everything and loved to teach other people.

And boy was he patient. Every day Thomas had worked for him, Mr. Ivanoff never lost his patience — even when Thomas messed up. Unlike Mrs. Johnson, who made him feel like he was in the army every time she barked her commands or scolded him for another mistake.

He watched Mr. Ivanoff walk down to the roundhouse where they did maintenance on the railroad engines. Maybe he could catch him later today and ask him for help.

If anyone could teach him about how to be a man, it'd be John Ivanoff. And maybe he could teach him more about the Bible too.

Allan stared up at the ceiling for a long time. Sleep was slow in coming and unfortunately that gave him more than enough time to think. He thought about his trip to Alaska and all that he'd hoped to accomplish and realized that very little of it had been done.

He'd found John and had been able to ask about his father's death, but the answers had been less than helpful. He'd found his own love of Alaska and undeniable feelings for one of her daughters. Cassidy Ivanoff was unlike the women he'd known in Seattle. Even his sisters were far more concerned about their appearance or the quality of their furnishings. Many of the women who moved in his family's social circles didn't even know how to cook, much less enjoy it as much as he'd heard Cassidy did.

But always there was a barrier between them.

"I can't very well pursue her unless I resolve my anger with her father and Dad's death," he whispered to himself.

But Allan wasn't even sure that anger still existed. For so long he'd been mad at John and what had happened. Even worse, Allan had been mad at God. He still was. God had given him the very best of fathers and then, like a greedy child — had taken him back. No warning. No concern for the people who were left with the loss. God had even chosen the very poorest of timing. Allan hadn't been able to be there to comfort his mother when she learned of her husband's death.

"It wasn't fair." He shook his head. "You aren't fair. You demand too much."

It was the first time he'd talked to God in a very long time, and for a moment, despite his mix of emotions, Allan felt a connection that had long been absent. It was as he'd felt when he and his father had prayed together. The feeling passed much too quickly, however, and the anger and disappointment returned. Would he ever be able to put this behind him? Would he never find peace again?

11

The cloudy skies and drizzly rain reflected Allan's mood. The week since the President came through flew by with more training from John, plans for future expeditions, and preparation for nature walks and fishing trips. His brain felt at times like it would explode with all the information. But what was worse? The misery he felt. He'd asked for John's patience with him after the older man had sought forgiveness. And everything within him wanted to like and respect John. A lot.

Not only John, but his beautiful daughter as well.

A couple of times this past week, he'd spotted her hiking up Deadhorse Hill long before anyone but the night crew were awake, her long dark hair in a simple braid down her back. That familiar pull whenever he was near her tugged at him again. But he had no idea what to do with his feelings. He was not in a good place right now.

All his dreams about Alaska were coming true. He just hadn't expected to meet John. Or to like the man. He wanted to forgive him. He did. But how?

And then there was Cassidy. Loyal, dedicated, fun-loving, encouraging Cassidy. The more he was around her, the more he was drawn to her.

She probably didn't even have a clue the attention she generated around the hotel. From wealthy guests all the way down to Thomas — the men adored her. And not just her attractive looks. But the way she made everyone feel loved and special. How did she do that? Allan didn't even like himself half the time.

Walking to the front desk, Allan tried to corral his thoughts back to the tasks of the day. Somehow he needed to shake off this gloomy attitude.

"Mr. Brennan, you have a letter." Mrs. McGovern waved it in the air.

"Thank you." Taking the envelope, he saw the return address was from Seattle. He checked his watch. Not enough time to go back to his room, but he could head downstairs to the section gang dining room and find a little privacy.

As he opened the envelope and read the

first few lines, he wished he'd saved it for later.

Allan,

Hopefully you know that I think of you as the son I never had. And so I must speak my mind. I am appalled to find out that you are apprenticing for the very man who killed your father. As your father's longtime friend and business partner, I must advise you against any further work with this man. He is not to be trusted. He should never be allowed to work again as a guide. How dare he masquerade as an expert? To the presidential delegation as well! I'm horrified.

What does your mother think? Have you told her? I can only imagine the heartache this will bring to her. It's time you gave up this foolishness and returned home. I can't stand by and watch you destroy your relationship with your family by befriending the very man who took it all away. In fact, I think you need to go to the legal authorities and find out if there's a way to press charges against this man. Just the thought of him makes my blood boil. It should do the same for you.

I await your response,
Frank

While Allan knew that Frank blamed John and that he cared for the Brennan family as if they were blood, he also knew that hatred and anger couldn't be the answer here. Hadn't he just decided it would be right to forgive John?

But Frank had been family for a long time. What if Allan had been wrong to trust John? Was he a charlatan? Or was Frank the one who was lying? Allan hated to admit it, but over the years — with all Allan had witnessed — he didn't really trust Frank.

How could he find out who was truly responsible for his father's death?

The walk from the water tower to the hotel was short. Too short. John needed more time to think, so he turned around and started back. The reservations from the wealthy flowed in on a daily basis, and with them came the requests to be taken on "real Alaskan adventures" — the men wanted to fish and see bear, and the women wanted to see the mountains and flowers. Most of these people had enough money to do whatever they wanted, but they were choosing to come to Alaska and give up amenities they were accustomed to so they could lay claim to conquering this last frontier.

The groups that had come in so far had been a little shocked at how "primitive" the Alaska Territory was compared to the city life they knew. No real cities to speak of. Not much development. Very few roads; only the railroad connected Fairbanks to Seward. People living without electricity and running water. Leaning shacks were labeled as hotels or roadhouses. The list could go on and on — all the interesting facts about this land that surprised the tourists.

But how he loved this land. This had been a great dream for him to come and be the expedition guide for the hotel.

Then Allan had arrived. Only God could have orchestrated that one — to bring the very son of the man he'd lost on Denali to his doorstep. And not just to the hotel, but to work for him. John hadn't been the same since. All those emotions roiled each day when he saw Allan.

But it had to stop. Allan might never truly forgive him. And John needed to be all right with that. He wasn't doing his job as well as he should with this weight pressing down on him every day, and in Alaska that could turn deadly. Cassidy worried about him, even though he'd tried to convince her he was fine.

At this point, he was just surviving from day to day. That wasn't good enough.

Allan was eager to learn, even though things were often strained between them, and John couldn't blame the young man for that. But his apprentice needed the Lord. Plain and simple.

John's heart ached for him — not just for the loss of his father, but for Allan's eternity — and he prayed for wisdom, but God seemed to be silent on this one.

As his steps took him past the water tower and to the very edge of Curry, the churning in his thoughts increased and John cried out to the Lord.

It's too much, Father. This burden. I can't carry it any longer, but I know You can. Please take this from me. Show me what I need to do, because I'm lost in this shadow of grief. Grief for the Brennan family's loss, but also for the loss of my dreams through it. I've admitted to Allan that I take full responsibility, but for all these years, I didn't want to. I didn't want to think that I had failed in any way. Please forgive me, Father.

John found himself at the river's edge, tears streaming down his face. He hadn't even realized he'd been crying. But a new peace flooded him. And the weight was gone. Why hadn't he given this over to the Lord weeks ago?

A memory came to mind — a pleasant one of the wife he'd lost so many years ago. Eliza had been wise beyond her years. Perhaps that was due to being the child of a preacher or from living on the mission field, but whatever it was, she seemed to have unusual insight for one so young.

John wanted to please Eliza's parents, and when he heard her mother say she'd like to have her walkway rocked, John saw it as the perfect opportunity to win her over. That night while everyone slept, John dug and carried load after load of rock in sacks on his back to the worn dirt paths that constituted the walkways. The sacks rubbed blisters on his back, and the strain on his muscles left him miserable the next day. However, the walkway had its rock and Eliza's mother seemed pleased, although she never said so. At least not to him.

The next day, John saw Eliza watching him as he struggled to tend to his chores. Surely she knew that he'd been responsible for the improvement to the walk. With his shirt off, he also knew she could see the sores on his back, yet she chided him rather than offer praise.

"You bore a burden no one asked you to bear, John Ivanoff, and now yer sufferin' for it."

And here he was doing it again decades later.

"Well, that seems to be the way with me." He glanced heavenward and smiled. "It's all Yours, Lord."

With a new lightness and determination to his step, John headed back to the hotel. He had excursions to plan and an apprentice to guide. The rest he would leave in God's hands.

The morning passed in a blur of activities. John and Allan sat together at one of the section gang tables in the basement, planning day-trips. Papers and maps were strewn across the length of the eight-foot table.

"Mr. Ivanoff!" Thomas came down the stairs and missed the bottom step but caught himself before he fell. "Here's a telegram for you." He straightened his tray. "I've got to get back to the kitchen, but Mrs. McGovern asked me to bring it to you straightaway."

"Thank you, Thomas." John took the envelope and tried to cover his smile. He glanced at Allan, who also appeared to be struggling to keep a straight face.

"You're welcome, but I have to get right back. Mrs. Johnson will have my hide if I don't see to the trash." With that Thomas darted back up the stairs.

"It's amazing he hasn't broken a leg or an arm, isn't it?"

Allan nodded. "I remember being clumsy as a kid, but I've never seen the likes of it. I'm surprised Mrs. Johnson allowed him to come back to the kitchen."

"Cassidy said she wasn't overly keen on it, but they needed the help. A kitchen that big requires a lot of hands to get things done."

Smiling, Allan gave a shrug. "It can't be all that helpful if you have to redo things because someone makes a mess of them the first time through."

The smile on his face proved to John that the younger man was working through his issues. Perhaps they were both learning to lay their demons to rest.

"So I take it that must be another request?"

John turned the envelope over. "Most likely." He opened it with a sigh. The summer schedule kept getting busier and busier. Eventually, they would be so full that they'd have to turn people away. He'd heard rumors that the railroad already planned to expand the Curry Hotel.

Unfolding the missive, he glanced it over:

23 July 1923

Group of twenty experienced riders wish to trek into new N.P. (stop)Will pay top dollar for horses and supplies (stop)Hear you are the expert (stop)Wish to see glaciers and Denali up close (stop)Arriving 25 July (stop)
    George Barker and company

"Good grief, they don't want much, do they?" Allan stretched his arms behind his head.

John pulled out the large calendar they'd been working on, and Allan lowered his arms and leaned forward. He pointed to the schedule. "Even if we leave on the twenty-sixth, that only allows four days before our next major commitments. With the new signs we just put up and the trails trimmed, there's other staff who could handle a few of the nature walks without us. Even Cassidy could do it if Mrs. Johnson would spare her."

He pointed to one of the date squares with a star on it. "We've got to be back for the thirty-first. It's a good fifteen miles to the Ruth Glacier, which would be the only logical place to take them. But we'll have to get a boat to take us and the horses across the Susitna River. Once across, we'll climb the ridge and cross Troublesome Creek and then the Chulitna River."

"Even with mountainous terrain, the fifteen miles *could* be accomplished in a day." Allan studied the map.

John nodded. "Yes, but I'm not sure about how 'experienced' these riders truly are. We could definitely tell them that is the goal for the first day. Then again, they might make that first ridge and see everything they want to see and decide to head back. I suppose we should just be grateful they aren't asking to climb one of the mountains in the range. I'm always amazed at the people who show up here thinking they can just launch into a full-scale mountaineering experience. I wish they'd seek information about these things prior to showing up." The words were no sooner out of his mouth than John wished he could take them back. He hadn't meant to give any reminders to the past.

The room was silent for several seconds. John looked up but couldn't read the young man's expression.

"Wouldn't that be nice?" Allan's words were clipped as he tapped the table. "Excuse me, I think I need some fresh air."

John didn't have to guess at what caused Allan's sudden distress and struggles. No matter the job before them, there was always something between them. Henry Brennan.

Laying the telegram on the table, John placed his palms on either side of the calendar and map. It's a good thing he'd given this over to the Lord because there wasn't any way humanly possible he could carry this burden.

12

The busy summer season thrilled Cassidy. While there wasn't a lot of extra time to spend with her father, she did enjoy the hustle and bustle. Pulling the deboned chickens she'd worked on that morning from the icebox, Cassidy went to work on the stuffing. The kitchen was busy, but no more so than usual. Quiet conversations between the staff echoed off the walls.

Every day newspapers from around the country would arrive at the hotel detailing the President's visit, the completion of the railroad, and tall tales about gold, mountains, and an untamed land.

Dad told her about a group coming in that he planned to take to the Ruth Glacier. She wished she could go along, but gone were the days of Cassidy getting to follow her dad around on one of his jaunts. She had a job of her own now. And one she loved.

Now that she'd mastered Mrs. Johnson's

soufflé recipe, she'd been given a new recipe each day to learn and conquer. Cassidy loved that the head cook trusted her and relied upon her. It made her feel . . . special.

Now if she could just break through the older woman's tough shell. They'd worked together for months and while Mrs. Johnson seemed to trust her more than anyone else, the woman stayed distant from everyone. Did she ever feel lonely like Cassidy? Did she even have any friends?

Cassidy wondered the same about herself. Could she say that she truly had any friends in Curry? They all knew each other well enough, but she wasn't ever invited to any of the young women's get-togethers because she was above most of them as assistant cook. And truth be told, most of the kitchen maids her age were interested in things Cassidy didn't even want to think about or consider.

Secretly, she blamed it on the lack of church. If these young people just knew what they were missing, they wouldn't be caught up in all the worldly nonsense, right?

With the stuffing made, she grabbed the twine to stitch the birds back up before they were roasted. The tangy sweet smell of the stuffing with onions, celery, and sage made her mouth water.

Thoughts of church and their church family back in Tanana made her weepy and even more hungry. Oh, how she missed the days of church socials, Sunday morning services, Wednesday evening Bible studies, and the occasional song service on a Saturday afternoon where everyone brought instruments and picnics and they went from one song to another for hours. They didn't even have any church services in Curry. Her dad led a small Bible study with a few others on Sunday afternoons, but other than that, they had no other fellowship. What was the world coming to?

"Cassidy Faith," Mrs. Johnson's fiery voice broke through. "Are you day-dreaming again?"

Cassidy blinked and looked at her supervisor, then down at the large needle threaded with twine in her hand. "Um, yes, ma'am. I guess I was."

"I should say so." The woman had her hands on her hips. "You've been standing there with that needle in the air for nigh unto two minutes."

"I'm sorry, Mrs. Johnson. But this is the last one. I'll have it ready in a jiffy."

"See that you do." The woman barked and walked out of the kitchen into the dining room.

Cassidy finished up the chickens and looked down the list at her next task. Dessert. She could handle that without too much thought. But something bothered her about Mrs. Johnson's demeanor. Granted the woman was never the friendliest of people, but something didn't seem right today.

Taking a quick glance at the clock, Cassidy washed her hands and went in search of her boss.

She didn't have to go far. Mrs. Johnson stood in the dining room, hands still on her hips.

Cassidy cleared her throat. "I'm sorry to bother you, but I wanted to check on you."

"No need. I'm fine." She didn't even turn around. "Just get on with your work."

"Well, the chickens are done and I was about to start on the dessert." Cassidy shifted her weight from one foot to the other. "It seems like something is bothering you, and I wanted to see if I could help."

The older woman turned, tears at the edges of her eyes. "Help? You can't help me, Cassidy Ivanoff. With your sunny attitude, your smiles, and your laughter. No, you can't help me. Especially not today."

What did that mean? "Why not today? I don't understand. I really do want to help and want to be here for you."

The woman huffed and shook her head. "You just can't let it be, can you? Well, all right then, I'll tell you why. Today would have been my brother Larry's birthday — but he's dead. I don't expect you to understand since you think the world is covered in gumdrops and rainbows, and while I appreciate your positive attitude, it doesn't do me any good today."

The words stung, but Cassidy couldn't allow the woman to hurt and feel she was alone. "But I do understand. And more importantly God understands —"

"Don't give me that God understands nonsense. Because He doesn't. If He did, my entire family — all of them — wouldn't have died of the influenza five years ago."

Cassidy gasped. The flu outbreak of 1918? It had killed millions of people around the world. Tears sprang to her eyes. This dear woman had lost everyone? How devastating!

Mrs. Johnson huffed again. "Don't get all teary-eyed on me, we have work to do. This is exactly why I didn't want to say anything to begin with, and you just need to let me be."

"But I can't." She wiped her face and took a deep breath. This was her chance to share her faith and she couldn't miss it. "God doesn't want you to carry this burden any longer. He hates to see you suffer."

"I find that all balderdash." Mrs. Johnson pointed her finger in Cassidy's face. "If He hates seeing me suffer, then He would have spared my mother and father, my brother, his wife, their three children, my sister, and her son. No, I'd say God rather enjoyed seeing me suffer, don't you? Either that, or He simply doesn't care how I feel." Her last words were full of anguish and anger. She marched back toward the kitchen. "Now, I won't have any more of this nonsense. We have dinner to prepare and I don't want to hear another word."

Cassidy thought to comment but held back. She walked to the kitchen with Mrs. Johnson's comments churning through her head.

"But I don't expect you to understand since you think the world is covered in gumdrops and rainbows. . . ."

Did Mrs. Johnson really think that was how Cassidy saw the world? All she'd ever wanted to do was present a positive spirit. There was enough sadness and bitterness in the world to go around, and Cassidy wanted only to offer a smile and an encouraging word. But Mrs. Johnson sounded as if she thought Cassidy foolishly naïve.

She frowned and felt her brows knit together. "Perhaps I am."

There was only an hour before Allan needed to be back in the lobby to help John with the next fishing group. He'd paced his room for almost thirty minutes trying to form a response to Frank, but nothing came. And it needed to get in the mail today. He couldn't wait any longer, or who knew what Frank would do.

The battle raged inside his mind. He'd been watching John day in and day out. More than anything, he wanted to know the truth about the man.

"Looks can be deceiving and few people are the sum total of their appearance," his father had once said. "Their actions are far more important."

Allan had taken that advice to heart in dealing with people all of his life. Why should he handle things any different with John?

Making a mental list, Allan began to assess John Ivanoff. First the positives. John seemed to care about each person. And no matter how great or small the expedition ended up being, he arranged it all with great care and structure. No room for slacking or careless mistakes. No detail left undone. No request unimportant. The man honestly knew his stuff and Allan had to admit — John Ivanoff was an expert.

The negatives? Frank believed John responsible for Henry Brennan's death.

But the depth of his internal war was so much more than John. And if Allan were to be honest, he'd have to admit that it wasn't just John who held his thoughts. He needed to know the truth about the man because of his daughter. The employees of the Curry Hotel couldn't avoid each other. Whether it was meals or staff meetings or just bumping into one another on the stairs or in the lobby — Allan couldn't avoid her. And he wasn't even really sure he wanted to anymore. In fact, he'd sought her out every day to talk to her. Even if it was only for a few minutes. He'd told himself it was just to be friendly. But who was he kidding?

As the past few years had rolled past, Allan felt the growing need for a companion — a wife to come alongside him. His father never failed to praise Allan's mother for being the one person to stand with him through his darkest hours. There had been too many dark hours for Allan since the war.

"One day, son, you will find a woman who strikes your interest and then without realizing

exactly when it happens, you'll find that she's the part of you that was missing and you can't be whole without her," his father had told him once.

Was that how it would be with Cassidy? Already he found himself thinking about her all the time. At first he'd tried to convince himself that it was just because she was John's daughter, but he couldn't pretend that any longer.

Frank admonished him to have nothing to do with John Ivanoff, but Allan couldn't just walk away. He couldn't avoid John because he still needed answers about his father, and he couldn't avoid Cassidy because he needed answers for his heart. Marching over to the chair at the desk, he determined to get the response written.

Frank was used to getting his way after all these years, and Allan had allowed the man to boss him around after Henry Brennan's death. But no more. It's not that he didn't respect Frank anymore; it was just time for Allan to show that he no longer needed anyone telling him what to do. He was twenty-eight years old and had a college education and a good head on his shoulders. The company was part his — he probably needed to start acting like it. He came to Alaska to follow in his father's footsteps and to find answers.

And find answers he would. Right now things didn't add up.

Perhaps the only way to find out what had really happened to his father would be to climb the mountain himself. If so, that's what he'd do.

Frank would just have to deal with it until Allan was satisfied.

Heat from the oven blasted Cassidy's face when she opened the door to the big range. The intensity took her breath away. As she stocked the oven with all the loaves of bread ready to bake, it reminded her of Shadrach, Meshach, and Abednego from the book of Daniel. What had the heat been like when they'd been thrown into the fiery furnace? Much worse than this hot oven, and it was more than Cassidy could stand for a few seconds.

Closing the oven, she thought of her chat with Mrs. Johnson the other day. Things had been stiff between them ever since and Cassidy hated it. The older cook was the closest thing Cassidy had to a friend.

But even more than that. Cassidy realized something big that day. Bigger than just being seen as a naïve girl who thought the world a beautiful, happy place. She'd never really been challenged in her faith. Not to stand strong, or to defend it, or to even really witness in the way she should. Oh, she'd shared the gospel with lots of people. John 3:16 was her favorite verse. But it had never gotten as intimate as it had with Mrs. Johnson. Hadn't that been what she'd prayed for? Ever since her chat with Thomas on Deadhorse Hill, she'd prayed for opportunities to be like Daniel and to share her faith no matter the cost.

Was this her chance? The even bigger question — would Mrs. Johnson listen?

And for that answer, Cassidy knew she'd have to wait. She understood now why the head cook was closed off. She even understood that almost impenetrable exterior around the woman was in place to protect her from further pain. Unfortunately, it also blocked out the opportunity to take in love. It would take a miracle to break through that armor.

Good thing she knew Someone in the miracle business.

She'd just have to wait for the right time. God had a plan for Cassidy here at the hotel. She knew it. And maybe she did look at the world through rose-colored glasses, but that didn't mean that being positive was wrong. God had blessed Cassidy with so much that she couldn't help but praise Him for it, and part of that praise was to have a merry heart, even in times of adversity. After all, the Bible said that "a merry heart doeth good like a medicine." Cassidy paused for a moment, remembering the latter half of that proverb.

"But a broken spirit drieth the bones." She barely whispered the words. Both her father and Mrs. Johnson were broken in spirit right now. Allan Brennan too. Cassidy shook her head and sighed. "But what can I do to help them?"

Mrs. Johnson entered the kitchen and approached Cassidy. "Miss Ivanoff, I owe you an apology for the other day." Her voice was low and raspy.

Cassidy was a bit shocked. The head cook never apologized for anything.

"I'm sorry for taking out my hurt and anger on you."

She swallowed. "I'm sorry for pushing, Mrs. Johnson. You were having a day of grief and I butted in."

The older woman gave a hint of a smile. "The truth is, you've grown on me. And I haven't allowed anyone to do that for a very long time. We always hurt the ones we love the most, don't we?"

Tears sprang to Cassidy's eyes. "Yes,

ma'am. We do." She reached over and hugged the woman.

Mrs. Johnson gasped and then squeezed Cassidy back. As she pulled away, she wiped a tear from her eye. "Now, we mustn't let anyone see us like this."

"No, ma'am." Cassidy glanced around the room. She knew others had seen the display of affection, but all heads were down and it was eerily quiet. Maybe now was her chance to stand up for what she believed. "You know, Mrs. Johnson, what you said about God the other day really got me to thinking."

"Oh?" She went to the other side of the table and began kneading more dough.

"You see, to me, God is loving and comforting. He's always there for me. Even when I'm the most down."

Mrs. Johnson shook her head. "But you're rarely down, are you? How could you be when your life has been so sweet?"

"It *hasn't* always been 'sweet.' And I really don't see the world as all gumdrops and rainbows."

A frown lined the older woman's face. "I was wrong to say that."

"But it did make me think. I haven't always considered how others regard me. Being happy was important to me because my father always told me it would benefit me far more than being sad. But it doesn't mean I don't feel pain or realize that there is a great deal of tragedy in the world. But God has always been there as my loving heavenly Father." Cassidy grabbed a ball of dough and starting kneading it as well.

Thunk. The dough hit the table with a puff of flour as Mrs. Johnson stared at it. "I don't see God that way, I'm sorry to say."

"But why?"

"He's more like a harsh taskmaster to me. Just sitting up there waiting to punish His children for wrongdoing."

Cassidy's dough hit the surface with an even louder *plunk.* "But how could you think that? He's not like that at all."

"Life experience, my dear. Life experience."

"No, what you're talking about isn't life experience, it's circumstances. We live in a sin-filled world, and that's what causes all the bad things around us to happen."

"Humph." She slapped her dough down again. "So now you're saying all the bad has happened because of my sin? That I caused my family to all die from influenza?"

Cassidy let her dough rest. With all the thudding and slapping and plunking, the rest of the staff were beginning to stare.

"No, that's not what I'm saying at all. Bad things do happen in this world because of man's sin — but that's only because we messed up the perfect world we had by sinning in the first place. As soon as we let it in, it ate away at the very fabric of joy-filled life. I couldn't live without my faith, Mrs. Johnson."

"That's the difference between us. I could. And I do."

"But maybe that's why you're so unhappy!" Cassidy regretted the words as soon as she said them. She covered her mouth with a flour-covered hand. "I'm sorry. I shouldn't have said that."

A few moments passed as Mrs. Johnson worked on the dough. "It's all right, I know you didn't mean it spitefully. And it's not like I don't want to be happy. Doesn't everyone want to be happy? But the difference is this: your life has always been a fairy tale. Mine has not. You've never been truly hurt. I have. More times than I care to remember." She sighed. "And each time, I've asked, 'Where is God?' "

Cassidy watched the woman for several seconds. If only her dad weren't off on the expedition to the glacier. She could really use his advice right now. All she could do was shoot a prayer heavenward and forge on ahead. "That's a valid question, and one I'm sure many people have asked, long before you and me." She lowered her voice. "But I've asked it too, Mrs. Johnson. That's something you need to understand."

"No, I doubt that. Not you, Miss Sunshine." Cook shook her head.

Emotions she'd buried long ago came back. Dare she tell the truth? "Yes. Me." She leaned forward and whispered. "My mother died soon after she gave birth to me. I never knew her. And then my grandparents abandoned my father and me because of my father's native heritage. They disowned me. And they never knew me." Cassidy took a deep breath. "And deep down inside, I have to admit that it hurt worse than anything I could have imagined. Why didn't they want me? Their daughter was their only child! I'm angry at the prejudice and hate toward people's heritage and skin color. I'm angry that I never got to hear stories of how my mother grew up or what she was like as a child. I'm angry that my mother died and left me. But I've put it to good use. I've always had compassion for the little guy — the ones left behind, the ones not chosen, the awkward, the less fortunate."

"Because you think that if you can help

someone else not feel rejected, then you will feel better about yourself too?"

"No, because I know that's what God has called me to do."

"I don't understand what you mean sometimes, Cassidy."

"It's simple. As believers, we're all chosen to share the gospel and show God's love to everyone. No matter their station in life or the color of their skin."

Mrs. Johnson shaped loaves out of her mound of dough. "While I appreciate your words, Cassidy, it still doesn't help me understand God. But I give you a gold star for trying."

"Well, that's a start." Cassidy smiled.

"Of course, you would think that." She shook her head. "Always the optimist."

"No one ever died from optimism, Mrs. Johnson."

13

The day had not gone as planned.

Frank eyed the papers in front of him. He had created all the documentation he needed to frame Louis Brewster — Henry's son-in-law — for the embezzling. Now he just needed a signature from the man. But that proved more difficult than he'd originally thought. Especially since he didn't want him reading any of the documents.

Maybe he could get him to sign off on something else and then have a forgery made?

It was a possibility. Frank tapped his chin with his pen. Why couldn't the whole Brennan clan just disappear? He was tired of having to do all the work for only part of the reward.

A swift knock preceded Lucy's entrance into his office. She handed him an envelope with one hand and then finished putting on her sweater. "Sorry to barge in, but this just

221

arrived and I've stayed much too late as it is tonight, Mr. Irving."

He grunted at her in response and she rushed out the door, closing it behind her. Whatever happened to help who stayed as long as the boss did? He shook his head. Terrible society they lived in nowadays. Perhaps he should go back to having a man as a secretary. Men were so much easier to handle.

He opened the envelope and read the contents:

25 July 1923

Dear Frank,
Thank you for your note. I appreciate your staunch dedication to my family and the memory of my father, but rest assured, I've got the situation under control. John Ivanoff is a wealth of information, and I'm certain that over time I will find out the truth of what happened to my father.

My mother and sisters are aware of my location. Thank you for your concern for their welfare. Please continue to look after them in my absence. On my return, I think it's time that I stepped up into a new role at the company. It's what my father would have wished.

As soon as I have any word, I will get the information to you.

Sincerely,
Allan Brennan

Wadding the paper into a ball, Frank threw it against the wall. Stupid boy! Who did he think he was dealing with?

Interference with his plans wouldn't be tolerated. He'd worked too long and hard to accomplish what he had. He began to pace.

He went to the locked cabinet where he kept his liquor. Fumbling with his keys, he finally found the right one. Nothing could be simple. He unlocked the door and opened it to reveal his choices. Picking the bottle of Scotch, he poured himself a generous portion.

He tossed back the drink, then poured another.

He thought of the ridiculous magic show he'd been forced to attend a few nights earlier. The tricks were accomplished by distraction — sleight of hand. Along with that, the magician had the help of a few props and an assistant.

Frank took the drink with him to his desk. He sank to the chair and studied the amber

223

liquid in his glass. Perhaps with a few props and an assistant he could accomplish his desires — perform his own magic.

With any luck at all he might well rid himself of the Brennan interference in the business.

There might even be an opportunity to rid himself of not just Henry's son, but of John Ivanoff as well. Maybe murder was required after all.

He smiled, then downed the scotch. Only time would tell.

All the staff gathered in the lobby as Mr. Bradley worked to quiet them.

Cassidy leaned up against the banister of the staircase. Her feet were killing her. It'd been such a long day.

"All right, all right." The manager rubbed his hands together. "Today, we found a station that will be broadcasting news in just a few minutes. There's a slight crackle, so we ask that everyone remain quiet so we can all hear."

The staff quieted. Cassidy noticed that several of the guests of the hotel had joined them in the lobby as well. Mr. Bradley had made the announcement at dinner regarding the radio, but few had even seemed interested. Radio broadcasts were most likely the norm for them anyway.

A touch on her shoulder brought her attention around. Allan held a chair for her. It was from the dining room; he must have carried it all the way over. "Would you like to sit? You look done in."

She sighed. "Thank you. That's very kind. Will you sit with me?"

He nodded and left for a moment, bringing another chair back with him.

The radio man and Mr. Bradley fiddled with knobs as they all waited. Crackling and sizzling was heard, and then a long hiss.

"It's supposed to start in about two minutes, so please be patient." Mr. Bradley nodded at the man.

Allan leaned toward her and whispered, "Your lemon soufflé the other night was delicious."

"Thank you. How did you know I made it?"

"Mrs. Johnson made an announcement — she's very proud of you."

How had she missed that? Warmth spread through her. Maybe she was finally getting through to the older woman.

"So is your dad. He talks about you all the time."

"Of course he does. I'm his only child. But it is nice to hear." She studied him for a moment. If only they had the time to talk all evening. This man beside her definitely gave her mixed emotions. "He speaks very highly of you as well."

"I'm glad to hear it. He's been very patient with me as I learn and work through everything since my father's passing."

"He's a good man." She straightened in the hardback chair. Did Allan truly see that now? More than anything, she wanted to trust this man beside her. She also wanted to know the truth about what had happened. Maybe as much as he did. Cassidy felt almost certain that until then, neither of them would be free to move forward.

She glanced at Allan to find him watching her. He offered her a slight nod as if having read her thoughts. Cassidy lowered her head, feeling her cheeks grow warm. She was glad to be sitting, as she was almost certain her knees would have given way at the rush of emotions that washed over her.

Allan made her feel things she'd never felt before. Was that a good thing?

The radio hissed and crackled to life. "We open our broadcast tonight with sad news for our nation. At 7:30 p.m. last night, August the second, President Warren Harding died suddenly in his hotel room in San Francisco."

Gasps were heard throughout the room, and Mr. Bradley quickly shushed them.

Everyone leaned forward.

"His countrywide trip — 'The Voyage of Understanding' — was drawing near to the end and he hadn't felt well for several days. Mere weeks ago, on June twentieth, the President gave one of the first presidential speeches to be broadcast live by radio. Just recently, he hammered in the golden spike to complete the Alaska Railroad and enjoyed a tour of the Alaska Territory as the first President to visit the Far North. Last week, he gave a speech predicting that Alaska would become one of the United States. And now today, we mourn his passing. We will take a moment of silence to remember President Warren Harding, the twenty-ninth President of the United States."

Music played in the background as Cassidy sat there in shock. Hadn't they just served the man a couple of weeks ago? How could this be?

While she wasn't really sure she liked him, she did have a lot of respect for the leader of the country. Of course, there were the rumors that he had a mistress, and the staff noted arguments behind closed doors. But Cassidy had been taught all of her life to ignore rumors. The President had been gra-

227

cious and kind to her and the staff . . . and he'd come all the way to Alaska when no other President had.

The hissing returned to the radio in the middle of the song.

"We must have lost the signal." The man fiddling with the radio furrowed his brows.

Conversations started all over the room in a gentle hum.

"This wasn't at all what I expected to hear the first time I listened to the radio." Cassidy wrung her hands. "How very sad."

Allan sat next to her in silence, shaking his head

"He didn't look at all like he was that ill, did he?"

"No, I can't say that he did." He shifted in his seat. "He looked a bit tired after we'd climbed up the hill a ways, but the schedule they had kept up to that point was ridiculously full."

Much of the staff dispersed as Mr. Bradley turned off the radio. No one seemed to be in a mood to socialize after the word they'd just received.

Allan turned in his chair to face her. "Do you think, perhaps, you'd like to take a walk with me? The fresh air might do us some good after such news."

She nodded. "Yes, I'd like that very

much." Cassidy stood and smoothed her apron. As Allan picked up their chairs and returned them to the dining room, she watched him and tried to calm her insides. They'd indeed had a rough start — that was for certain — but she couldn't deny the way she felt drawn to him.

He returned and offered his arm. Placing her hand in the crook of his elbow, she allowed him to lead her out the front door and onto the large wooden platform.

"How about we walk down to the roundhouse? There's a trail we could take from there if you'd like to walk farther." His brow was furrowed again.

"That sounds fine."

"My sisters would want to know everything about you if they knew I'd asked you on a walk."

The thought made her laugh. "Well, there's not much to know. I'm just me."

"I beg to differ. You are fascinating, Cassidy."

"I'm glad you think so, but you do realize I'm pretty simple, right?"

"Maybe in your tastes and expectations, but I don't think there's anything simple about you."

His words made her stomach flip. "And you're no longer angry with my father?"

"You keep asking me that, so it must be very important to you." He sighed. "Your father has proven over and over again to me that he's not the kind of man to leave my father to die." He stopped and turned to look into her eyes. "I still want to know what happened up there, but I don't blame your father anymore. I just don't know what to think."

The fire in his green eyes blazed through her. "I can understand that. And I really do appreciate your honesty. I can't imagine what you've had to go through. Have you had a chance to tell my father that you . . . forgive him?"

Allan looked at her oddly. "No, because until just now I wasn't sure I had. But now, talking to you, I realize he doesn't need to be forgiven. He did nothing wrong."

She smiled. "Still, I know it would mean the world to him to hear those words."

He turned forward again and started walking. For several minutes neither one said anything, and Cassidy worried that she'd once again pushed too hard. When would she ever learn a balance?

"The thing is, Cassidy, I've never met anyone like you." Allan's words came without warning. "And even though I'm still struggling with the death of my father, I want to know you . . . and your father better."

What exactly did that mean for her? She didn't quite have the gumption to ask. At least not yet. She had to change the subject. "Speaking of my father, what did you think of the glacier?"

Allan studied her face for a moment. "It was beautiful. More beautiful than anything I'd ever seen." He seemed momentarily to have lost his thoughts. Finally, he continued. "I was quite amazed to learn the glaciers are always moving. It seems strange to imagine."

"Ruth Glacier is one of my favorites. But I think I like the Kahiltna Glacier better. Maybe because of the view you get between Denali and Sultana. Snowshoeing is beautiful there."

"You've been there?" His jaw dropped.

She laughed again at his expression and squeezed his arm with her other hand. "Of course. You forget I was born and raised up here. Those mountains are home to me."

"Have you climbed McKinley?"

"Gracious, no. I'm not up for that. Dad says one of the most important things about life in Alaska is to recognize your limitations, otherwise you'll get hurt. But you never know . . . maybe one day."

"Your dad and I are planning a climb for next year. We wanted to keep it a secret to start with, since it will take much planning and preparation, but I'm excited. It will be a dream come true."

"That's wonderful. Even though it scares me a little." It scared her a lot. Who was she fooling? The last time her father climbed that mountain, one of the men didn't return. What if that happened this time? She didn't even want to think of losing her father. And what about Allan? Was he up to the challenge?

"Cassidy?"

He'd caught her lost in her thoughts. She smiled and pressed on, changing the subject to a safer topic. "Were your clients up for the challenge? I didn't hear too many complaints from my father. That's always a good sign. It always upsets him when people bite off more than they can chew."

"The group was interesting. They were very experienced riders and had obviously done other excursions, but probably not anywhere so remote. There were a few odd glances and questions at times, but for the most part, they were good sports and good travelers. I admit it made the trip that much easier." Allan's brow furrowed again. "So why is the Ruth Glacier named that? I meant to ask your father and I forgot. I like the other glacier name you said. What was it? It sounded so much more . . . Alaskan."

"The Kahiltna is the other one I mentioned. It's the longest glacier in all of the Alaska Range, I think. Stretches for miles and miles and miles. And as to the Ruth Glacier, Frederick Cook named it after his stepdaughter Ruth Hunt when I was a child. Apparently, the name stuck."

"I've heard a lot of controversy surrounding Cook."

"Dad says there will always be men who will actually accomplish what they set out to do and others who won't. Then there will be those who speak for and against those men. Every one of them will have their own reasons and motivations. If Cook didn't actually summit Denali, the loss is ultimately his."

"Yes, but he claims to have been the first, and that was important to a great many people."

Cassidy shrugged. "There are a lot of unimportant things that people call important. I think the measure of a man is his honesty. I don't abide anyone lying about their exploits, but neither am I inclined to give such matters more attention than they deserve. It's just not how I want to spend my time — my life."

They walked in silence for a few moments, and Cassidy enjoyed holding on to Allan's strong arm. She felt safe. And comfortable.

"So what is it that you really want to do with your life, Cassidy? What dreams do you have?"

She continued to hold his arm with both hands and took her time, but gave him a smile. "You're the only person other than my father who's ever asked me that question." She took a few more steps. "More than anything, I want to serve the Lord. Whatever that might look like. I know He's got a great plan. I would love to have a family of my own one day. And, of course, I want to stay in Alaska. But I also really love to cook. It'd be fun to be head chef one day. Maybe." She bit her lip. "Although it is a lot of work. While I'm young, it might be fun, but I can't imagine doing it at Mrs. Johnson's age. I think I'd be plumb worn out. But she doesn't have a family to take care of, so maybe she pours everything into her work. I know it gives her satisfaction and she loves it."

Allan laughed out loud at that one. "She's a tough woman, Mrs. Johnson. How is it, working for her?"

"Oh, we get along just fine. Underneath

all her bluster is a tender heart." She grew thoughtful. "A wounded one, but tender with love as well."

"I think you're probably the only person who would say as much."

She shrugged. "Sometimes you just need to look deeper. People have commented that you are rude and think yourself too good to associate with the rest of us. I've paid it no more attention than what they say about Mrs. Johnson."

Allan looked stunned. "People have said that about me?"

"Well, you have to admit you have very little to do with anyone other than Dad. Even then, you don't say a whole lot — unless, of course, it has to do with work."

"But that doesn't mean I think myself better than others."

She looked deep into his eyes and shook her head. "No. It means you're just as wounded as Mrs. Johnson, and you've built a wall up to keep others out. For some reason you both think that if you keep that wall in place, you won't be hurt again. But what's really sad is that you're still wounded. Never mind getting hurt again."

For a moment he said nothing, and Cassidy thought she'd offended him just as she'd done with Mrs. Johnson. Why couldn't

235

she learn to keep her opinion to herself?

"You know," he said after a few more moments of silence. "I think you're right."

"I didn't mean to cause you pain."

He shook his head. "I needed to hear it, and coming from you . . . well . . . it didn't seem harsh at all. You are about the most optimistic and inspiring person I think I've ever met." He stopped and looked at her. "You simply amaze me."

She breathed a sigh of relief. "Well, I will take that as a compliment."

"You're good for me, Cassidy . . ." He paused. "What's your middle name, if you don't mind my asking?"

"Faith."

"I should have known. How appropriate. As I was saying, you're good for me, Cassidy Faith Ivanoff. I need more positive influences in my life." The brooding look was back on his face. "Now, if I can just figure out how to tear down the wall and let them in."

She wished more than anything she could take away his pain. If he'd been Mrs. Johnson, she might have given him a hug. But if he'd been Mrs. Johnson, she wouldn't be dealing with the war of emotions that threatened to betray her at any moment.

"Well, it is getting late, even though it's

still plenty light. Deceiving this time of year, isn't it? I better get you back before your father sends out a search party." He smiled again, that half smile that made his face even more handsome.

She frowned. She hadn't seen her father since before the radio broadcast. "Allan, did you know where my father was going after dinner?"

"He wanted to check on the trail for the hiking group tomorrow."

"He should've been back by now, wouldn't you think?"

"I would have thought so." Allan looked off toward the trail. "Don't worry. You go on in and I'll go check. I'm sure he's fine."

14

The evening light in Alaska never ceased to amaze Allan. It looked like it was still only five or six o'clock and yet it was pushing 11:00 p.m.

He hadn't wanted to say anything in front of Cassidy, but he'd forgotten about John. And the man should've been back before they ever left for their walk.

Guilt gnawed at his gut. He should have paid closer attention to the time. Instead, he'd been absorbed by Cassidy's presence. What if something had happened to his boss, and Allan was the only one who even knew the experienced guide had gone out to do what he always did — double-and-triple check everything. All for the care and safety of others.

A mile up the trail, Allan spotted a waving red bandana. He couldn't see John, which meant the man was down. He ran ahead. If only he'd been more observant. Had he been more vigilant . . . had he been more like John . . . maybe this wouldn't have happened.

He came upon his mentor and wanted to retch. Blood stained his shirt and left trouser leg.

John lowered his bandana, his other arm tight about his middle and rasped, "I knew you'd find me."

"John, I'm so sorry it took me so long. What happened?"

He shook his head. "You couldn't have known, son. It's all right." He took a deep breath, which looked like it exhausted him. "I came upon a mama moose and her two calves. There wasn't any time to react; I just rounded this bend and there they were." He leaned his head back on the ground. "I backed up quietly, trying to put some space between us, but the mama probably thought I was after her babies, and she came after me with her hooves. She got in a couple of swift kicks and knocked me down. Then she left. Thankfully, she didn't stay to trample me some more."

Allan went into survivor mode. John had lost a lot of blood and it was more than a mile back to the hotel. He quickly took off his jacket and button-up shirt.

"Here." John lifted his jacket to Allan.

"Use this too."

Tearing the bottom of his shirt into long strips, Allan used the material to bind John's leg. Then he folded John's jacket and pressed it against the wound in his abdomen and used the top of his shirt with the long sleeves to wrap around John's midsection as a bandage and tied it as tight as he could. "This will have to do for now, but maybe it will help us get back to the hotel."

"Thank you." John's words were weak.

"Stay with me, John. I need you to stay awake."

"I'll do my best."

Allan assessed the situation. He was going to have to carry him down the trail. John had lost too much blood to leave and come back with help. "This isn't going to be comfortable, but I'm going to have to lift you like a sack of potatoes over my shoulder if we're going to make it back. Hopefully that jacket will give the wound in your abdomen some padding, but I don't know how else to do it."

"Do what you have to do. I'll make it."

Helping John to his feet, Allan hoped he'd have the strength to make it back. His boss was a solid, muscular, and tall man. He crouched down and let John lean over his shoulders and back. Allan grabbed John's right arm and right leg and lifted. As he balanced the man's weight on his shoulders, John moaned.

"I'm sorry, John."

"It's all right. Now that I'm up, I'm okay."

Brave words. But Allan knew they weren't true. Now he just needed to make it back to the hotel in time.

Step after step down the trail, Allan tried not to jostle his cargo too much. John had long since passed out. Probably from the pain or the loss of blood. It didn't matter. Just made it all the more urgent.

Allan's thoughts returned to Cassidy and their conversation earlier. A realization hit him square in the face. He cared about these people. A lot. Somewhere along the way they had managed to find a hole in his wall.

John was more than just his boss. He'd become his friend. Allan respected him and wanted to learn all he could from him. The more he thought about it, the more he realized that John reminded him of his father. All the best parts of him.

And then there was Cassidy. With her dark, inquisitive eyes. And her constantly positive outlook.

He couldn't deny it. He wanted their

friendship to grow.

"Mr. Brennan! Mr. Brennan!"

Allan couldn't see anyone yet, but that sure did sound like Thomas — and what a beautiful sound it was.

Footsteps got closer and then he could see the young man running up the path.

"Mr. Brennan, is Mr. Ivanoff all right?"

Allan kept moving down the trail, afraid to stop and lose the steady momentum. "He's been kicked by a moose. I need you to run back and tell Mr. Bradley. Ask him to get the medic and to prepare a room in the hotel for John. It's not pretty."

"Yes, sir." Thomas nodded and took off at a sprint.

The sight of Thomas renewed Allan's energy. They would be ready to help John as soon as he made it to the hotel, so he simply needed to place one foot in front of the other and make his way down the trail.

Cassidy paced the lobby of the hotel while a few of the other men went out to help Allan the rest of the way.

When they entered the front door, Allan had her father over his shoulders. He looked exhausted, but his eyes found hers and pierced her heart. He nodded to her and went down to his knees, while three other men lifted her father off of him.

She followed them down the hallway but looked back at Allan, still kneeling in the lobby. His white undershirt was soaked in blood. Her father's blood.

Cassidy's voice choked. "Thank you." She didn't wait for his response but hurried to join her father.

The medic wouldn't let her in the room and had placed Mr. Bradley as guard at the door. "This isn't something your father would want you to see. Right now he needs the medic's full attention and you would be a distraction. I'll come get you as soon as we know anything."

"I'm not going anywhere, Mr. Bradley. I'll just wait out here."

He nodded and closed the door.

She leaned against the wall and then slid down it, pulling her knees up to her chest. She couldn't hold the tears back any longer. *Lord, please don't let him die. He's all I have.*

All the conversations from the past few days sprang into her mind. That she was little Miss Sunshine, had lived a fairy-tale life, and was always positive.

She didn't feel so optimistic right now. Instead, loneliness gripped her again. What would she do if she lost her father? He'd always been there.

Sobs shook her shoulders and she buried her face in her apron.

An arm wrapped around her shoulder. "Cassidy, shhh, it's okay. I'm here." Mrs. Johnson's voice sounded almost lyrical. "Allan came and got me. He thought you might need a shoulder."

Lifting her head, she sobbed harder and threw herself into the woman's arms. They sat on the floor rocking for what seemed like hours. She owed Allan so much. He knew . . . somehow he knew that she'd need comfort from a motherly figure. And even though Mrs. Johnson could be all prickles and rough edges, she was the only one Cassidy wanted right now. Other than her father.

A tap on her shoulder brought her awake in a snap. Cassidy sat up. "Dad?" The medic stood before her, blood on his jacket.

"He's all right. And he'll mend. Took quite a beating and lost a lot of blood, but I've got him stitched up. I don't think there's severe internal damage, but we'll keep an eye out for swelling in the abdomen and blood in his urine. There will be a lot of bruising, and we'll have to watch him for infection, but I think in a few weeks, he'll be back to full strength."

She nodded. "Thank you . . . ?" It hit her that she didn't even know the man's name.

"It's Larry. And you're welcome."

She scrubbed her face with her hands and looked at Mrs. Johnson. How appropriate that the medic's name was Larry.

Mrs. Johnson was all smiles.

Cassidy looked back at Larry. "Thank you. May I see him?"

"Yes. He was asking for you earlier, but he's sleeping pretty hard now."

"That doesn't matter. I just want to see him."

The medic nodded and walked away.

Mr. Bradley greeted her at the door. "Your father is a strong man, Miss Ivanoff. I'm sure he'll have a full recovery."

"Thank you, Mr. Bradley. For everything."

"Not a problem, my dear. He's the best man I've got. We'll take good care of him. Barring any complications to his condition, he should be able to get up and around in about a week and then he'll have to take it slow for a week or two after that."

She nodded and looked at her father. He'd always been so strong. The vision of health. Now he looked pale and tired.

Leaning over his bed, she kissed his forehead. "I love you, Daddy. Now you just concentrate on getting better. I'll be praying for you."

"It's probably best you just let him sleep." The manager patted her shoulder. "Looks like you could use some sleep as well. We'll make sure someone comes to get you as soon as he's awake again. Never fear, someone will be with him throughout the night."

"All right." Cassidy headed for the door and saw Mrs. Johnson and Allan both waiting for her outside.

Mrs. Johnson came forward and grabbed her hands. "Go get some sleep. I don't even want to see you before noon."

"But —"

"Don't argue with me, Cassidy Faith. You sleep and get some time in with your father. There will be plenty of work to do later."

Cassidy couldn't help but smile at the glint in the woman's eye. "Yes, ma'am."

Mrs. Johnson waved and walked away. "Not before noon!"

Cassidy looked at Allan for a moment. There was so much she wanted to say to him, but there were no words. Without even thinking about it, she went straight into his arms. She hugged him for all she was worth. "Thank you."

It only took a moment before his strong arms wrapped around her. She'd never been held by a man other than her father, and she didn't know if it was the emotion and relief of the moment, or simply that it was Allan who held her. But she never wanted to leave.

15

Six o'clock in the morning came all too soon after such a long night. Allan hadn't gotten much sleep between his thoughts of Cassidy and John. With his boss laid up, the full schedule of excursions would fall on his shoulders. But mainly his thoughts were of Cassidy.

As he went over the schedule for the next few days, his thoughts wouldn't stay on task. It was hard to imagine he'd only known the Ivanoffs a month. And even though he hadn't treated them very well, they'd shown him nothing but kindness. It didn't make sense.

His walk with Cassidy last night had opened up his heart, but he never could have prepared himself for what his heart would do when she hugged him. He wanted to treasure her and protect her, but he didn't have that right. At least not before he made things right — truly right — with her father.

Allan felt so convicted for the thoughts he'd held toward John. Now that he knew the man, and had seen his true character over and over again, he couldn't imagine how he ever believed the man had been responsible for his father's death. But how could he have known? And why did Frank hate John so much? Because he needed someone to blame for the loss of his friend? Or was there something else to it?

He didn't want to go there — but there had been things over the years that made Allan doubt Frank's loyalty to the Brennan family.

Dad, what do I do?

He stared at the ceiling. No answer came. But oh, how he wished one would. Since he'd lost his father, he didn't have anyone to talk to about the tough decisions. Allan had relied on his father for guidance and wisdom in every aspect of his life. Henry Brennan often scolded him for it. Told him that he should be relying on God. Not man. But Allan idolized his father.

As for God . . . he shook his head. For the longest time he'd worked to convince himself that he didn't need God anymore.

During the war, after learning of his

father's death, he'd often considered his father's faith. He knew his dad would have been disappointed — crushed more like it — that his death would drive his son away from God. Of course, Allan didn't allow himself those thoughts. Not in the trenches. His commanding officer was fond of quoting the old French poet Jean de La Fontaine, who said, "Death never takes the wise man by surprise, he is always ready to go."

His commander had been a Christian, and would usually add that a man could only be truly ready when his spirit was at peace with God.

At the time, Allan forced himself to be logical about it. His father was dead and eventually he would die as well. Whether here or in his bed as an old man. Death was death.

But even now his father's words whispered in his ear.

"For to me to live is Christ, to die is gain."

His father didn't fear death, nor did he dread life. He'd been completely at peace with both, and Allan wanted the same.

Shaking off the regret and the endless void that dogged him, Allan headed out to the equipment shed. In time he would speak to John and tell him the truth — that he did forgive him. For now, however, he needed to focus on the job at hand. That's all. John was injured — lucky to be alive, but that meant Allan would need to put all his energy into performing his duties, as well as John's.

The morning passed in a wild-flower hike with city ladies who found the beauty inspirational and the dangers thrilling. They walked in their dainty fashion with their very pretty dresses and thin-soled shoes and marveled that anything so rustic still existed in the modern world. At noon he delivered them back to the hotel safe and sound, with each of the ladies speaking in animated excitement about how they'd faced the dangers of the wild frontier and survived.

What would they have thought if they'd truly had to face all that Alaska had to offer? Allan's growling stomach reminded him that he'd forgotten breakfast. Not a smart thing to do. Especially when he had to spend the afternoon taking a group out fishing. He pulled out his pocket watch — just enough time to check on John and get his advice if he was awake, and to eat a quick lunch.

As he headed to John's room, one of the kitchen boys caught him by the sleeve.

"Mr. Brennan, here's a telegram for you."

"Thank you."

The boy dashed off.

Opening the envelope, Allan stayed in the hall. He hoped it wasn't anything too urgent — especially not another group requesting anything, but John received most of those requests.

4 August 1923

```
Concerned about Brennan/Irving
(stop)Not all appears as it
should (stop)Anna believes
Frank involved in shady deal-
ings (stop)Please advise
(stop)
                        Louis
```

Allan leaned against the wall and reread it. His sister Anna was the quietest out of all of them, but also the most observant. Whenever she brought something to their attention, she was correct.

For Louis to send the telegram also gave a strong hint. Louis was capable and independent. He never communicated unless it was necessary. Things must be very bad indeed.

But how could Allan deal with the matter from here?

Shoving the paper back in the envelope, he strode the rest of the way to John's room.

He knocked softly.

"Come in." Cassidy's sweet voice called out.

When he opened the door, he was over-joyed to see John sitting up and with color in his face. "You look a hundred times better than you did last night."

John reached out a hand.

Allan took it in a firm grip and shook it.

"Thank you for finding me."

"You would've done the same for me." Allan sat in a chair on the other side of John's bed. Not only could he see his boss, but he had a good view of Cassidy as well. However, with her there, Allan didn't feel he could speak to John about forgiveness. That was still too personal.

"I wanted your advice about the fishing expedition this afternoon."

John smiled. "Just take them to Deadhorse Creek. The salmon are starting to run, and they will be so stacked in there that no one should have a problem catching at least one."

"Yes, sir. I knew you would know exactly where to go." He looked down at the envelope in his hand.

"Something bothering you, Allan?"

His head shot up. Just like Dad. The man could read him. "Well, yes, sir. As a matter of fact there is."

"Since I've got nothing else to do, would you like a listening ear?"

Allan looked at John and then at Cassidy. Compassion shone in both their eyes. They really cared about him. The thought struck him. He didn't deserve their friendship, but he was thankful for it. He nodded. "I would appreciate your insight, John." He pulled the telegram out and handed it over.

John read it and sighed. "Not the news you wanted to hear." He handed the paper back.

"No, sir."

"Do you trust Louis? He's your brother-in-law, correct?"

"Yes, sir. On both accounts. And my father loved Louis. Knew he could rely on him for anything. He's always been honest to a fault."

Cassidy leaned forward. "Is this something about your father's company?"

Allan nodded. "Yes, and it's my company now — along with Frank. My eldest sister, Ada, and her husband, Stanley Meyers, helped out a lot while I was at war. But Stanley's family owns a grocery business, and a few years ago it came time for Stanley to step up into his role there managing the stores. Anna is married to Louis and he's worked at Brennan/Irving for years. Dad trusted all of them implicitly. Louis is a good man. But I haven't really taken ownership like I should have. I guess I was grieving the loss of my father too much and just left Frank to do what he pleased." He handed the telegram to Cassidy.

She read it. "Oh my." She turned to her father. "Frank is the other man from the expedition, isn't he?"

"Yes." John frowned and shifted a bit on his bed. He closed his eyes and grimaced. "Sorry, gotta get used to the pain."

Cassidy stood and leaned over her father. She looked at Allan and then back at John. "Don't you think he deserves to know your insight?"

Allan puzzled over that statement. He leaned toward John. "Yes, please, John. Tell me."

"I'm not one to tarnish a man's reputation. Especially since I know how being wrongly judged feels." His eyes opened and he fixed his gaze on Allan. "I don't want to cause problems where none should exist."

"I know that, sir. But if there's something you know that could give me guidance here, I'd greatly appreciate it."

John shook his head. "I don't really know anything. It's just a gut instinct."

"I'd still like to hear it."

"I never felt like I could trust Frank on that mountain. And that frightened me. There was something . . . shifty about him that I couldn't put my finger on." John breathed heavily. "Completely different than your father. I would have put my life in Henry's hands and felt totally comfortable."

"But you didn't feel that way about Frank?" Allan pressed.

"No. I'm sorry to say." John held a hand up. "Now, I'm not saying that I saw him do anything wrong. He just always went for the easy way out. I'd ask him to do things — important things — and he'd only do them halfway. He always seemed distracted, like he was deep in his own little world. I got the feeling the most important person in Frank Irving's world was Frank Irving. Seemed like a weasel to me, to be honest. Always manipulating things. But your father trusted him."

Allan stood up and walked over to the window. "Frank is definitely a manipulator. We all know that. And he likes to have his way. But Dad always had a system with him. Could handle him." He turned back to John and Cassidy. "As to the trust. Well, that goes back to when they were kids. Dad fell out of a tree and broke his arm. Frank gave Dad his coat and ran all the way home to get help." He thought about it for a minute. "You know, Frank was the whiner, the doubter, while Dad was the positive, always optimistic dreamer. Whenever Frank would get down and needed affirmation, Dad would always remind him of that good deed he did. Almost like he knew Frank needed the encouragement to stay on the up and up."

"Sounds like Henry." John nodded. "Your father was encouraging him every step up the mountain. I doubt Frank would have made the summit if not for your father's determination to see him there."

"So now I need to ask for your advice. What do you think I should do?"

John and Cassidy looked at each other. Then John spoke. "Well, I think you need to follow your own gut. And if you have full trust in Louis and know he wouldn't contact you unless he absolutely had to, then you need to find out what's going on. The only caution I have is that Frank is a smart cookie. He probably already has a plan." His mentor sighed. "It could just be that Frank never recovered from Henry's death. People do strange things when they've lost someone they love."

Allan clenched his jaw. But he had a feeling Frank knew exactly what he was doing. And maybe had been all along. "I'll see to it after the fishing trip."

He got up, then remembered what he wanted to say to John, and decided to forge ahead even with Cassidy in the room. He opened his mouth to share his heart just as Mr. Bradley bustled into the room.

"I've come to see our patient."

"As you can see I'm on the mend," John announced.

Allan slipped from the room. There would be another time.

The fishing trip only took two hours because the men were so excited to catch so many fish, they couldn't wait to get them all back to the hotel. One man even pulled out two with his bare hands.

But even the cheers and pats on the back couldn't rid Allan of the black cloud he felt covered him. He didn't want to think Frank could turn his back on the Brennan family, but maybe that is what happened. Maybe he had turned on them that day back in 1917 when his father was lost on the mountain. Maybe he was the reason his father died. It was a terrible thing to consider, but after listening to John, Allan knew he had no other choice. Frank very well could have the answers that Allan needed.

As he stowed the fishing gear in the shed, Allan thought through his response to Louis. How should he advise his brother-in-law?

Maybe he just needed to return home. But would that solve anything? It's not like he'd been highly involved in the business at any point of his life. But how could he leave now? John needed him.

Shutting the door, he realized he just wanted to talk to John again.

Thomas rounded the corner. "Mr. Brennan, there's a telegram for you."

Another one? "Thank you, Thomas. Did it just arrive?"

"Yes, sir."

Allan watched him run back to the main building. The young man's eagerness to please was apparent. It'd been a decade since Allan was that age, but he couldn't imagine going through those tough years without parents. It was hard enough to not have his dad now, and he was twenty-eight.

He opened the envelope and read the second telegram for that day.

4 August 1923

Received letter (stop)Anxious

for you to be a part of your
father's legacy (stop)Sad news
to report (stop) Louis embezzling (stop)Fired him today
(stop)No other way (stop)

                        Frank

Fury burned in his gut. None of it added
up, and Allan *would* find out the truth. No
matter what.

He marched straight to the front desk. "I
need to send a couple of telegrams."

"Certainly, Mr. Brennan." Mr. Clark, the
railroad clerk, stood behind the desk and
passed two slips of paper and a pencil
toward him. "Write them out here, and I'll
get them out straightaway."

"Thank you."

He penned the first one to his mother's
brother — an accountant.

4 August 1923

In need of your assistance
(stop)Embezzling at Brennan/
Irving (stop)Need an audit of
company books (stop)Rush
(stop)

                 Allan Brennan

The second one, he took a bit more care

writing. Frank needed to know that Allan was serious about taking on a more substantial role, and that he wouldn't be taking Frank's word as truth. Not anymore.

16

Thomas watched for Cassidy down the hallway. She had to be coming out soon. Mrs. Johnson would have his hide if he didn't get back to the kitchen, and he didn't want to risk her anger just when she'd finally agreed to let him work for her full-time again.

But he wanted to be there for Cassidy. She was the only one who smiled and encouraged him no matter what blunder he made. Not only that, but she made him feel special, and no other girl had ever done that.

He brushed a dirt smudge off his pants and propped his foot up against the wall behind him. He wanted to tell her how he felt, but every time he tried it felt like he had a mouth full of cotton. If only he could talk to someone and get advice on how to court a lady. The only one he could talk to, though, was Mr. Ivanoff, and he was Cassidy's father. So that made the situation impossible.

A door closed and it brought his attention up. There she was.

Carrying a tray, she blew a strand of hair out of her face.

He raced toward her, doing his best not to get his feet tangled. "Here. Let me take that for you, Miss Cassidy."

"Why, thank you, Thomas." She handed him the tray and smoothed her hair back with her hands. "My hair was making my nose itch and I best get it back under control before we reach the kitchen. There's lots of food to prepare, and I don't think the guests would like my hair to be in it."

They laughed together as they walked. She always could make him laugh. That was one of his favorite things about Cassidy. It didn't hurt that she was so pretty. He loved her dark eyes and hair. He didn't even think he'd mind if her hair got in his food.

"Uhh . . . how's your . . . dad doing?"

"A little better. He makes a poor patient. He wants to be up and back to work. It's hard on him not being able to do what he loves."

"At least he knows what he loves." Thomas felt his face flush and hurried to change the subject. "I know the guests have asked about him."

"I know. I've had several ask me as well. He's definitely missed."

She worked on winding her hair around and around, and Thomas forgot what he was going to say and just stared. Was her hair as soft as it looked? When they reached the kitchen, he was so fascinated with the knot she'd made at the back of her head that he must not have been paying attention, because all of a sudden, she turned around.

"Thomas, I —"

Too late he realized his mistake and the tray slammed into the front of Cassidy. The rest of Mr. Ivanoff's soup and fruit now covered the front of Cassidy's apron and dripped off her face.

Allan knocked on John's door.

"Come in."

He turned the knob and entered the room where his boss was recuperating. "Sorry to bother you, John."

"Not at all."

"I was hoping you might have a few minutes to talk."

John pushed up with his fists. "No matter how hard I try, I keep sinking down into this bed."

"Here, let me help." Allan moved forward

and lifted a pillow up while John situated himself.

"I didn't realize how sore my muscles would be." John rubbed his midsection.

"That mama landed quite a kick, so you better follow the doctor's orders."

He took a sip of water. "All right, now what can I help with?"

"It's Thomas."

John raised his eyebrows.

"I just came from a meeting with Mrs. Johnson and Mr. Bradley. Apparently, he had another clumsy moment and spilled a tray all over Cassidy. So Mr. Bradley thought he should assign Thomas to me, since you are laid up and I could use the help."

John chuckled. "Go on."

"Well, last time you took him on when Mrs. Johnson had had enough of him, and while we weren't without mishap, he did do so much better for you. That's why I need your advice. I don't want to lose my patience with him."

"Ah, I understand."

"So?"

"So what?"

"How did you do it?"

His mentor looked out the window and then smiled at him. "You might not like

265

hearing this, but I try to look at Thomas like God looks at me."

"What exactly is that supposed to mean?" He scratched his head. Maybe this wasn't such a good idea.

"It means that I know I'm a messed-up sinner. I make lots and lots of mistakes. And yet God loves me so much, He looks past all of that and sees what I am underneath — washed clean. Without any of those mistakes."

"I'm not sure you've hit on all sixes today, John. Has that medic given you some medication that's made you a bit . . ." He lifted his eyebrows and wiggled them.

John laughed. "Oh, don't do that. Don't make me laugh, that hurts too much." He patted his middle again. "No, this isn't any medication talking. It's just plain ol' truth. The point is, how dare I think that I'm better than anyone else? No matter if I'm clumsy or beautiful and graceful, no matter the color of my skin or where I was raised. No matter if I have lots of money, or if I have none. God loves us all. Exactly the same. Not one of us can earn our way into heaven."

"I remember hearing my dad say the same thing. But how do you not get frustrated with him?"

John smiled. "With God or with Thomas?"

Allan shook his head and couldn't help but smile. John seemed to be able to read his mind. "Well, both, but for now — Thomas. It's hard to have patience when someone is making another mess while you're still busy trying to clean up the last one."

"We make a mess of things from time to time. When I err, when I make a mess of things, I want to be forgiven. I figure others feel the same way."

The words hit Allan and he knew he could no longer avoid the topic of forgiveness. Not that he even wanted to.

"John . . . I've been wrong to hold Dad's death against you." He looked down at his hands, uncertain he could continue. "I was . . . angry. When I heard about Dad, I was angrier than I'd ever been. I was angry that the war had kept me from going with him on the climb. I was angry that you had somehow failed to keep him alive, and I was angry at God for taking Dad away from me."

When John said nothing, Allan forced himself to look up. There were tears in John's eyes. "I want to do the right thing regarding my family and the business, but I'm almost afraid that what I'll uncover will

267

be worse than what I ever imagined." Allan drew in a deep breath. "But I want you to know that I don't hold you responsible for anything that happened. And . . . I hope that you'll forgive me."

John smiled and wiped at his tears. "Son, you've always had my forgiveness."

"I appreciate that — even if I don't deserve it."

Allan got to his feet, but John wasn't finished with him. "You know, you've got God's forgiveness too. You just need to seek it."

Allan looked past John to the open window. This man was so full of knowledge. Just like his father. And he missed his father. More than he could even say. But John was asking for more than Allan could give. He was asking for Allan to say it was okay for God to take away his father. And to admit that he couldn't handle any of this on his own. Ever since coming home from the war, he'd done a pretty good job of taking care of himself — at least he'd built a pretty good fortress to hide inside.

He drew a deep breath and let it go. "I know."

So young Allan Brennan was getting wise.

Frank was livid. He'd done everything he

could to gain complete control of the business — the business that was *his.* His! Henry had been the one in the way, but he'd gotten rid of him. Then that stupid will had to show up. He'd never forgive himself for that giant mistake. Then the son-in-law, Louis, started poking around and meddling. Like he had any say whatsoever. And now Allan thought he could just defend his family and take sides with John Ivanoff. Who knew what stories that man had planted?

Frank threw the glass bottle in his hand up against the wall and watched it shatter and fall. He glanced back down at the telegram. No doubt, the kid had hired his uncle's firm to audit. But Frank had another card up his sleeve. All he had to do was make a phone call.

"Two can play at this game." The words drifted on the air.

17

The crème brulées were just about done. Cassidy prepared to take the water baths out of the oven so the custards could finish cooling and setting. Then they would have several hours to chill before dinner.

Checking the clock, she realized she had just enough time to pull them out and then to whip the dressing for the salad before luncheon.

Mrs. Johnson strode into the kitchen. "Cassidy, those custards look lovely."

She couldn't help smiling under the praise. "Thank you, Mrs. Johnson."

"I wanted to speak to you a bit before lunch."

"Yes, ma'am?" The rest of the kitchen staff might have been afraid of the head cook starting off with that statement, but Cassidy had gotten to know the woman little by little.

"First, I think you probably need to have

a conversation with Thomas soon."

"Oh? About what?"

"I'm pretty sure the poor lad has a crush on you. And the sooner you nip it in the bud, the easier it will be for him to recover."

That was unexpected. Cassidy blinked. "I had no idea."

"Of course you didn't. Which makes you even more likeable. But you should be aware, half the male staff has a crush on you, my dear. And with you smiling and encouraging and laughing with everyone, they all probably think they have a chance to win your heart." Mrs. Johnson looked at her. "That doesn't mean you've done anything wrong. It just means your sunny personality is attractive."

"Oh."

"And I'm thinking that you're okay with the thought of one Mr. Allan Brennan being one of your admirers?" She tossed some flour onto the worktable and went to work on her roll of dough.

Cassidy bit her lip. Was she okay with that? She liked Allan very much. But there was still so much he needed to resolve. "Allan is a very nice man."

Mrs. Johnson laughed out loud, which was a rare occurrence. "Oh, Cassidy Faith, you do beat all."

"Yes, ma'am. I'm sure I do." She tried her best not to smile.

The head cook took a pinch of flour and blew it toward Cassidy's face. "And you're ornery too."

"Yes, ma'am." She wiped the flour off her face and continued whipping the dressing. "I'm sure I have learned that from the very best."

"If you are insinuating that I have taught you to be ornery . . . well . . . I really don't have any room to talk, now do I?" Mrs. Johnson winked at her and folded the dough in thirds. "I have to admit that I wanted to speak with you on another matter." Her voice lowered in volume.

"Yes?"

Mrs. Johnson's expression took on a look of discomfort and her mouth tightened. Whatever it was she wanted to say it wouldn't come easily. Cassidy wondered if she should say something to ease the tension, but it seemed waiting for the older to woman to speak was best. Finally the words came.

"How did you not lose faith yesterday?"

"What do you mean?" Cassidy's heart skipped a beat. Mrs. Johnson was actually initiating a conversation about God and she didn't want to do anything to discourage her.

"Last night, when your father was found injured. We spent hours together sitting on that floor waiting for news. And even though you were devastated and crying, you kept talking to God like He was right there. You never lost hope."

Cassidy stopped the whisking. She wiped her hands on her apron and prayed for wisdom. "I didn't lose hope, Mrs. Johnson, because my hope is in the Lord. No matter what might happen. But that doesn't mean that I didn't worry about losing my father. I was almost sick with worry over him — wondering what would happen if I lost him. I was a newborn when my mother died, so although the hurt of losing her is quite real, I never knew her. But with my dad, it's hard to imagine my life without him. That was a hurt unlike anything I'd ever experienced.

"And when you said I talked to God like He was right there — well, that's because He was. And still is. I didn't realize I'd been praying out loud, but I do that a lot, so I'm not surprised."

Mrs. Johnson didn't look at her but pinched off pieces of dough to be shaped. "And you believe that He hears you? And wants to hear from you?"

"All the time. Yes, ma'am."

"The way you view God is so very different than anything I've ever known."

Cassidy smiled. "My relationship with God is unlike anything else I've ever known."

Mrs. Johnson nodded. "I'm not saying I'm ready to buy into what you believe, but I do know that I admire you for how you handled the situation. And . . . if I'm honest, I have to admit that I often want what you have. The light that shines out of you all the time. It's refreshing. And makes me want it too."

Cassidy smiled at her boss. It was a step in the right direction, and she praised the Lord in her heart for that.

The intimacy of the moment was obviously a little too overwhelming for the older woman. She hurried to the counter on the opposite side of the room. "Now, let me get a tray fixed for you and your father. I want you to take at least an hour to spend with him." She held up a hand before Cassidy could even respond. "No arguments. It's an order."

The group of tourists who requested a hike up Deadhorse Hill were likely to be Allan's undoing. Women with inappropriate footwear, men with bellies too stout to balance on the side of a hill, and then there were the three boys. Their parents were part of the group, but Allan couldn't say who they actually belonged to, since the adults seemed too preoccupied with their blathering conversations about this and that.

In fact, Allan wondered if there was a lick of sense found among the whole group.

Thomas led the way up the hill, since the three youngsters had way more energy than the adults in the group, and Allan wanted to be prepared to catch whoever would fall next. He hated giving such a huge responsibility to Thomas, but the lad seemed excited to take on a challenge.

And a challenge it was. The boys ranged in age from eleven to fifteen — or so he'd been told — but frankly, they acted like five-year-olds. Pushing, shoving, tripping each other. And covered in dirt. Each one of them from head to toe.

Allan just hoped that none of them had any brilliant ideas of jumping off cliffs.

"Mr. Brennan, did you say that we might see moose?" The stoutest man of them all stopped for a moment. Probably to catch his breath.

"It's a strong possibility, sir, but with all the ruckus we're making, I doubt the moose will venture anywhere near us."

"Oh, well, that's too bad. I hear they're awfully cute and awkward-looking." One of the ladies adjusted her parasol and huffed.

Allan knew he should bite his tongue, but he couldn't contain it. "Actually, ma'am, it's better if we don't see them. They are very dangerous animals."

"Well . . ." she huffed again. "That's not what I've heard." She strutted up the hill, wobbling on her silly shoes.

How did John do this? Day in and day out. The man had the patience of a saint. Of course, what was he thinking? John *was* a saint. The man's forgiving spirit and patient endurance was a credit to him. He saw the good in everyone — at least if there was good to be found. Apparently there hadn't been much of that when it came to Frank Irving. Allan had been so blinded by his sense of injustice and need to blame someone that he'd very nearly missed the deception and underhanded actions of his father's former partner.

Whoops and hollers echoed down from above and brought Allan's attention back to the distasteful task at hand.

While the other adults seemed content to meander their way up the hill, Allan began to worry about Thomas and those boys. And what they could get into.

"If you all believe that you are doing all right, I'd like to check on the youngsters, so I'll go on ahead."

"Oh, please do. That Billy of mine can be quite a prankster." Another of the ladies plopped down in the grass. "And I'm quite worn out already and these mosquitoes are pesky and annoying."

Great. A prankster.

With nods and murmurs from the rest of the group, Allan headed up at a faster clip. While the fresh air invigorated him, the steepness of the trail made it slower going than he'd hoped.

The last twenty yards or so, Allan heard voices.

"Come on, Thomas! Don't you want to try it? Everybody else is . . ." one of the boys' voices squeaked.

"No, and neither should you." Thomas sounded so much older than before.

"It ain't hurtin' nobody. Don't be such a killjoy."

"Hand 'em over, Billy."

Allan was impressed. When push came to shove, it looked like Thomas was made of sterner stuff than he'd given him credit for. Creeping up the hill, he listened and tried not to be noticed.

"No way! My parents gave 'em to me."

"That's a bunch of baloney and you know it." Thomas's voice deepened even more, but his tone was even. "I will speak to them about this as soon as they get here."

The younger boys all seemed to be laughing.

"They won't make it up here. They just want to pretend to be adventurous. Besides, why would they listen to you? You're nothing but the help — a worker. They'd never believe you over their own son. And it's three against one."

"Come on, fellas, we need to smoke these while we have the chance." Billy seemed to be the ringleader. He pulled a matchbook out of his pocket and lit his cigarette. He puffed and didn't even choke on it.

The other two clambered forward and lit matches and then their cigarettes.

Thomas walked in the other direction. What was he doing? After standing up to them, now he was just going to walk away?

Allan waited and watched.

Then the coughing began. First, the shortest kid, then Billy. He actually looked a little green now. Then the last one succumbed to a coughing fit and dropped his smoke.

Before they knew what was happening, the grass was on fire as well as Billy's pant leg. The boys all started screaming like little girls.

"I'm on fire! Do something!" Billy looked toward Thomas.

Allan jumped up but saw Thomas racing toward them. He reached the boys and dumped water from his hat and an entire canteen onto the small fire, effectively quenching it.

So that's where he'd gone. To the creek. To fill the canteen and his hat with water.

That moment was as good as any for him to appear, so Allan walked the rest of the way to the boys. The three troublemakers looked up at him with fear in their eyes.

"How's your leg, Billy? Did it get burned?"

"A little, sir." A single tear slipped down his cheek. "So . . . you saw?"

"Yup. I sure did." Allan checked the boy's leg. The hair was singed, but no other damage except to his pants. He held out his hand. "I'll take the rest of those cigarettes and matches."

"Aw, man. You and your stupid ideas, Billy." The older of the two boys kicked the dirt.

Once he had checked all their pockets, Allan gave them a speech about fire safety, especially in the wilderness, and told them to sit right where they were until the adults joined them. Then he told them if they moved, he'd tell their parents everything.

Surprisingly, the threat worked.

Allan turned to Thomas. "I'm proud of you. That was awfully brave standing up to them."

"It was the right thing to do."

"And when you walked away?"

"My plan was to just dump water over their heads to teach them a lesson. I didn't know they'd be dumb enough to catch themselves on fire."

He slapped the young man on the back while he laughed. "You did good, Thomas."

"Thank you, sir." He straightened his shoulders and stood even taller. "I don't know if I would have before I learned about Daniel."

"Daniel?"

"You know, from the Bible? Cassidy told me about him a while back. So then I asked Mr. Ivanoff about him, and we've been studying together, since he can't do much else. Cassidy inspired me when she said she wanted to be like Daniel." Thomas puffed his chest out. "I want to be like Daniel too." He walked away and stood over the boys.

A tinge of jealousy sparked through Allan. The seventeen-year-old had bested him. He wondered if maybe John had space in his Bible study to include a rather wayward twenty-eight-year-old.

18

John shifted in his bed and moaned. Good thing Cassidy wasn't in there to hear him. He'd tried not to let her see how much the bruising affected him, but he had a feeling she knew anyway. And he had to admit, he wasn't getting any younger. Two kicks from a moose had done a number on him. It had been three days and still he hadn't been able to stand up yet. The first few days were to be the worst. He knew that.

A knock sounded at the door. "Mr. Ivanoff?" Thomas's voice preceded his head as he peeked around the door. "You've got a letter."

"Thank you, son."

Thomas handed him the letter and nodded. "I'll be back later to check on ya, but I need to help Mr. Brennan."

The postmark caught John's attention as Thomas left.

Ireland.

It had been twenty-three years since he'd seen that on an envelope.

Tearing it open, he held his breath. Only one page. But as he read it, it packed a wallop.

Eliza's parents were reaching out from the other side of the world.

And they were asking for forgiveness.

John awoke later with tears dried at the corners of his eyes. Wiping away the crusty remains, he took one more look at the letter. He'd waited for so long to hear from them, it pleased him to no end to hear they'd had a change of heart. But could he put his daughter through the ups and downs of hope and possible rejection?

His body ached. Confounded bed. He hated being stuck in it.

Tucking the letter back in its envelope, he put it under his pillow. Best to just let this one sit on the back burner for a while. He had more important things to worry about. Like getting through the summer lineup and planning an expedition up Denali.

But first, he had to heal. And quick.

He wanted to be back out there. Not just to be with his daughter, but he felt an urgency to help Allan.

His apprentice could do the job — of that

John was certain. But something else in his heart prodded him on. Ever since Allan's appearance in July, John's mind had churned with the details of the trip up Denali, the loss of Henry, and Frank's demeanor. None of it added up. So what had he missed?

And then there was Allan. He was still struggling and seeking to fill the void in his heart with remembrances of his father. But John knew — better than most — that the void could only be filled by God.

"Lord, I'm not sure why You've got me laid up in this bed right now, but I'm betting it's for a good reason. Maybe it's because I needed to spend more time talking to You. Well, here I am. Allan needs You, Father. And I feel inadequate in leading him. So I need Your direction and Your words. Then there's Cassidy. I know You love her more than I do and want the best for her. I've had this feeling in my gut that You brought Allan here for her. If that's Your will, Lord, let it be done. Bring Allan back to You, Father. Keep Cassidy strong through all of this. And Father God, I know it's asking a lot, but I'd appreciate Your help in healing this flesh of mine —"

"— because You know he's not a very good patient." Cassidy's voice cut in.

284

John chuckled. "Yes, Lord, You know it's true. In Jesus' name I pray, amen."

"Amen." Cassidy set down the tray she'd brought in and held out a hand to him. "Sorry to intrude on your prayer, but I came to see how you are doing."

He grabbed her hand and squeezed. "Other than feeling my age with these bruises, I'm doing all right." The letter popped into his brain. Should he tell her? No. Now was not the time.

"Liar." She squinted at him. "And you're only forty-five. That's never slowed you down before, so I don't think you can use age as an excuse."

"Okay, okay. I'm hurting a lot. And sick of being in this bed."

"But it won't be too long now. Didn't they say that the first few days would be the worst? Everything on your insides is bruised. Let it heal."

"Prayerfully it won't be long now. I'd like to get back to walking pretty soon."

"Well, that leg is pretty beat up too. Doc said no real walking for a week — just a few more days. Then after that, I'm sure it won't be any time at all before you're up and at 'em again." She laid a napkin across his lap. "Now, it's time to eat so you can build up your strength, and if you eat everything, then you may have dessert." She brought him a plate with a sandwich and beamed him a smile. "I want to hear about all the stories Allan has shared."

"Poor man. He's had his fill of tourists for the summer, I think."

"I can only imagine. Thomas came into the kitchen and told us about the fire the other day." She poured them both a glass of lemonade. "We were all so proud of him. You know, it's amazing, he hasn't had an accident or fallen down once since then."

John picked up half of his sandwich. "He's a good lad. And he's got a knack for tracking as well, I've noticed." He ate a bite and then took a sip of lemonade. "He also seems to be a bit smitten with you, daughter."

She cringed and laid her own sandwich down. "I was afraid you were going to say that. Mrs. Johnson said as much."

"And?"

"Well, I'll talk to him. I don't want to hurt his feelings, though. I like Thomas a lot."

He reached over and patted his daughter's hand. "I know. We all do. But from the first time he came to me to talk about studying Daniel and said you inspired him, I could tell by the gleam in his eyes that he was over the moon. Not that you're not worth being over the moon for, but I have an inkling that your feelings tend to drift toward a certain blond-haired gentleman."

Cassidy was silent for several moments as she chewed. John hoped he hadn't overstepped with his precious daughter.

After a long look out the window, Cassidy turned back to him. "I admit I'm drawn to Allan, Dad. But I know that nothing can come out of it — at least not for the time. He has so much he needs to figure out. I want to be his friend, and of course I'm praying for him." She fell silent for a moment. "I didn't think it would be so hard."

"What?"

"Seeing his pain and knowing I can't make it better. I'm praying for him, but it seems so little to do for someone I've come to care for. It hurts me as well. And it's not just where Allan's concerned, but Mrs. Johnson as well."

John's heart overflowed with love and admiration for this girl the Lord had so graciously given him. "Your mother would be so proud of you. As am I. The Lord has given you a tender heart for those who are hurting and lost. He'll also give you the wisdom and strength to bear up under the burden. Remember, He never asks you to bear anything alone."

Cassidy smiled. "I know, but I'm glad you

are reminding me. It's easy to forget when my heart gets all tied up in knots."

He winked at her. "Your mother used to tie my heart up in knots, so I know how that is. I think Allan is a wonderful man, and I know God isn't done with him yet — in fact, I've seen some mighty important changes. Just give him time."

Cassidy scrunched up her nose like she used to as a little girl when she didn't like something. "If he wasn't such a brooder . . ."

"A little brooding can actually do the soul good," John countered.

"And his smile. He's such a handsome man, but his smile never quite reaches his eyes. Like he's guarded about something. I think my one wish is to see a real smile on his face. One that makes his green eyes sparkle."

He just about spewed lemonade on that one. "Well, I don't know, anything about his sparkling eyes, but let's keep praying for him, shall we? God's the only one who can fill the void in Allan."

"Deal." Cassidy stuck out her hand.

He shook it.

"Thanks, Dad."

"For what?"

"For always being there and always listening."

"Anytime, Cass." He hadn't used her nickname in a long time. She'd grown up so fast and into such a beautiful and delightful woman. Eliza would be proud indeed. "Now, did I hear something about dessert?"

She giggled. "You and your sweet tooth . . ."

A knock sounded at the door.

"Come in." Father and daughter spoke at the same time. Cassidy laughed again and walked over to the tray.

Allan peeked in and smiled. "I just wanted to see how you were doing and if I could keep you company for a while, but I see you already have a better visitor than me."

"Nonsense." Cassidy handed John a spoon. "Please stay. In fact, Dad would probably love to hear how your morning went while he eats his dessert." Her eyes had a new sparkle in them. One John couldn't miss.

John smiled to himself. Oh, to be young again.

"Don't go getting all spoiled on me, but I admit I made your favorite — chocolate mousse." She handed him a bowl. She turned to Allan. "And I have another one right here, if you'd like it, Allan."

John raised his eyebrows as he took the first bite. To separate Cassidy from her chocolate was quite an ordeal. The fact that she offered it up freely spoke boatloads to him. He looked from one to the other.

Allan accepted the dish with a nod. "It's one of my favorites as well, so I won't pass it up." He glanced at the tray. "But what about you? Isn't this yours?"

Cassidy took her fork and pointed toward John's bowl. "Nope. You go ahead. I'll just steal a bite or two from Dad."

John enjoyed the lively conversation about the guests and the fun things Cassidy was concocting in the kitchen, but after a few minutes, she gathered up the dishes.

"I've got to get back." She leaned over and kissed him on the forehead. "You and Allan have a nice visit, and then I think you need a nap. You look tired."

He shook his head. "Only because I am."

She smiled and left the room.

John looked at Allan. "What's on your mind, son?"

"I was wondering if once you are recovered, we could continue the plan to climb up McKinley — Denali." Allan cleared his throat. "I know we have plenty of time, but I had an idea. I was hoping we could work at two different routes to see which one would be best suited for other climbers in the future."

"That's an excellent idea."

"I know you understand that I want to climb the mountain myself for personal reasons, but I've had three other men — guests from the hotel — ask if expeditions up the mountain would be offered in the future."

John nodded. What he'd always hoped for, in fact. "We don't need to wait for me to recover to plan. We can start now." He tried to sit up straighter, the adrenaline and excitement pushing past the pain. "I'll need you to go to my room and on the shelf above my desk, there's a dark brown leather book next to my mother's Bible. Go get that and bring it back." He rubbed his hands together. "This is just what I need to get my mind off being laid up."

The hour with John had been exhilarating. After he'd grabbed the book, they'd pored over John's notes together. The man was meticulous and had research from every angle of the great mountain. The maps were glorious. And Allan could taste it. He would finally, truly follow in his father's footsteps. He imagined his father sitting with John and going over the same details. He could almost feel his presence when John described the dangers of climbing on the glaciers. Had his father felt the same surge of excitement when John showed him the best places to make their camps?

Allan gave a sigh. *Dad, I wish I could have been there with you. Maybe then you'd be here now, with me.*

Their dream of climbing Mount McKinley together would never come to fruition, but at least he could honor his father by climbing it in memory of him. When he'd first talked to John about planning an expedition, his heart hadn't been right — and he didn't feel the true excitement that he felt now. But something else had changed too. While he couldn't pinpoint the reasons, it didn't matter.

"No matter how much planning goes into the climb and the equipment needed," John said as he absent-mindedly rubbed his abdomen, "things always go wrong. Harry Karstens would tell you that himself. You try your best to plan for the worst, but sometimes the worst isn't at all what you thought it would be."

"How so?"

John continued to rub his stomach. "Well, for me, and I think Harry would tell you the same was true on his climb, you think of things like how to deal with the storms and wind. You know there are certain problems you'll face, like crevasses opening up where you least expect it or avalanches. You're less expectant of tent seams ripping and having no way to repair them or of oil stoves clogging — even setting the tent on fire. Then there are the bodily things. Fingers and toes that never quite seem to thaw out."

"You lost two toes, I recall Cassidy mentioning." Allan couldn't imagine how difficult that must have been.

"I did, but it's not unusual. Frostbite will do damage to your face and extremities and in some cases you could lose a finger or toe. You try to take care of those things, but it's difficult to master some of the day-to-day work with heavy gloves and mitts on your hands. You soon learn that even ordinary things like relieving yourself becomes an exercise not without its dangers."

Allan stretched his arms. "You're right, those are things I honestly hadn't given a lot of thought. Dad and I did several mountain climbs together, but never were they as high or isolated as this."

"And that's the danger I think we'll find with so many of the folks who come here to climb. I fear that it won't be long before throngs of people will make their way up here and just climb without much planning or a guide. They'll figure it to be no more dangerous than their other climbs."

"You really should work with Superintendent Karstens and create some kind of a guidebook, John. Then even if the people do come without bothering to check in with Mr. Karstens or seek to hire someone to guide them, at least they'd have the book."

John gave several slow nods as he seemed to consider this. "You know, that isn't at all a bad idea. In fact, it's something you could even sell along with your outdoor gear."

"I like that idea. Maybe a series of books based on various climbs."

"Why limit it there? You could create books that would give detailed listings for hiking trails and let the reader know the degree of difficulty and what amenities are available — you know, like fresh water, sheltered camping, paths to accommodate horses or pack animals. Those kind of details might very well save lives."

Allan slapped his leg, getting caught up in the excitement. "My father used to say that with all the modern conveniences, a lot of folks no longer know how to live off the land or survive in bad situations where there's no one else to help them, and very little in the way of equipment. We could teach folks how to make a shelter out of nothing but pine boughs and how to find dry wood and kindling in a rainstorm. We could detail how to set up a fire to benefit them the best for cooking and heating." He had to admit the ideas were coming faster than he could share them. "I remember my dad telling me that starting and maintaining a good camp-fire was paramount to deeming the success or failure of survival. We could even teach folks how to start a fire when matches aren't available."

"And then how to make certain the fire is extinguished before leaving the area. I've seen some sorry situations arise from care-lessness in that area," John admitted.

"You know, I really think we have some-thing here. Especially where Denali is concerned. Most would be unaware the tree line is at one thousand feet. So the lack of wood for fires and shelter will make for even harsher conditions. There aren't very many men who could offer true wisdom regarding the climb and what's needed to make it suc-cessful. Even if we start small and just cre-ate a booklet, I think this would be a very useful thing. We could work on it throughout the winter."

"Then you plan to stay?" John raised his eyebrows.

His question caught Allan by surprise. He

hadn't really considered that possibility. He knew at some point he would have to go back to Seattle and deal with the problems at hand. Not only that, but there was the matter of his personal possessions and other things he'd need to start a new life in Alaska.

He couldn't help but grin. "You know what, John? I just might."

"Well, may I offer a bit of advice?"

Allan was taken aback. "Of course you can. I think you know that by now. Next to my father, you're the only man I respect enough to listen to." He smiled. "What is it?"

"Pray about it." John held up his hand as if expecting a protest from Allan. "I know you've had some rough waters where the Almighty is concerned, but, Allan, you will never be happy until you put those matters to rest. Allow for the fact that even though you don't understand Him or still have questions regarding why He allowed your father to die, He still knows best and is quite willing to show you what's best."

"But . . . well . . . I'm still so angry with Him." Allan surprised himself by being willing to speak the words aloud.

"Then forgive Him."

Allan shook his head. "Forgive God?"

John smiled. "Well, not exactly. God

doesn't need our forgiveness, after all. But since we're human and think in such ways, it might help you to consider it. See, forgiving is all about letting go — about giving over our right to retribution. It isn't approval, like some folks think, and therefore won't offer it. It's a release." A weariness came to John's expression. "And until you find a way to let it go — you'll always be stuck in the same place."

As Allan walked back to the equipment shed to prepare for this afternoon's hike, his thoughts drifted to Cassidy and of staying in Alaska. Mostly, however, he thought of John's words regarding forgiveness. John was wise — like Dad. Dad always stressed the importance of forgiveness. Over the years since losing his father and enduring the war, Allan had truly given little thought to forgiveness. Now since coming to Alaska, it seemed that issue was all he could think on. And while he'd learned to forgive John — even seek his forgiveness — Allan wasn't sure how to go about making things truly right between himself and God.

If Cassidy were here, she'd no doubt tell him it was simple. Just do what needed to be done. Life seemed very straightforward for her — and John. He envied them that and the love they shared.

The relationship Cassidy had with her father was special — just like Allan's with his father had been. But the Ivanoffs had something different. Perhaps it was due to the death of Cassidy's mother or maybe because they lived in such an isolated location.

Their love for one another seemed so easy and sure. And their laughter, happiness, and sunshine really did seem to radiate out of Cassidy's skin. The more he got to know her, the more he realized that her optimistic and shining outer shell truly was a reflection of her inside. She wasn't offering up pretense. She spoke her mind and shared her feelings without being overly concerned about how someone might take it. It wasn't that she sought to be cruel either. She just wanted the truth on the table, as his father might have once said.

John and Cassidy hadn't known that he'd been outside the cracked door listening to their earlier conversation about him. Or how their words had affected him. Was God really the only person who could fill the void inside of him? Allan would have adamantly said no a few months ago. Now he wasn't so sure. Especially after witnessing the strength in John. And in Cassidy as well.

She attracted him like no one else ever had. But she thought he was a brooding man. That didn't conjure up images of romance.

But even so . . . it was apparent she liked him. But found him lacking.

He looked up to the brilliant blue sky for guidance.

Maybe he needed to learn how to let his smile reach his eyes.

The summer sun of August in Alaska beat down on Cassidy's head. Even in the evening hours, the heat could be brutal. She fanned herself as she walked next to Allan, both to cool her face and to keep the mosquitoes from it.

How could it already be the twenty-second of August? In the past two weeks, a lot of things had changed at the Curry. The Annex behind the T-shaped building of the hotel was now housing overflow. The night cook and his staff were having to increase their preparations so the kitchen would be ready for the following day. Mr. Bradley was even talking about the need for additional cooks for the next summer, much to Mrs. Johnson's protests. He assured her she'd still be in charge, but the woman had only harrumphed and exited the room. Cassidy couldn't help but smile at the memory. Mrs. Johnson might put up a fight, but in the long run she'd come around.

Besides the endless hours of work required in the kitchen, there was the laundry and its problems. The laundry now serviced up to thirteen thousand pieces a month between the railroad dining cars, the Anchorage and Nenana hospitals, and the hotel. The hotel alone accounted for half that number of fresh linens. There wasn't just bedding to consider, but kitchen and serving towels, cleaning and polishing rags, aprons, table-cloths, and linen napkins. There were also the staff's clothes and of course the towels and washcloths for all of the bathrooms. Cassidy knew the laundry worked round the clock to meet the needs, and Mr. Bradley felt additional staff was needed there as well.

The differences at the hotel weren't the only changes. Cassidy and Allan spent more time together visiting with her dad in his room while he recovered. Then they began taking him for short walks once he was up to it. The last few days, Dad was walking without a limp but still tired easily. And as he would head back to his room in the evenings, she and Allan would continue their walk together. They fell into the new routine easily, and Cassidy marveled at the ease in conversation.

Allan smiled more often now too. Especially when he talked about their plans for a Denali expedition and the guidebooks they were working on. The more time she spent with him, the more she liked him, and the greater urge she felt to pray for his heart. What had been a dear friendship to her was already becoming much more than that. She couldn't be certain, but Cassidy feared she'd already fallen in love with him.

Could she lose her heart to Allan Brennan?

"Your dad was telling me about 'Cassidy Lane' this afternoon." Allan's steps were slow down the path. He looked at her with such warmth. "How does it feel to have a dangerous cliff named after you?"

That was another thing. He made her laugh quite often, and she loved it. "I guess I could take it a couple of different ways, but I'd like to think that it's endearing rather than ominous."

"I agree. I thought the story was quite charming. Apparently, my father did too." He clasped his hands behind his back as he walked and his smile faded a bit.

"Your father sounds like he was an amazing man." This topic always threw Cassidy for a loop. Her own father loved to talk about Henry now — but in a positive and almost joyous tone. It always seemed the opposite for Allan. His memories were fraught with sadness and pain. But maybe that was because no one ever encouraged it to be otherwise.

"That he was." Allan turned toward her again. "I wonder if there's some ridgeline up there that I can name in my father's memory?"

"You never know. You might get up there and find the perfect spot. There are many places that have been named by those who've gone before. I'd bet my father would remember someplace where your dad was particularly happy or in awe of the scenery."

"That's a good idea," Allan responded. "I hadn't considered that possibility."

Cassidy drew a deep breath and let it out slowly. "You must have been quite special to your father."

Allan cocked his head to one side. "Why do you say that?"

"Dad told me you were the only son in your family. Sons have a special place in their father's hearts."

"Daughters do too." He smiled. "My dad was always doting on my two sisters."

"Oh, I agree, but you must allow that there is something unique between a father and son. I always wished Dad could have had a son."

Allan surprised her by laughing. "I think he's more than content with what he has in you. You light up his world."

"But I'm sure he misses having a son."

"How can he miss what he's never had?"

"I miss my mother and I never had her." Cassidy saw him wince and wished she could have taken the words back. She began walking again, uncertain what to say.

Allan easily caught up with her. "I'm sorry, Cassidy. I didn't think before speaking. Of course you miss your mother, but don't you see — she existed. The memories of her were able to be shared with you, and even though you didn't have a chance to know her personally, you've learned to know her through the hearts of others."

"I never thought of it that way."

"It makes a big difference. Not that a person can't long for something. I'm not saying that at all. I long for a great many things. I'm sure your father would have loved a son, but when I watch him with others — even in how he deals with me — I think he has found great purpose with the sons of other men."

"He does love people. He always has. He's always been so generous with his time and love. There isn't a person back in our village who didn't love him." She smiled at a memory. "In fact, my father could have remarried many times over. There were always women who tried to win his affection."

"Why didn't he take another wife?"

She stopped and met his gentle expression. "He said he could never love anyone as much as he loved my mother. He didn't think it was fair to make another woman live in her shadow."

Allan nodded. "Your father is indeed a very wise man."

"I like to think so. He's given me great insight and wisdom over the years. He's always encouraged me — like with my cooking. He knows how much I enjoy it and he helped me get the job here. He's always telling me to seek the desires of my heart."

"And what are those desires?" Allan asked in a barely audible voice. She wasn't sure, but she thought he also might have moved just a little closer.

She longed to change the subject, but wasn't sure how. Her knees seemed to weaken as she stood there so close to him, gazing into his eyes. The thought of sharing a kiss came to mind and Cassidy felt her face flush.

Footsteps behind them broke the moment

as they both turned to look.

Thomas ran up waving an envelope. "A telegram just came in for you, Mr. Brennan."

"Thank you, Thomas."

The young man ran back to the hotel while Cassidy waited for Allan to open it.

He stared at it.

"Would you like me to give you some space? I can head back by myself."

"No." Allan tore the envelope. "I'd like for you to stay." He read the contents quickly and then grimaced and sighed. He handed it to Cassidy. "Here, read it."

```
22 August 1923

Coming to Alaska (stop)Need
to discuss business (stop)Ex-
pect me on the 28th (stop)
                        Frank
```

She handed it back to him. "What do you think it means?"

"I have no idea." Allan looked at the river. "I haven't heard anything about the audit, and Louis hasn't sent anything either." He tapped the paper against his palm. "It makes me wonder what Frank is up to."

The heat of the kitchen drained the life out of a person. Cassidy couldn't remember the last time she had perspired so much. And it wasn't a pleasant thought. She wiped sweat off her neck with a towel and went back to assembling the puff pastry stuffed with asparagus and lemon zest. The buttery pastry was one of her favorites. It made her mouth water to think of the glorious flavors melding together.

But the heat. Goodness, it was almost enough to make her wilt. If they didn't need the ovens on, it sure would help with the temperature. But the ovens ran day and night to simply keep up with the bread needs for the hotel.

Mrs. Johnson was red-faced and dripping herself, but the woman kept everything going like clockwork. No one could ever complain about the food at the Curry. It was always, *always* delicious and on time.

Her thoughts drifted to Allan and their walk. Ever since that telegram from Frank, he'd been quiet. And had gone back to brooding. She missed her friend, but she also prayed for him in a new way. The weight of taking care of his family rested firmly on his shoulders. And no matter what she did or thought, something about Frank didn't sit well with her.

Lord, only You know our hearts. I don't want to judge Frank without knowing the truth, but my heart aches for Allan and his family. Something scares me about Frank coming here, but I don't know what it is. Please help to calm my heart. Draw Allan to You. And help me to show Your love to Frank as well.

"Cassidy, you're looking mighty warm." Mrs. Johnson came to her station.

"Yes, ma'am. It's hot today." She didn't dare comment on how warm the head cook appeared.

"Well, I know I'm about to melt into a great big puddle, so I imagine you're pretty uncomfortable yourself." The woman pulled out a fan and leaned closer. "You're doing a fabulous job. Especially considering the heat. Thank you."

Compliments from her boss were few and far between. Cassidy smiled up at her. "If it gets any worse, though, I'm going to want to jump in the frigid Susitna."

Mrs. Johnson chuckled. "You and the rest of us! Wouldn't that be a sight? The kitchen staff all floating down the river." She fanned herself some more. "I wonder what they would do about dinner." Raising an eyebrow, the older woman smirked.

"They would never make it without you, Mrs. Johnson."

The rest of the staff seemed busy across the kitchen, so Cassidy decided to brave a question. "I've thought about what you said regarding Thomas. I want to say something to him, but I don't know how to go about it. He's so sweet and I don't want to hurt him. I thought maybe you could advise me on what to do — what to say."

Mrs. Johnson grew quite serious. "Honesty is always the best. Of course, don't embarrass him by speaking to him in front of others. That wouldn't be right."

"Of course not."

"You might not believe this, but I had my share of young men who I had to disappoint."

Cassidy smiled imagining a younger, but just as fierce, Margaret Johnson. "I certainly can believe it."

"Letting others down gently isn't easily done, that's to be sure. Even so, it is always best to just explain the situation and move on. Find a time when you can be alone with Thomas. Start with a kindness and then explain the truth of the matter."

"What do you mean?"

Mrs. Johnson frowned. "Tell him he's a nice young man or that you admire the way he's worked hard to change his everlasting clumsy ways. I don't know. Just say something nice so that it's easier when something not so nice follows."

"Do you suppose that will really make it any easier?"

Mrs. Johnson shook her head. "No, I doubt it. He's quite batty over you, and nothing will make it any easier when he hears that you don't feel the same way." She reached over and patted Cassidy's arm. "Just be gentle and kind. Don't give him any reason to think you're looking down on him or making light of his feelings."

Cassidy nodded. "I would never do that. Thomas is such a fragile soul in so many ways. He told me how hard things were growing up in the orphanage. How the missionaries there forced God upon the children but taught them very little about His love. I'm sure Thomas longs for love more than anything else in his life."

"We all do," Mrs. Johnson admitted. Then as if she'd said too much, she turned away and took on her gruff, bossy façade. "Now, I want everyone to pick up their pace. These meals don't prepare themselves!"

The platform outside the hotel wasn't any cooler than anywhere else. Allan paced the length of the hotel and back, but nothing could get rid of the gnawing in his gut. He'd telegrammed Louis but had no response. What was going on? And why on earth was Frank coming here?

His long strides ate up the boards but did nothing to ease the anguish.

"Thomas said I'd find you out here." John stood under the awning, his arms across his chest. "Here, this letter came for you." He held out an envelope.

Allan walked over and took it. He checked the postmark — Seattle, and nearly two weeks past. Flipping it over, he saw Louis's name. "Thanks, John. Let's hope this has some answers in it."

"Anything I can do to help, or do you just need to read?"

"I'd like it if you would stick around while I read it. I might need your advice."

"I'll be here." John walked over to a bench, took off his hat, and sat down, fanning himself.

Opening the letter, Allan prepared for the worst.

14 August 1923

Dear Allan,

I'm sorry to say that the news I must share with you is grave.

I've been fired from Brennan/Irving for

embezzlement. Frank actually accused me of stealing. But it's worse than that. He has accused the whole family of being in on it, stating that we were unhappy with Henry's will (that Frank inherited half of Henry's stake in the company). Your mother slapped Frank and ordered him from the house.

Before I go any further, I must tell you, emphatically, that I have never stolen from the company. The accusations from Frank are untrue.

But the story doesn't end there. Frank has told Mother that he is going to sue if she takes one more penny from the company. He says that he's been terribly hurt by the unkind treatment and doesn't understand how we could do this to him. Even worse, he's been telling the story to other business relations in Seattle. He has tarnished the Brennan name. Your mother says it wouldn't be right for us to try to defend ourselves right now — it would just feed into the story Frank has told. But this has crushed her. She trusted Frank like a brother all these years.

Uncle Melvin's firm did indeed do a thorough audit. I'm sorry to be the bearer of more bad news, but somehow the books have been swapped. (I know this for certain because the books presented at the auditor's findings were NOT the ones that we used day in and day out.) I don't even know where to begin to find the real ones, and now my hands are tied, since I am not allowed anywhere at the company.

We brought in Josiah Biedermeier to attempt to straighten out the mess, but he's hit a major roadblock. The audit was done by a family firm that we hired. The man who Uncle Melvin put in charge of the audit was a Mr. Ephraim Henderson. Uncle Melvin assured us he trusted the man. But now Mr. Henderson has disappeared. Along with all of the files from his office.

I know this must be terrible to hear, but it was too much to put in a telegram. I've decided to assist a man our lawyer has hired in the search for Mr. Henderson. Somehow, Mr. Henderson must be the missing link to all this confusion.

Through it all, your mother and sisters are well. Emotionally this has devastated them, but they have bucked up under the weight of it and are ready to carry on. We believe that we must be united. There is sufficient money set aside for the running of the household and day-to-day needs. Your father, as you know, was not one to invest all of his money in one place. I will continue to oversee the finances, unless of course you feel me unworthy in light of what has happened. You must think of your mother and sisters first. However, I pledge you and them my loyalty.

As to Frank, he played the martyr well, or perhaps he truly is hurt thinking that we have wronged him. But rest assured, we will continue to seek the truth.

Your mother, Anna, and Ada all send their love and prayers. They had a prayer vigil for you last night, knowing that the receipt of this letter would be difficult.

I will, most likely, not be available for a few weeks as we search.

As to the company, I will leave that up to you to decide what is best. We will do our part to ascertain the facts, and if I have any news, I will telegram immediately.

Your brother-in-law,
Louis

Allan growled and crumpled the paper in his hand. "That man is lower than a snake."

"Let me guess. You're talking about Frank Irving."

Allan met John's knowing gaze. "None other. The man has treated my family abominably. He has accused the entire family of robbing him blind. And he has ordered them to stay away from the business, fired my brother-in-law, accusing him of embezzlement, and told my mother she is not to have any more proceeds from the company."

"Are they left destitute?"

Allan shook his head. "No, thank God."

John smiled. "Do you mean that?"

"Mean what?"

"That you're thankful to God they aren't destitute?"

For a moment Allan considered the question. Then he nodded. "I am. It will take God's intervention to make this right. Frank Irving is quite astute, and it's obvious he's the one responsible. I'm willing to bet that if money is missing — he's the one who has it. Or who had it. Dad said that while Frank had a head for books and the overall running of the office, he was a poor steward of his money. It seemed Dad was always loaning him money or allowing him to draw from the profits, even though they paid themselves a reasonable dividend every quarter. My brother-in-law has brought in the family lawyer to help, so that should afford me an edge."

"Are you to return to Seattle, then?"

"I don't know what I'm going to do. My brother-in-law says things are under control and that my mother and sisters are fine. As he points out, my father was good to diversify his holdings so the loss of Brennan/Irving would be hard, but would not leave my family in financial ruin."

"So Frank would steal the company out from under you? Would you allow for that?" John watched Allan the entire time.

"It's not the company that matters. I only have a fourth interest in it anyway. And there's no reason I can't start up my own company and do it bigger and better. Dad was the one who had the ideas for new gear, and between you and me, I'm certain we could continue along those lines."

John smiled but said nothing. Allan knew he'd presumed upon the older man's willingness to participate, but at the moment that was the least of his concerns.

"What matters is my father's good name. I won't have the likes of Frank Irving running it into the ground the way he has the company."

"And how will you stop him?"

Allan let out a heavy sigh. "I don't know.

He'll be here soon, however, and I need to have a plan in place."

"I'd like to help if that's possible."

"I appreciate that you would help me. I'm afraid I'm at a complete loss as to how to handle this. I've known Frank all of my life, but I don't think I really know him at all. I can't help but wonder if Dad knew how underhanded and deceptive he was."

"Well, it's possible that even Frank is being duped."

Allan's eyes narrowed. "What are you saying? Do you think my brother-in-law is lying? That he's really responsible for embezzlement?"

"No, not at all. I'm merely suggesting it is possible that someone else in the company could have done it."

The idea wasn't without merit. It was possible that someone could be working behind the scenes to frame Louis. Perhaps he had an enemy at the company — one who was envious of his position. Perhaps wanted his job.

"You're right. There I go jumping to conclusions again. I trust Louis implicitly, so it seemed obvious to find Frank at fault."

John shifted and stretched his legs out in front of him. "I'm not saying Frank isn't to blame, but I think you should consider all

317

the possibilities. Frank isn't stupid. If this is his doing, he will have planned it out and had a whole lot more time to consider all the details. If he's set this up to blame your brother-in-law, as you suspect, then he's no doubt created the necessary proof. You're going to have to find some way to reveal the truth."

"Well, Frank's going to be here in a matter of days. That means he won't be at the office. I could arrange for someone to go through everything. Everyone makes mistakes and Frank is no exception. I'm going to get word to Louis. He was well liked, and he's bound to have friends in the company who would be happy to help him get the information we need."

"That's a good idea. Perhaps that lawyer might arrange for some legal papers that would help. I'm sure there is probably something that a judge could do."

"You're right, John." Allan felt a glimmer of hope. "I appreciate talking to you. It's helped more than you know." He unclenched his fist and looked at the wadded-up letter. "I just want to make sure I do all I can to make this right."

"Well, there is one more thing I would advise."

Allan looked up and met John's smile.

"What's that?"

"Pray. We all need to pray on this and ask God to reveal the truth."

20

Cassidy couldn't stop thinking about that moment with Allan before Thomas interrupted them and how she thought Allan might kiss her — and how she'd hoped he would. Her thoughts had been a jumble ever since. She knew Allan was gradually working through his issues with God and that he'd asked her father for forgiveness. The two were, in fact, becoming quite close.

The two most important men in her life had become friends. Her father commented just the night before about how he had seen great changes in Allan spiritually and felt certain he was finally on his way to working things out with the Almighty.

That, of course, gave Cassidy great joy. She couldn't allow herself to fall in love with a man who didn't love and serve God. Nor would her father ever sanction any such union. No, if she were to marry anyone, he would have to put God first.

Marriage. Where had that thought come from? She didn't even know for sure that she was in love, although she highly suspected that was the reason for her confusion and sense of elation. Goodness, but was it like this for everyone? It didn't seem a minute went by without some thought of Allan going through her mind.

"Cassidy Faith, what in the world is wrong with you?" Mrs. Johnson came and forced the measuring cup from Cassidy's hand. "That's salt — not sugar."

"Oh my." Cassidy looked at the cup and then to Mrs. Johnson. "I'm sorry. I guess my mind was elsewhere."

"Why don't you go work on the hollandaise — you've never had any trouble with that."

"I don't know what's wrong with me." Cassidy quickly moved away to do as Mrs. Johnson requested. Whirling around, however, caused her to collide with several newly washed pots. They went flying off in several directions, crashing to the floor in a loud metallic clatter.

"Cassidy!" Mrs. Johnson shook her head. "Have you been taking lessons from Thomas?"

Two of the young women who helped in the kitchen came running to see what the problem was. They stood in amusement, pointing at the pans and Cassidy, giggling all the while.

"And you two . . ." Mrs. Johnson stalked to where the girls now stood, trying to compose themselves. "You have potatoes to peel and vegetables to cut up. I'm almost certain you couldn't possibly have completed it in the few minutes you've been at work."

"No, ma'am," one of the girls replied. The other cast her head down.

"Then get to work! I won't have you dawdling about my kitchen."

Cassidy had just retrieved one of the pans by the time Mrs. Johnson turned back to address her. "I want a word with you. In the other room. Now."

She swallowed the lump in her throat and put the pot aside. Following Mrs. Johnson, Cassidy knew she'd have to explain herself.

"You've been making mistakes all morning. First it was dropping that crock of cream. Then it was burning the rolls. I've never seen the likes."

"I am sorry." Cassidy forced herself to meet Mrs. Johnson's displeased gaze. "I haven't been myself."

"I should say not. What in the world is wrong with you? You weren't even this distracted when your father got hurt. Now he's up and on his feet again, but you seem completely daft."

Cassidy folded her hands. "Mrs. Johnson, have you ever been in love?"

The older woman's mouth dropped open, but no words came.

"I'm sorry if that was an inappropriate thing to ask, but . . . well . . . you see . . ."

"You fancy yourself in love." It was more statement than question. Mrs. Johnson led Cassidy by the hand to a chair. "Sit and tell me everything."

They each took a seat and Cassidy cleared her throat. "I don't know if I'm in love. I think it's very possible, but I've never had anyone around to tell me what a girl feels when she's in love."

"And what do you feel?" It looked as if Mrs. Johnson was trying to keep from smiling.

"Confused, mostly."

"Sounds about right." This time Mrs. Johnson did smile. "Go on."

Cassidy shook her head. "I find myself thinking about him . . . Allan. I think about him all the time. I find myself wondering what his favorite food is and what he thinks about. I wonder if he ever thinks about me and if maybe he feels the same way.

"One minute I think I have a good grasp on it — on my thinking and my heart, but then I see him and find myself quite overwhelmed. Sometimes when we walk together I'm so nervous I can't even speak. My knees get all weak, and my hands get sweaty. Then just as I get control of that, he says something and I find myself feeling quite . . . well . . . I don't even know what to call it. I don't know what I'm feeling."

Mrs. Johnson nodded. "It sounds like love all right. Never felt quite as useless as when I was in love. I couldn't seem to do anything right until I accepted I'd contracted the fever and gave in to it."

"You make it sound like a disease." Cassidy laughed. "But I suppose it does feel like that. I feel like I've come down with something. I wasn't even this bad off when I had the measles."

"Falling in love is never easy."

"Do you think Allan knows how I feel?"

Mrs. Johnson snorted. "He's too blinded by his own feelings to know much of anything."

"What do you mean?" Cassidy frowned.

"I mean he's batty for you. Even more so than Thomas. I've seen the way he looks at you. He watches you all of the time. I feel quite certain he is just as caught up in this sickness as you are."

Cassidy felt a surge of joy at Mrs. Johnson's declaration. "So what do I do? Do I just go and tell him how I feel?"

"I have no advice on that matter. You see, love is a very individual thing. Much like your measles. Some folks take a light case and others fight for their lives. It all depends on the people involved." She looked past Cassidy and seemed to forget she was even there.

"When I fell in love, it was all I could do to keep food down. Like I said, I wasn't any good to anyone until I gave in to it. But in my case, he was very vocal. He wooed and courted me in spite of my initial disinterest. He proposed several times, and I laughed at him and told him I wasn't of a mind to marry. The darn fool wouldn't take no for an answer, though. He told me that sooner or later I would be his bride."

"It sounds very romantic to me."

Mrs. Johnson looked back at her with a sad smile. "It was. And I miss him very much."

Cassidy reached over and took hold of the older woman's hand. "But do you regret it — love, that is? Do you regret having fallen in love?"

The look on her face changed to one of

pure joy. "No, Miss Cassidy Faith. I do not regret it. Falling in love was the best thing that ever happened to me."

The deck of the steamship was crowded as Frank edged his way to the bow. Now that the seas had calmed, everyone wanted fresh air.

He just wanted them all out of his way.

A plan had formulated in his mind over the last week. He could play the martyr — and a changed man all at the same time. The Brennans were all churchy, Bible-thumping, give-everyone-a-second-chance type of people. Frank could use that to his benefit. The devastation of the family embezzlement drove him to God. And there, he'd changed. Now he only wanted forgiveness and to offer forgiveness. Oh, he would make them feel so guilty that they wouldn't challenge his legal rights. All would be right with the world.

Let them think that anyway.

The years of patiently waiting for his due were over. This time, there wouldn't be any mistakes.

Little by little he'd let various men know about his plight. Men he felt certain were and would remain on his side. Sympathy had poured in for him from business associates across Seattle when they'd heard the news about the embezzlement. Frank had to admit, he liked the attention, even if he had to keep playing the wounded victim for a time.

He'd paid a reporter to put a story in the paper. Nothing that shared any real detail, but instead gave just a hint of scandal and the question of responsibility. This brought other reporters to his doorstep and allowed Frank to portray himself as the wronged individual who refused to point the finger at any one party, but felt unfairly taken advantage of by some betraying source.

The only pieces of the puzzle standing in his way were Allan and John. Frank had thought he could have what he wanted in spite of them, but that wasn't proving true. Allan wasn't as easily manipulated as he had been at first. Given time, he would no doubt conspire with Ivanoff — if he hadn't already done that. Ivanoff had never liked Frank — it was almost as if he could read his thoughts and knew the darkness in his soul. All the time on their descent from the mountain, Frank had been certain John was suspicious. Frank had been sick and played it to the hilt to avoid John's endless questions about what had happened. However, he hadn't been too sick to realize John suspected him of foul play. Once they were back in Anchorage, Frank rallied from his illness to point the finger at John. He had heaped copious amounts of blame on the man — condemning his leadership skills and calling him negligent. He hoped it might even lead to John's arrest, but it seemed there was no real law in Alaska. People dying on a mountaintop didn't seem all that unusual. He laughed in spite of himself.

People dying anywhere in the wilds of Alaska didn't seem all that unusual. In fact, it was expected. After all, death was around every corner for the trained and untrained alike. With any luck at all, Frank would use this to his benefit. With any luck at all, he'd soon be free of any entanglements. John Ivanoff and Allan Brennan would no longer be a problem.

The hike for the morning had been canceled due to rain, and Allan was glad for the respite. He and John planned to meet in the basement reading room of the hotel to plan a little more for their Mount McKinley expeditions and guidebooks. Allan realized over all the talks he'd had with John that he preferred the native name, Denali. It rolled off the tongue and sounded regal and fitting for such a mountain as the High One.

Even though he knew that John was using the distraction of planning the climb to keep his mind off Frank's arrival, thoughts bombarded him hourly. He still had no idea how to learn the truth about what had happened to his father, nor what was happening back in Seattle. John had been right about one thing: Frank was crafty.

Allan took the stairs down at a brisk clip and shuffled the papers in his hands. While John had several maps of the Alaska Range, there was still so much unknown about each mountain. Glaciers were everywhere, icefalls and sheer granite walls were prevalent. And the crevasses. They were mostly unseen until upon them. Or falling into them.

Every other expedition that they knew of had come into the Alaska Range from the north. The successful summit in 1913 and his father's own summit in 1917 had both taken the Muldrow Glacier up. And that was after the serious trek into the national park all the way from Nenana.

Even the entrance to the national park was far north of where they were in Curry. If they journeyed by train up there, it would only be wasted time and energy. Whereas at Curry they had the prime location to start.

As he laid the papers out on the table, excitement built in Allan. Curry's location was not only perfect for the railroad as a needed stop between Seward and Fairbanks, but once the ridge to the west was crested, the views of the Alaska Range were incomparable. And they were so close. In fact, Curry was only forty miles away from Denali "as the crow flies." Wouldn't it be wondrous to one day open up the Curry Hotel as the premier location to venture into the national park and climb the tallest mountain in North America?

Thoughts of staying in Curry long-term appealed to him. More than he'd ever imagined they would. He enjoyed working with John and knew the man's dream would be to lead expeditions up the mountains. He thought it more than a little exciting to be a part of that. Even plans to create and publish guidebooks gave him a sense of satisfaction that had long been missing in his life.

Then there was Cassidy. Just the thought of spending time with her thrilled him. He had to admit it. There were feelings present.

But she held back. And with good reason. Allan had come here under different pretenses. Granted, he still wanted to find out what happened to his father, but before, he'd thought John was responsible. And he'd blamed God. Admittedly, he still did.

Allan hadn't quite come to terms with that, but at least now he actually wanted to. He also knew he'd have to figure that out before he could advance his relationship with Cassidy.

He shook his head. One step at a time.

"Just wait until you see this latest map." John entered with a huge smile on his face holding a long roll of paper. "Karstens has been working on it for the government and he allowed me to copy it. It took a while, but I believe I was able to duplicate it correctly."

"Let's open it up." Allan felt like a little boy planning his first tree house.

"Now, if you look here" — John pointed with his pen — "I believe that for our first ascent we could take the Ruth Glacier up to the east side of the buttress. From there it would be very steep, but the south summit is doable, depending on the icefalls and crevasses. Since we already have a decent trail blazed from here to the Ruth, we would just need snowshoes and a dogsled team to go up the glacier for about thirty or so miles and then our climbing equipment from the wall here. Base camp could be here, in the northwest fork of the glacier that climbs up."

Allan studied the idea John had. "This looks outstanding. The most distance will be covered on the glacier, correct?"

"Yes, but the most time-consuming will be above ten thousand feet. And that's after we reach the wall here."

"I like it. So for the second ascent, what were your ideas?"

"I haven't studied it enough, but the Kahiltna Glacier seems to be the next logical step. I'm familiar with the glacier, but not with that side of Denali."

Allan nodded and studied the map a bit more. "Well, then, I think you're right. We should start with what we know and go from there. There's bound to be more than one good way to reach the summit, right?"

John laughed. "Yes, but sometimes, you find several other ways that do not reach it at all. I've explored the possibilities and discussed it at length with Karstens. I've even read things written by others who attempted to explore the area."

"I've climbed a few fourteen-thousand-foot peaks in the States with my father. But that's been years and, of course, not this far north. Should we attempt a smaller peak in the range first, for training purposes?"

"That would actually be very wise. We could try for the Child first if you would like. That would get you used to the sleds, snowshoes, and other climbing apparatus.

As well as the weather."

"When should we plan?"

"I'd say March or April for the smaller mountain. And then aim for a June expedition on Denali."

"That will give us plenty of time to put away more stores of food."

John brought over another piece of paper and a pen. "Karstens wrote this down for me — it's how they sustained themselves in 1913. Granted, they had to take lots of time away from the expedition to hunt and then prepare it, but we have the upper hand. We can start on it now and preserve it to take with us."

Studying the paper, Allan was fascinated. Rather than taking cans of pemmican with them, they made their own. He read aloud. ". . . A fifty-pound lard can, three parts filled with water, was set on the stove and kept supplied with joints of meat. As a batch was cooked we took it out and put more into the same water, removed the flesh from the bones, and minced it. Then we melted a can of butter, added pepper and salt to it, and rolled a handful of the minced meat in the butter and moulded it with the hands into a ball about as large as a baseball. We made a couple of hundred of such balls and froze them, and they kept perfectly. When all the boiling was done we put in the hocks of the animals and boiled down the liquor into five pounds of the thickest, richest meat-extract jelly, adding the marrow from the bones. With this pemmican and this extract of caribou, a package of erbswurst, and a cupful of rice, we concocted every night the stew which was our main food in the higher regions."

Putting the paper down, Allan looked back to John. "I've had the canned store-bought pemmican on other expeditions with my father, and it wasn't pleasant at all. This actually sounds good. When should we go hunting?"

Another laugh. "As soon as we have another break in the schedule. I don't think Mr. Bradley will mind at all. Especially since he knows that we are doing all of this to expand the experience for future guests of the Curry."

"Mr. Brennan!" Thomas's voice carried down the stairs. He rounded the corner and strode purposefully to Allan. "Another telegram."

"Thank you, Thomas." Allan tore the envelope and muttered, "I swear the telegraph company is the one benefiting from this fiasco."

John patted Thomas on the shoulder.

"And thank you for all your hard work lately. We have appreciated you."

"Thanks, Mr. Ivanoff. I'm finding that even though I like kitchen work, I like the outdoors and hiking a lot more. Especially when we go fishing." The boy, who was really almost a man, smiled at them both. "Of course, I don't get to see . . . ah . . . some of the folks in the kitchen when I'm working outside."

Their conversation faded behind Allan as he walked away and read the brief note.

26 August 1923

```
Frank coming to you (stop)
Found evidence of foul play at
Henderson's (stop) Police on
the case (stop) Be wary (stop)
Best not to tell him you heard
from me (stop)
                          Louis
```

A thousand questions clamored for attention in his mind. Henderson was the auditor who worked for his uncle. What kind of foul play? Did that mean the man was dead? How did Louis know Frank was coming to Alaska? Or did the police suspect something and they tried to warn the family?

"Allan?" John's voice broke through his thoughts. "Everything all right?"

"I don't think so."

21

As he made his way back to the kitchen, Thomas thought about Cassidy. She and Mr. Brennan seemed to be spending a lot of time together lately. And he liked Mr. Brennan a lot. But what if Cassidy did too?

"If she does, it's because I haven't told her how I feel," he murmured. It made perfect sense that Cassidy would want to share her time with someone. Thomas just had to find a way to let her know how he felt.

The object of his thoughts appeared and she jumped back.

"Goodness, Thomas." She put a hand near her throat. "I didn't realize you were right there."

"Sorry to startle you, Miss Cassidy. I guess I wasn't paying attention."

"That's all right." She took a deep breath and folded her hands in front of her. "I actually wanted to talk to you."

"Really?" His insides quivered and he couldn't help the smile that covered his face. She'd looked for him! Maybe explaining his feelings wouldn't be so hard after all.

"Yes." Then she gave him one of her beaming smiles that had the potential to melt all the snow on Mount McKinley. "Why don't we go sit in the dining room?"

He nodded and followed her. Anything she wanted. He'd follow her anywhere. He pulled out a chair for her and then took a seat on the other side of the table so he could look into her expressive eyes. She really did have the most beautiful eyes.

She placed her hands in her lap. "I hope you know I think very highly of you, Thomas. I've seen you work hard to make changes around here and you've borne up under that stress with great dignity." She paused and cleared her throat. "I also want you to know that I like you very much."

"I like you too." More than he could say. In fact, his brain couldn't come up with anything better to say and his mouth felt like it was stuffed with dry bread.

Another brilliant smile. "I just want to make sure that I haven't confused you."

He furrowed his brow. Confused him? She seemed to be the only person who could explain things to him where he actually understood.

"Let me start again." She looked down and then back into his eyes. "It has come to my attention that you might perhaps think of my friendliness toward you as if it's in a romantic way. And it wouldn't be fair for you to keep thinking like that." She drew a deep breath and continued. "Not that you aren't deserving of a girl's romantic feelings toward you — you are a wonderful young man — it's just that I would never have wanted to give you the wrong impression. I'm so sorry if my actions to you have been untoward."

Thomas didn't understand. He blinked several times as his eyes felt dry and then he thought he might burst into tears at any moment. "Are you saying that you *don't* like me in that way, Miss Cassidy?"

She bit her lip for a moment and shook her head. "I'm sorry, Thomas. I never meant to lead you astray. I do like you very much . . . as my friend. And I hope we will remain friends for the rest of our lives."

He looked down at his lap. "Is this because I'm an orphan? Am I not good enough? Too clumsy?"

"Heavens, no! You're wonderful just the way you are. It isn't like you have a sign hanging over your head that you're a bad person because you're an orphan. That's never mattered to me. I grew up without a mother and my grandparents wanted nothing to do with me. People can't help what happens to their folks."

"I didn't know your grandparents didn't want you."

Cassidy nodded. "Sometimes it really bothers me. My mother had no choice, but they did and it hurts to know they walked away." She squared her shoulders. "But enough about that. I just want to assure you that your being an orphan has nothing to do with my feelings for you. As for your abilities, you must remember, I was much clumsier than you at one point."

"I don't think you've ever been clumsy, Miss Cassidy." He felt a growing sadness wash over him. It was like he was all alone again.

"Thomas, I will still be here for you, and there are a great many people here who truly like you." It was as if she'd read his mind. "One day you are going to find the perfect young woman to fall in love with."

But I already love you. He left the words unspoken.

"And when you find her, then you'll realize what I'm talking about when I say that our kind of love is more like that of a brother and sister." She squeezed his arm. "Thomas, you are the last person in the world I wanted to hurt. If I was untoward, then please forgive me. I truly do think you are an incredible young man and I am blessed to have you as my friend."

"I'm blessed too, Miss Cassidy. And I don't think you have been untoward. You've been my friend. And I really appreciate that." He stood up. "I need to go now."

He hurried from the room fighting back tears. There wasn't any way to explain the emotions that surged through him. But he did understand that Cassidy Ivanoff didn't love him like he loved her.

Cassidy fanned herself on the train platform. She'd agreed to wait with Allan and her dad to greet his father's partner, Frank Irving. But tensions were high. And it wasn't just the heat that seemed to strain everyone's nerves. She didn't know the full extent of problems that existed with Mr. Irving, but it was evident that both Allan and her father were less than pleased to have the man coming to Curry.

The whistle sounded in the distance, which meant the train was almost there. She turned to Allan. "Are you all right?"

"Yep." His lips were a thin line.

"You don't look all right."

"Well, I don't know what to expect."

Dad placed a hand on Allan's shoulder. "I've been praying for you."

Allan's brows knit together. For a moment Cassidy thought he might protest, but then he gave a curt nod. "Thank you, sir." His eyes remained on the tracks.

Dad leaned back behind Allan and caught Cassidy's eyes. His look covered a gamut of thoughts. Allan wasn't ready for this. And he was obviously still angry at God, or at least dismissive of prayer, even with all the healing he'd come through the past few weeks. The arrival of Frank Irving could be disastrous to his tenuous thread of hope.

She took a deep breath and watched the steam engine ease toward them as it came to a stop. No sense worrying about what was about to happen. She had a front row seat to watch it unfold whether she liked it or not.

The seconds ticked by as if they were minutes. Passengers disembarked. Luggage was gathered.

Then an elegantly dressed man with silver hair showing around his ears descended the steps.

Cassidy felt Allan tense next to her.

The man headed straight for their group. He looked into her eyes, and even though his were a brilliant blue, they made her feel cold even in the insufferable summer heat.

All of a sudden the man smiled. "Allan, my boy! So good to see you." He clapped a hand on his shoulder. Before Allan could reply, he dropped his hold and turned.

"And my, my, if it isn't John Ivanoff?" Frank nodded toward Dad. "How long has it been, John?"

"Six years." Dad took Frank's proffered hand and shook it. "Welcome to Curry."

The man removed his hat and fanned himself. "Thank you. I didn't remember the heat being so intense." He looked at Cassidy. "And you must be Miss Cassidy Ivanoff, of Cassidy Lane fame." The man bowed a bit, took her hand, and kissed it.

"Um, yes. I guess I am." She wasn't quite sure what to make of this man. But he seemed . . . oily, and she immediately wanted to wash her hand.

"Why don't we get you settled in a room, Frank?" Allan extended an arm toward the hotel's entrance.

Dad took that opportunity to take her elbow and lead her toward the door, but she realized she wanted to hear what Frank would say next and so she kept her steps slower than usual and her ear attuned to the men behind her.

"It's so good to see you, son." Frank's voice seemed smooth as cream. "I have to admit that one of the reasons I wanted to come all this way in person is to make sure you — my partner — were all right. That everything is well between us. Especially after that terrible disaster with Louis." The man *tsk*ed several times. "After all, one can't choose who their family members are, but you can choose who to trust. Business partners need to have the utmost trust, don't you agree?"

"I do." Allan cleared his throat. "Quite adamantly, I must say."

"I also came to tell you that while your family has hurt me deeply, I am a changed man from the Frank Irving of the past. I'm hoping we can move forward into the future with no regrets."

Mr. Bradley allowed for some of the staff to eat with John, Cassidy, Allan, and Frank Irving in the main dining room after the rest of the guests had been served. It had been a lovely dinner Cassidy was quite proud of, but now that she sat down for a few moments, her feet ached, and her head wanted nothing more than to hit her pillow for the night.

But the men continued talking. Hiking, climbing, and the latest gear seemed to be the topics of the evening.

"It appears, Miss Ivanoff, that we have lost your attention." Mr. Irving's comment brought her head back to the conversation at hand.

"I apologize, Mr. Irving. Did I miss something important?"

"We were just discussing your father's plans to find other suitable approaches to climb Mount McKinley." Those cold blue eyes drilled into hers in an almost accusing manner, even though a smile seemed plastered to his lips in contradiction. Something about it made her uncomfortable.

"Well, he is an expert in that area, Mr. Irving." She brought her water glass to her mouth and took a drink.

"That he is. That he is." Frank tapped the table. He leaned back in the chair as if he owned the place. "I say, why don't we put a climbing expedition together while I'm here?"

Cassidy sputtered on her water. Quickly grabbing a napkin, she dabbed her mouth.

The man turned to Allan and patted his back. "The idea has been on my mind the entire trip north. I suppose because the last time I made this journey, that was the excitement and motivation. As I get older, however, I find it important to act quickly on our desires. None of us knows how much time we have on this earth." He looked around the table. "Not only that, but I've been wanting some good exercise and fresh air. It's been some time since I've gone mountain climbing."

Allan looked to Cassidy, his jaw clenching. "It's a little more than just good exercise. I don't know if that's a very good idea, Frank. It's late in the season and we'd have a lot to do to prepare."

"Seems to me the weather is just fine. The heat today could have melted my hat."

Allan shook his head. "That's all well and good, but it takes a lot of time to plan . . ."

"And my father . . ." Cassidy hated to interrupt, but she had to. "It's only been a few weeks since his accident."

"An accident, you say?" Frank's attention shot to Dad. "John, you look healthy as a horse. What happened, man?"

Her father picked up his own water goblet and swirled the contents. "Nothing too major. Just had a run-in with a moose." His pointed glance at her made her insides jumble. She knew better than to contradict him.

What was going on?

"Well, then?" Frank smiled around the table. "Shall we give it a go? If the weather did turn bad, we could turn back. It's not like we'd have to climb to the top. I've already done that, as have you, John, and Allan . . . well, he'd have plenty of opportunities in the future. No, I think we should just strike out and do as much as the weather and our energy allows."

When no one said anything in response, Frank continued. "Not only that, but such an endeavor would allow me time to make plans. It would give Allan and me time together to discuss business. I could get some good ideas for equipment to supply, and we'd get to build trust together as we planned it."

Murmurs around the table did nothing but encourage Frank. The idea seemed to excite the other staff.

But Cassidy felt a knot growing in her stomach.

Thomas entered the dining room with a tray. "They're already planning a trip. You should see the maps — whooo-eee."

Frank pointed to Thomas. "See? It's meant to be." He slapped Allan on the back. "I've never seen you decline such a wonderful challenge."

"Well, it's just that . . ."

"And it would give us a chance to bond. I know you always wanted to climb it with your father. I could help you accomplish that dream." Frank put a hand over his heart. "And we could talk about what *God* has done in my life."

Why did he sound so fake? The men weren't buying this man's story, were they?

Her dad looked toward Allan. "We have done a lot of the legwork and planning already. If we took a couple weeks to finalize the details, we could leave after the last booked fishing trip. Mr. Bradley has already voiced his support. He won't mind us moving up the timeline, since it will probably help with advertising for next year, and that means next year we'll be available for more trips."

What was her dad saying? He actually agreed with Mr. Irving?

"I don't know . . ." Finally, Allan was being a voice of reason.

Cassidy sat back and crossed her arms. She knew she liked him.

"I agree the time is too short . . ." Allan leaned forward. "But it's even more important to stay ahead of the weather. I think we should do it."

She took it back. They were all a bunch of

harebrained, ridiculous men. And she didn't want anything to do with them.

22

Whatever had possessed him to volunteer to climb that stupid mountain again? Frank paced his room, smoking a cigar.

There wasn't any real logical explanation other than the fact that as soon as Allan and John shared their excitement about their future plans, Frank saw it as a way to get rid of them both. He'd killed Henry that way, hadn't he? It seemed ironic that he should eliminate his other problems the same way.

But he had no desire to go trekking up a mountain again. Sleeping in tents. Eating food that was only worthy for dogs and gutter rats. There had been nothing about that trip six years ago that had been worth the time and money. With exception to Henry's death, of course, and even that didn't satisfy as much as Frank had hoped it would.

As the night escalated with the men's plans, Cassidy left, citing a headache. He was just as glad to see her go. The young woman was rather unnerving. She seemed to gauge that something wasn't quite on the up and up, and Frank didn't need to have to worry about her interference. Especially when there were details to iron out and plans to be made. Way too many plans.

In the end it was concluded that John's Ahtna-Athabaskan tribal people would help. Frank was less than excited when he heard this. The fewer people around the better. It would force Frank to wait on his plans until they were able to leave them all behind at the lower camp. He sighed at the thought of the work that would have to be done. They'd have to do a lot of snowshoeing and use dogsleds again. There would be that ever annoying need to walk hunched over, poking a stick into the ground to make sure that the trail wouldn't give way to some endless glacial hole. And then there was the cold.

Frank shook his head.

He really should stop complaining. He'd provided the perfect scheme. He wouldn't have to climb all the way up. Just once they left base camp with the helpers and dogs behind, he'd have to look for his opportunity.

He walked over to his bag. This time, he'd

come even better prepared. Unwrapping a brown paper package, he pulled out a thirty-eight revolver and a brand-spanking-new hunting knife he'd taken from The Brennan/Irving Company. It didn't have to look like an accident, because there wouldn't be any witnesses. And because of the very accommodating nature of the glacier, he'd have no trouble ridding himself of the bodies.

He'd be the only one to come back alive. And of course — he'd be grief stricken.

Cassidy slammed the pie crust dough down on the worktable. All morning long, the staff had been abuzz about the team climbing Mount McKinley. After she'd snapped poor Marie's head off with her words about the stupidity of the idea, the rest of the group left her alone. No one here had ever seen her in less than a positive spirit. And they definitely hadn't seen her lose her temper. Well, they were getting an eyeful *and* an earful today.

The wooden rolling pin sped across the dough. There wouldn't be any issue getting the crust thin enough today. She was mad enough to roll it out as thin as paper.

"Cassidy Faith." The kitchen was hushed at Mrs. Johnson's voice. "I'd like to see you in the dining room, please."

Cassidy nodded but kept rolling.

"Now." Mrs. Johnson's voice was sharp.

She blew the hair off her forehead, set the wooden pin down, and wiped her hands on her apron. "Yes, ma'am."

In the dining room, Cassidy crossed her arms. Deep down, she knew she was acting like a toddler throwing a tantrum, but her anger ruled out everything else.

Her boss turned to look at her as soon as she shooed everyone else out of the room. "Let's get one thing straight right now, missy. I will not abide you taking out your ill-mannered and uppity temper on the other staff in this hotel. You seem determined to prove to me that you aren't all gumdrops and rainbows, but I assure you there is no need. Nor desire. No matter what, you will treat the others with respect."

"I didn't —"

Mrs. Johnson cut off her protest mid-sentence.

She stepped closer to Cassidy and pointed her finger. "I don't want excuses. For someone who I never thought could have a bad day, you sure do beat them all. Did you know that Mrs. McGovern just had to speak with me because you lit into one of the maids and she hasn't stopped crying since?" The older woman began to pace. "I don't know what has gotten into you, but it needs to stop."

Cassidy bit her lip.

"Well? Do you have anything to say for yourself?"

A few moments passed, but then Cassidy couldn't take it any longer. "I don't think they should go."

"You don't think who should go where?"

She rolled her eyes. Now she knew she was being impertinent. "The men. I don't think they should go up the mountain."

"And they need your permission *why* exactly?"

The woman knew how to stab her where it really hurt. "They don't. But my father is just now healing and last time he went up there, he lost a man coming down —"

"But it's not your decision."

"But neither one of them even thought about me and what I —"

"Aha. So there it is." Mrs. Johnson put her hands on her hips. "You're offended that your dad and Allan didn't consult you before making the decision."

Pretty much.

All her life, her dad had talked things through with her. But now he didn't need her. He talked to Allan instead. And Allan . . . well, he should know better. At least, if he cared about her, he should. Maybe that's what really ate at her. Maybe Allan didn't feel the same way she did.

Mrs. Johnson's arms came around Cassidy and pulled her in for a hug. "It's hard being in love, isn't it?"

He hadn't seen Cassidy all day, and when Allan asked Mrs. Johnson about her, she gave him a scolding glance and shooed him away.

It didn't seem right. Almost every day now, they walked in the evenings together, but Cassidy was nowhere to be found. And Allan couldn't wait to share everything with her. He paced the spot where they usually met and considered all that was happening.

It had all moved so fast. Once the decision had been made, momentum took off. Sure, their timeline wasn't ideal, but all the pieces were fitting into place nicely. John dug out the equipment he'd had from the last expedition, and they'd spent the day trying on gear, patching the tents, and making lists. Frank wasn't his ideal climbing partner — or business partner for that matter — but Allan was still excited. The man had several stories of how his life was now changed. He was even going to church. Could the conniving Frank of the past be gone? Maybe Louis and his family just didn't know.

Allan's dream of climbing Mount McKinley would finally be realized. Not only that, but Allan had it in the back of his mind that once they were actually on the mountain away from everyone else, he could finally get Frank to tell the truth. The truth about the business and about his father. Especially if the man was being honest about God changing his life.

Allan's questions could be put to rest. His dreams come to fruition. Maybe they could even square away the disaster that happened with the company.

It was funny — although he didn't trust Frank, Allan thought him far less imposing than he'd expected. The man was accommodating and even pleasant. When he made suggestions and John or Allan overruled them, he yielded. Often he was even self-abasing, admitting how little he knew and how grateful he was for their wisdom. Maybe he really had changed.

Allan wasn't entirely sure they were being all that wise, given the way they were advancing their plans. John had always been a very cautious man who gave heavy regard to the details. This time . . . there wasn't that luxury. Now they had to scramble for everything from gloves and mittens to thick woolen socks and backpacks.

It was a good thing John had gotten that info from Karstens regarding the food. Last week's hunt had been prosperous, and they had enough homemade pemmican balls made to make it through the whole trip. Of course they still needed a variety of other stores, but Mr. Bradley had been generous after their promise to repay. They were blessed.

Now if he could just talk to Cassidy, all would be right with the world.

He glanced at his watch. It was well over an hour past the time they usually met. Something must have happened to keep her occupied. It wasn't like they had any promises to meet there. But until now — she had come with regularity.

Allan couldn't help feeling the loss of her company. Cassidy affected him in a way he'd never known. She'd encouraged his love of Alaska and of Denali. The mountain was no longer just the place where his father had died. It had become a steadfast companion, constant and in many ways comforting. Through Cassidy's eyes, Allan had learned to look for the positive things in life — the good in people — joy in the moment. She had a passion and a love for life and

Alaska that exceeded anything Allan had ever experienced. He wondered if there would ever be a chance . . . a time when she could love Allan with that same degree of passion.

He looked down at his watch and then once more in the direction Cassidy had always come in the past. Nothing. He put aside his disappointment and headed for the staff sleeping quarters. They had an early morning fishing trip planned with some guests, so he'd better head on to bed. He'd have to find Cassidy at luncheon tomorrow.

For two straight days, she'd managed to avoid him, but Allan couldn't figure out why. Sure, their schedules were jam-packed, but that hadn't stopped them from finding time to chat before. John said that he hadn't spoken to Cassidy either, which was doubly strange. Maybe Mrs. Johnson had some major event coming that the men didn't know about. That would explain it. But he decided to wait in the dining room anyway. Just in case.

Allan sat down with a paper from Seattle and decided to catch up on the news from last month. Between the President's visit, then subsequent death, and everything else at the Curry, Allan had no idea what was going on in the rest of the world. Frank happened upon him shortly after Allen finished with the front page.

"We've had so little time to talk since my arrival," Frank said, taking a chair opposite Allan. "I know there's much to be said between us."

Allan put the paper aside. "Yes, I suppose there is."

"I'm sure you have questions about Louis."

With a nod Allan fixed his gaze on Frank. "Yes. A great many."

"Well, I suppose the temptations were just too great. I've been suspicious of the man for years. I tried to overlook the occasional discrepancy for the sake of the family, but the loss became far too regular."

"And you questioned him about this?"

"It wouldn't have done any good," Frank countered. "He would never have admitted to it. I think the fact that you called for an audit of the books left him trembling in his boots. I was quite grateful that you made the decision for that. It took some of the pressure off of me."

"I would still like to hear what Louis has to say."

"Oh, I'm sure he would have some sort of

excuse — if he admitted to any of it. I think for the sake of the family it's probably best to just let bygones be bygones."

Allan knew better than to believe Frank — at least the old Frank. But what about now? "So you don't intend to press charges?"

"Well, I had considered it. I'm not one to treat thievery lightly. I always figure it just encourages others to take advantage. However, in this circumstance, there are only a handful of people who know the truth. To have him arrested would force your entire family into scandal. Your good name would be dragged through the courts and I fear it would spell disaster for the company."

"I'm not afraid of that." Allan could see his statement caused Frank to squirm. "In fact, I would welcome a trial. I want to get to the bottom of it. I want the truth to be told. If Louis has done what you say he did, he deserves to go to prison."

Allan heard Cassidy's distinctive laugh. He had to speak to her. He turned back to Frank. "If you don't mind, I have some business to attend to."

"As do I." Frank jumped up, seeming only too happy to put an end to the conversation. "I hope you have a productive day, my boy. I find it most difficult to wait for our impending journey." He gave Allan a nod and made his way from the dining room just as Cassidy entered. Allan watched as she stepped aside to let Frank pass. He gave her a nod and then disappeared.

Allan thought she looked relieved. At least until she turned back and saw him. Anxiety mixed with what appeared to be distaste filled her expression.

"What's wrong?" He stood and crossed the room to be near her.

She shook her head. "Nothing."

"I don't believe that for one minute, Cassidy." He stepped closer to her. "I thought we'd just been too busy to see each other, but now, by the look on your face, I'm thinking that I've done something to upset you."

Her hands fidgeted in front of her. She looked down for a moment and then looked back into his eyes. "I . . . I . . ."

The hurt he saw there was almost his undoing. For the rest of his days, he never wanted to see her look like that again. He took her hands in his. "Go on. What is it?"

"I'm worried."

Her words took him aback. "Worried about what?"

"You . . . my father . . . the expedition. All of it."

Was that all? He smiled. "Oh, Cassidy, there's nothing to worry about. That's why I was waiting for you. I wanted to talk to you about all the exciting things —"

"That's just it." She pulled away. "It's going to be mid-September when you leave. The temps will still be moderate most likely, but I've seen the snow fly here in early September. Snow down here means major snow up there. And you're heading into the wilderness knowing this! My father used to always say that June, July, and August were the best times to do any climbing in Alaska. I just don't understand. You were planning an expedition for *next* year. And then Frank comes along and says, 'Hey, let's do it now' and you all just think it's a grand plan? Why do you even trust the man?" She placed her hands on her hips.

Allan had never seen her feisty like this. She'd always been so positive and upbeat and now she seemed . . . well, to be honest, she seemed angry. He held up both his hands. "I came up here wanting to climb Mount McKinley eventually. You knew that. I thought you'd be happy for me."

"Happy? How could I be happy? The time of year is a disaster, the time crunch is a disaster, my dad is still healing *from* a disaster, and you stubborn men are dashing

362

around to make all these plans, and you didn't even think to ask how I felt about it when the two men I care most about in all the world —" She slapped her hand over her mouth.

The words were like a punch to the gut. But a good one — if there could be such a thing. She was worried about him and she cared for him. Sweeter words couldn't have ever been said.

Allan took hold of her arms with a new confidence. "Cassidy . . . I'm sorry. It was wrong for us to not include you." He inched closer to her again, intent on doing what he'd wanted to do for a very long time — kiss her. "Forgive me?"

Tears spilled out of her eyes and without a word she pushed him away so hard that he nearly lost his balance. Allan steadied himself and started to call out to her, but she was already gone.

He thought about going after her, then decided against it. She obviously needed time, and he knew what that felt like. A slow smile formed and Allan couldn't resist whirling on the heel of his boot. She cared about him. In that moment he felt like he could have run straight up the side of Denali.

Cassidy could hardly see for her tears by the time she crested Deadhorse Hill. She found her favorite rock and plopped down to have a good, long cry. Why did things have to be so complicated? Why couldn't Allan and her father understand how hard this was for her?

She buried her face in her hands and sobbed. She had a terrible feeling that something horrendous was going to happen to them on that mountain, but no one cared. No one would listen to anything she had to say about it.

Rustling sounded in the brush behind her. Cassidy stiffened. She'd been foolish to fly up here without her rifle. She drew in a deep breath to force her nerves to calm.

"Cassidy?"

Thomas peeked around the rock, looking apologetic. "I'm sorry, but I saw you come up here and thought you looked upset."

She let down her guard. "Oh, Thomas, you are probably the only one in the world who cares what I feel right now."

He climbed up on the rock. "Why do you say that?"

Cassidy shook her head and straightened

out the tangles of her skirt, then dried her eyes on the hem of her apron. "I don't know. Besides, it's not fair to burden you with my worries."

Thomas shrugged. "You said we were friends — that we'd always be good friends. Don't friends share their burdens?"

She was humbled by his gentle words. "Of course they do. I'm sorry. It's just been so hard these last few days. I'm terribly worried about my father making this climb."

"Don't you think he knows what he's doing?"

The question was asked innocently enough, but hit Cassidy like a slap to the face. Of course her father knew what he was doing. He'd never been one to take unreasonable chances. He was born and raised here, and he knew full well the dangers and how to avoid them.

"Thomas, you are quite amazing." She forced a smile. "Of course my father knows what he's doing. I suppose I'm being childish. He didn't talk to me about it and I felt left out. Then when I tried to talk to Allan about it he . . . well . . . he didn't help matters."

"Your dad is the smartest man I know. He's real careful too. I've learned a lot from him about how to do things so as not to get yourself or someone else hurt. You should trust him."

She nodded. "I do. And I know I shouldn't worry."

"No, you shouldn't." Thomas sounded quite the authority. "In my Bible study with your father he told me worry was a sin. It's like saying that God doesn't care enough to take care of the problem."

Again she received his gentle chastisement with a smile. "And we both know there isn't anything God doesn't care about. I've been such a ninny, Thomas, and you were a good friend to deal with me honestly."

He returned her smile. "I've never really had a friend until you, Miss Cassidy."

"I'm certain you will make many friends as the years go by, Thomas. I'm sure my father already considers you one, and Allan too."

"You like him a lot, don't you? Mr. Brennan, that is."

She was momentarily taken aback. Dare she be honest with him about her feelings for Allan, or would that only serve to reopen his wounded heart?

Thomas seemed to understand. "It's all right, Miss Cassidy. I know you love him."

"You do?" She shook her head. "How can you possibly know that?"

He shrugged. "Because I know what love looks like. You look like you feel things for him that I felt for you."

"Oh, Thomas. . . ." She looked away, afraid she might start crying all over again.

Thomas touched her arm. Cassidy forced herself to look at him. He was such a sweet boy.

"Don't be sad, Miss Cassidy. Love is a good thing to feel."

23

The entire staff of the Curry and most if its guests were standing in the grass by the dock on the Susitna River.

The day had finally arrived. September the fourteenth, 1923.

Allan could hardly believe it. Today, they'd start their journey to Denali.

Frank came up beside him and patted his back. "This takes me back, son. I can't tell you how privileged I am to have shared this with your father and now with you."

"Thanks, Frank." He had an instinct to want to cringe every time Frank called him "son," but he held himself in check.

The past few weeks had been exhausting but worth it. Nothing could put a damper on the joy he felt to be on his way to a dream. Nothing except saying good-bye to Cassidy.

She'd apologized to him for her treatment of him that day in the dining room but hadn't resumed their evening walks. Their conversations had been few and far between the past couple of weeks, but she appeared supportive, and he appreciated that effort. The time away would give them both a chance to really think about their future and what they wanted. Allan was confident that he already knew that he wanted Cassidy for his wife, but first he had to settle things with Frank and finally lay his father to rest.

The boat arrived that would take them downriver and south a bit to a better location to cross the ridge to the west. Frank headed toward the boat. "Guess we better get going." He walked down the dock.

John said good-bye to Thomas and Mr. Bradley and thanked them for their help and support. Then he hugged his daughter good-bye.

Allan couldn't hear their words to each other, but he noticed a long hug. John waved to the crowd and walked down the dock as well.

Then Cassidy came to Allan. He'd been hoping she would spare a moment for him.

"Hi." He had nothing profound to say.

"Hi." She smiled. "Well, this is it, isn't it?" Reaching forward, she grabbed both his hands in hers. Allan forced himself not to show his surprise. "I'll be praying for you every day."

"Thank you. I'm sure we'll need it."

She nodded. "Dad gave me your basic itinerary, so we'll know about where you'll be. Just be safe and don't ever risk the weather."

"Yes, ma'am." He winked at her.

Tears formed in her eyes. "I'll be looking forward to when you get back."

"Me too." There weren't words to describe how he felt, but hopefully she knew. And when he returned, he'd tell her.

"Please watch over Dad. He's . . . well . . . you know."

He smiled. "He'll be just fine. I'll see to it."

She nodded and reached into her apron pocket for a hankie and an envelope fell to the ground. "Oh, goodness! I'm so sorry. I almost forgot. This came for you just before breakfast." She wiped her nose and her eyes and handed over the envelope. "Please be careful."

"I will." He tucked the telegram into his jacket pocket, certain it was something that couldn't wait, but he didn't want Frank to see it. "You too."

He tapped her nose with his finger and headed to the boat. Waving to the crowd, he wondered if Cassidy would think about him as much as he thought about her.

The first day passed without incident, although Allan was a bit saddlesore from the number of miles they'd covered. And they'd made it all the way across the Sus- itna by boat and then the Chulitna River and beyond by horse. Their first camp was made without mishap at the base of the Ruth Glacier.

John's friends from the Ahtna tribe had a hot meal waiting for them and told them of the journey for the next few days. They'd be snowshoeing once they made it to the top of the glacier, and the sled teams would carry their supplies.

The thrill that rippled through him now was unlike anything he'd ever felt. Here he was at the base of a glacier, with Denali in his majesty towering in the distance. Allan couldn't take it all in.

Blue ice walls rose from the rock below him in great ripples. Their jagged edges looked sharp and uninviting. He couldn't help wondering what his dad had thought when he'd first seen this sight.

Their team had left the trees much earlier in the day. John had explained that the tree line was at its height at one thousand feet because of the glaciated land around them.

It was all so beautiful and amazing.

Their camp was several hundred yards away from the actual glacier so that just in case the glacier walls calved in the night, they wouldn't be buried in glacial ice.

Allan listened to the native Athabaskan tongue flow off the men. John joined in and laughed. What a beautiful language and what incredible people. These men were tough as nails and yet loved to teach Allan new things. The one Allan questioned the most never seemed to lose patience with him. No wonder John was the amazing man he was.

Frank stood up and stretched. He'd been quiet most of the day and went from friendly to wearing a scowl as soon as they'd met up with the Athabaskan party. "I'm tired. I think I'll hit the hay for the night."

Allan nodded. "All right."

After Frank left, one of the Athabaskan men walked over and sat by Allan. "Your friend isn't very friendly."

"No, he doesn't seem to be."

"But he's not looking forward to this adventure the way you are, is he?" The man's eyes twinkled.

"No, he's not. And you're right, I'm excited about this adventure."

"Anyone who respects the Great One like

you do will be blessed." He looked down at the pile at Allan's feet. "Do you need help with those?"

"As a matter of fact, I do. These are different snowshoes than I've used before."

"That's because they're *tsistl'uuni.*"

"Chist-loo-nee? What does that mean? Do I have the wrong ones?"

The man laughed. "No. These are hill snowshoes. What you will need to climb the glacier."

"Oh yes. Thank you." Allan watched intently as the native man demonstrated with grunts. John had told them before they met up with the natives that they would learn the men's names if and only if the men told them. It wasn't polite to ask, and they had to earn each other's trust. Allan found it all fascinating.

The man nodded once Allan finally latched the shoes correctly. "Here." He handed Allan a paper-wrapped packet. "For your journey."

"What is it?" He leaned down and took a whiff.

"Natsak'i."

Allan tried to say it. "Nat-sa-kee."

The man laughed. "Close enough. It's smoked salmon strips. To keep your mind clear as you travel up the mountain."

"Thank you, my friend. This is a wonderful gift."

The native man walked away and went to his tent. Such fascinating people. Hardworking. Giving. Simple.

As Allan placed the packet of salmon into his coat pocket so he could carry his snowshoes to his tent, his hand brushed on the envelope Cassidy had given him that morning. He'd completely forgotten about it.

With everyone else occupied or asleep, he opened it up.

```
13 September 1923

Henderson found dead (stop)
Murdered (stop)Witness and
evidence point to Frank (stop)
Pray you are safe (stop)
Please let us know update
(stop)
                              Louis
```

He read through it three times as a chill settled over him. Glancing at the tent where Frank had gone, Allan thought momentarily about confronting him with the news. He put that thought aside, however. If he caused a confrontation, there was no telling what Frank might do. Was the man's story

374

about a changed life all a sham?

He glanced around for John and found him on the far side of the camp reloading his backpack. Making his way across the camp, Allan cast a concerned glance at Frank's tent. Had he murdered Henderson, and if so, why? Had the man threatened to expose him? Perhaps he had simply served his purpose and Frank felt it necessary to get rid of the man. Had that been how he felt about Allan's father?

The thought of Frank being responsible for actually ending his father's life sickened him. He had been fully accepting that negligence or even his father's confusion at high altitude had resulted in Henry Brennan's death — but murder was something entirely different.

John looked up as Allan approached. He gave him one of his customary smiles, but when Allan didn't return it, John's expression sobered.

"Is something wrong?"

Allan prayed for clarity. What was the truth? The Frank of the past, or the jovial story of a changed-life Frank?

Allan squatted down beside John, the weight of the truth hitting him. "We've got a killer in our camp."

24

Three days had passed since the men left on their expedition. Everyone still talked about where they were or what might be happening, but for the most part, life just kept going at the Curry Hotel. Trains came in and trains left, bringing with them interesting passengers, miners, and railroad workers. There were fewer tourists, but enough that elaborate meals were still required. Cassidy tried to keep her mind on the task at hand, but it became more difficult with each passing day. She couldn't shake off the feeling that something was very wrong.

She looked to the west several times during the day and prayed. She prayed that the weather would hold and the temperatures remain well above freezing. She prayed that they would be safe from harm and that her father's previous injuries wouldn't put him at risk. Most of all she prayed that time would pass faster and they would all return home safely.

Walking back to the kitchen from her room, Cassidy had to stop suddenly to keep from running into Thomas. "Whoa there. Where are you headed in such a hurry?" She reached back to straighten the bow in her apron.

"Actually, I was coming to fetch you, Miss Cassidy. Mr. Bradley says he needs you right away in his office." He gulped in a few breaths.

"Thank you, Thomas. Would you mind letting Mrs. Johnson know where I am?"

"Sure. I'll go right now."

"But you don't have to run." Cassidy laughed over her shoulder.

His retreating steps slowed.

As she headed to the manager's office, she wondered what concoctions Mrs. Johnson planned for the Asian diplomats they expected this weekend. That must be what Mr. Bradley wanted to speak to her about. He'd been all excited to host the dignitaries.

Cassidy reached the manager's office and knocked on the door.

"Come in." Mr. Bradley opened the door.

Immediately, she noticed the older, gray-haired couple sitting in front of the manager's desk. Then she noticed that he closed the door behind her — making both doors to the office shut. Unusual for this time of day.

"Have a seat, Cassidy," Mr. Bradley directed.

She looked to the couple and then to her boss as she took her chair. "Is there something wrong?"

The manager cleared his throat. "Cassidy, this might come as a surprise to you, but I'd like to introduce you to your mother's parents, Mr. and Mrs. Callaghan."

Had she not been seated, she probably would have fallen over. What? Her mother's parents? Here? Words wouldn't form, but she felt her mouth drop open and couldn't do a thing about it.

"I know this is a shock for you." Mrs. Callaghan spoke first. "We sent a letter first, several months ago, but we weren't sure your father had received it."

Had Dad gotten a letter? He hadn't mentioned it.

"We planned to speak with your father first, but Mr. Bradley informed us of his whereabouts, so we felt we had no choice but to come to you." She paused and looked at the old man before continuing. "We've come to make amends." Tears streamed down her cheeks.

Of all the things that could have happened to her on that day, this was the one that Cassidy would never have expected. Her grandparents had never been a part of her life. There had never been so much as a single word from them in twenty-three years. Now here they sat as if those years meant nothing.

"Yer hair and coloring is darker, but ye look like yer mother." Sobs shook the woman.

Dad often told her she was as beautiful as her mother, but Cassidy knew her dark hair and dark eyes were from her father. She looked native Alaskan and she knew it. Still the thought of looking like her mother sent a little thrill through her.

Mr. Callaghan rose from his chair, his hat in his hand, and then slowly knelt in front of Cassidy. "My granddaughter." His voice cracked on the words. "We've wasted too much time, and we've come to apologize."

Cassidy blinked and closed her mouth. "I . . . I don't understand. You left us. You wanted nothing to do with my father or me."

Mrs. Callaghan sniffed and spoke again. "We were missionaries from Ireland. We'd come to this beautiful land to teach the native people. And we shouldn't have been surprised that your mother would fall in love with one of the men, but we were. We were terrified of him as a half-Indian" — she corrected herself — "half-Athabaskan man. All those years we served with our holier-than-thou attitudes, knowing that we had the knowledge of the one true God and how He loved everyone and died for the world. And yet, we didna truly understand.

"We were angry with John for taking away our only daughter. And then when you were born and she died, we could bear it no longer. We felt we were being punished. We said some very ugly things to your father. Things that should never have been thought, much less spoken."

After all these years. She had more family. They were here. Apologizing. And yet, Cassidy couldn't move.

Mr. Callaghan reached for her hand. "Our attitude and behavior toward your father has haunted us these many years. When God finally got ahold of my stubborn heart, I knew we had to come and repent to you both as well, but sadly, we lacked the funds and the courage until now."

Her grandmother — yes, her very own grandmother — stood. "You see, we're old. It couldn't wait any longer. We wanted to see you — to know you not only because you're all that remains of Eliza, but because you are our only grandchild. And . . . we are hoping that ye'll forgive us and let us be a part of your lives."

Cassidy blinked and looked around the room at each face. This couldn't be real. Suddenly, she stood, opened the door, and ran back to the kitchen as fast as she could. She couldn't imagine what they would think of her, but at the moment she didn't care.

The clatter of the kitchen was comforting as Cassidy ran in and found Mrs. Johnson. Before she knew it, she started sobbing all over the woman.

Mrs. Johnson's warm arms came around her and guided her into the dining room. "What on earth is going on? Are you all right?"

Cassidy pulled her apron up to her face and sobbed into it. Then she lowered it and started telling Mrs. Johnson everything that had just transpired.

The cook was stunned as well. "I can say that's one I never expected." She leaned back in her chair. "And you just left them and ran in here?"

"I didn't know what to say. The shock was just a bit too much, and then my stomach started flooding with all these nasty feelings. I couldn't believe they'd left us the way they did. The way they'd been prejudiced against the very people they were trying to minister to. And all the hurt from my childhood of growing up without them — without their love — and knowing they were out there just overwhelmed me."

"I see." Mrs. Johnson leaned forward. "And so you don't want them in your life?"

"I didn't say that."

"You *do* want them in your life?"

"I didn't say that either. I'm so confused." The sobs shook her again.

"Cassidy." Mrs. Johnson's hand engulfed hers. "Remember when I told you that I lost my entire family a few years ago?"

"Yes."

"I didn't have a choice to keep them as family or to let them go. I didn't have the choice for them to come back."

"I know. And I'm so sorry to come to you with all this. It's not very sensitive of me."

"Oh, hogwash. My point is this: They're family and you have a chance to start anew. You need to forgive them for the past and leave it there — in the past. Losing them the first time was a loss you couldn't fix. But to lose them again now would be devastating — and your fault. I would give anything to restore relationships with my family if they were still here. . . ."

The words sunk in and Cassidy nodded. Her heart broke looking at Mrs. Johnson's face so full of regret. She threw herself into the older woman's arms. "I hope you know that *you're* my family now too. And I love you." Before the woman could respond, Cassidy kissed her cheek and ran back to the manager's office.

Her grandparents were waiting.

She could see the apprehension on the faces of the two elderly people. No doubt they had been completely surprised by her reaction.

"I want to apologize." She looked first to her grandmother and then to her grandfather. It was funny that their blood flowed in her veins, but they were strangers.

"There's no reason to," her grandmother assured. "We put a terrible shock on you. Please say that you'll forgive us — both for the shock and for all the lost years."

Cassidy sank onto the chair she'd only recently vacated. "Of course I do. I can't tell you how many years I dreamed of a meeting just like this — prayed for it too. I think after a while I gave up hope of it, but God had other plans."

Her grandmother smiled. "I'm glad to hear you speak of God."

"My father raised me on the Bible and

taught me the value of hope in God. He also told me stories about my mother, but of course he had so few. I would very much like to hear more about her."

"We would love to tell you."

John watched the clouds above as they trekked farther up the glacier. The wind had a nasty bite to it. The weather had definitely changed.

Two days ago, they'd all snowshoed in their shirt-sleeves when the sun had been so warm reflecting off the snow and ice. But today, they were bundled up. Of course, they'd also climbed a couple thousand feet in elevation. He didn't like the change from warm to cold.

But he didn't like much right now. After Allan shared the news of the telegram with him, John made it his job to keep a constant watch on Frank's whereabouts. Everything the man did or said was suspect. If Irving knew just how closely he was observed, he didn't show it. Frank was as jovial as ever when it was just the three of them. But when the native men were anywhere around, his mood changed. And two of the Ahtna had told him that they didn't trust Frank.

Not a good sign.

But what reason did they have for turning

around and quitting? Unless the weather changed drastically, John realized they couldn't let Frank know that they were suspicious. Irving knew how much Allan wanted to succeed, and he also knew how much they'd paid the native men to help and for all the supplies.

The only way out seemed to be if they hit some weather they couldn't manage.

So John prayed for a storm.

A big one.

25

The evening meal passed in relative quiet — at least for a bustling hotel. But Cassidy couldn't wait to spend more time with her grandparents. Nothing could put a damper on the joy she'd felt the last day getting to know them.

As soon as she'd gone back and forgiven them, a beautiful blanket of peace seemed to rest on her shoulders. Now she couldn't wait for Dad to get back so he could share in this joy.

Grandmother Callaghan sat at a table in the dining room with her tea, waiting for Cassidy to be done.

"Grandmother." Cassidy plopped in a chair across from her. "Thank you for waiting for me."

"Not to worry, my dear one. It has been fun to watch you work." She pointed at her bowl with her spoon. "What is this delicious dessert you created?"

"Lemon soufflé. It's Mrs. Johnson's secret recipe."

"It's delightful."

"Thank you." Praise from the woman who gave birth to her own mother gave her more happiness than she could have known. "Where is Grandfather?"

"He's been so tired from the travel and excitement of finding you that he went to bed. He hoped you wouldna mind."

"Not at all." Cassidy smiled and folded her hands. "Would you tell me more about the family?"

"I'd love to." The lines on her face crinkled around her eyes. "Did you know you were named after my family?"

"Yes. My dad told me that my name was the last gift that my mother gave me before she died."

"Cassidy is a good, strong, noble Irish name. It was my family name. My father's name — your great grandfather — was Ewan Cassidy."

"What does it mean?"

Grandmother laughed. "It means 'clever one' or 'one with the twisted locks.' But your mother's hair didn't have a bit of curl, and neither does yours."

Cassidy wondered if that was why dad always called her "Clever Cassidy" as a little girl. The memory brought a smile to her face. "Tell me about my mother, please."

"Oh, she was such a sweet girl. She was our pride and joy. Voice like an angel. She loved to help with church — especially with the children. And the children loved her. She was always so happy. Her father — your grandfather — used to say she was 'as sunny as the day she was born.' Nothing ever seemed to make her sad — unless it was some injustice done to someone she loved." Her grandmother frowned. "Like the way we treated your father."

"Was it really just that Dad was part Athabaskan?" Cassidy hadn't really meant to ask the question aloud, but now that it was out, there was no taking it back.

Grandmother sighed. "No. At least not for me. I think it was more about losing my daughter. You see, we knew we wouldn't stay in Alaska forever, but if Eliza married your father, I knew she would never leave — because I knew your father would never leave. It was clear how much he loved this land.

"I think there was a part of me that was jealous of the affection Eliza held for him." She shook her head. "I was so wrong. I had my piety and my religion, but no charity — no love. I can only pray your father will find forgiveness in his heart."

Cassidy smiled. "I don't think you have to worry about that. I've never seen Dad refuse someone forgiveness."

"Perhaps no one has ever hurt him as much as we have."

Shrugging, Cassidy didn't feel she could countermand the woman's statement. "With Dad it's never been about the degree of wrong done him. He forgives openly and willingly because he wants forgiveness in return. At least that's what he's always telling me. If I know him as I think I do, he'll be seeking your forgiveness."

"Oh, but he doesn't need to. The only thing we ever held against him was loving your mother — and we both know that wasn't a sin or anything that needs to be forgiven."

Now that they were talking about her father, Cassidy couldn't help but let her worries creep to the front of her thoughts. If something happened up there, she wouldn't get word until long after the fact. He could die . . . they could both be killed by an avalanche or lose their footing and fall off the mountain and Cassidy wouldn't know about it until days, even weeks afterward. She truly regretted having spent any time in anger toward Allan and her father.

"I can see you are far away." Grandmother stifled a yawn.

"I was just thinking of my father up there on the mountain." Cassidy stood and forced a smile. "But I've kept you up way too late as it is. Why don't you let me walk you to your room?"

"I'd like that very much."

The frailty of her grandmother's arms couldn't be hidden by the woman's thick sweater. Cassidy slowed her pace and once again sent a prayer heavenward, thanking God for the opportunity to be reunited with family before it was too late.

Once she had her grandmother safely delivered to her room, Cassidy walked outside. The summer days of long light were gone and now the skies were dark. At least here she had the glow of electric lights to mark her way, but on the mountain they had nothing more than their lanterns.

She looked in the direction of Denali and wondered where they were. Were they safe? Wrapping her arms around her body, Cassidy couldn't help the thought that came to mind.

Why didn't she tell Allan that she loved him?

The wind was stronger than any he'd ever

390

felt. Allan bundled up inside the tent he and John shared and drank the tea before it lost all its heat. He also wrestled with his conscience and God. For so long now he had blamed God for his father's death, but now that he was here . . . near to where his father had died, Allan felt he had to make his peace.

I don't really know where to start. He tried to imagine God sitting on His throne in His full majesty. *I've been so wrong — so angry. I knew it wasn't right to blame You or John for Dad's death, but I had to blame someone . . . and . . . well, I couldn't blame Dad. Even though he was the one who made the decision to come. He knew all the risks, but came anyway.*

I think for a long time I've been mad at him more than anyone else, but I couldn't admit it. Not to myself or anyone else, and certainly not to You. Allan had been considering this for most of the climb that day and now that he'd allowed himself to realize the truth, it was like a dam had burst. His emotions and memories flooded down over the years.

"I need Your forgiveness." The words were barely whispered but seemed to echo in Allan's head. "Please, God — Father — forgive me." For a moment the wind ceased and there was absolute silence. With it came peace to Allan's weary heart.

Then just as quickly the wind started up again and the tent shook harder than before.

John entered as he tried to shake off all the snow. "It's not good."

Allan nodded. "I guess that storm you prayed for is upon us." He didn't speak very loud, but he knew John heard him.

"Yes. I knew God answered prayers, but I guess I didn't realize what I was asking for." John sat down by the camp stove and extended his hands. "I tried to convince Frank to join us here, but he refused."

It had been three days since they'd left the native men, sleds, and dogs at a camp on the glacier. Each day, they'd made a little progress, but John and Allan purposefully slowed their pace. Frank had been edgy and irritable, but the weather had been nice, so they'd pushed on. Today, they made it over a towering wall and could no longer see the camp below them. Which meant the men from the camp couldn't see them either. And that made Allan's hackles rise. Up until this point, they'd had other people around them. But now, they were truly alone with Frank. And they didn't know what he had planned.

A strong sense of foreboding filled him.

John sat cross-legged on the floor and then

pulled out his notes and a map. "We're in dangerous territory. Not good in the middle of a storm."

"Do you think Frank will suspect if we suggest we turn around?" Allan handed him a tin cup with hot tea. John took it and sipped it before answering. He set the cup aside and returned his attention to his book of notes.

"Probably. At least if we don't wait a few days to let the storm pass. We have enough provisions." John closed his book. "And Frank will remember from the last time that we had to hunker down and wait more than once. There's also the possibility that this storm will last for a week or more. Up here on the mountain it's not at all unusual. Maybe if it continues we can convince him that it's impossible to go on — that we simply waited too late in the season."

Allan nodded. "I think we have grounds to declare that now. It's obvious the snows are going to be heavy. We can remind him how difficult it is to break a path through new snow. I'm sure he must remember that."

John grimaced. "I don't know if you've noticed, but he's miserable up here. He doesn't want to be here."

"Sure, I've noticed."

"Well, that means he came here for an entirely different reason than just to climb. A reason that made him willing to risk his own comfort — possibly his own life. What isn't clear is what he has planned. I think you and I should sleep in shifts so that one of us is always awake. I just don't trust him."

The gravity of the situation before them scared Allan.

"I suggest we pray. It's the only surety we have."

John smiled, seeming to sense the change that had taken place in Allan's heart. "I couldn't agree with you more."

Another day, another train. Cassidy watched the southbound train pull in. No doubt filled with hungry men from the railroad. The workers had been flooding in and heading south the past couple days now that their work was complete up north. A lot of them wanted to get home before the snow started to fall. And she couldn't blame them.

She went back into the kitchen to see what needed to be finished up for dinner. Time with her grandparents had been wonderful, but she still couldn't wait for the return of Dad. The time with her grandparents had also taught her that time was short — if Al-

Ian Brennan came back and told her he cared for her, then she would sit him down and tell him that he needed to let go of his anger toward God before she could give him her heart. No more mincing of words. No more waiting for him to see the light. She cared about him. A lot. Enough to tell him the truth.

The railroad agent, Mr. Fitzgerald, entered the kitchen and called out, "Miss Ivanoff!"

She wiped her hands and went over to him. "Yes, sir."

"We've just gotten terrible news that there's a massive storm sitting over the mountains. Some of the men say the natives told them it was worse than anything else they've seen." He looked down at the floor. "I hate to be the bearer of bad news, but I wanted to tell you personally."

A hand flew to her mouth. Her worst fears had just come true. She'd been so consumed with her grandparents and her own thoughts that she'd hardly given the weather any thought.

After dinner, Cassidy received permission from Mrs. Johnson to take the rest of the evening off.

Racing up Deadhorse Hill in her apron

and dress, she didn't care a lick about her attire or any danger that might befall her. She just had to see for herself. Had to get a glimpse of what the men were all talking about around the tables. The light was fading fast, which only made the urgency greater. She stumbled on something and barely righted herself before hugging the ground. Another time, the thought might have amused her.

When she finally reached the top, an icy wind cut across her. The temperature had dropped considerably since earlier in the day. Cassidy drew in her breath and held it before turning to face the view. Thick, black, swirling clouds to the west told her the story she didn't want to hear. The Great One was completely engulfed, and the storm was moving toward the hotel at a rapid pace. For a moment she was mesmerized and then a blast of cold wind hit her face. She let out the breath she'd been holding and fell to her knees. "Oh, God, please don't take them from me! Please!"

Her mind raced to remember their plan. If they'd followed the itinerary, Dad and Allan . . . and Frank would be close to ten thousand feet up the mountain. This storm could cover them in hours, and they might be buried alive. They might already be! The temperatures would be subzero and there would be no place to take refuge except the tents they'd carried with them. And depending on how quickly the storm came up, they might not even have had time to erect the tents.

"No, Dad would have been more aware of the weather than that," she told herself aloud. It did little to comfort her.

"Miss Cassidy, Miss Cassidy!" Thomas's voice drifted up to her. "Miss Cassidy!"

She tried to collect herself and stood. "I'm here, Thomas."

"Miss Cassidy, we need to get down from here right now. The storm is coming this way. Mrs. Johnson told Mr. Bradley where you went and they sent me to fetch you. They're preparing for a doozy down at the hotel."

She nodded. "I just had to see for myself." She pointed toward the mountains.

When Thomas's gaze followed her finger, he gasped. "Oh no! But I'm sure Mr. Ivanoff and Mr. Brennan are hunkered down and waiting it out. Nobody is as smart as your dad when it comes to that mountain." He grabbed her hand. "But we've got our own problems. We've got to get down."

Sheets of rain began to pelt them with no mercy, and Cassidy half ran, half slid her way down the top part of the hill. The wind was a constant opponent, leaving her exhausted, just fighting to stay upright. Finally, Cassidy gave up and plopped down. She began to work her way down, letting her backside anchor her to the ground. It kept her center of gravity lower, and her feet could at least guide her over rocks. Thomas looked at her like she was crazy, but he soon joined her, offering whatever help he could. He stayed beside her the whole time, making sure she didn't get to going too fast.

By the time they reached the bottom of the hill, the rain had turned to snow. And by the time they made it to the hotel doors, it looked like a full-on blizzard.

If it was this bad down here, how bad was it up on Denali?

Oh, Lord God. Please help them!

26

Morning came without a break in the storm. The howling of the wind did little to offer any hope of an end to the blizzard. Allan nudged John. "Are you awake?"

"I am. I'm just trying to stay warm."

"Should one of us go check on Frank?"

"I was just thinking that, but didn't want to leave my warm blankets." John pushed the warm bedding aside. "Fool of a man. He did this last time we climbed — refused to share a tent with anyone else."

Allan nodded. Frank had always been a bit of a recluse — even a snob. "I don't trust him, but I also don't want to see him die, so maybe we should invite him over here."

John donned his outer gear. "I'll do that. You stay here and heat us up something to drink."

"I can do that."

The wind roared around them and when John opened the flap of the tent, a blast of air took Allan's breath away. "Hold on to the rope!" he yelled, but doubted John could hear him over the noise of the storm.

Several minutes passed and Allan pulled on his coat to go check on the men. But just then John entered the tent with his hands over his head, Frank right behind him.

Frank shoved John to the ground, revealing a gun in his right hand. "I've had about all of this I can take," he shouted. He motioned to Allan. "Do up the flap."

"What are you doing?" Allan shook his head. "Frank, you've lost your mind. Put the gun down." He edged slowly to the opening and grabbed the flap as it beat mercilessly against the tent. With one eye on Frank and the other on what he was doing, Allan managed to reclose the opening.

"You two think I haven't known what you've been up to, but I have. You've been plotting a way to get rid of me, but little did you know I was doing the same."

"We've been doing no such thing, Frank." Allan looked at John. There was a nasty gash on his head. Frank must've hit him with the gun before they came to the tent. "What have you done?"

"What have I done? What have *I* done?" A hideous laugh spewed out of the man's lips.

It was clear he'd gone mad. "I'll tell you what I've done. One — I've waited for years to have sole ownership of my company. Your father was supposed to die and I was supposed to get it all. But no . . . he had to leave half of his share to his sniveling brat of a son who wanted nothing to do with it. So I killed him for nothing."

"You killed my father?" Allan lunged.

Frank stuck the gun in his face. "I'm not finished." He hissed. "Yes, I killed your father. When this fool stopped to find our trail marker, it gave me just enough time. I positioned myself in the perfect place, and when your father joined me I held his attention by asking him to help me clear my goggles. While he did that, I untied the rope from around his waist. It almost cost me my fingers because I had to take off the thick mittens in order to work the knot." He laughed in a maniacal manner and waved the gun.

Allan noted that he wore only a thin pair of the woolen gloves they'd brought. With his hand wrapped around the cold metal of the gun, his fingers would have to be extremely stiff.

"Then I shoved him over a cliff. How's that for lifelong friends?" The man's eyes were crazy. "Let's see, where did I leave off?

Oh yes . . . Two — I've had to deal with your pious family sticking their nose into everything they shouldn't. Three — I've lost a fortune because I've been waiting for the rest of my money to invest in my other ventures. And four — I had to resort to stealing money from the company to make it all work. Then, of course, your brother-in-law had to get in the middle of all that, and then there was that stupid auditor —"

"How many have you killed, Frank?" Allan couldn't take any more. He pushed forward, but Frank stuck the barrel of the gun on his forehead.

"I don't think you want to press me."

Allan pulled back an inch. Frank had gone over the edge. He was insane. It wouldn't do his family any good for him to allow the man who'd taken his father away to take his life as well. But one question haunted him. "You did it all for money?"

"Of course."

He gritted his teeth. "Why? My father would have given you all the money you wanted."

"I don't care. He didn't deserve it. And he didn't deserve his family and all the respect of the community. He didn't deserve any of it. He made plans and they turned golden. I made plans and they turned to ash. It wasn't fair." His voice took on a shrill, almost screeching tone. "I had plans that were good. I had ideas and dreams."

Out of the corner of his eye, Allan saw John slowly reach for his ice axe. He needed to stall. "Frank. Please. Why don't you let John go and I'll sign over the whole company to you now. It'll be yours. All yours." He held up his hands. "Nobody else needs to get hurt."

He lowered the gun almost as if he'd forgotten all about it. "Do you think I'm stupid? John could just go tell the authorities everything."

"No. He wouldn't. Not if I asked him to promise. We could help each other down the mountain and you'd own the company."

"You're dumber than your father, Brennan —"

John rose up with the axe and took Frank by surprise. The gun fired.

John fell to the ground, a circle of red growing above his knee.

Allan took that moment to lunge at Frank and tackled him to the ground. Wrestling with him, Allan knew that this could be the end. But he had to save John.

For Cassidy.

Another shot fired from the gun.

■ ■ ■ ■

Three weeks had passed since the expedition team left the Curry Hotel. Cassidy was a bit beside herself. The storm had cleared but had left two feet of snow in its wake.

Now the sun was shining once again and the snow began to melt. Unfortunately her fears would not.

Every day she looked toward the west. Did they survive the storm? Would she ever see her father again? And Allan?

She regretted not sharing her heart with him earlier. Now it might be too late. The thoughts threatened to overwhelm her, but she held on to hope.

Through it all, her grandparents and Mrs. Johnson had been a rock beside her. In fact, Mrs. Johnson seemed to be slowly coming around. Each morning she asked Cassidy to share a Scripture with her and then asked what it meant. She might have only been doing it to force Cassidy to think on something other than the missing men, but Cassidy knew God's Word would never return void.

Maybe there was hope to break down those seemingly impenetrable walls as well.

Nothing was impossible with God.

Not even sparing her father and the man she loved from a killer storm.

Allan awoke to a dog licking his face. Where was he?

Every muscle in his body ached as he tried to sit up.

But then spots danced before his eyes. Thoughts of Cassidy surged through his mind. Would he see her again? He never got to tell her that he loved her. Or that he'd gotten himself straight with God. He wanted to see her face when he told her.

But maybe it wasn't meant to be.

The rushing of his own heartbeat filled his ears.

Everything went black.

27

Mrs. Johnson and Cassidy spent the morning cleaning sweet Alaskan blueberries and preparing them for jelly. While she appreciated Mrs. Johnson's efforts, she hadn't realized the woman could come up with just about anything to keep them busy — including traversing hills and gullies to pick berries.

But it had kept her mind off the fact that her father and Allan hadn't returned yet.

"Now, you finish with those and then work on this bucket," Mrs. Johnson instructed, hoisting the bucket alongside the first. "I'm going to check on those silly girls and make sure they've properly cleaned the pots and pans." She hurried away before Cassidy could reply.

Once her work was finished, Cassidy planned to talk to Mr. Bradley about letting her ride out with Thomas and maybe a couple of other men to look for her father.

She was certain the storm would have ended their ascent and they surely were making their way back. They had to be. They couldn't be dead.

She'd know if they were. Wouldn't she? Tears threatened.

Cassidy straightened for a moment and closed her eyes. Drawing a deep breath, she calmed herself and sighed. God was in control. Not Cassidy Ivanoff.

As she reached for another bucket of berries, hands came over her eyes and she gave a squeal of fright. She immediately recognized the warm chuckle of the man she'd fallen in love with. She turned and found herself in Allan's strong arms.

"What . . . ? How . . . ?" She hugged him tight around the neck and spotted her father behind him.

His leg and head were bandaged, and he leaned on a cane, but he was there. In front of her. "Dad!" She ran to him and hugged him too.

Mrs. Johnson and the others had come to see what the ruckus was all about. They broke into a round of cheers, clapping all the while. There were very few dry eyes.

Cassidy couldn't believe it. She grabbed one of each of their hands and dragged them to the dining room, where she knew everyone would follow to hear the story of their mountain expedition. After she sat her father down, she kissed his cheek. "Tell me everything. I can't wait to hear what happened."

John shook his head. He looked around the room at the anxious gathering. "It's not a pretty story, Cass. But I think Allan should tell you the hardest part first."

She turned to Allan. "The hardest part was waiting for you to come home. I think I can face anything now that you're both here."

His eyes were clear and bright and when he smiled at her, it reached his eyes and melted her all the way down to her toes.

"Go on," Dad prodded.

Allan nodded and his expression sobered. "Frank is dead. He planned to kill us both up there."

Gasps were heard around the room.

As the story unraveled, Cassidy cried and grabbed her father's hand. The fact that he had survived being shot on the side of a mountain was a miracle in and of itself.

". . . After I realized that it wasn't me who was shot, I saw Frank's empty eyes. But there wasn't time to worry about him. I knew your dad was bleeding and I had to get him down the mountain. But we were still in the middle of the storm. So I cleaned his wound and pulled the bullet out. After I had him bandaged up, I prayed the bleeding would stop. And wouldn't you know, it did.

"Then I prayed for the storm to stop so we could get down the mountain. And within the hour everything calmed. So then, I thought, 'As long as I'm praying, I might as well ask for a miracle to get down the mountain.' So I prayed some more. I knew I couldn't carry your dad and too many provisions, so our survival depended upon me getting us down to the base camp as quickly as possible.

"The first day was excruciating. The snow was deep. I was tired and coming to grips with what Frank had done. And then we hit the big wall on the east buttress. John was passed out, no doubt from the pain, and I didn't know if I could go on any farther. And then all of a sudden, I looked down and could see the camp. It was a long ways down, but someone was waving at me. It gave me the encouragement I needed.

"Next thing I knew, I woke up with a dog licking my face and a huge knot on my head with every muscle in my body aching."

John laughed.

Cassidy couldn't stand it. "What do you

mean? What happened? How did you get down?"

Allan and her dad shared a look. They both smirked.

Then Dad leaned forward. "Apparently we slid the rest of the way down."

"What?" Cassidy couldn't believe it. "There's no way you could survive that. Could you?" Others murmured around the table.

"Well, let's just say that I shoved the pack with our meager provisions over the edge to see what would happen — and if there were any obstacles or crevasses along the way. It bounced and then rolled and turned into a huge ball of snow but showed me a decent path to take. I started over the edge, but it was steeper than I thought. With your dad over my shoulders, my equilibrium was way off and I was worn out. So I prayed some more — asking God to get us down. About a third of the way, I completely lost my balance and landed on my backside. I slid for a ways, but our combined weight was too much for me to stay upright and not go head over heels, so I leaned back and tried to keep John behind me. But along the way, I must have hit a rock with my head because I don't remember anything after that."

Dad laughed. "Don't look at me. I don't

remember anything because I was passed out, but our friends at the bottom said we gave them quite a show."

"And then we had the opportunity to tell them about the power of prayer." Allan patted her father on the back.

The weariness in Dad's eyes made his pale complexion more intense. And Dad wasn't pale. Ever. "Enough storytelling for now. You need to be in bed." She motioned to Thomas. "Please help me."

"What about me?" Allan asked, looking almost hurt.

Cassidy laughed. "I would love to spend more time with you, but you should probably go and rest too." She knew there would be plenty of time to make her declaration of love, and she had no desire to do so in front of a bunch of people. She helped get her father into bed, then asked Thomas to bring him some lunch. The boy smiled and hurried off to do her bidding.

"Once you've rested, there's someone here to see you. In fact, two someones."

Her father eyed her with a raised brow. "Cassidy Faith, what kind of mischief have you been up to?"

She grinned. "Only the very best kind."

With her father settled, Cassidy found her grandparents and shared the joyous news of

411

the men's return. She explained that she hadn't told him of their arrival, only that there were two people who wanted very much to see him. After that, she joined the others for lunch, including the Ahtna men who had escorted them all the way back down the mountain to the hotel. Allan was nowhere to be found. Maybe he'd taken her suggestion to go rest.

"We were just hearing about how your father and Allan were rescued," Mrs. Johnson declared, pulling back a chair at the table for Cassidy.

She took a seat. "I want to hear it all."

Her father's Ahtna friends began filling in the missing details of what had happened. "We had already decided to go after them, but then we saw them on top of the ice. Then before we knew it, they were falling. But it wasn't like any fall I'd ever seen. It was slow — almost like unseen hands were lowering them."

Cassidy felt the hairs on her arm prickle. Unseen hands indeed. God's hands.

"We managed to get to them and get them off the glacier. They were banged up and bruised, and both were unconscious. They slept for days and we figured it was best not to move them."

They continued answering the questions

412

thrown at them by the others, but after about twenty minutes Cassidy had heard enough. She made her excuses to Mrs. Johnson, then slipped from the room eager to find Allan. She didn't have far to go. He stood leaning against the hallway wall as if waiting for her to join him on some pre-arranged date.

Cassidy smiled. "I was just coming to find you. I have something I need to say."

Allan pushed off the wall. "I have something I need to say to you, as well."

She felt a delicious shiver run through her. Cassidy had little doubt he loved her. He offered her his arm and she took hold of him.

She found herself wanting to pour her heart out to him but not knowing where to start. So she chose to quietly walk beside him as they made their way back to the main lobby. Cassidy was glad to see it deserted.

Allan led her to the fireplace. "I'm afraid it's going to take me a few days to feel warm again."

Cassidy laughed and took his hands. "I'm so glad you're all right." She felt a blush creeping up her neck. "And I need to thank you for saving my father."

"He's a wonderful man." He stepped

closer and took her chin in his hand. "One I hope to call father myself, Lord willing."

For a moment his words confused her and then it hit her. "Oh! Do you . . . I mean . . . does this mean . . . that you . . . ?"

He got down on one knee and looked up into her eyes and took hold of her hand. "Cassidy Faith Ivanoff, I've already gotten your father's permission, and so I'd like to ask you if you'd give me the honor of becoming my wife."

"Don't you want to know first whether or not I love you?"

He chuckled and shook his head. "I already know that, you silly goose. I can see it in your eyes. I hear it in your voice." He stroked the back of her hand with his thumb and grew serious. "I knew the only thing left to settle was my anger at God. I did that on the mountain."

She felt tears come to her eyes. "Oh, Allan, I'm so happy."

He gave her a lopsided grin. "Does that mean you're saying yes?"

"Yes!" She pulled him back to standing and jumped into his arms. "Yes, yes, yes!"

28

Cassidy held her father's arm tighter than she intended. Thomas stood in the center of the new suspension bridge over the Susitna waving at her, and she watched the bridge sway.

When Allan told her his idea to get married across the river and up on the ridge, she thought it sounded terribly romantic. But now as she faced crossing the wooden planks in her white wedding gown, she wasn't sure she'd been thinking straight.

But she did love him. More than she'd thought possible. And she'd follow him anywhere. Even across a footbridge and up a mountain so they could stand in the shadow of Denali and take their wedding vows.

"I'm so glad Grandfather and Grandmother could be here for the wedding. It means the world to me that we're all a fam-

415

ily again."

Her father nodded. "It would mean the world to your mother as well. I like to think she knows."

Cassidy nodded and squeezed his arm. "I do too."

For several seconds they said nothing more. Then with a smile, her father pulled her forward. "Well, they're all waiting for us. Now, if we can just keep Thomas from bouncing too much on this thing, we might make it across without mishap." Dad had a twinkle in his eye.

"It is a bit disconcerting, isn't it? Knowing there's nothing in the middle holding us up?" Cassidy wasn't sure how she felt about the gently moving bridge and she leaned over the railing to look down. "But today of all days, I'd rather not give the bridge a hug."

Dad laughed heartily. "Me neither, sweetheart. Although that would be a story you could pass down to your grandkids one day."

"Oh, there will be plenty of those."

Her dad looked at her. "Grandchildren or stories?"

"Both." She patted his arm. "You can just tell them about all my clumsiness."

Cassidy took a tentative step. She knew on the other side of the bridge and up the

416

ridge her groom awaited her with friends and family who wanted to be a part of their wedding.

With each step, her courage grew. God had indeed blessed her.

The walk up the ridge trail wasn't easy in her pretty dress, but Cassidy kept reminding herself it was worth it. They had plenty of time and she enjoyed the conversations she shared with Dad and Thomas.

Grandmother had sewn her dress — a stylish drop-waist satin creation, with layers of filmy white chiffon below the wide satin sash forming a beautiful handkerchief hem. It was the most beautiful dress Cassidy had ever seen, and she loved it even more since it was created by her grandmother.

So many memories to cherish today. She didn't want to forget any of it. Not the sway of the bridge, the smell of the flowers, the sunlight sparkling off the river, or even the climb up the ridge. Because she knew, at the top, she'd see Allan.

Thomas raced on ahead to let everyone know they were almost there.

Dad stopped and took her hands. "This is it, my daughter. You have my blessing and I love you with all my heart."

Blinking away tears of joy, Cassidy swallowed hard. "Don't you dare make me cry, Dad." She breathed in deep. "Thank you. For your blessing, and for your love. I love you too." She turned forward again and could see the last twenty steps or so leading to the top of the ridge. "Now, let's get moving. I'm ready to get this shindig under way."

He laughed and held out his elbow to her.

Thomas stood above them, turned, and nodded real big.

As Cassidy took the final steps, she heard the words of the doxology wash over her. The whole wedding party sang it together, and it echoed over the ridge in beautiful harmony. As she reached the top, she looked to her groom. He was all smiles, and it lit up his whole face.

To the west was the most glorious sight. Denali stood in all his majesty — not a cloud in view.

The crowd continued to sing until John brought her to stand beside Allan.

"Who gives this woman to be married?" Their pastor from Tenana had come all this way to perform the ceremony.

"I do," Dad answered with a slight break in his voice.

The pastor continued on.

Her soon-to-be-husband leaned over to whisper to her. "I hope the journey was worth it."

She giggled. "Oh, definitely. And you'll be proud — I didn't hug the ground even once."

Before she knew what was happening, Allan wrapped his arms around her and kissed her with a passion she wasn't expecting. Then he pulled back and chuckled. And then he kissed her again.

The crowd applauded and laughed.

The pastor cleared his throat. "We're not to that part yet, young man."

More laughter surrounded them.

Allan straightened, tucked her hand into his elbow, and pulled her closer. "I'm sorry, sir, I couldn't resist." He breathed in deep. "I'll behave."

Cassidy tried to cover her laughter. She looked at Allan, his face now serious and focused on the pastor. Oh, the joy to be with this man.

She tried to keep a straight face, but she just couldn't help it. Her smile generated from her toes today.

The pastor leaned in, a twinkle in his eyes. "May I continue?"

"Yes. Please do."

Now her dad started chuckling as well. At least it was a joyous occasion. And one they would all remember for the rest of their lives.

"Ladies and gentlemen, we are gathered here today in the sight of God and in the shadow of Denali, to join this man and this woman in holy matrimony . . ."

DEAR READER

Thank you for joining us for the beginning of THE HEART OF ALASKA series.

Our heroine — Cassidy Faith Ivanoff — is very dear to our hearts, and yes, she has a lot of Cassidy Faith Hale's real personality traits. In fact, the saying, "I guess the floor needed a hug" was a direct quote from this special girl. We hope you enjoyed the light from her legacy.

Curry and the Curry Hotel are fascinating pieces of Alaska's — and our country's — history. For many years, Curry was the heart and hub of not only the railroad but of all who visited the great Territory. There are conflicting reports about the actual layout of the Curry Hotel in 1923. Alaska Rails cites that the kitchen was originally in the basement and then moved, where the original floorplans for the hotel show the main kitchen on the main level and the section gang kitchen in the basement. Alaska

Rails also states that the Annex was built in 1923 while other sources claim that it was built later. We've chosen to follow the original floorplans for our story and added the Annex in.

The book *Lavish Silence: A Pictorial Chronicle of Vanished Curry, Alaska* by Kenneth L. Marsh is a fascinating read and provided us with wonderful research for *In the Shadow of Denali,* but there are discrepancies with other sources in some matters of the history, buildings, and layout. Over the years, the Curry Hotel changed. The town changed as many other buildings were constructed. While we tried to be as accurate as possible, we did take a few liberties to fit our story when all the sources didn't line up. We'd like to thank Ken Marsh for all his work and his incredible help sharing his research about Curry.

Today, the only remaining structure is the historic Curry Lookout, sitting high above the Susitna River on Curry Ridge (which, by the way, the lookout was not the President's idea, but we had fun putting that conversation into the story). It's not easily accessible. (We even tried to get in by helicopter, but the weather didn't cooperate.) You can find a couple of pictures at www.alaskarails.org/historical/curry/

lookoutview.jpg and www.alaskarails.org/historical/curry/lookout.jpg.

The location where Curry existed can be visited by riding the amazing Alaska Railroad, but since the suspension bridge has been gone for several decades, there's no way across the river to the lookout. Coming in from the west, you can drive the Parks Highway to where the future South Denali Visitor's Center will be (and the preliminary plans show a hiking trail to Curry Lookout), but this is still several miles west of Curry Ridge, and there are no trails to Curry Lookout at this time. At one time there was a snowmobile and ski trail, but it seems to be gone as well. Remember, Alaska is still wild and untamed — and Curry and the Curry Lookout are in the "bush" of Alaska and off the road system. But to know that these pieces of history are still there thrilled us as authors.

For simplicity's sake, we have named the railroad throughout the book as the Alaska Railroad. In actuality, the history of the Alaska Railroad includes the Alaska Central Railroad, the Alaska Northern Railroad, the Tanana Valley Railroad, and the Alaska Engineering Commission.

The President and First Lady really did visit Curry on their journey to Fairbanks.

There are some fascinating pictures and stories of this time. Be sure to check out Kim's blog at http://kimandkaylawoodhouse .com for pictures of the "Presidential Special" railroad car that now resides in Fairbanks at Pioneer Park. To be historically accurate, we spent hours and hours researching President and Mrs. Harding and their cross-country trip. Facts about the formal dedication of Mount McKinley National Park and the presidential visit in 1923 were taken from reports made to the Department of the Interior.

The First Lady's line to Thomas about "If I had a son . . ." would have been accurate for the private lady. Most people are unaware that she had a son before marrying Mr. Harding, and the son died in 1915, long before this story took place. What is fascinating though, is that very few during Harding's presidency ever knew that she even had a son. She never mentioned him either, which gave us an interesting twist to use.

The views from Talkeetna, Curry Ridge, and the South Denali Viewpoint on the Parks Highway are my favorite views of The High One. Even though the entrance to Denali National Park is one hundred miles north of these locations on the highway, Curry had the most ideal location to become a climbing expedition starting point since it was barely forty miles away as the crow flies. Even though Curry didn't survive, the quaint little town of Talkeetna did, and today that is where you find the Park Ranger Headquarters to climb Denali. If you go there, say hi to Missy for me (Kim). She was, once again, an invaluable source of information.

On June 7, 1913, the first ascent of the main summit (the southern peak) of Denali was achieved. The expedition was put together by Howard Stuck, but the first man to reach the summit was a native Alaskan, Walter Harper. The first superintendent of Mount McKinley National Park, Harry Karstens, was also part of this historic group and the real leader. (Harry Karstens is a fascinating man, and you will get to read more about him and his incredible work there in the rest of THE HEART OF ALASKA series.)

After the successful summit of 1913, nineteen years would pass before another known party attempted the climb. So for our story, we obviously took some artistic liberty and thought how fun it would be to have a party attempt the climb after Mount McKinley was officially named a national park. When the *Brooklyn Daily Eagle* delegation went to dedicate the park, it really was a party of seventy, but from what we found in doing research, there's no mention of the staff of the Curry helping in any way. But we had fun adding that into our story since it is a significant part of history.

We also used *The Ascent of Denali* by Hudson Stuck several times in *In the Shadow of Denali.* In chapter twenty, we used the actual description in the book for how they prepared their meat for the expedition. It's hard to imagine the time and preparation it took for their group to tackle the monumental task of climbing North America's tallest mountain. A free e-book of *The Ascent of Denali* by Hudson Stuck is provided by www.gutenberg.org/files/26059/26059-h/26059-h.htm.

In 2016, the national parks across the country celebrated the one hundredth anniversary of the creation of the National Parks Service. And in 2017, Denali National Park will celebrate its one hundredth year. We pray this book honors that in some small way.

A big thank you goes out to Dr. John Smelcer for his invaluable work on the *Ahtna Dictionary and Pronunciation Guide.* His love for his native people and the desire to preserve a dying language is evident in the care and immense amount of time he's taken over the years to provide this free resource. For this book, we've used the western dialect of Ahtna, the tribe whose native land was the setting of our story.

We've so enjoyed weaving in the people and historical facts that were part of this amazing time, but please remember this is a work of fiction.

Randy and Jackie Hale, thank you for giving us the honor of sharing Cassidy with the world.

As with all our other books, we would be lost without the team at Bethany House Publishers. It is a joy and a privilege to work with the whole team there. From editing to marketing to cover design and everything in between, they are top-notch. Thank you, BHP, for all you do.

Thank you — our readers — for your notes of encouragement and anticipation for each new book. We couldn't do this without you.

Last and ultimately most important, Thank You, Lord for giving us the opportunity to write for You.

Until next time . . .

Let it shine, let it shine, let it shine.

Kim and Tracie

ABOUT THE AUTHORS

Tracie Peterson is the award-winning author of over one hundred novels, both historical and contemporary. Her avid research resonates in her stories, as seen in her bestselling HEIRS OF MONTANA and ALASKAN QUEST series. Tracie and her family make their home in Montana. Visit Tracie's website at www.traciepeterson.com.

Kimberley Woodhouse is a multi-published author of fiction and nonfiction. A popular speaker and teacher, she's shared her theme of "Joy Through Trials" with hundreds of thousands of people across the country. She lives, writes, and homeschools with her husband of twenty-plus years and their two awesome teens in Colorado. Connect with Kim at www.kimberleywoodhouse .com.

The employees of Thorndike Press hope you have enjoyed this Large Print book. All our Thorndike, Wheeler, and Kennebec Large Print titles are designed for easy reading, and all our books are made to last. Other Thorndike Press Large Print books are available at your library, through selected bookstores, or directly from us.

For information about titles, please call:
  (800) 223-1244

or visit our Web site at:
  http://gale.cengage.com/thorndike

To share your comments, please write:
  Publisher
  Thorndike Press
  10 Water St., Suite 310
  Waterville, ME 04901

1/17